Contents

KT-382-983

Beijing

"All you've got to do is decide to go
and the hardest part is over.

So go!"

TONY WHEELER, COFOUNDER – LONELY PLANET

TAO IMAGES LIMITED / GETTY IMAGES ©

YADID LEVY / GETTY IMAGES ©

(left) Architectural detail, Forbidden City (p52)

....

(above) Hòuhǎi Lakes area (p118)

....

(right) Sìchuān chicken dish and steamed buns (p36)

....

JEN VOO PHOTOGRAPHY / GETTY ©

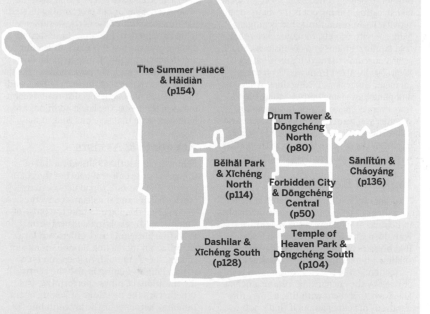

The Summer Palace & Hǎidiàn (p154)

Drum Tower & Dōngchéng North (p80)

Sānlǐtún & Cháoyáng (p136)

Běihǎi Park & Xīchéng North (p114)

Forbidden City & Dōngchéng Central (p50)

Dashilar & Xīchéng South (p128)

Temple of Heaven Park & Dōngchéng South (p104)

Welcome to Běijīng

As the capital of the country set to dominate the 21st century, Běijīng is a city intoxicated by the spirit of change.

Food Heaven

Food is an obsession for the Chinese and the dazzling array of different dishes you'll encounter in Běijīng reflects the sheer joy locals take in eating. Dining out is the main social activity; it's in restaurants that Beijingers hang out with friends, romance each other, hold family reunions and do business. You'll swiftly succumb to the delights of eating Běijīng-style. Apart from what's on the local menu – succulent Peking duck, delicious dumplings, awesome hotpot – there's food from every corner of China in the capital. Whether you want to sample fiery Sìchuān dishes, the Central Asian–inspired Uighur cuisine or the delicate flavours of the southwest, there's a restaurant serving it here.

Imperial Delights

No other city in China can match the extraordinary historical panorama on display in Běijīng. At its heart is the magnificent Forbidden City, a royal palace on a scale that beggars belief. Běijīng is also home to sublime temples that aspire to cosmological perfection, while the city centre is crisscrossed by the enchanting *hútòng*, ancient alleyways that teem with life, as they did hundreds of years ago. As if that's not enough, the majestic Great Wall snakes its way across the hills north of town.

Architectural Ambition

The locals think they live at the centre of the world, and the jaw-dropping structures that line their streets are a very visible sign that Běijīng is not shy about proclaiming its status as China's capital. Some of the world's most innovative modern buildings have sprung up here over the last few years, as leading architects vie for the chance to make their mark on the new global powerhouse. Like the temples and palaces of the ancient past, and the vast and imposing socialist realist monuments of the 1950s, the latest additions are built on a scale that screams 'look at me'.

Acrobats & Artists

Běijīng isn't just the political capital of China – it's the cultural heart of the country too. The nation's top artists, writers, movie-makers and musicians converge here, making this *the* place to take the pulse of China's rapidly evolving cultural scene. With fine museums and galleries galore, as well as an increasing number of music venues, there's enough to keep you busy day and night. Běijīng is also the centre for the traditional Chinese performing arts. Whether it's the mystique of Peking opera, tumbling acrobats or the graceful lines of Chinese classical dance that entrance you, the capital has it and more.

Why I Love Běijīng

By Daniel McCrohan, Author

I love the food, the overabundance of restaurants, the lack of table manners and the cheap beer. I love eating outside in summer, then huddling around a hotpot in winter. I love drinking freshly ground Italian coffee in a Qing-dynasty courtyard. And I love the fact that I can cycle everywhere, even to the Great Wall! But most of all, I love the *hútòng* – their mishmash architecture, their *fēngshuǐ* design, their chess-playing elderly residents and their peaceful, village-in-a-city vibe. Běijīng has many remarkable qualities, but it's the *hútòng* that make this exceptional city so utterly loveable.

For more about our authors, see p304.

Nanluogu Xiang (p86)

Běijīng's
Top 13

The Great Wall (p166)

1 Not only is this China's most famous landmark, it's one of the superlative manmade sights on earth. The Great Wall snakes its way across northern China for almost 9000km, but nowhere beats Běijīng as a base for mounting your assault. Scattered throughout the municipality are more than a dozen fragmented stretches, from the perfectly chiselled to the charmingly dilapidated. You can get to them by bus, by train, by taxi...even by bike. And the adventurous can hike along it for days. The question isn't whether to see the Great Wall; it's how. THE JĪNSHĀNLǏNG (P174) SECTION OF THE GREAT WALL

◉ *The Great Wall*

The Forbidden City (p52)

2 The largest palace complex in the world, the Forbidden City is the be-all and end-all of dynastic grandeur, with imposing halls, splendid gates and age-old relics. No other place in Běijīng teems with so much history, legend and imperial intrigue. You could spend hours wandering its vast squares and high-walled passageways, which lead to delightful courtyards, gardens and minimuseums, and give you plenty of time to contemplate the enormity of shuffling your way around the place that 24 consecutive emperors of China called home.

◉ *Forbidden City & Dōngchéng Central*

LUIS CASTAÑEDA INC./ GETTY IMAGES ©

JOHN BANAGAN / GETTY IMAGES ©

Tiān'ānmén Square (p60)

3 The world's largest public square is a vast desert of paving stones at the heart of Běijīng. The stringent security can be off-putting, but such is its iconic status, few visitors leave Běijīng without coming here. Crowds gather, children stamp around, and tourists huddle together for the obligatory photo opportunity with the great helmsman's portrait. Get up early and watch the dawn flag-raising ceremony, or wander by later on to see the surrounding buildings lit up at night.

⊙ *Forbidden City & Dōngchéng Central*

Temple of Heaven Park (p106)

4 The ultimate expression of the eternal Chinese quest for order, the Temple of Heaven is sheer geometric perfection: a series of stunning shrines where the sons of heaven, China's emperors, came to pray for divine guidance. Everything about them – colour, shape, sound – has an esoteric significance that's mind-boggling to contemplate. Surrounding them is a delightfully soothing park, where the locals come to stroll and dance, or to sit under the gnarled cypress trees planted hundreds of year ago during the Ming dynasty. HALL OF PRAYER FOR GOOD HARVESTS (P107)

⊙ *Temple of Heaven Park & Dōngchéng South*

Hútòng (p220)

5 The heart and soul of Běijīng are its *hútòng*, the intoxicating alleyways that criss-cross the centre of the city. Still home for many locals, these unique lanes not only tie the capital to its ancient past but offer the chance to experience Běijīng street life in all its raucous and cheerful glory. Wandering or cycling the *hútòng*, dating back 800 years in some cases, during the day, and repairing at night to some of the many bars and restaurants that now inhabit them, is an absolutely essential part of any visit to Běijīng.

⊙ *Historic Hútòng*

The Summer Palace *(p156)*

6 The imperial summer playground, the Summer Palace is a beguiling, superbly landscaped collection of temples, pavilions, gardens, lakes, bridges and corridors. Less formal than the Forbidden City, there is still more than enough elegance and beauty in its many structures to take your breath away. Clamber up Longevity Hill, pausing for breath at the various temples that dot it, for splendid views across Bĕijīng, or promenade around Kūnmíng Lake and imagine what it must have been like to have had this place all to yourself. BUDDHIST FRAGRANCE PAVILION (P157)

◉ *The Summer Palace & Hăidiàn*

Lama Temple *(p82)*

7 Bĕijīng's largest, most important and most atmospheric Buddhist temple, the serene Lama Temple used to be home to legions of monks from Mongolia and Tibet and was where the reincarnation of the Panchen Lama was determined. These days it is still an active temple, although tourists now outnumber the monks. There are five beautiful central halls, the last of which houses the world's largest sandalwood Buddha.

◉ *Drum Tower & Dōngchéng North*

Peking Duck (p31)

8 You can't leave Běijīng without sampling its most iconic dish. Once reserved for emperors and mandarins, Peking duck began to feature on the menus of the lower orders at the beginning of the 20th century. Now, there are a number of specialist *kǎoyā* (roast duck) restaurants and the dish is as much a part of Běijīng's fabric as the streets themselves. And these are no ordinary birds. Reared on special farms, the ducks are cooked in a variety of styles steeped in history. By the time it reaches your plate we guarantee your mouth will be watering.

🍴 *Eating*

Chinese Performing Arts *(p226)*

9 Whether it's the chance to experience the intricate, highly stylised Peking opera, or tumbling, spinning and high-wire-walking acrobats, to say nothing of shaven-headed Shàolín monks showing off their supreme fighting skills, Běijīng is a great place to catch a show. There are performances every night of the week, giving you no excuse to miss out. And don't be put off by the language barrier; most shows are easy to follow. Acrobatics in particular is a stunning spectacle. Just don't try to repeat at home what you see here.

☆ *Arts*

Drum & Bell Towers *(p84)*

10 Standing watch over one of the most charming corners of Běijīng, these two magnificent ancient towers, facing each other on either side of a small public square, used to be the city's official timekeeper, with drums beaten and bells rung to mark the times of the day. Climb the Drum Tower to listen to a body-rumbling performance played out on replica drums or climb either tower for a bird's-eye view of the surrounding *hútòng*. Alternatively, perch yourself on a rooftop cafe by the square and enjoy them both in a single glance.

◉ *Drum Tower & Dōngchéng North*

Hòuhǎi Lakes *(p118)*

11 These three interconnected lakes are one of the great outdoor areas in Běijīng and a prime spot to watch, and join, the locals at play. Ringed by bars and restaurants, the lakes themselves provide much of the entertainment. In the summer, flotillas of pedalos take to the water. During the winter, the lakes are the best place in the capital to ice skate. Then there's fishing, kayaking and swimming (for the brave). But perhaps the most amenable option is simply meandering around them, enjoying the sight of Beijingers letting their hair down.

🏃 *Běihǎi Park & Xīchéng North*

798 Art District (p138)

12 Housed inside the cavernous buildings of a disused electronics factory, 798 has become the city's premier art district. It celebrates its proletarian roots via retouched red Maoist slogans decorating gallery interiors and statues of burly, lantern-jawed workers dotting the lanes, while the voluminous factory workshops are ideally suited to ambitious projects requiring lots of space. Cafes dot the streets, making this a pleasant spot for lunch before you plug yourself in to the world of some of China's leading artists. AT CAFE (P144)

👁 *Sānlǐtún & Cháoyáng*

KYLIE MCLAUGHLIN / GETTY IMAGES ©

Pānjiāyuán Market (p148)

13 Save some time at the end of your trip to visit this treasure-filled outdoor market and head home with armfuls of unusual souvenirs. Pānjiāyuán is easily the best place in Běijīng to shop for arts, crafts and (mostly fake) antiques, and even if you don't want to buy anything, it's fun to wander through the clutter. You might not find that rare Yuan-dynasty vase, but what's on view is no less than an A to Z of Middle Kingdom knick-knacks.

🏛 *Sānlǐtún & Cháoyáng*

What's New

Cooking Classes

One of the joys of visiting Běijīng is sampling the superb food on offer, and many people want to replicate the mouthwatering dishes they've tasted once they return home. Now you can, by taking one of the short courses on offer at the variety of cooking schools, run by established chefs, that have mushroomed in the city. Learn to chop like a Chinese cook, as well as how to make delicious dumplings, handpulled noodles or even tongue-numbing Sìchuān dishes.

Bike Sharing

In an effort to get people back on board the mode of transport most associated with the capital, Běijīng's government is making 50,000 bicycles available at 1000 kiosks around the city – and at the knockdown price of ¥1 per hour (¥300 deposit).

National Museum of China

It's been a long wait but finally this mammoth museum has reopened. As well as offering a guide to 5000 years of Chinese history and culture, there are rotating exhibitions from both home and overseas. (p62)

Temple Restaurant

The fine dining scene in Běijīng has exploded in recent years, but the opening of this shrine to contemporary European cuisine has really upped the ante. As an added bonus, the Temple is located in a long-out-of-bounds 600-year-old temple complex. (p70)

Micro-brewing

Běijīng is undergoing a brewing revolution, with a number of micro-breweries offering a welcome alternative to the ubiquitous Yanjing and Tsingtao beers.

New Metro Lines

The roads are more jammed than ever, but compensation has come in the form of new metro lines. Line 9 especially has opened up the previously hard-to-reach southwest, and made it much easier to get to Běijīng West Train Station.

Běijīng Railway Museum

Trainspotters will be in seventh heaven at this newly reopened museum located in the historic former Qiánmén Railway Station. (p109)

Driving Licences

Anyone on a short-term tourist visa can now obtain a temporary driving licence at Běijīng Airport's Terminal 3, opening up the prospect of day trips and more beyond the capital.

Běijīng Natural History Museum

Dinosaurs and creepy-crawlies to keep the kids happy await at this museum, which has reopened its doors after a lengthy closed period. (p109)

For more recommendations and reviews, see **lonelyplanet.com/beijing**

Need to Know

Currency
Yuán (¥; 元)

Language
Mandarin

Visas
Required for almost all nationals. A 30-day visa is standard. Allow three to five working days to process.

Money
Most ATMs accept foreign cards. Most large banks change money. Credit cards are not widely used, so carry cash at all times.

Mobile Phones
Local SIMs can be used in non-locked phones. Local phones are cheap. Smartphones can use China's 3G network (with roaming charges) or free wi-fi spots.

Time
GMT plus eight hours

Tourist Information
Tourist information offices are aimed at domestic tourists. Foreigners are better off using tourist information desks at hotels or, better still, at hostels.

Your Daily Budget
Daily costs can easily spiral into the thousands on a top-end budget. The following are average costs per day.

Budget under ¥200
➡ Staying in hostel dorms

➡ Eating and drinking in locals' restaurants

➡ Travelling by bicycle or public transport

➡ Restricting yourself to one main tourist sight a day

Midrange ¥200–750
➡ Staying in standard private rooms

➡ Eating in a mix of restaurants; drinking in bars

➡ Travelling by taxi

➡ Seeing all the sights

Top end over ¥750
➡ Staying in luxury accommodation

➡ Eating at international restaurants

➡ Drinks at cocktail bars

➡ Guided tours

Advance Planning

Three months before Check your vaccinations are up to date. Book your flights. Sort out your visa. Start learning Mandarin.

One month before Decide which neighbourhood to base yourself in. Scout around for hotel deals.

One week before Have your accommodation booked. Consider possible day trips.

Useful Websites

The Beijinger (www.thebeijinger.com) Eating and entertainment listings, blog posts and forums.

The Běijīng Page (www.beijingpage.com) Online directory with reams of practical info on the city.

Běijīng Cultural Heritage Protection Center (www.bjchp.org) Info on campaigns to help protect Běijīng's *hútòng* (alleyways).

Wild Wall (www.wildwall.com) William Lindesay's website on the Great Wall.

Thorn Tree (www.lonelyplanet.com/thorntree) The China branch of our long-standing travel forum includes plenty of info on Běijīng.

Lonely Planet (www.lonelyplanet.com/china/beijing)

WHEN TO GO

April/May or October/November are pleasant. December to February, dry and cold. June to September, hot and polluted (rainstorms offer respite); oddly, this is peak season.

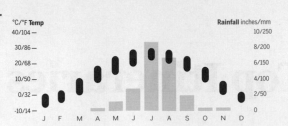

Arriving in Běijīng

Běijīng Capital International Airport Airport Express (¥25, 30 minutes, 6.30am to 11pm) links up with subway system. If taking a taxi (¥80 to ¥100), use official taxi rank only.

Běijīng Train Station On subway Line 2.

Běijīng West Train Station Soon to be on subway Line 9. Until then, 20-minute walk from Military Museum subway station on Line 1 (walk directly north then turn right at the end).

Běijīng South Train Station On subway Line 4.

 For much more on **arrival** see p242

Getting Around

➡ **Bicycle** The most fun, and often the quickest, way to get around. Almost every road has a bike lane. Bike rental per day is ¥30 to ¥50.

➡ **Walking** The best way to see Běijīng's *hútòng*.

➡ **Subway** Quick, modern and easy to use, but often overcrowded. Per trip ¥2.

➡ **Buses** Dirt cheap and extensive, but difficult for non-Chinese speakers to negotiate, and often overcrowded. Per trip ¥1, with travel card ¥0.4.

➡ **Taxis** Cheap by Western standards but at certain times hard to find, and traffic jams can really slow things down. Flag fall is ¥10.

 For much more on **getting around** see p248

Sleeping

Accommodation is of a decent standard in Běijīng, but can be expensive. Hostels provide best value for money, with traveller-friendly facilities and staff with good English-language skills. Budget travellers can also tap into Běijīng's ever-growing couch-surfing community. The city's courtyard hotels are wonderfully atmospheric, and plant you right in the thick of the *hútòng* action, but they lack the facilities of top-end hotels in the same price bracket. You can book rooms over the phone, or directly through hotel websites. Or else use one of the following:

Useful Websites

➡ **airbnb** (www.airbnb.com) Private rooms for short-term (even daily) rent.

➡ **CTrip** (www.english.ctrip.com) Discounted hotels.

➡ **Couch Surfing** (www.couchsurfing.org) Stay with locals for free.

➡ **Hostel Bookers** (www.hostelbookers.com) Hostel bookings, ratings and reviews.

 For much more on **sleeping** see p188

Top Itineraries

Day One

Temple of Heaven Park & Dōngchéng South (p104)

 You're jet-lagged anyway, so what the heck? Get up at the crack of dawn and head straight for **Temple of Heaven Park**. Běijīng is blessed with some fabulous city parks, but this is arguably the most captivating of all, and early morning, when it's filled with locals rather than tourists, is the best time to visit. Wander around its ancient cypress trees watching Beijingers perform taichi, fly kites or practise their favourite opera songs, then pay a visit to the magnificent **Hall of Prayer for Good Harvests** – Ming-dynasty architectural perfection.

> **Lunch** Sample folk cuisine from Yúnnán province at Lost Heaven (p110).

Forbidden City & Dōngchéng Central (p50)

Join the crowds of domestic tourists on their pilgrimage-like tour of China's most famous public space, **Tiān'ānmén Square**, before spending the afternoon exploring the immense palace grounds of the **Forbidden City**.

> **Dinner** Běipíngjū (p123) offers excellent-value Peking duck.

Drum Tower & Dōngchéng North (p80)

Start your evening with cocktails in **Mao Mao Chong**, just a few doors down from the restaurant, before working your way along the numerous bars of **Nanluogu Xiang** and finishing off with some live music in **Mao Livehouse**.

Day Two

Drum Tower & Dōngchéng North (p80)

 Ease yourself into Day Two with a calming stroll around the incense-filled courtyards of the **Lama Temple** before visiting the equally peaceful **Confucius Temple**. Grab a coffee at nearby **Confucius Cafe** before heading for lunch.

> **Lunch** At Qì Shān Miàn (p90) try delicious Xī'ān-style noodles.

Summer Palace & Hǎidiàn (p154)

Time to escape the city centre and head to the western outskirts for an afternoon trip to the **Summer Palace**, where the imperial court used to decamp to flee Běijīng's midsummer heatwaves. Built around the cooling waters of the huge Kūnmíng Lake, the palace grounds and its buildings demand at least a couple of hours of your time. Stay too long, though, and you'll miss your date with the **Peking opera**. Head to Húguǎng Guild Hall, the most atmospheric of Běijīng's opera venues.

> **Dinner** Dūyīchù (p112) is more refined than your average dumplings joint.

Dashilar & Xīchéng South (p128)

Join the backpackers – and the *hútòng* vibe – with a drink at Helen's Restaurant & Bar (p132) in Dashilar.

Day Three

Forbidden City & Dōngchéng Central (p50)

 Start your day early in another city park. **Jǐngshān Park** is also one of our favourites. It's smaller than Temple of Heaven, but it's usually bursting with colour, thanks to its flower-filled gardens and the ribbon-waving locals who come here to dance the morning away. After joining in with a game of *jiànzi* (keepie-uppies with an oversized shuttlecock), climb Coal Hill for splendid views of the Forbidden City. If you have time, hop over to neighbouring Běihǎi Park for a dash of history and a spot of boating.

Lunch Zuǒ Lín Yòu Shè (p70) does Běijīng grub in a no-nonsense setting.

Drum Tower & Dōngchéng North (p80)

Catch one of the shudderingly loud drumming performances inside the **Drum Tower** before walking across the square to climb the equally sublime **Bell Tower**. Save some time to walk over to **Pénghāo** to enjoy an am-dram show in this small *hútòng* venue.

Dinner Try charming Dàlǐ Courtyard (p90) for stylish Yúnnán cuisine.

Drum Tower & Dōngchéng North

Depending on your musical tastes, catch some live music at **Jiāng Hú**, **Jiāng Jìn Jiǔ** or **Yúgōng Yíshān**.

Day Four

Sānlǐtún & Cháoyáng (p136)

 Head out to **798 Art District** in the morning (not too early, though; nothing opens before 10am) to immerse yourself in Běijīng's art scene. Wander the galleries, stop for coffee and chat to young artists whilst eyeing up your possible options for lunch.

Lunch 798's first cafe, At Cafe (p144) is still popular with local artists.

Sānlǐtún & Cháoyáng

You're in *the* district for shopping. Either head to the ultra-modern, and ultra-cool, at **Sānlǐtún Village** or dive into the curio chaos at **Pānjiāyuán Market**. Save time to catch an **acrobatics show** before dinner. Cháoyáng Theatre is nearest, but Tiānqiáo Acrobatics Theatre is better.

 Dinner Nàjiā Xiǎoguǎn (p140) – imperial cuisine with an old-Běijīng vibe.

Sānlǐtún & Cháoyáng

For a rough-and-ready finale, catch a metal band at **Dos Kolegas**. For something more refined, head to the roof terrace at **Migas** or sip cocktails in **Apothecary**.

If You Like...

Imperial Architecture

Forbidden City Sitting at the very heart of Běijīng, this vast 9000-room palace made up of hundreds of buildings is China's best-preserved reminder of its imperial past. (p52)

Temple of Heaven This collection of extraordinary altars and halls is the supreme expression of Ming-dynasty architecture. (p106)

Summer Palace A harmonious marvel of landscaping on the outskirts of the city that features hilltop temples and elegant pavilions all set around a lake. (p156)

Drum & Bell Towers Dating back to the Mongol occupation of Běijīng and still standing guard over the surrounding *hútòng* (narrow alleyways). (p84)

Gate of Heavenly Peace Chairman Mao's portrait may adorn it, and he proclaimed the founding of the People's Republic of China (PRC) from atop it, but this was the largest gateway to the old imperial city. (p63)

Workers Cultural Palace Not a very promising name, but this little-visited and quiet park was once an important place of worship for China's emperors and is home to some superb imperial-era halls. (p63)

Southeast Corner Watchtower Splendid Ming-dynasty structure that rises above the last remaining stretch of the former city walls. (p109)

Prince Gong's Residence An imperial-style home and the finest example of a traditional

LONELY PLANET / GETTY IMAGES ©

Silk Market (p148)

courtyard house, only on a very grand scale. (p118)

Foreign Legation Quarter Imperial, but in the Western fashion rather than the Chinese; an incongruous slice of colonial-era European architecture in Běijīng. (p64)

Ming Tombs The Unesco-protected final resting place of 13 of the 16 Ming-dynasty emperors showcases some of Běijīng's largest and most-impressive imperial structures. (p181)

Parks

Fragrant Hills Park Superb in the early autumn, when Beijingers flock here to see the maple leaves turn red against the green backdrop of the hills. (p161)

Běihǎi Park Hire a boat and spend a lazy day floating on the lake, or just amble around watching the locals at play. (p116)

Temple of Heaven Park A prime spot for people-watching, as Běijīng's senior citizens dance or practise taichi in the shade of thousands of ancient cypress trees. (p106)

Jǐngshān Park Climb the man-made hill for fine views over the Forbidden City. (p62)

Rìtán Park A soothing escape from the hustle of the nearby CBD, fly a kite by the altar to the sun that's located here. (p139)

Dìtán Park Home to Běijīng's most popular temple fair during the Spring Festival. (p86)

Hòuhǎi lakes Not strictly a park, but still one of the most happening open spaces in Běijīng; a playground by day and nightlife hub come sundown. (p116)

Markets

Pānjiāyuán Market Hands-down the most fun market in the city, a chaotic jumble of antiques, calligraphy, carpets, curios, furniture and Mao memorabilia. (p148)

Mǎliándào Tea Market All the tea in China, or at least most of it, with tea shops galore around it for those in search of tea sets. (p134)

Silk Market Still one of the essential stops for many visitors to the capital, its collection of counterfeit clothes and bags is as popular as the genuine silk sold here. (p148)

Hóngqiáo (Pearl) Market Pearls and more pearls, of wildly different quality, as well as all manner of ephemera. (p113)

Temples

Lama Temple A former royal palace that is now home to chanting monks, this impressive, ornate complex is Běijīng's most popular Buddhist temple. (p82)

Confucius Temple Lovely, tranquil retreat from the hustle of Běijīng's chaotic streets and surrounded by atmospheric *hútòng*. (p86)

Dōngyuè Temple Perhaps the strangest temple in the capital, certainly the most morbid, this thought-provoking and very active Taoist shrine has halls dedicated to ghosts and the God who manages the 18 levels of hell. (p139)

White Cloud Temple Founded in AD 739 and tended by top-knotted Taoist monks, White Cloud Temple is the HQ for China's Taoists and home to a fabulous temple fair during Spring Festival. (p118)

For more top Beijing spots, see the following:

➡ Eating (p30)

➡ Drinking & Nightlife (p40)

➡ Entertainment (p42)

➡ Shopping (p44)

Fǎyuán Temple Secluded and very ancient shrine, dating back to the 7th century AD, and still busy with worshippers. (p130)

Wǔtǎ Temple A distinct oddity, with its five striking pagodas, and more reminiscent of an Indian temple than a Chinese one. (p158)

Fine Dining

Maison Boulud With a menu that changes with the season and fabulous service, the opening of this superb French restaurant signalled the capital's emergence as a fine-dining destination. (p110)

Temple The hip destination of the moment for Běijīng's gourmands, with a contemporary European menu and a fabulous location in a former temple. (p70)

Capital M Classic Mediterranean meets North African dishes and views over Tiān'ānmén Sq at this Běijīng outpost of a celebrated Shànghǎi restaurant. (p111)

Dàlǐ Courtyard Ever-changing menu centred around the exquisite flavours of southwestern Yúnnán province and with a romantic courtyard. (p90)

Duck de Chine A France-meets-China take on the capital's favourite bird in industrial-chic surroundings. (p142)

Běi Smart, sophisticated restaurant that specialises in north

Asian dishes, taking the best of northern Chinese, Japanese and South Korean cuisines. (p142)

Courtyard The setting right by the Forbidden City couldn't be better – book ahead for a window seat – and the food and wine list are top class. (p70)

Source Swish Sìchuān, with the spices toned down for Western palates, in a delightful courtyard house in the heart of *hútòng* land. (p91)

Tiāndì Yījiā Hushed and refined courtyard restaurant in the shadow of the Forbidden City, whose menu ranges across China, from dim sum to Peking duck. (p74)

Grill 79 Fantastic views over Běijīng (on a clear day), serious steaks and a superb wine list. (p142)

Museums & Galleries

Capital Museum Běijīng's finest; containing superbly informative galleries on the evolution of the city and its customs, and all in a bright, user-friendly environment. (p119)

798 Art District A maze of galleries devoted to the weird and wonderful world of Chinese contemporary art; be prepared to be alternatively bemused and captivated. (p139)

Poly Art Museum The place to see some of the ancient treasures, including incredible bronzes, that weren't pillaged by invading armies in the 19th Century. (p67)

Běijīng Police Museum Brothels, opium dens, class traitors, gangsters and spies; the past and present Běijīng underworld revealed in all its fascinating, sometimes gruesome, glory. (p64)

Military Museum Something of a propaganda exercise perhaps, but plenty of detail on China's martial past and lots and lots of guns, swords, tanks, missiles and planes. (p161)

Běijīng Ancient Architecture Museum Little-visited but excellent museum housed in a former Ming-dynasty temple that offers a great guide to how the imperial city was built. (p130)

Red Gate Gallery The original gallery devoted to modern Chinese art, and still a trailblazer in the artists it showcases. (p109)

National Museum of China Newly renovated, extensive trawl through 5000 years of Chinese history and culture. (p62)

Chinese Performing Arts

Tiānqiáo Acrobatics Theatre Perhaps the finest tumbling, spinning, high-wire-walking show in town, and less touristy than other venues. (p132)

Húguǎng Guild Hall Fantastic, historic venue for Peking Opera, with the audience close to the action and superb balconies overlooking the stage. (p132)

National Centre for the Performing Arts One of the key hubs of Běijīng cultural life, as well as one of the city's most striking buildings, with China's top orchestras and classical dance troupes regular performers. (p123)

Lao She Teahouse A little bit of everything takes place here on a nightly basis: Peking Opera, shadow-puppet and folk-music performances especially, but also crosstalk: traditional Běijīng stand-up comedy. (p132)

China Puppet Theatre Shadowplay and puppetry every weekend, and a great place to take kids who've had enough of sightseeing. (p98)

Live Music

Yúgōng Yíshān Chinese and foreign bands and electronic knob-twiddlers, as well as an audience-friendly vibe, make this the top venue for seeing live music in the capital. (p97)

Mao Livehouse Big enough to make you feel like you're at a real event, but small enough to still feel intimate, a sound booking policy and a cracking sound system. (p98)

East Shore Jazz Café The number one spot in town for jazzers with a prime location by the side of the Hòuhǎi lakes, a relaxed feel and cool tunes late into the night. (p123)

Dos Kolegas A little bit out of the way, but this is a grungy gem of a venue that puts on a lot of the local punk and alternative bands. (p147)

Temple Bar The owners are tattooed and pierced metal and punk fiends, but all sorts of bands take to the stage at this friendly place. (p97)

Jiāng Jìn Jiǔ A cafe by day that puts on a lot of folk and ethnic minority acts, especially Uighur and Mongolian, which you won't hear anywhere else once the sun goes down. (p97)

What? Bar Years ago this tiny place was just about the only venue in town; it still has loads of character and it's a good place to see up and coming new bands. (p75)

Month by Month

China follows both the *yánglì* (Gregorian) and the *yīnlì* (lunar) calendars. Traditional Chinese festivals are calculated according to the lunar calendar and fall on different days each year according to the Gregorian calendar.

January

Běijīng shivers at the beginning of the year, with temperatures dipping down to −10°C or below. But there are far fewer visitors in town, so this is a great time to see the Great Wall or the Forbidden City without the crowds.

✸✸ Western New Year

With the Spring Festival as their New Year bash, the Chinese treat the Western New Year (元旦; Yuándàn) on 1 January as an excuse just to party and have fun. But don't expect any fireworks.

✸✸ Spring Festival

As big as Christmas in the West, the family-oriented Spring Festival (春节; Chūn Jié) is the most joyous celebration of the year. Fireworks illuminate the night sky and everyone is more relaxed and friendly. It usually falls sometime between late January and mid-February, depending on the lunar calendar. In 2014 it starts on 31 January.

February

Not a good month for air pollution and it's still cold, but the end of the Spring Festival means winter is drawing to a close.

✸✸ Valentine's Day

China has its own festival for lovers (held on the seventh day of the seventh month of the lunar year), but it's not nearly as popular as the Western version, Valentine's Day (请人节; Qíngrén Jié). Book ahead if you want to eat out.

✸✸ Lantern Festival

Celebrated 15 days after the first day of the Spring Festival, the Lantern Festival (元宵节; Yuánxiāo Jié) is a very colourful time to visit Běijīng, as the Chinese devour *yuánxiāo* (glutinous rice dumplings with sweet fillings), while firework shows explode all over town.

March

It's almost time to put away the winter wardrobe. The domestic tourists who came for the Spring Festival have gone, but foreign ones are arriving in numbers.

✸✸ International Literary Festival

The excellent International Literary Festival (国际文学节; Guójì Wénxué Jié) sees writers and bibliophiles convening at the Bookworm (www.chinabookworm.com) for a two-week bonanza of readings and talks. With a very strong line-up of international authors and local writers, it's one of the key cultural events of the year. Get tickets early.

✿ Guanyin's Birthday

Held on the 19th day of the second moon, the birthday of Guanyin (观世音生日; Guānshìyīn Shēngrì), the Buddhist Goddess of Mercy, is a fine time to visit Buddhist temples. It falls on 19 March in 2014.

April

One of the nicest months of the year to be in Běijīng, as a fresh wind keeps the sky clear and willow catkins (*liŭxù*) flutter through the air. It's getting warmer.

✿ Tomb Sweeping Day

A day for worshipping ancestors, Tomb Sweeping Day (清明节; Qīngmíng Jié) falls on 5 April (4 April in leap years). People visit and clean the graves of their departed relatives, placing flowers on tombs and burning ghost money for the departed. It's an official public holiday.

✿ Midi Festival

China's longest-running music festival, Midi (迷笛音乐节; Mídí Yīnyuè Jié), normally takes place in Hăidiàn (or sometimes in Tōngzhōu on the eastern outskirts of Běijīng) on the last weekend of April. Both domestic and international bands and electronic acts play. It's a great chance to mingle with local music fans.

May

The temperature starts to soar; the beginning of the fiercely hot and humid Běijīng summer. May also

(Top) Procession for Spring Festival
(Bottom) Lanterns for Mid-Autumn Festival

marks the beginning of the peak tourist season.

✨ May Day

May Day (五一; Wǔyī) on 1 May kicks off a much-needed three-day national holiday for Chinese, who swamp tourist sights the length and breadth of the nation.

June

Hot and sweaty days and balmy nights. But this month is also the peak time for rainfall in Běijīng. The main tourist sites are packed.

✨ Dragon Boat Festival

Held on the fifth day of the fifth month of the lunar year (usually June), the Dragon Boat Festival (端午节; Duānwǔ Jié) races are sometimes staged on Běijīng's reservoirs and you'll see people all over town scoffing *zòngzi* (delicious parcels of sticky rice and meat or vegies wrapped in a bamboo leaf).

🎟 Affordable Art Beijing

Normally held at the 798 Art District, Affordable Art Beijing (买得起艺术博览会; Mǎidéqǐ Yìshù Bólǎnhuì; www.affordableartchina.com) showcases emerging contemporary Chinese art-

ists and, as its name suggests, prices are reasonable.

September

The crowds are thinning out a little at the main tourist sites and the heat has mercifully relented. But this month sometimes sees major gatherings of the Chinese Communist Party (CCP) in the capital, which means enhanced security around Tiān'ānmén Sq.

✨ Mid-Autumn Festival

Also known as the Moon Festival, the Mid-Autumn Festival (中秋节; Zhōngqiū Jié) is marked by eating *yuèbǐng* (moon cakes), gazing at the full moon and family reunions. In 2014 it falls on 8 September.

October

Autumn is a fine time to visit Běijīng as it enjoys high clear skies and perhaps its best weather of the year. It can feel crowded, though, as domestic visitors descend on the capital during Golden Week.

✨ National Day

Crowds flock to Tiān'ānmén Sq for a huge party on National Day (国庆节; Guóqìng Jié), on 1 Oc-

tober, followed by a massive week-long national holiday where the Chinese blow their hard-earned savings on travelling and enjoying themselves in what is known as Golden Week.

✨ Beijing Music Festival

Usually staged throughout October, this classical-music festival (北京国际音乐节; Běijīng Guójì Yīnyuè Jié; www.bmf.org.cn) showcases foreign orchestras and musicians and has become increasingly high-profile in recent years. It's a must for Běijīng culture vultures.

December

Běijīng can feel gloomy once winter descends and it becomes relentlessly cold. But a white Christmas is a real possibility, and you can strap on the ice skates and take to the Hòuhǎi lakes.

✨ Christmas Day

Not an official Chinese festival perhaps, but Christmas (圣诞节; Shèngdàn Jié) is a major milestone on the commercial calendar, when Běijīng's big shopping zones sparkle with decorations and younger Chinese get into the Yuletide spirit.

Temple of Heaven Park (p106), Jǐngshān Park (p62), Rìtán Park (p139) or Cháoyáng Park (Map p298).

With Kids

The Chinese have a deep and uncomplicated love of children and openly display their affection for them. Běijīng may have less child-friendly facilities than equivalent-sized cities in the West, but the locals will go out of their way to accommodate your kids.

Need to Know

Discounts Kids are often half price; under 1.2m in height are usually free.

Nappies Baby essentials are widely available at supermarkets.

Non-smoking Most restaurants are smoky. Sit outside if you can. We've reviewed non-smoking restaurants with a special icon.

Bike seats Rent baby seats and helmets from Bike Běijīng (p77).

Seatbelts Only in the front of taxis.

Getting Lost Always arm your child with your hotel's business card.

Toddlers

Parks

Toddlers will love running around Běijīng's parks, exploring their dinky pathways and dancing along to bands of local singers. They're also perfect for family picnics. Try

Young Kids

Lakes

The lakes at Hòuhǎi (p118) provide pedal-boat action. Historic Běihǎi Park (p116) also has a large boating lake. Come winter, the lakes at Hòuhǎi freeze and become central Běijīng's biggest playground. Rent ice-skates, ice-bikes and even ice bumper cars! The rest of the year, try Le Cool Ice Rink (p153) inside the China World Shopping Mall.

Swimming

For water slides, try the outdoor pools at Cháoyáng Park, Tuánjiéhú Park (Map p298) with its mini beach, or Qīngnián Hú Park (p103). For something bigger, head to the indoor Happy Magic Water Park (p153).

Toy Markets

The Toy Market (p113) behind Hóngqiáo Pearl Market is full of cheap toys that whiz, whir, beep and flash. Try also New China Children's Store (p76).

Kite-Flying

Buy a traditional Chinese kite (p126) and head to one of the parks to join Běijīng's legion of kite-flying enthusiasts.

Museums & Shows

Try the vast China Science & Technology Museum (p140) or the Běijīng Natural History Museum (p109), which has dinosaurs! Kids will love the China Puppet Theatre (p98) or an acrobatics show (p132).

Teenagers

Hiking & Cycling

Older kids will love the adventure of hiking along The Great Wall (p166); just be sure they know the dangers. Cycling tours (p225) around the *hútòng* (narrow alleyways; p220) can also be fun.

Like a Local

Eat pancakes off a cycle rickshaw, use a shuttlecock for keepie-uppies, and walk backwards, barefoot, along pebbled pathways; you're in Běijīng now, where people do things a bit differently.

LONELY PLANET / GETTY IMAGES ©

Outdoor dining near Lu Xun Museum (p120)

Eating

Běijīng Cuisine

Běijīng has pretty much every type of world cuisine covered – be it Chinese or international – but there are still a few restaurants knocking out genuine old-Běijīng tucker.

Breakfast

Skip the expensive fry-up and coffee in your hostel and head to any restaurant between 6am and 8.30am that has bamboo baskets stacked up at its entrance. This indicates that they do dumplings. Order *'yītì bāozi'* (a basket of dumplings) with *'yīwǎn zhōu'* (a bowl of rice porridge), and tuck in. You'll pay less than one US dollar. Other favourite breakfast combos here include *yóutiáo* (油条; fried dough sticks) with *dòujiāng* (豆浆; soy milk); and *húntún* (馄饨; wonton soup) with *shāobing* (烧饼; sesame-seed roasted bun).

Snacks & Street Food

Things to look out for in the evenings include *yángròu chuàn* (羊肉串; lamb skewers) – any place with a large red neon 串 sign does them. During the day, look for *jiānbing* (煎饼; savoury pancakes), often cooked off the back of a cycle rickshaw.

Food Markets

Western-style supermarkets are on the rise, but thankfully there are still some atmospheric food markets in Běijīng where you can stock up on fresh fruit as you watch locals pick their favourite frogs and fish. Try Rùndélì Food Market (Map p294) near Hòuhǎi Lake or Xīnmín Food Market (Map p290) in Dōngchéng North.

Park Life

Group Dancing

Locals often congregate in parks for a hearty singsong or a good old dance. Large-group formation dancing, accompanied by heavily amplified, patriotic songs is the order of the day, and passers-by are always welcome to join in. It isn't just parks that attract group dancing; any large paved area of the city, especially public squares (although not Tiān'ānmén Sq), are prime locations come early evening. Try the square between the Drum and Bell Towers, or the lakeside Hòuhǎi Park (Map p294).

Flying Kites

The all-time classic Chinese pastime is as popular as ever and Běijīng's parks are a great place to join in. Buy a kite (p126) then head to any park; the northeast corner of Temple of Heaven Park (p106) is a good spot.

Games

Card games are very popular, as is *jiànzi*; an oversized shuttlecock that's used for keepie-uppies. Older people enjoy the soothing nature of *róuʔqiú* (taiji softball). Whatever the game, locals are almost always happy for you to join in. So, don't just stand there taking photos; play!

Working Out

All Běijīng parks have exercise areas with low-tech apparatus, such as pull-up bars and leg curls. Hòuhǎi Exercise Park (Map p294)is a popular lakeside version. Some areas include a pebble path. Try walking barefoot along them; good for your circulation, apparently, especially if you do it backwards.

Taichi

You'll notice some trees in parks have a worn out ring of bare ground around the base of their trunk. This marks out the tree as a taichi spot. Every day, usually early in the morning, someone will come to this tree to perform his or her preferred taichi movements. It's fascinating to watch.

Other Activities

Cycling

Cyclist numbers are declining, but they are still huge, and cycling along with the masses is a great way to feel like you are a part of the everyday city flow. It's also the perfect way to explore Běijīng's *hútòng*.

Table Tennis

It's easy to understand how China dominates world table tennis when you see how easily available the sport is. Schools have whole floors of buildings dedicated to table tennis, and there are free-to-use tables dotted around the city, in most parks and most residential areas. If you fancy being on the wrong end of a ping-pong thrashing, head to Jǐngshān Table Tennis Park (p77). Hòuhǎi Exercise Park also has tables.

Ice Swimming

Every day of the year a group of dedicated Beijingers go swimming in the lakes at Hòuhǎi. Nothing strange about that, until it gets to December, when temperatures plummet and the lake freezes over. Instead of taking a winter break, they rise early each morning, smash a hole in the ice and go for the coldest swim imaginable. Head to Hòuhǎi Exercise Park if you want to watch or, heaven forbid, take a plunge yourself.

Nightlife

KTV

Bars and clubs are a Western influence. Most locals just go for a slap-up meal if they fancy a night out. If they do go anywhere after dinner, it's usually to a karaoke joint, aka KTV. You're locked away in your own private room, so it's pretty boring on your own, but if you get the chance to join a group of Chinese friends, take it; the Chinese enthusiasm for belting out pop classics is incredible, and most KTV joints have an English song list available too.

Báijiǔ

We don't recommend you drink this stuff – it is lethal – but the few old Beijingers who are serious drinkers, tend only to drink *báijiǔ* (白酒); a potent liquor made from sorghum. If you do get goaded into a *báijiǔ* session at a local restaurant (no one drinks *báijiǔ* in bars), take care. The protocol is to down glassfuls in one hit, whilst declaring '*gānbēi!*' ('dry glass!'), so getting blind drunk doesn't take long.

For Free

Běijīng may not appear at first sight to be a city overburdened with freebies. But dig a little deeper and there are a plethora of places to see, things to do and worthwhile experiences to be had that don't involve cash changing hands.

Free Activities

Hòuhǎi Lakes
Join the locals as they promenade around the lakes (p118), offer them advice on their kite-flying technique, or scrounge a bat and play them at table tennis. The fearless can dive into the water for a free swim.

Hútòng
Walk your shoes off through the myriad of ancient alleyways that crisscross central Běijīng. There's something to see almost every step of the way.

Pānjiāyuán Market
Best visited early on Sunday morning, this market (p148) is a fantastic place to browse, although with so much on offer you will be tempted to spend money.

798 Art District
One of the very best freebies in town is spending a day perusing the numerous galleries of this art district (p138) inhabiting a former electronics factory. They're mostly closed on Mondays.

Free Museums
All you have to do to get into the following for free is bring your passport.

Capital Museum
The best museum (p119) in the city, with a host of galleries and exhibits relating to Běijīng's history.

Military Museum
Guns, planes, rockets and tanks. Hours of warlike fun and all things military (p161).

National Museum of China
Visit the National Museum (p62) for a crash course in 5000 years of Chinese history.

Free Sights

Tiān'ānmén Square
Stroll with the hordes of domestic visitors, catch the flag-raising and lowering ceremonies at dawn and dusk, and watch the kite-flying in the world's largest public square (p60).

Chairman Mao Memorial Hall
It doesn't cost a máo to shuffle reverently past the Great Helmsman's mummified remains in this memorial hall (p62).

Foreign Legation Quarter
Enjoy a walk past the imposing European architecture of this area (p64).

Ming City Wall Ruins Park
The sole remaining section of the Ming city walls (p109) that once enclosed Běijīng, this slice of history comes gratis.

Qianmen Dajie
Tourist tacky perhaps, but Qianmen Dajie (p110) is still a great place to watch the locals at play.

Wǔtǎ Temple
Free admission on Wednesdays for the first 200 visitors to the temple (p158).

Dōnghuámén Night Market (p73)

 # Eating

Běijīng is a magnificent place for culinary adventures. With upwards of 60,000 restaurants serving up not only local specialities but also cuisines from every corner of China and the world, some of your most memorable Běijīng experiences will take place around the dining table. So do as the locals do – pick up those chopsticks and dive in.

Peking duck

Peking Duck

Undoubtedly the capital's most-iconic dish, you'd have to be quackers to leave Běijīng without trying Peking duck. While its fame has spread around the world, nothing beats sampling it in the city where it comes from. Its origins go back as far as the 13th century and the Yuan dynasty, when it was listed in royal cookbooks. But it wasn't until imperial rule in China came to an end in 1911 that most ordinary people got the chance to try it when the former palace cooks set up roast-duck restaurants around Běijīng.

Chefs go through a lengthy process to prepare the duck. First the birds are inflated by blowing air between the skin and body. The skin is then pricked and boiling water poured all over the duck. Sometimes the skin is rubbed with malt sugar to give it an amber colour, before being hung up to air dry and then roasted in the oven. When roasted, the flesh becomes crispy on the outside and juicy on the inside. The bird is then meticulously cut into slices and served with fermented bean paste, light pancakes, sliced cucumbers and green onions.

Vegetarians & Vegans

China has a long history of Taoist and Buddhist philosophers who abstained from eating animals, and vegetarianism can be traced back over 1000 years. But try telling that to your waiter when he brings out a supposedly pristine veggie or tofu dish decorated with strips of pork or chicken. The majority of Chinese have little understanding of vegetarianism and many consider it a strange Western concept.

NEED TO KNOW

Price Ranges

The following price ranges are used in all our listings and represent the cost of a meal for one person.

$ less than ¥50
$$ ¥50 to ¥100
$$$ more than ¥100

Opening Hours

Běijīng restaurants are mostly open from around 10am to 11pm, although there are quite a few that run 24/7. Many shut after lunch and reopen at 5pm. Generally, the Chinese eat much earlier than Westerners, lunching from 11am and having dinner at about 6pm.

Menus

Be warned that some restaurants in tourist areas still fob off foreigners with an English menu (英文菜单; *yīngwén càidān*) that has higher prices than the Chinese menu (中文菜单; *zhōngwén càidān*). Generally, though, most places have picture and/or English menus now.

Service

With the exception of upmarket restaurants, service can often be erratic and/or lackadaisical. Unless you're in a restaurant serving foreign food, don't expect the waiting staff to speak English.

Smoking

There are nonsmoking signs in most Běijīng restaurants these days, but that doesn't mean they are adhered to. Smoking is still commonplace in many eateries. Our listings note if an establishment is tobacco-free.

Tipping

Tipping is not standard practice in Běijīng. Leave a tip in a local restaurant and the waiter will likely come after you saying you've forgotten your change. Some upmarket Western places, though, do tack on a service charge to the bill, as do high-end hotel restaurants.

With a long history of poverty and famine in China, eating meat is a sign of status and symbolises health and wealth. Vegetables are often fried in animal-based oils,

Above: Dumplings
Left: Vegetables for sale at *hútòng* stall

and soups are most commonly made with chicken or beef stock. Saying you don't eat meat confuses many Chinese, and trying to explain why you don't eat meat leads to even more head-scratching.

However, in the major cities vegetarianism is slowly catching on and there are an increasing number of vegetarian (吃素的人; *chīsùderén*) eateries, while many Buddhist temples also have vegetarian restaurants. Nevertheless, vegetarian food consists often of 'mock meat' dishes made from tofu, wheat gluten and vegetables. Some of the dishes are almost works of art, with the ingredients sculpted to look like spare ribs or fried chicken and 'bones' created from carrots and lotus roots.

Etiquette

Strict rules of etiquette don't really apply to Chinese dining, with the notable exception of formal banquets. Table manners are relaxed and get more so as the meal unfolds and the drinks flow. Meals can commence in Confucian fashion – with good intentions, a harmonic arrangement of chopsticks and a clean tablecloth – before spiralling into Taoist mayhem, fuelled by never-ending glasses of *píjiǔ* (啤酒; beer) or *báijiǔ* (白酒; white spirit) and a procession of dishes. At the end of a meal, the table can resemble a battlefield, with empty bottles, stray bones and other debris strewn across it.

A typical dining scenario sees a group seated at a round table. Often, one person will order for everyone and the dishes will be shared; group diners never order dishes just for themselves. Many foreigners get asked if they mind dishes that are *là* (辣; spicy); if you don't, then say '*bú yào tài là*' (not too spicy). The Chinese believe that a mix of tastes, textures and temperatures is the key to a good meal, so they start with

Eating by Neighbourhood

The Summer Palace & Hǎidiàn
Korean and Japanese eateries in Wǔdàokǒu

Drum & Bell Towers

Drum Tower & Dōngchéng North
Courtyard restaurants, vegetarian and Ghost St

Běihǎi Park & Xīchéng North
Local and foreign places around Hòuhǎi lakes

Sānlǐtún & Cháoyáng
Largest selection of foreign restaurants

Forbidden City & Dōngchéng Central
Foreign places, dumpling joints and Sìchuān

Dashilar & Xīchéng South
Muslim food around Niújiē Mosque

Temple of Heaven Park & Dōngchéng South
Peking duck and Western food

Xiba River
Hucheng River (City Moat)
Liangma River
Xīhǎi Lake
Hòuhǎi Lake
Qiánhǎi Lake
Nanluogu Xiang
Běihǎi Park
Jǐngshān Park
Zhōnghǎi Lake
Forbidden City
Nánhǎi Lake
Yùyuāntán
Yongding River
Tiān'ānmén Square
Tonghui River
Temple of Heaven
Hucheng River (City Moat)
Hucheng River (City Moat)

cold dishes and titbits and follow them with a selection of hot meat, fish and vegetable dishes. Bear in mind that waiters will expect you to order straightaway after sitting down and will hover at your shoulder until you do. If you want more time, say '*wǒ huì jiào nǐ*' (I'll call you).

At big tables, the dishes are placed on a lazy Susan, which revolves so everyone can access the food. Rice often arrives at the end of the meal but if you want it before, just ask. The mainland Chinese dig their chopsticks into communal dishes, or spoons will be used to ladle out the food, but don't root around for a piece of food. Instead, identify it first and go directly to it without touching what's around it. Bones can be deposited in your side dish, or even on the table itself. If you're in doubt about what to do, just follow the example of the people around you.

Běijīng Bites

Off the main roads is a world of steaming food stalls and eateries teeming with activity. Eat this way and you will be dining as most Beijingers do. Breakfast can be easily catered for with a *yóutiáo* (油条; deep-fried dough stick), a sip of *dòuzhī* (豆汁; bean curd drink) or a bowl of *zhōu* (粥; rice porridge). Other snacks include the crunchy, pancake-like *jiānbǐng* (煎饼). The heavy meat-filled *ròubǐng* (肉饼; cooked bread filled with finely chopped pork) are lifesavers and very cheap. A handy vegetarian option is *jiǔcài bǐng* (韭菜饼; bread stuffed with cabbage, chives,

leek or fennel and egg). *Dàbǐng* (大饼; a chunk of round, unleavened bread sprinkled with sesame seeds) can be found everywhere, and of course there's *mántou* (馒头; steamed bread).

Hóngshǔ (红薯; baked sweet potatoes) are cheap and filling and sold during winter. *Málà tàng* (麻辣烫) is a spicy noodle soup that's very warming in winter, and has chunks of *dòufu* (豆腐; bean curd), cabbage and other veggies – choose your own ingredients from the trays. Also look out for *ròu jiāmó* (肉夹馍), a scrumptious open-your-mouth-wide bun filled with meat, chilli and garlic shoots. But perhaps the most ubiquitous Běijīng snack is *kǎo yángròu chuàn* (烤羊肉串; lamb kebabs), which are sold throughout the city at all times of the day and night.

Desserts & Sweets

The Chinese do not generally eat dessert, but fruit is considered an appropriate end to a good meal. Western influence has added ice cream to the menu in some restaurants, but in general sweet stuff is consumed as snacks and is seldom available in restaurants.

One exception to the rule is caramelised fruits, including apples (拔丝苹果; *básī píngguǒ*) and bananas (拔丝香蕉; *básī xiāngjiāo*), which you can find in a few restaurants. Other sweeties include shaved ice and syrup (冰沙; *bīngshā*); a sweet, sticky rice pudding known as Eight Treasure Rice (八宝饭; Bābǎofàn); and various types of steamed bun filled with sweet bean paste.

Regional Cuisines

All of China's cuisines converge on Běijīng, from far-flung Tibet to the hardy northeast, the arid northwest and the fecund south. In fact, you can eat your way around the country without ever leaving the capital. The most popular cooking styles are from Sìchuān, Shànghǎi, Hong Kong, Guǎngdōng (Cantonese) and Běijīng itself. If you want to explore China's full compendium of cuisines, Běijīng is *the* place to start.

BĚIJĪNG

Běijīng's native cuisine (京菜; *jīngcài*) is classified as a 'northern cuisine' and is in one of the four major styles of cooking in China. Peking duck apart, many popular dishes, such as hotpot (火锅; *huǒguō*), have their origins in Mongolia and arrived in the wake of Genghis Khan. Běijīng's bitter win-

---

CHOPSTICKS

Most people get to grips with chopsticks quickly out of necessity (it's either that or go on an involuntary crash diet), but don't feel embarrassed if you struggle at first; there's no shame in dropping a dumpling.

Until recently, only posh places handed out their own, reusable chopsticks, while cheap joints relied on disposable wooden ones. The disposable ones are more hygienic but with China producing 63 billion pairs of them a year, which is an awful lot of bamboo, they are not environmentally friendly. If you don't want to use them but are worried about cleanliness, consider carrying your own chopsticks.

ters mean that warm, filling dishes are essential. Typically, they are made with wheat or millet, whose most common incarnations are delicious dumplings (饺子; *jiǎozi*) or noodles, which are preferred to rice in the capital. Vegetables are more limited, so there is a heavy reliance on freshwater fish and chicken; cabbage and turnips, as well as yams and potatoes, are some of the most ubiquitous vegetables found on menus.

Two of the region's most famous culinary exports – Mongolian barbecue and Mongolian hotpot – are adaptations from Mongol field kitchens. Animals that were hunted on horseback could be dismembered and cooked with wild vegetables and onions using soldiers' iron shields on top of hot coals as primitive barbecues. Alternatively, each soldier could use his helmet as a pot, filling it with water, meat, condiments and vegetables to taste. Mutton is now the main ingredient in Mongolian hotpot.

Roasting was once considered rather barbaric in other parts of China and is still more common in the northern areas. The main methods of cooking in the northern style, though, are steaming, baking and 'explode-frying' (爆炒; *bàochǎo*), a rapid

MǍIDĀN!

The Chinese pride themselves on unwavering generosity in public and the arrival of the bill (买单; *mǎidān*) among a group of diners is an excuse for some elaborate histrionics. People push each other aside and almost fight for the right to pay, but generally it is the host who does and if he didn't he would lose face.

Splitting the bill is less common here than in the West, so if you invite someone out for dinner, be prepared to foot the bill. And remember that most places will expect you to settle it in hard cash; only top-end restaurants take credit cards.

method of cooking in which the wok is superheated over a flame and the contents tossed in for a swift stir-frying. The last of these is the most common, historically because of the scarcity of fuel and, more recently, due to the introduction of the peanut, which thrives in the north and produces an abundance of oil. Although

Wángfǔjǐng Snack Street (p74)

northern-style food has a reputation for being salty and unsophisticated, it has the benefit of being filling and therefore well suited to the region's punishing winters.

SÌCHUĀN

Famed as China's fiercest food, Sìchuān cuisine (川菜) must be approached with caution and lots of chilled H_2O or beer. A concoction of searing red chillies (introduced by Spanish traders in the early Qing dynasty), star anise, peppercorns and pungent 'flower pepper' (花椒; *huājiāo*), a numbing herb peculiar to this cuisine, Sìchuān dishes are simmered to allow the chilli peppers time to seep into the food. Meats are often marinated, pickled or otherwise processed before cooking, which is generally by stir- or explode-frying.

Landlocked Sìchuān is a long way from the coast, so pork, poultry, legumes and *dòufu* (豆腐; bean curd) are commonly used, and supplemented by a variety of wild condiments and mountain products, such as mushrooms and other fungi, as well as bamboo shoots. Seasonings are heavy: the red chilli is often used in conjunction with Sìchuān peppercorns, garlic, ginger and onions. Hallmark dishes include camphor-smoked duck, Granny Ma's bean curd (*Mápó dòufu*) and spicy chicken with peanuts (*gōng bǎo jī dīng*).

CANTONESE

Cantonese cuisine (粤菜) is what non-Chinese consider to be 'Chinese' food, largely because most émigré restaurateurs originate from Guǎngdōng (Canton) or nearby Hong Kong. Cantonese flavours are generally more subtle than other Chinese styles – almost sweet – and there are very few spicy dishes. Sweet-and-sour and oyster sauces are common. The Cantonese are almost religious about the importance of fresh ingredients, which is why so many restaurants are lined with tanks full of finned and shelled creatures. Stir-frying is by far the favoured method of cooking, closely followed by steaming. Dim sum (点心; *diǎnxīn*), now a worldwide Sunday institution, originated in this region; to go *yám cha* (饮茶; Cantonese for 'drink tea') still provides most overseas Chinese communities with the opportunity to get together at the weekend. Dim sum can be found in restaurants around Běijīng.

Expensive dishes – some that are truly tasty, others that appeal more for their 'face'

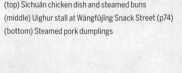

(top) Sìchuān chicken dish and steamed buns
(middle) Uighur stall at Wángfǔjǐng Snack Street (p74)
(bottom) Steamed pork dumplings

value – include abalone, shark's fin and bird's nest. Pigeon is a Cantonese speciality served in various ways but most commonly roasted.

SHÀNGHǍI

Generally sweeter and oilier than China's other cooking styles, Shànghǎi cuisine (上海菜) features plenty of fish and seafood, especially cod, river eel and shrimp. Fish is usually *qīngzhēng* (清蒸; steamed) but can be stir-fried, pan-fried or grilled. Crab-roe dumplings *(xièròu jiǎozi)* are another Shanghainese luxury. *Dàxháxiè* (大闸蟹; hairy crabs) are a Shànghǎi speciality between October and December. They are eaten with soy, ginger and vinegar and downed with warm Shàoxīng rice wine. They are delicious but can be fiddly to eat. The body opens via a little tab on the underside (don't eat the gills or the stomach).

Several restaurants specialise in cold salty chicken, while drunken chicken gets its name from being marinated in Shàoxīng rice wine. *Bāo* (煲; clay pot) dishes are braised for a long time in their own casserole dish. Shànghǎi's most famous snack is *xiǎolóngbāo* (小笼包), small dumplings containing a meaty interior bathed in a scalding juice.

Vegetarian dishes include *dòufu;* cabbage in cream sauce; *mèn* (焖; braised) *dòufu;* and various types of mushrooms, including *xiānggū báicài* (香菇白菜; mushrooms surrounded by baby bok choy). Tiger-skin chillies are a delicious dish of stir-fried green peppers seared in a wok and served in a sweet chilli sauce. Fried pine nuts and sweet corn *(sōngzǐ chǎo yùmǐ)* is another common Shanghainese dish.

UIGHUR

Uighur cuisine (新疆菜) reflects the influences of Xīnjiāng's chequered past. Yet, despite centuries of sporadic Chinese and Mongol rule, the strongest influence on ingredients and methods is still Turkic or Middle Eastern, which is evident in the reliance on mutton for protein and wheat as the staple grain. When rice is eaten, it is often the Central Asian version of pilau *(plov)*. Nevertheless, the infusion of Chinese culinary styles and ingredients makes it probably the most enjoyable region of Central Asia in which to eat.

Uighur bread resembles Arabic *khoubz* (Indian naan) and is baked in ovens based on the *tanour* (Indian tandoor) model. It is often eaten straight from the oven and sprinkled with poppy seeds, sesame seeds or fennel. Uighur bakers also make excellent *girde nan* (bagels). Wheat is also used for a variety of noodles. *Laghman* (拌面; *bàn miàn*) are the most common: noodles cooked al dente, thick and topped with a combination of spicy mutton, peppers, tomatoes, eggplant, green beans and garlic. *Suoman* are noodle squares fried with tomatoes, peppers, garlic and meat, sometimes quite spicy. *Suoman goshsiz* is the vegetarian variety.

Kebabs, both shashlik (羊肉串; *yángròu chuàn*) and tandoori styles, are common, as they are throughout the Middle East and Central Asia. *Samsas* or *samsis* (烤包子; *kǎo bāozi*) are the Uighur version of samosas: baked envelopes of meat. Meat often makes an appearance inside *chuchura* (dumplings; 饺子汤, *jiǎozi tāng*), which can be steamed or fried.

Foreign Fancies

Běijīng's emergence as a true world city has revolutionised its dining scene. Now, a whole host of ambitious chefs, including Michelin-starred legends, have descended on the capital, meaning that if you're pining for a taste of home, you won't have to travel too far to find it.

Korean and Japanese restaurants are especially plentiful because Běijīng hosts large expatriate communities from those countries, and there are many places specialising in contemporary Mediterranean cuisine, as well as standard Western comfort food such as pizza, pasta, steaks and hamburgers. But whether you're hankering for African or Turkish food, a burrito or a rogan josh, it's being served somewhere in the city. For restaurant listings, check the monthly expat magazines.

Self-Catering

Avoiding restaurants in Běijīng is easy, as even the most selective chef will be able to find just about any ingredient they might want. But if you're staying in an apartment, you might be stumped by the lack of an oven in the kitchen; Chinese cooking doesn't call for them.

If you're after Western food, the following supermarkets and stores cater for foreigners and stock such esoteric delights as imported cheese, foreign wine, English tea and peanut butter.

Běijīng Dàdǒng Roast Duck Restaurant (p73)

Carrefour (6b Beisanhuan Donglu; ⏰8.30am-10.30pm; [S]Liufang) The best supermarkets in Běijīng belong to the French hypermarket chain Carrefour, which moved into China early on. Carrefour stocks just about everything you need, as well as providing ATMs and taking credit cards. Its supermarkets are open every day and are always crowded.

Olé (Map p298; 48 Dongzhimenwai Dajie, Basement Ginza Mall; ⏰10am-10pm; [S]Dongzhimen) Olé is a reliable supermarket chain, with a number of branches around town. This branch is in the Ginza Mall in Dōngzhímén.

April Gourmet (Map p298; 1st fl, Lianbao Mansion, Xingfucun Zhonglu; ⏰8am-midnight; [S]Dongsi Shitiao) A rival of Jenny Lou's for the affections of Westerners starved of home cooking, April Gourmet operates three stores in Běijīng. Its selection isn't quite as extensive as Jenny Lou's, but the prices are similar. Cheese, fresh bread, butter, wine, sauces, Western soups, coffee, milk, meats and frozen food are all available. This branch stays open till midnight.

Lonely Planet's Top Choices

Dàlǐ Courtyard (p90) Beautiful courtyard restaurant with an ever-changing menu of subtly flavoured Yúnnán specialities.

Běijīng Dàdǒng Roast Duck Restaurant (p73) The leanest duck in town in a busy and bright setting.

Nàjiā Xiǎoguǎn (p140) Old-school Běijīng place with an esoteric menu of Manchu favourites.

Maison Boulud (p110) Consistently excellent French restaurant and the best service in the city.

Bǎihé Vegetarian Restaurant (p90) Serene setting and inventive dishes at one of Běijīng's few veggie eateries.

Best by Budget

¥

Qí Shān Miàn (p90)

Tàn Huā Lamb BBQ (p91)

Zhāng Māma (p93)

Bocata (p142)

Bāozi Pù (p93)

¥¥

Jīn Dǐng Xuān (p91)

Xiǎo Wáng's Home Restaurant (p142)

Lǎo Zhái Yuàn (p70)

Vineyard Café (p92)

Veggie Table (p91)

¥¥¥

Běi (p142)

Lost Heaven (p110)

Capital M (p111)

Courtyard (p70)

Tiāndì Yījiā (p74)

Best by Cuisine

Best Peking Duck

Lìqún Roast Duck Restaurant (p111)

Biànyífāng (p112)

Duck de Chine (p142)

Jīngzūn Peking Duck (p141)

Qiánmén Quánjùdé Roast Duck Restaurant (p111)

Best Dumplings

Din Tai Fung (p141)

Bǎoyuán Dumpling Restaurant (p142)

Dūyīchù (p112)

Hángzhōu Xiǎochī (p74)

Gǒubùlǐ (p130)

Best Hotpot

Yáng Fāng Lamb Hotpot (p88)

Little Sheep (p92)

Lǎo Chē Jì (p164)

Chóngqìng Kǒngliàng Huǒguō (p92)

Róng Tiān Sheep Spine (p90)

Best Regional

Crescent Moon Muslim Restaurant (p70)

Home Sweet Home (p70)

Jíxiángniǎo Xiāngcài (p141)

Kǒng Yǐjǐ (p121)

Middle 8th (p143)

Best Sìchuān

Chuān Bàn (p72)

Jìngyuán Chuāncài (p72)

Source (p91)

Méizhōu Dōngpō Jiǔlóu (p144)

Fèitáng Yúxiāng (p142)

Best Běijīng

Yáojì Chǎogān (p88)

Bàodǔ Huáng (p141)

Zuǒ Lín Yòu Shè (p70)

Lǎohéjiān Donkey-Meat Restaurant (p93)

Best Foreign

Temple (p70)

Rumi (p143)

Hútòng Pizza (p123)

Café De La Poste (p92)

Elephant (p144)

Grill 79 (p142)

Best Asian

Purple Haze (p144)

4Corners (p121)

Café Sambal (p93)

Salang-Bang (p161)

Indian Kitchen (p144)

Drinking & Nightlife

It's staggering to contemplate, as you sip a martini in the latest hotspot or dance to a big-name European DJ, but until 20-odd years ago there weren't any bars or nightclubs, outside a few hotels, in Beijing at all. Now, as more and more locals take to partying, the capital is home to an increasing number of sophisticated nightspots.

Hútòng Bar-Crawling

Until recently, Sānlǐtún was the undisputed centre of Běijīng nightlife – not any more. A host of bars have sprung up in the ancient heart of the city. Former courtyard homes have been converted into some of the finest and liveliest drinking destinations in town. They range from bohemian joints to distinctly chic cocktail bars. Nanluogu Xiang (lane) led the way in making the *hútòng* an integral part of the city's nightlife; now many *hútòng* across Dōngchéng north are almost as popular.

Drink Like a Local

Although wine and whisky are gaining ground among the middle classes, the two most popular alcoholic drinks in Běijīng remain *píjiǔ* (beer) and *báijiǔ* (a pungent, potent white spirit). The commonest brews are Yanjing Beer (the local favourite), Beijing Beer and Tsingtao. None are very distinguished, and all are weaker than most foreign beers. You can pick up a large bottle of Yanjing or Tsingtao, the closest to a European-style lager, for around ¥3 on the streets; Beijing beer is usually served on tap.

Báijiǔ is super-strong and has a unique taste that few foreigners can stomach. But if your preferred tipple is paint stripper, you'll love it. It's cheap too; a small bottle of the locally distilled Èrguōtóu costs about ¥5.

Drinking & Nightlife by Neighbourhood

● ●

➡ **Drum Tower & Dōngchéng North** *Hútòng* bars and cafes aplenty, with Nanluogu Xiang especially drawing the crowds.

➡ **Běihǎi Park & Xīchéng North** The shores of the Hòuhǎi lakes are awash with bars, although many are squarely aimed at the out-of-town domestic crowd.

➡ **Sānlǐtún & Cháoyáng** Clubbing central, especially around the west gate of the Workers Stadium, and also home to upmarket cocktail bars.

➡ **The Summer Palace & Hǎidiàn** The Wǔdàokǒu district of Hǎidiàn is Běijīng's principal student zone and buzzes come nightfall.

KARAOKE

Karaoke is the number-one leisure pastime in China. There are well over 100,000 karaoke joints on the mainland, ranging from giant chains where the prices are as high as some of the notes you'll hit to seedy operations that are often fronts for prostitution. As alien as it can seem to be singing along to a TV in front of people, karaoke is one of the best ways of getting to know the locals. And you'll be surprised at how quickly crooning cheesy pop standards becomes addictive.

Lonely Planet's Top Choices

Apothecary (p144) Huge range of cocktails lovingly made from fresh ingredients.

El Nido (p94) Always jammed and the archetypal neighbourhood *hútòng* bar.

Haze (p145) The best DJs in town and an authentic, sweaty basement vibe.

Migas Bar (p144) Wildly popular roof terrace in the summer and a hip crowd.

Best Hútòng Bars

Bed Bar (p96)

Ball House (p95)

12SQM (p95)

Drum & Bell (p95)

If (p95)

Best Cocktail Bars

Mao Mao Chong (p95)

Mài (p96)

Atmosphere (p145)

Yĭn (p75)

d Lounge (p146)

Best Clubs

Cargo (p147)

Destination (p146)

Mix (p146)

Chocolate (p145)

Best Cafes

Zá Jiā (p95)

Lush (p164)

Alley Coffee (p74)

Bridge Café (p164)

Best Neighbourhood Bars

Tree (p145)

Passby Bar (p96)

Paddy O'Shea's (p146)

First Floor (p145)

NEED TO KNOW

Business Hours

Most bars in Běijīng open their doors in the late afternoon and close them at 2am. But many stay open longer, especially on weekends, while others shut up shop around midnight. Cafes open much earlier and sometimes close early, too. Clubs can go all night, depending on their mood.

Prices

The cost of drinking in Běijīng's bars depends very much on your personal tastes. If you want to gargle with a Guinness, you'll pay more (¥40 to ¥50) than if you drink a bottle of Tsingtao (¥20 to ¥25). Mixed drinks start at around ¥35 in most places, but in a swanky bar expect to pay Western prices, ¥60 and up, for a proper cocktail. Many bars, though, have happy hours (usually 5pm to 8pm) when you can imbibe more cheaply.

PLAN YOUR TRIP DRINKING & NIGHTLIFE

☆ Entertainment

There's far more to Běijīng than imperial palaces, temples and museums. As the cultural capital of China, it's the best place to be if you're interested in seeing anything from ballet and contemporary dance to jazz or punk bands. Then there's the traditional local pastimes such as Peking opera (jīngjù) and acrobatic shows, as well as movies, theatre and Běijīng's various sports teams.

Live Music

While there might be an instinctive Chinese fondness for Taiwanese boy bands, Beijingers have always been at the forefront of the more soulful end of the Chinese music scene. Now, you can find all sorts of bands – indie, alternative, punk, metal, folk and jazz – lifting roofs every night of the week. Sadly, though, the capital remains a backwater for international rock and pop acts, very few of whom make it out here.

Acrobatics & Peking Opera

Two thousand years old, Chinese acrobatics is one of the best shows in town and there are daily performances at a number of different theatres. Look out too for the legendary, shaven-headed Shàolín monks, who pass through the capital regularly to put on displays of their fearsome fighting skills.

Far more sedate, but equally intriguing, is Peking opera, also known as Běijīng opera. It might seem impenetrable to foreigners, its mystique reinforced by the costumes, singing style and, of course, the language, but live performances are actually relatively easy to follow. Plot lines are simple (rather like Shakespearean tragedy, including the low comic relief) and the shows are a more interactive experience than you might imagine.

Spectator Sport

The Chinese are avid football (*zúqiú*) fans, with many supporting the top teams in England, Italy and Spain. Now, the China Super League is emerging as a force of its own in Asia, with increasing numbers of foreign players arriving to lift standards. The local heroes are the Běijīng Guo'an, who play their home games at the Workers Stadium.

Even more popular than football is basketball. A number of Chinese players have followed in the footsteps of national icon Yao Ming to play in the NBA. The capital's team is the Běijīng Ducks; they draw a big crowd at the Wŭkēsōng Arena in Hǎidiàn.

Entertainment by Neighbourhood

➡ **The Forbidden City & Dōngchéng Central** Prime district for culture vultures, with classical music, opera and theatre venues.

➡ **Drum Tower & Dōngchéng North** Home to many of the best live music venues in town.

➡ **Běihǎi Park & Xīchéng North** Key cultural hub thanks to the impressive National Centre for the Performing Arts.

➡ **Dashilar & Xīchéng South** The Húguǎng Guild Hall is the most atmospheric Peking opera venue of them all.

➡ **Sānlǐtún & Cháoyáng** Acrobatics shows galore and movie multiplexes.

Lonely Planet's Top Choices

Yúgōng Yíshān (p97) Great space and super booking policy make this the number one spot for live music.

National Centre for the Performing Arts (p123) Extraordinary building that is now Běijīng's cultural centre.

Tiānqiáo Acrobatics Theatre (p132) The most agile and graceful acrobats in town.

Húguǎng Guild Hall (p132) Beautiful and historic venue to watch Peking opera in.

Best for Alternative, Punk & Metal Bands

Dos Kolegas (p147)

Mao Livehouse (p98)

13 Club (p164)

Temple Bar (p97)

What? Bar (p75)

Star Live (p98)

Best for Folk & Jazz Bands

Jiāng Jìn Jǐu (p97)

East Shore Jazz Café (p123)

Jiāng Hú (p97)

Modernista (p96)

Best for Classical Music & Dance

Forbidden City Concert Hall (p75)

Běijīng Concert Hall (p126)

Poly Plaza International Theatre (p147)

National Library Concert Hall (p164)

Best for Peking Opera

Cháng'ān Grand Theatre (p75)

Mei Lanfang Grand Theatre (p123)

Líyuán Theatre (p133)

Lao She Teahouse (p132)

Best for Acrobatics & Plays

Universal Theatre (p147)

Cháoyáng Theatre (p147)

Red Theatre (p112)

China Puppet Theatre (p98)

Pénghǎo Theatre (p98)

Capital Theatre (p75)

NEED TO KNOW

Business Hours

Ballet, classical music and Chinese folk or contemporary dance performances generally start at 7.30pm at the big concert hall venues. Acrobatics and opera houses often have two shows a day, starting at 5.15pm or 6.30pm and then again at 7.30pm. Live music venues mostly open their doors around 8pm and don't close till the wee hours.

Information

Specific opening hours are listed in all reviews. Check the monthly expat magazines, which can be picked up around town, for the latest news on events and who is playing when and where.

Prices & Tickets

Some live music venues don't levy an entrance fee, but if a popular local band or any international act is playing they will, and it's advisable to reserve tickets in advance. You'll need to book ahead if a famous foreign orchestra or ballet company is in town too.

PLAN YOUR TRIP ENTERTAINMENT

🛍 Shopping

With much of the nation's wealth concentrated in Běijīng, shopping has become the favourite pastime of the young and the rising middle class in recent years. Whether you're a diehard shopaholic or just a casual browser, you'll be spoiled for choice with shiny shopping malls, markets, specialist shopping streets, pavement vendors and itinerant hawkers all doing their best to part you from your cash.

Arts, Crafts & Antiques

Běijīng is a great place to pick up curios such as embroidered purses, paper cuttings, wooden and bronze Buddhas, paper lanterns, Chinese musical instruments and kites. Carpets, jade and pearls of varying quality can be found in abundance too.

Remember it's not just DVDs and clothes that are pirated in China: antiques, ceramics and carpets get the facsimile treatment too, so be wary before paying for that supposed Ming-dynasty vase. Be aware, too, that technically items dating from before 1795 cannot be exported from China.

Clothing

Sīchóu (silk) is an important commodity in Běijīng and excellent prices for both silk fabrics and clothing can be found. Top places for silk in Běijīng include the Silk Market and Ruìfúxiáng. If you have the time, there are excellent tailors who will turn your silk into made-to-measure clothing, such as traditional Chinese gowns (*qípáo*, or *cheongsam* in Cantonese). *Yángróngshān* (cashmere) from Inner Mongolia is also a good buy in Běijīng.

If you're on the hunt for genuine Western clothing, you'll pay much the same as you would at home.

Contemporary Art

With Chinese contemporary art still in demand from collectors around the world, artwork can be a great investment. If you're here in June, the annual Affordable Art Fair held in the 798 Art District is a fine place to find reasonably priced work. Otherwise, visit reputable galleries like Red Gate Gallery. Realistically, you'll need to spend at least US$1000 for something from an up-and-coming artist that will subsequently increase in value.

Shopping by Neighbourhood

➡ **The Forbidden City & Dōngchéng Central** Wangfujing Dajie is Běijīng's premier shopping street, home to malls and more.

➡ **Drum Tower & Dōngchéng North** Trendy and offbeat boutiques abound in Nanluogu Xiang and Gulou Dongdajie, and the capital's finest kite shop is also here.

➡ **Temple of Heaven Park & Dōngchéng South** Hóngqiáo Market and its oceans of pearls is the main draw, but there's also the renovated Qiánmén Dajie shopping strip.

➡ **Dashilar & Xīchéng South** Some of the city's oldest emporiums, and the antiques, arts and crafts hub of Líulìchǎng.

➡ **Sānlǐtún & Cháoyáng** Mall central, as well as home to most of Běijīng's finest markets.

Lonely Planet's Top Choices

Shard Box Store (p149) Utterly unique exquisite shard boxes in all sizes.

Ruìfúxiáng (p134) Purveyors of all kinds of silk in every conceivable pattern.

Plastered 8 (p99) Ironic T-shirts with Běijīng-centric themes.

Grifted (p99) Great for souvenirs and almost everything here is made locally.

Three Stone Kite Shop (p126) Glorious handmade kites at this family-run place.

Yuèhǎixuān Musical Instrument Store (p134) Esoteric instruments from across China.

Best Markets

Pānjiāyuán Market (p148)

Mǎliándào Tea Market (p134)

Hóngqiáo Market (p113)

Centergate Como (p165)

Best Clothing Stops

Sānlǐtún Yashow Clothing Market (p149)

Silk Market (p148)

Village (p148)

Place (p149)

77th Street (p126)

Best Shopping Streets

Wangfujing Dajie (p76)

Líulichǎng Xijie (p133)

Dashilar (p130)

Nanluogu Xiang (p86)

Qiánmén Dajie (p110)

Best Buys

Silk (p134)

Jade (p76)

Carpets (p148)

Pearls (p113)

Best for Art

798 Art District (p138)

Red Gate Gallery (p109)

Róngbǎozhāi (p134)

Arts & Crafts Emporium (p76)

NEED TO KNOW

Business Hours

Most shops in Běijīng open earlier than in the West and close later; they usually open between 8am and 8.30am and shut between 9pm and 10pm. Open-air markets generally run from dawn to around sunset, but might open later and close earlier.

Bargaining

Always remember that foreigners are likely to be quoted an inflated price in Běijīng. Prices in malls are fixed, but bargaining is very much standard practice elsewhere and vendors expect it. In all markets, haggling is essential. It's always best to bargain with a smile on your face. Remember, the point of the process is to achieve a mutually acceptable price, not to screw the vendor into the ground.

Paying

Most large department stores take Western credit cards, but many smaller ones only take Chinese ones, so check before paying. Markets deal in cash only. In some shops, a salesperson will give you a ticket for your goods and you then go to a separate till to pay and get your ticket stamped, before returning to the salesperson who will give you your purchase.

Explore Běijīng

BĚIJĪNG'S
TOP SIGHTS

Neighbourhoods at a Glance

❶ Forbidden City & Dōngchéng Central (p50)

Packed with essential sights, and the very heart of Běijīng, this is the area you'll likely be spending many of your days in. Imperial palaces, temples, socialist-realist architecture, parks and museums jostle for space here, but it's also where you'll find the capital's premier shopping street, Wangfujing Dajie.

❷ Drum Tower & Dōngchéng North (p80)

The *hútòng* in this part of town are the most numerous and best-preserved and offer a fantastic insight into local life. Many, like Nanluogu Xiang and Fangjia Hutong, are also home to an ever-increasing number of hip bars and restaurants. With some lovely courtyard hotels to stay in and key sights

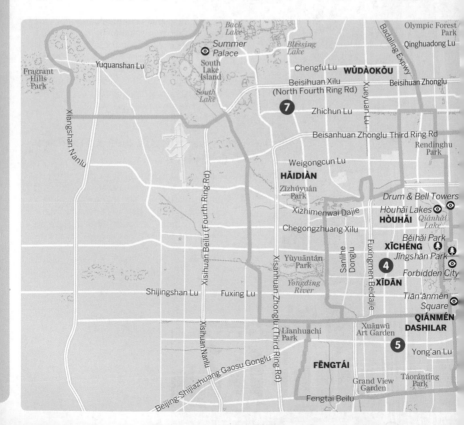

scattered around too, it's the most visitor-friendly neighbourhood in all Běijīng and makes a great base.

❸ Temple of Heaven Park & Dōngchéng South (p104)

Encompassing the former district of Chóngwén, this is an area both grand – dominated by the magnificent Temple of Heaven – and down-at-heel, a place where ordinary Beijingers have long resided. Now, it houses some of the finest Peking duck restaurants in the capital, as well as an increasing number of excellent Western eateries, and the restored shopping street of Qianmen Dajie.

❹ Běihǎi Park & Xīchéng North (p114)

Northwest of the Forbidden City, Běihǎi Park and the adjacent Hòuhǎi lakes act as one big playground for Beijingers. During the day, they are a great spot to kickback, while at night locals carouse at the bars and restaurants that surround them. Also a temple and *hútòng*-rich neighbourhood, the Capital Museum, Běijīng's finest, can be found here too.

❺ Dashilar & Xīchéng South (p128)

With the historic shopping street of Dashilar providing a focus, and the many hostels in the nearby *hútòng* (narrow alleyways) making it Běijīng's backpacker central, this neighbourhood southwest of Tiān'ānmén Sq is both handy for the major sights and has plenty of character. Formerly known as Xuanwu district, it's also home to the best acrobatics and opera shows in town.

❻ Sānlǐtún & Cháoyáng (p136)

Big and brash and a key nightlife zone, with many of the most popular bars, clubs and restaurants clustered in the Sānlǐtún area. While Cháoyáng lacks the history of other districts, most of the city's top-end hotels and shops are also located here. Further out, the 708 Art District is the centre of the Chinese contemporary art scene.

❼ Summer Palace & Hǎidiàn (p154)

Home to many of Běijīng's universities, as well as museums and parks, the buzzing student district of Wǔdàokǒu makes for a fine contrast with the regal Summer Palace and the tranquil, rural delights of the Fragrant Hills, which occupy Hǎidiàn's northwestern edge.

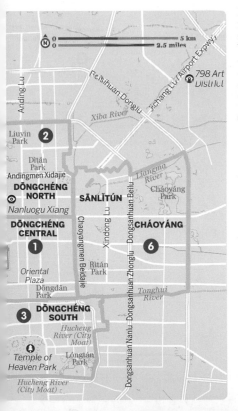

NEIGHBOURHOODS AT A GLANCE

Forbidden City & Dōngchéng Central

Neighbourhood Top Five

1 Marvel at the might and splendour of the awe-inspiring **Forbidden City** (p52), the world's largest palace complex and one-time home of 24 emperors of China.

2 Place yourself at the symbolic heart of the Chinese universe with a visit to iconic **Tiān'ānmén Square** (p60).

3 Explore the area's **imperial hútòng** (p71) on our cycling tour of the historic alleyways surrounding the Forbidden City.

4 Rise early to get the most out of this area's wonderful **imperial parks**; **Jǐngshān Park** (p62) is our favourite.

5 Peruse some of the city's best **museums and galleries**. For starters, try the **National Museum of China** (p62), the **Poly Art Museum** (p67) and the photography exhibition inside **Front Gate** (p66) on Tiān'ānmén Sq.

For more detail of this area see Map p286 and p288 ➡

Explore: Forbidden City & Dōngchéng Central

The most historically significant part of Běijīng, Dōngchéng Central comprises much of what was once the Imperial City, at the heart of which lay the Forbidden City, from where emperors ruled China for more than 500 years.

The *hútòng* (alleyways) fanning out to the north and east of the Forbidden City were where the members of the imperial court once lived.

You'll need at least a couple of days to visit all the best sights in this history-rich neighbourhood; figure on half a day for the Forbidden City alone.

Food options are fabulous, with local no-nonsense restaurants and busy street-food markets sharing quarters with some of the city's more unusual fine-dining establishments. Nightlife, though, is thin on the ground.

Local Life

➡ **Food** Tuck into authentic Běijīng grub at Zuǒ Lín Yòu Shè or sample donkey-meat pastry pockets at Dōngzi Lǘròu Huǒshāo. The street-food markets near Wángfǔjǐng may be fun, but locals find them touristy and overpriced. Enjoy your barbecued skewers from a hole-in-the-wall *hútòng* joint instead; spot the red neon 串 sign, and you're good to go.

➡ **Parks** Jǐngshān Park and Zhōngshān Park are two of Běijīng's most colourful – and locals, particularly the elderly, love to spend their mornings in them; dancing, singing and exercising with their friends. April and May are particularly popular as both parks burst into bloom during their annual flower fairs.

➡ **Table Tennis** At Jǐngshān Table Tennis Park you'll find a host of spritely octogenarians queuing up to give you a ping-pong thrashing.

Getting There & Away

➡ **Subway** Tian'anmen West, Tian'anmen East, Wangfujing and Denghshikou are all useful subway stations, and the handy Line 8 extension south to the Chinese Museum of Art should be up and running by the time you read this.

➡ **Bus** Bus 5 runs south from the Drum Tower, passing Jǐngshān Park, the west side of the Forbidden City and Tiān'ānmén Sq. Buses 专线1 and 专线2 go from the north gate of the Forbidden City down to Tiān'ānmén Sq, handy if you left your bikes near the south entrance, or want to hook up with the subway system.

Lonely Planet's Top Tip

Be very wary of rickshaw drivers outside the north gate of the Forbidden City; they regularly trick tourists into paying over the odds. As a rough indicator, you shouldn't be paying much more than ¥20 per rickshaw to get from here to the Drum Tower.

⊙ Best Places for History

➡ Forbidden City (p52)
➡ National Museum of China (p62)
➡ Front Gate (p66)
➡ Gate of Heavenly Peace (p63)
➡ Workers Cultural Palace (p63)
➡ Zhìhuà Temple (p67)

For reviews, see p52 ➡

✕ Best Places to Eat

➡ Zuǒ Lín Yòu Shè (p70)
➡ Courtyard (p70)
➡ Crescent Moon Muslim Restaurant (p70)
➡ Home Sweet Home (p70)
➡ Lǎo Zhái Yuàn (p70)
➡ Temple (p70)

For reviews, see p69 ➡

🔒 Best Places to Shop

➡ Oriental Plaza (p76)
➡ Wangfujing Dajie (p76)
➡ Háoyuán Market (p76)
➡ Arts & Crafts Emporium (p76)

For reviews, see p76 ➡

TOP SIGHTS
FORBIDDEN CITY

Home to 24 Chinese emperors, spanning two complete dynasties and more than 500 years, the astonishing Forbidden City (故宫; Gù Gōng) is the largest palace complex in the world and an absolute must-see for any visitor to Běijīng.

Located at the geographical centre of China's capital, the palace occupies a primary position in the Chinese psyche. To communists, it's a contradictory symbol: a politically incorrect yarn from a pre-Revolutionary dark age, but also one spun from the very pinnacle of Chinese civilisation. It's therefore not surprising that violent forces during the Cultural Revolution wanted to trash the place. But Premier Zhou Enlai, perhaps hearing the distant tinkle of the tourist dollar, stepped in to calm down the Red Guards.

Although you can explore the Forbidden City in a few hours, a full day will keep you occupied and the enthusiast will make several trips. More than half of the complex is closed to the public, but a massive chunk remains, focussing mainly on the hugely impressive ceremonial halls, which line the central axis. Marvel at these by all means, but don't miss the delightful courtyards, pavilions and mini-museums within them on each side of the central axis. This is where the emperors actually lived, and it's fun to explore the passageways and courtyards that link them.

Information & Warnings

As you approach the ticket office you may be encircled by a swarm of pushy guides. Note that their English levels vary and the spiel can often be tedious and formulaic. The bet-

DON'T MISS

➡ Clock Exhibition Hall

➡ Ceramics Gallery

➡ Changyin Pavilion (opera house)

➡ Western Palaces

PRACTICALITIES

➡ 紫禁城; Zǐjìn Chéng

➡ Map p288

➡ ✆8500 7114

➡ www.dpm.org.cn

➡ admission Nov-Mar ¥40, Apr-Oct ¥60, Clock Exhibition Hall ¥10, Hall of Jewellery ¥10, audio tour ¥40

➡ ⏰8.30am-4pm May-Sep, 8.30am-3.30pm Oct-Apr

➡ 🚻

➡ Ⓢ Tian'anmen West or Tian'anmen East

ter and cheaper alternative is to rent a funky automatically activated audio tour, which comes in 30 languages.

Don't confuse the Gate of Heavenly Peace with the Forbidden City entrance. Some visitors purchase a Gate of Heavenly Peace admission ticket by mistake, not realising that this admits you only to the upstairs portion of the gate. The Forbidden City ticket booths are on either side of Meridian Gate – walk north until you can't walk any further without paying and you will spot the queues nearby.

Restaurants, cafes, ATMs and toilets can be found within the Forbidden City.

Wheelchairs (¥500 deposit) are free, as are pushchairs (¥300 deposit). Smoking is not permitted anywhere in the Forbidden City.

Pushy rickshaw and taxi touts wait at the north gate to take advantage of weary visitors exiting the complex. Be very clear when negotiating a fare with them. A common trick is for them to add a zero onto your pre-agreed price, claiming language-barrier confusion as their excuse. Better still, walk a few hundred metres away from the exit and pick up a normal taxi on the road.

History

Constructed on the site of a palace dating to Kublai Khan and the Mongol Yuan dynasty, the Ming emperor Yongle established the basic layout of the Forbidden City between 1406 and 1420, basing it on the now-ruined Ming dynasty palace in Nánjīng. The grandiose emperor employed battalions of labourers and craftspeople – by some estimates there may have been up to a million of them – to build the Forbidden City. The palace once lay at the heart of the Imperial City, a much larger, now-vanished walled enclosure reserved for the use of the emperor and his personnel. The wall enclosing the Forbidden City – assembled from 12 million bricks – is the last intact surviving city wall in Běijīng.

This gargantuan palace complex – China's largest and best-preserved cluster of ancient buildings – sheltered two dynasties of emperors (the Ming and the Qing), who didn't stray from their pleasure dome unless they absolutely had to. So highly rarefied was the atmosphere that nourished its elitist community, it was as if a bell jar had been dropped over the whole spectacle. A stultifying code of rules, protocol and superstition deepened its otherworldliness, perhaps typified by its twittering band of eunuchs. From here the emperors governed China, often erratically and haphazardly, with authority occasionally drifting into the hands of opportunistic court officials and eunuchs. It wasn't until 1911

ENTERING THE FORBIDDEN CITY

Tourists can only enter the Forbidden City via the south gate, known as **Meridian Gate**. It's a massive U-shaped portal that in former times was reserved for the use of the emperor. Gongs and bells would sound imperial comings and goings, while lesser mortals used lesser gates: the military used the west gate, civilians the east gate. The emperor also reviewed his armies from here, passed judgement on prisoners, announced the new year's calendar and oversaw the flogging of troublesome ministers.

Note that although tourists can only enter via Meridian Gate, they are allowed to exit the Forbidden City via the south, north or east gates. There are places to lock bicycles by the south and northeast gates of nearby Zhōngshān Park.

WALKING TOUR

After entering through the imperious Meridian Gate, resist the temptation to dive straight into the star attractions and veer right for a peek at the excellent **1 Ceramics Gallery** housed inside the creaking Hall of Literary Glory.

Walk back to the central complex and head through the magnificent Gate of Supreme Harmony towards the Three Great Halls: first, the largest – the **2 Hall of Supreme Harmony**, followed by the **3 Hall of Middle Harmony** and the **4 Hall of Preserving Harmony**, behind which slopes the enormous Marble Imperial Carriageway.

Turn right here to visit the fascinating **5 Clock Exhibition Hall** before entering the **6 Complete Palace of Peace & Longevity**, a mini Forbidden City constructed along the eastern axis of the main complex. It includes the beautiful **7 Nine Dragon Screen** and, to the north, a series of halls, housing some excellent exhibitions and known collectively as The Treasure Gallery. Don't miss the **8 Pavilion of Cheerful Melodies**, a wonderful three-storey opera house.

Work your way to the far north of this section, then head west to the **9 Imperial Garden**, with its ancient cypress trees and pretty pavilions, before exiting via the garden's West Gate (behind the Thousand Year Pavilion) to explore the **10 Western Palaces**, an absorbing collection of courtyard homes where many of the emperors lived during their reign.

Exit this section at its southwest corner before turning back on yourself to walk north through the Gate of Heavenly Purity to see the three final Central Halls – the **11 Palace of Heavenly Purity**, the **12 Hall of Union** and the **13 Palace of Earthly Tranquility** – before leaving via the North Gate.

Water Vats

More than 300 copper and brass water vats dot the palace complex. They were used for fighting fires and in winter were prevented from freezing over by using thick quilts.

Entrance/Exit

You must enter through the south gate (Meridian Gate), but you can exit via south, north or east.

ticket offices

Guardian Lions

Pairs of lions guard important buildings. The male has a paw placed on a globe (representing the emperor's power over the world). The female has her paw on a baby lion (representing the emperor's fertility).

Kneeling Elephants
At the northern entrance of the Imperial Garden are two bronze elephants kneeling in an anatomically impossible fashion, which symbolise the power of the emperor; even elephants kowtowed before him.

Nine Dragon Screen
One of only three of its type left in China, this beautiful glazed dragon screen served to protect the Hall of Imperial Supremacy from evil spirits.

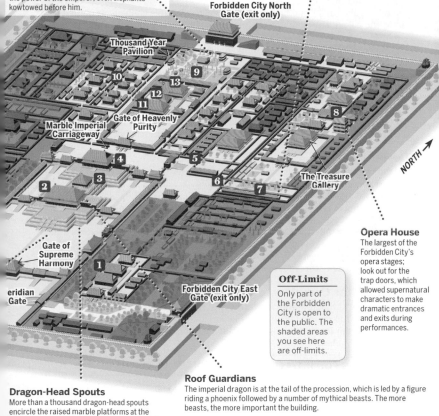

Forbidden City North Gate (exit only)

Thousand Year Pavilion

10
13
9
12
11
8

Gate of Heavenly Purity

Marble Imperial Carriageway

4
5
3
2
6
7

The Treasure Gallery

NORTH →

Gate of Supreme Harmony

1

Meridian Gate

Forbidden City East Gate (exit only)

Off-Limits
Only part of the Forbidden City is open to the public. The shaded areas you see here are off-limits.

Opera House
The largest of the Forbidden City's opera stages; look out for the trap doors, which allowed supernatural characters to make dramatic entrances and exits during performances.

Dragon-Head Spouts
More than a thousand dragon-head spouts encircle the raised marble platforms at the centre of the Forbidden City. They were – and still are – part of the drainage system.

Roof Guardians
The imperial dragon is at the tail of the procession, which is led by a figure riding a phoenix followed by a number of mythical beasts. The more beasts, the more important the building.

that revolution eventually came knocking at the huge doors, bringing with it the last orders for the Manchu Qīng and dynastic rule.

Its mystique diffused (the Běijīng authorities prosaically call the complex the Palace Museum, or *gùgōng bówùguǎn*; 故宫博物馆), the palace is no longer off limits. In former ages the price for uninvited admission would have been instant death; these days ¥40 to ¥60 will do.

Most of the buildings you see now are post-18th century. The largely wooden palace was a tinderbox and fire was a constant hazard – a lantern festival combined with a sudden gust of Gobi wind would easily send flames dancing in unexpected directions, as would a fireworks display. Fires were also deliberately lit by court eunuchs and officials who could get rich off the repair bills. It wasn't just buildings that burned, but also rare books, paintings and calligraphy. Libraries and other palace halls and buildings housing combustible contents were tiled in black; the colour represents water in the *wǔxíng* (five-element) theory, and its symbolic presence was thought to prevent conflagrations. Originally water was provided by 72 wells in the palace (only 30 have been preserved), while a complex system took care of drainage.

In the 20th century there were two major lootings of the palace by Japanese forces and the Kuomintang (KMT; Chiang Kaishek's Nationalist Party, the dominant political force after the fall of the Qīng dynasty). Thousands of crates of relics were removed and carted off to Taiwan, where they remain on display in Taipei's National Palace Museum (worth seeing). Some say this was just as well, since the Cultural Revolution reduced much of China's precious artwork to confetti.

Layout

Ringed by a picturesque 52m-wide moat that freezes over in winter, the rectangular palace is laid out roughly symmetrically on a north-south axis, bisected by a line of grand gates and ceremonial halls that straddle the very axis that cleaves Běijīng in two. The palace is so unspeakably big (over 1 million sq metres, with 800 buildings and 9000 rooms) that restoration is a never-ending work in progress, and despite the attentions of restorers, some of the hall rooftops still sprout tufts of grass. Many halls have been repainted in a way that conceals the original pigment; other halls, such as the Hall of Mental Cultivation (p8), however, possess a more threadbare and faded authenticity.

Entering the Complex

After passing through **Meridian Gate** (午门; Wǔ Mén) – the only one of the four gateways now used as an entrance to the Forbidden City – you enter an enormous courtyard. From there, you cross the Golden Stream (金水; Jīn Shuǐ) – shaped to

ROUTINES FOR ROYAL FROLICKING

With so many wives and consorts to choose from, a system was needed to help the emperor choose his bedtime companion. One method was to keep the names of royal wives, consorts and favourites on jade tablets near the emperor's chambers. By turning a tablet over, the emperor made his request for the evening, and the eunuch on duty would rush off to find her. Stripped naked (and therefore weaponless), the foot-bound woman was gift-wrapped in a yellow cloth, piggybacked over to the royal boudoir and dumped at the feet of the emperor, the eunuch recording the date and time to verify the legitimacy of a possible child.

According to an ancient Chinese belief, frequent sex with young girls could sustain one's youth, so all this frolicking had a more serious purpose: prolonging the life of the emperor.

Meridian Gate, Forbidden City

CLOCK EXHIBITION HALL

The **Clock Exhibition Hall** (钟表馆; Zhōngbiǎo Guǎn; admission ¥10; ⊗8.30am-4pm summer, to 3.30pm winter) is one of the unmissable highlights of the Forbidden City. Set in the **Hall for Ancestral Worship** (Fèngxiàn Diàn), the exhibition contains an astonishing array of elaborate timepieces, many of which were gifts to the Qing emperors. Many 18th-century examples were crafted by James Cox or Joseph Williamson (both of London) and imported through Guǎngdōng from England; others are from Switzerland, America and Japan. Exquisitely wrought, fashioned with magnificent elephants and other creatures, they display astonishing artfulness and attention to detail. Standouts include the **Gilt Copper Astronomy Clock** equipped with a working model of the solar system, and the **Gilt Copper Clock** equipped with a robot writing Chinese characters with a brush. The Qing court must surely have been amazed by their ingenuity.

Arrive at 11am or 2pm to see the clock performance in which timepieces strike the hour and give a display to wide-eyed children and adults.

resemble a Tartar bow and spanned by five marble bridges – on your way to the magnificent **Gate of Supreme Harmony** (太和门; Tàihé Mén). This courtyard could hold an imperial audience of 100,000 people.

First Side Galleries

Before you pass through the Gate of Supreme Harmony to reach the Forbidden City's star attractions, veer off to the west and east of the huge courtyard to visit the **Calligraphy and Painting Gallery** inside the **Hall of Martial Valor** (武英殿; Wǔ Yīng Diàn) and the particularly good **Ceramics Gallery**, housed inside the creaking **Hall of Literary Glory** (文化殿; Wén Huà Diàn).

Three Great Halls

Raised on a three-tier marble terrace with balustrades are the **Three Great Halls** (三大殿; Sān Dàdiàn), the glorious heart of the Forbidden City. The recently restored **Hall of Supreme Harmony** (太和殿; Tàihé Diàn) is the most important and largest structure in the Forbidden City. Built in the 15th century and restored in the 17th century, it was used for ceremonial occasions, such as the emperor's birthday, coronations and the nomination of military leaders. Inside the Hall of Supreme Harmony is a richly decorated **Dragon Throne** (龙椅; Lóngyǐ), from which the emperor would preside over trembling officials. The entire court had to touch the floor nine times with their foreheads (the custom known as kowtowing) in the emperor's presence.

At the back of the throne is a carved Xumishan, the Buddhist paradise, signifying the throne's supremacy.

Behind the Hall of Supreme Harmony is the **Hall of Middle Harmony** (中和殿; Zhōnghé Diàn), which was used as the emperor's transit lounge. Here he would make last-minute preparations, rehearse speeches and receive ministers. On display are two Qing-dynasty sedan chairs, the emperor's mode of transport around the Forbidden City. The last of the Qing emperors, Puyi, used a bicycle and altered some features of the palace grounds to make it easier to get around.

The third of the Great Halls is the **Hall of Preserving Harmony** (保和殿; Bǎohé Diàn), used for banquets and later for imperial examinations. The hall has no support pillars, and to its rear is a 250-tonne **marble imperial carriageway** carved with dragons and clouds, which was transported into Běijīng on an ice path. The emperor was conveyed over the carriageway in his sedan chair as he ascended or descended the terrace. The outer housing surrounding the Three Great Halls was used for storing gold, silver, silks, carpets and other treasures.

A string of side halls on the eastern and western flanks of the Three Great Halls usually, but not always, houses a series of excellent **exhibitions**, ranging from scientific instruments and articles of daily use to objects presented to the emperor by visiting dignitaries. One contains an interesting **diorama** of the whole complex.

Other Central Halls

The basic configuration of the Three Great Halls is echoed by the next group of buildings, which is accessed through **Heavenly Purity Gate**. Smaller in scale, these buildings were more important in terms of real power, which in China traditionally lies at the back door or, in this case, the back gate.

The first structure is the **Palace of Heavenly Purity** (乾清宫; Qiánqīng Gōng), a residence of Ming and early Qing emperors, and later an audience hall for receiving foreign envoys and high officials.

Immediately behind it is the **Hall of Union** (交泰殿; Jiāotài Diàn), which contains a clepsydra – a water clock made in 1745 with five bronze vessels and a calibrated scale. There's also a mechanical clock built in 1797 and a collection of imperial jade seals on display. The **Palace of Earthly Tranquillity** (坤宁宫; Kūnníng Gōng) was the imperial couple's bridal chamber and the centre of operations for the palace harem.

Imperial Garden

At the northern end of the Forbidden City is the **Imperial Garden** (御花园; Yù Huāyuán), a classical Chinese garden with 7000 sq metres of fine landscaping, including rockeries, walkways, pavilions and ancient, carbuncular cypresses. Before you reach the **Gate of Divine Prowess** (神武们; Shénwǔ Mén), note the pair of **bronze elephants** whose front knees bend in an anatomically impossible fashion just before you reach **Shùnzhēn Gate** (顺贞门; Shùnzhēn Mén. They signify the power of the emperor; even elephants kowtow before him!

Western & Eastern Palaces

About half-a-dozen smaller palace courtyards lie to the west and east of the three lesser central hall. They should all be open to the public, although at the time of research many of the eastern ones were closed for extensive renovation. It was in these smaller courtyard buildings that most of the emperors actually lived and many of the buildings, particularly those to the west, are decked out in imperial furniture. The **Hall of Mental Cultivation** (养心殿; Yǎng Xīn Diàn is a highlight, while the **Palace of Gathered Elegance** (储秀宫; Chǔ Xiù Gōng contains some interesting photos of the last emperor, Puyi, who lived here as a child ruler at the turn of the 20th century.

Palace Quirks

Attached to buildings, or standing incongruously in the corners of courtyards, are quirky objects that can easily go unnoticed.

The huge **copper and brass vats** that dot the Forbidden City were once full of water for dousing fires. There are 308 in total, all in various states of disrepair. They used to be draped in quilts or warmed with fires in winter to keep them from freezing over.

Pairs of stone or bronze **guardian lions** protect important buildings, with two particularly fine specimens in front of the Gate of Supreme Harmony. The male always has a paw placed on a globe (representing the emperor's power over the world), while the female has a paw placed on a baby lion (representing the fertility of the emperor's court).

More than a thousand **dragon-head spouts** encircle the raised marble platforms at the centre of the Forbidden City. They were, and still are, part of the drainage system. If you are unlucky enough to visit on a day of torrential rain, you will at least get to see water spouting out of their mouths.

Roof guardians adorn many important historic buildings in Běijīng. Here too, on the upturned eaves of significant halls, you'll find processions of mythical creatures leading and protecting the imperial dragon, which lies at the tail end of the line. The more mythical beasts in the procession, the more important the building, with nine guardians being the maximum.

From the back of the Hall of Preserving Harmony slopes the largest of the city's **marble imperial carriageways**. This beautifully carved, 250-ton block of marble, transported to the palace in winter on sheets of ice, acted as a VIP access ramp for the raised hallways. Sedan-chair bearers walked up the steps on each side, while the emperor was carried over a scene of marble-carved clouds and dragons.

Bronze turtles like the large one in front of the Hall of Supreme Harmony symbolise longevity and stability. On special occasions incense was lit inside it so that smoke billowed from its mouth.

Sundials also dot the complex. You can find one to the east of the Hall of Supreme Harmony. To the west of the hall, on a raised terrace, is a small pavilion with a **bronze grain measure**; both objects are symbolic of imperial justice.

Also look out for the round, football-sized **tether stones** dotted around the weed-covered corners of the large central courtyards. It is assumed that these were used for tethering horses to.

COMPLETE PALACE OF PEACE & LONGEVITY

A mini Forbidden City, known as the **Complete Palace of Peace and Longevity** (宁寿全宫; Níng Shǒu Quán Gōng) was built in the northeastern corner of the complex. During the Ming Dynasty, the Empress Dowager and the imperial concubines lived here. Now it houses quieter courtyard buildings, which contain a number of fine museum exhibitions, known collectively as the **Treasure Gallery** (珍宝馆; Zhēn Bǎo Guǎn; entrance ¥10). Enter the complex from the south – not far from the Clock Exhibition Hall. Inside the entrance is the beautiful glazed **Nine Dragon Screen** (九龙壁; Jiǔlóng Bì), one of only three of its type left in China.

Visitors then work their way north, exploring a number of halls and courtyards before being popped out at the northern end of the Forbidden City. Don't miss the Pavilion of Cheerful Melodies (畅音阁; Chàngyīn Gé)**, a three-storey wooden opera house, which was the palace's largest theatre.**

TOP SIGHTS
TIĀN'ĀNMÉN SQUARE

Flanked to the east and west by stern 1950s Soviet-style buildings and ringed by white perimeter fences that channel the hoi polloi towards periodic security checks and bag searches, the world's largest public square (440,000 sq metres) is a vast desert of paving stones at the heart of Běijīng. The square is also a poignant epitaph to China's democracy movement, which was driven from the square by the People's Liberation Army (PLA) in June 1989. The stringent security and round-the-clock monitoring hardly makes it the most relaxing of tourist sights, but such is its iconic status that few visitors leave Běijīng without seeing Tiān'ānmén Sq (天安门广场; Tiān'ānmén Guǎngchǎng). In any case, there's more than enough space to stretch a leg and the view can be breathtaking, especially on a clear, blue day or at nightfall when the square is illuminated.

DON'T MISS

➡ Chairman Mao Memorial Hall
➡ Front Gate
➡ Flag-Raising Ceremony

PRACTICALITIES

➡ 天安门广场; Tiān'ānmén Guǎngchǎng
➡ Map p286
➡ admission free
➡ Ⓢ Tian'anmen West, Tian'anmen East or Qianmen

History

Tiān'ānmén Sq as we see it today is a modern creation and there is precious little sense of history. During Ming and Qing times part of the Imperial City Wall (Huáng Chéng) called the Thousand Foot Corridor (Qiānbù Láng) poked deep into the space today occupied by the square, enclosing a section of the imperial domain. The wall took a 'T' shape, emerging from the two huge, now absent, gates that rose up south of the Gate of Heavenly Peace (p63) – Cháng'ān Zuǒ Gate and Cháng'ān Yòu Gate – before running south to the vanished Dàmíng Gate (Dàmíng Mén). Called Dàqīng Gate during the Qing dynasty and Zhōnghuá Gate during the Republic, the Dàmíng Gate had three watchtowers and upturned eaves and was guarded by a pair of stone lions. It was pulled down after 1949, a fate similarly reserved for Cháng'ān Zuǒ Gate and Cháng'ān Yòu Gate. East and west of the Thousand Foot Corridor stood official departments and temples, including the Ministry of Rites, the Ministry of Revenue, Honglu Temple and Taichang Temple.

Mao Zedong conceived the square to project the enormity of the Communist Party. During the Cultural Revolution, the chairman, wearing a Red Guard armband, reviewed parades of up to a million people here. The 'Tiān'ānmén Incident' is the term given to the near riot in the square that accompanied the death of Premier Zhou Enlai in 1976. Another million people jammed the square to pay their last respects to Mao in September that year.

Layout

The square is laid out on a north-south axis. Front Gate (p19), which can be climbed, lies to the south, while the Gate of Heavenly Peace (p19) – the gate that lends its name to the square – lies at the northern end, on the other side of the main road. Sitting innocuously in the middle of the square, is the Chairman Mao Memorial Hall (p13), which thousands of domestic tourists visit each morning.

In the square, one stands in the symbolic centre of the Chinese universe. The rectangular arrangement, flanked by halls to both east and west, to some extent echoes the layout of the Forbidden City. As such, the square employs a conventional plan that pays obeisance to traditional Chinese culture, but its ornaments and buildings are largely Soviet-inspired.

Activities

Early risers can watch the **flag-raising ceremony** at sunrise, performed by a troop of PLA soldiers drilled to march at precisely 108 paces per minute, 75cm per pace. The soldiers emerge through the Gate of Heavenly Peace to goosestep faultlessly across Dongchang'an Jie as traffic is halted. The same ceremony in reverse is performed at sunset. Ask at your hotel for flag-raising/-lowering times so you can get there early, as crowds can be intense.

Bicycles can no longer be ridden, or even walked, across Tiān'ānmén Sq, although you can ride along the north-south avenues on either side of the square.

Kite flying has also been banned.

Dangers & Annoyances

Unless you actually want a map you'll have to side-step determined map sellers and their confederates – the incessant learners of English – and just say no to the 'poor' art students press-ganging tourists to view their exhibitions; fending them off can be draining. Avoid invitations to tea houses, unless you want to pay in excess of US$400 dollars for the experience.

1989 PROTESTS

Tiān'ānmén Sq is best known in the West for the events of 1989, when live television pictures showed the army forcing pro-democracy demonstrators out of the square. Although it seems likely that no one was actually killed within the square itself, hundreds, possibly thousands, were killed in the surrounding streets. During the 10th anniversary of the 1989 protests, the square was shut for renovations.

Despite being a public place, the square remains more in the hands of the government than the people; it is monitored by closed-circuit TV cameras, Segway-riding policemen and plain-clothes officers who move faster than the Shànghǎi maglev at the sign of any disruption.

FORBIDDEN CITY & DŌNGCHÉNG CENTRAL TIĀN'ĀNMÉN SQUARE

SIGHTS

FORBIDDEN CITY — HISTORIC SITE
See p4.

TIĀN'ĀNMÉN SQUARE — SQUARE
See p11.

[FREE] NATIONAL MUSEUM OF CHINA — MUSEUM
Map p286 (中国国际博物馆; Zhōngguó Guójì Bówùguǎn; en.chnmuseum.cn; Guangchangdongce Lu, Tiān'ānmén Sq, 天安门,广场东侧路; audio guide ¥30, cafe coffee from ¥20, pastries & sandwiches ¥10-20; ⏰9am-5pm Tue-Sun; [S]Tian'anmen East) After years of renovation, China's premier museum, housed in the immense 1950s building on the eastern side of Tiān'ānmén Sq, finally reopened in 2011. It was a work in progress at the time of research, with some halls still closed, but much of what was open was well worth visiting. The **Ancient China** exhibition on the basement floor is outstanding. It contains dozens and dozens of stunning pieces, from prehistoric China through to the Qing Dynasty, all displayed beautifully in modern, spacious, low-lit exhibition halls. Look out for the 2000-year-old jade burial suit, made for the clearly well-endowed Western Han Dynasty king Liu Xiu, and the life-sized bronze acupuncture statue, dating from the 15th century. You could easily spend a couple of hours in this exhibition alone.

Also worth a look is the **Ancient Chinese Money** exhibition on the top floor. The **Bronze Art** and **Buddhist Sculpture** galleries, one floor below, are also impressive.

Many of the other halls housed temporary art galleries when we last visited, which were eye-catching, but lacked English captions. The museum, which is vast and energy sapping, also has a pleasant ground-floor **cafe**. Note, you must bring your passport along to gain museum entry.

[FREE] CHAIRMAN MAO MEMORIAL HALL — MAUSOLEUM
Map p286 (毛主席纪念堂; Máo Zhǔxí Jìniàntáng; Tiān'ānmén Sq; bag storage ¥2-10, camera storage ¥2-5; ⏰8am-noon Tue-Sun; [S]Tian'anmen West, Tian'anmen East or Qianmen) Mao Zedong died in September 1976 and his memorial hall was constructed on the southern side of Tiān'ānmén Sq soon afterwards. This squat, Soviet-inspired mausoleum lies on Běijīng's north-south axis of symmetry on the footprint of Zhōnghuá Gate (Zhōnghuá Mén), a vast and ancient portal flattened during the communist development of Tiān'ānmén Sq.

Domestically feted so his achievements forever eclipse his darker and more ruinous experiments, Mao is still revered across much of China. His portrait hangs over living rooms throughout the land and graces drum towers in far-off Guǎngxī villages and beyond. Mao's personality cult is recalled in the statues of the chairman that rise up across China while mute Mao-era slogans still fight the class war from crumbling walls in villages across the Middle Kingdom.

To this day the Chinese show deep respect when confronted with the physical presence of Mao, and you'll see some reduced to tears here. You are reminded to remove your hat and you can fork out ¥3 for a flower to lay at the foot of a statue of the Great Helmsman. Further on, Mao's mummified corpse lies in a crystal cabinet, draped in an anachronistic red flag emblazoned with hammer and sickle, as guards in white gloves impatiently wave the hoi polloi on towards further rooms, where a riot of Mao kitsch – lighters, bracelets, statues, key rings, bottle openers, you name it – ensues.

Bags need to be deposited at the **building** (Map p286) east of the memorial hall across the road from Tiān'ānmén Sq. And don't forget your passport. You won't be let into the hall without it.

JǏNGSHĀN PARK — PARK
Map p288 (景山公园; Jǐngshān Gōngyuán; Jingshan Qianjie; adult ¥2, in summer ¥5; ⏰6am-9.30pm; [S]Tian'anmen West, then bus 5) The dominating feature of Jǐngshān – one of the city's finest parks – is one of central Běijīng's few hills; a mound that was created from the earth excavated to make the Forbidden City moat. Called Coal Hill by Westerners during Legation days, Jǐngshān also serves as a *fēngshuǐ* shield, protecting the palace from evil spirits – or dust storms – from the north. Clamber to the top for a magnificent panorama of the capital and princely views over the russet roofing of the Forbidden City. On the eastern side of the park a locust tree stands in the place where the last of the Ming emperors, Chongzhen, hung himself as rebels swarmed at the city walls. The rest of the park is one of the best places in Běijīng for people-watching. Come early to see (or join in with) elderly folk going about their morning routines of dancing, singing,

performing taichi or playing keepie-uppies with oversized shuttlecocks. In April and May the park bursts into bloom with fabulously colourful peonies and tulips forming the focal point of a very popular flower fair. The park's south gate (Map p288) is directly opposite the Forbidden City's Gate of Divine Prowess (exit only).

WORKERS CULTURAL PALACE PARK

Map p288 (劳动人民文化宫; Láodòng Rénmín Wénhuà Gōng; ☎tennis court 6512 2856; adult ¥2, tennis court per hour ¥80, Supreme Temple ¥10; ⏰6.30am-7.30pm, tennis court 6am-11.30pm; [S]Tian'anmen East) Despite the prosaic name and its location at the very heart of town, this reclusive park, between Tiān'ānmén Sq and the Forbidden City, is one of Běijīng's best-kept secrets, and a bargain to boot. Few visitors divert here from their course towards the main gate of the Forbidden City, but this was the emperor's premier place of worship and contains the **Supreme Temple** (太庙; Tài Miào), with its beautifully carved interior roofing. If you find the Forbidden City either too colossal or crowded, the temple halls here are a cheaper, more tranquil and more manageable alternative. The huge halls of the temple remain, their roofs enveloped in imperial yellow tiles, beyond a quiet grove of ancient cypresses and enclosed within the **Glazed Gate** (琉璃门; Liúli Mén). Rising up to the splendid **Front Hall** (前殿; qiándiàn), the scene of imperial ceremonies of ancestor worship, are three flights of steps. Only gods could traverse the central plinth; the emperor was consigned to the left-hand flight. Note how the plaque above the Front Hall is inscribed in both Chinese and Manchu. Sadly this hall, as well as the **Middle Hall** (中殿; Zhōngdiàn) and **Rear Hall** (后殿; Hòu Diàn) behind, is inaccessible. The northern perimeter of the park abuts the palace moat *(tǒngzi hé)*, where you can find a bench and park yourself in front of a fine view. For an offbeat experience, practise your backhand within earshot of the Forbidden City at the **tennis court** in the park. Take the northwest exit from the park and find yourself just by the Forbidden City's entrance gate, or pop out of the eastern gate to Nanchizi Dajie. There is also a southern entrance.

TOP SIGHTS
GATE OF HEAVENLY PEACE

Hung with a vast likeness of Mao, and guarded by two pairs of Ming **stone lions**, the double-eaved Gate of Heavenly Peace (p19), north of Tiān'ānmén Sq, is a potent national symbol. Built in the 15th century and restored in the 17th century, the gate was formerly the largest of the four gates of the Imperial City Wall, and it was from this gate that Mao proclaimed the People's Republic of China on 1 October 1949. Today's political coterie watches mass troop parades from here.

Climb the gate for excellent views of the square, and peek inside at the impressive beams and overdone paintwork; in all there are 60 gargantuan wooden pillars and 17 vast lamps suspended from the ceiling. Within the gate tower there is also a fascinating photographic history of the gate (but only captioned in Chinese) and Tiān'ānmén Sq.

There's no fee for walking through the gate, en route to the Forbidden City, but if you climb it you'll have to pay. The ticket office is on the north side of the gate. For Forbidden City tickets, keep walking about 600m further north to the entrance at Meridian Gate.

DON'T MISS

- Mao's giant portrait
- Views of Tiān'ānmén Sq
- Impressive interior beams
- Photography exhibition

PRACTICALITIES

- 天安门; Tiān'ānmén
- Map p288
- admission to climb ¥15, bag storage ¥2-6
- ⏰8.30am-4.30pm
- [S]Tian'anmen West or Tian'anmen East

PITCHER PERFECT: RARE ATTACKS ON MAO'S PORTRAIT

The portrait of a benign Mao Zedong still hangs exaltedly from the Gate of Heavenly Peace in the same way that public statues of the Great Helmsman still keep guard over cities across China, from Dāndōng on the North Korean border to the far-flung Central Asian outpost of Kashgar and the ethnic Naxi town of Lìjiāng in Yúnnán. Mao's Běijīng portrait has reportedly been vandalised just twice during its long vigil overlooking Tiān'ānmén Sq: once in 1989 and again in 2007. During the pro-democracy protests of 1989, three men from Mao's home province of Húnán pitched paint-filled eggs at the portrait, while in 2007 burning material was thrown at the painting, scorching it in the process. Several copies of the portrait exist and replacement versions were speedily requisitioned in both instances. Such dissent is severely dealt with in China: the three egg throwers paid for their crime with spells in jail. One of them was journalist Yu Dongyue, who was jailed for over 16 years, emerging mentally ill upon his release in 2006. Two of the egg throwers fled China in 2009 to seek sanctuary in the US.

ZHŌNGSHĀN PARK — PARK

Map p288 (中山公园; Zhōngshān Gōngyuán; adult ¥3, Spring Flower & Tulips Show ¥10; ⏲6am-9pm; [S]Tian'anmen West) Named after Sun Zhongshan (Sun Yat-sen), the father of modern China, this peaceful park sits at the southwest corner of the Forbidden City and partly looks out onto the palace's moat and towering walls. A refreshing prologue or conclusion to the magnificence of the Forbidden City, the park was formerly the sacred Ming-style Altar to the God of the Land and the God of Grain (Shèjìtán), where the emperor offered sacrifices. The **Square Altar** (wǔsè tǔ) remains, bordered on all sides by walls tiled in various colours. Near the park entrance stands a towering dark-blue-tiled *páilou* (traditional Chinese archway) with triple eaves that originally commemorated the German Foreign Minister Baron von Ketteler, killed by Boxers in 1900. In the eastern section of the park is the Forbidden City Concert Hall (p26). As with Jǐngshān Park, north of the Forbidden City, April and May is a beautiful time to visit thanks to the hugely colourful **Spring Flower and Tulips Show**. The northeast exit of the park brings you out by Meridian Gate, from where you can enter the Forbidden City or cross the square to the northwestern gate of the Workers Cultural Palace. The south exit brings you out near Tiān'ānmén Sq. There is also a **west exit**).

MONUMENT TO THE PEOPLE'S HEROES — MONUMENT

Map p286 (人民英雄纪念碑; Rénmín Yīngxióng Jìniànbēi; Tiān'ānmén Sq; [S]Tian'anmen West, Tian'anmen East or Qianmen) North of Mao's mausoleum, and also in the centre of Tiān'ānmén Sq, the Monument to the People's Heroes was completed in 1958. The 37.9m-high obelisk, made of Qīngdǎo granite, bears bas-relief carvings of key patriotic and revolutionary events (such as Taiping rebels and Lin Zexu destroying opium at Hǔmén), as well as calligraphy from communist bigwigs Mao Zedong and Zhou Enlai. Mao's eight-character flourish proclaims 'Eternal Glory to the People's Heroes'. The monument is illuminated at night.

FOREIGN LEGATION QUARTER — HISTORIC BUILDINGS

Map p286 (租界区; [S]Chongwenmen, Qianmen or Wangfujing) The former Foreign Legation Quarter, where the 19th-century foreign powers flung up their embassies, schools, post offices and banks, lies east of Tiān'ānmén Sq. Apart from the Běijīng Police Museum, the **former French Post Office** (now a Sìchuān restaurant), and some of the Legation Quarter buildings, which have been turned into high-end restaurants and members clubs, you can't enter any of the buildings, but a stroll along the streets here (Taijichang Dajie and Zhengyi Lu) gives you a hint of the area's former European flavour.

BĚIJĪNG POLICE MUSEUM — MUSEUM

Map p286 (北京警察博物馆; Běijīng Jǐngchá Bówùguǎn; ☎8522 5018; 36 Dongjiaomin Xiang; adult ¥5, through ticket ¥20; ⏲9am-4pm Tue-Sun; [S]Qianmen) Propaganda aside, riveting exhibits make this a fascinating exposé of Běijīng's *dà gài mào* (local slang for the constabulary). Learn how Běijīng's first

Public Security Bureau (PSB) college operated from the **Dōngyuè Temple** in 1949 and find out how officers tackled the 'stragglers, disbanded soldiers, bandits, local ruffians, hoodlums and despots…' planted in Běijīng by the Kuomintang (KMT). There are also eye-opening accounts of how KMT spies Li Andong and Yamaguchi Takachi planned to mortar the Gate of Heavenly Peace, and a welcome analysis of how the Běijīng PSB was destroyed during the 'national catastrophe' of the Cultural Revolution. Altogether 9685 policemen were dismissed from their posts during the paroxysms of violence – spot the yawning gap among portraits of PSB directors from June 1966 to June 1977. The museum covers grisly business: there's Wang Zhigang's bombing of Běijīng Train Station on 29 October 1980 and an explosion at Xīdān Plaza in 1968, while upstairs the museum gets to grips with other morbid crimes and their investigations; for police weapons, head to the 4th floor. The through ticket includes some laser-shooting practice and a souvenir.

[FREE] ST JOSEPH'S CHURCH — CHURCH

Map p286 (东堂; Dōng Táng; 74 Wangfujing Dajie; ⏲6.30am-5pm; [S]Dengshikou) A crowning edifice on Wangfujing Dajie, and one of Běijīng's four principal churches, attractive St Joseph's Church is also known locally as the East Cathedral. Originally built during the reign of Shunzhi in 1655, it was damaged by an earthquake in 1720 and reconstructed. The luckless church also caught fire in 1807, was destroyed again in 1900 during the Boxer Rebellion and restored in 1904, only to be shut in 1966. Now fully repaired, the church is a testament to the long history of Christianity in China. A large piazza in front swarms with children playing, elderly folk resting and newlyweds posing for photographs. Mass is held in Chinese at 6.30am and 7am from Monday to Saturday, and at 6.15am, 7am and 8am on Sundays. An English version is held every Sunday at 4pm. The wide-screen televisions, bolted in place above parts of the aisles and showing non-stop recordings of Chinese hymns being sung, are a rather distracting recent addition.

BĚIJĪNG WÁNGFǓJǏNG PALEOLITHIC MUSEUM — MUSEUM

Map p286 (北京王府井古人类文化遗址博物馆; Běijīng Wángfǔjǐng Gǔrénlèi Wénhuà Yízhǐ Bówùguǎn; 1 Dongchang'an Jie, W1P3 Oriental Plaza; adult ¥10; ⏲10am-4.30pm; [S]Wangfujing) Archaeologists and anthropologists will be rewarded at this simple museum detailing the tools and relics (stone flakes, bone scrapers, fragments of bone etc) of Late Pleistocene Man, who once inhabited Běijīng. The discoveries on display were unearthed during the excavation of the foundations of Oriental Plaza in 1996. To find the museum, take Exit A at Wangfujing subway station.

[FREE] CHINA ART MUSEUM — MUSEUM

Map p286 (中国美术馆; Zhōngguó Měishùguǎn; 1 Wusi Dajie; ⏲9am-5pm, last entry 4pm; [S]National Art Museum) This revamped museum has received a healthy shot of imagination and flair, with absorbing exhibitions from abroad promising doses of colour and vibrancy. Běijīng's art lovers have lapped up some top-notch presentations here, from the cream of Italian design to modern artworks from the Taipei Fine Arts Museum. The latter offers a chance to compare contemporary mainland Chinese art – with its burdensome political baggage and recurring themes – with the light-footed, invigorating and more universalist conceptions from the island across from Fújiàn. English captions can be sporadic, but this is a first-rate place to see modern art from China and abroad and, just as importantly, to watch the locals looking at art. Lifts allow for wheelchair access. Note, you must bring your passport along to gain entry.

[FREE] DŌNG'ĀN MÉN REMAINS — RUIN

Map p286 (明皇城东安门遗址; Míng Huáng Chéng Dōng'ānmén Yízhǐ; Imperial Wall Foundation Ruins Park, cnr Donghuamen Dajie & Beiheyan Dajie; ⏲24hr; [S]Dengshikou or National Art Museum) In an excavated pit on Beiheyan Dajie sits a pitiful stump, all that remains of the magnificent Dōng'ān Mén, the east gate of the Imperial City. Before being razed, the gate was a single-eaved, seven-bay-wide building with a hip-and-gable roof capped with yellow tiles. The remnants of the gate – just two layers of 18 bricks – may make for dull viewing but of more interest are the accompanying bricks of the excavated **Ming-dynasty road** that used to run near Dōngān Mén. The road is around 2m lower than the current road level, its expertly made bricks typical of precisely engineered Ming-dynasty brickwork. The remains are located in the **Imperial Wall Foundation Ruins Park**

TOP SIGHTS
FRONT GATE

Front Gate, or Qiánmén (前门), actually consists of two gates. The northernmost of the two gates is the 40m-high **Zhèngyáng Gate** (正阳门城楼; Zhèngyáng Mén Chénglóu), which dates from the Ming dynasty and was the largest of the nine gates of the Inner City Wall separating the inner, or Tartar (Manchu), city from the outer, or Chinese, city. Partially destroyed in the Boxer Rebellion around 1900, the gate was once flanked by two temples that have since vanished. With the disappearance of the city walls, the gate sits out of context, but it can be climbed for decent views of Tiān'ānmén Sq and of Arrow Tower, immediately to the south.

Inside the upper levels are some fascinating historical photographs, showing the area as it was at the beginning of the last century, before the city walls and many of the surrounding gates and temples were demolished. Explanatory captions are in English as well as Chinese. **Zhèngyáng Gate Arrow Tower** (正阳门箭楼; Zhèngyángmén Jiànlóu; Map p286), directly south, can't be climbed. It also dates from the Ming dynasty and was originally connected to Zhèngyáng Gate by a semicircular enceinte (enclosing wall), demolished last century.

DON'T MISS

- Fascinating historical photographs
- Views of Tiān'ānmén Sq

PRACTICALITIES

- 前门; Qiánmén
- Map p286
- admission ¥20, audio guide ¥20
- ⌚9am-4pm, closed Mon
- [S]Qiánmén

(皇城根遗址公园; Huángchéng Gēn Yízhǐ Gōngyuán), a thin strip of park that follows much of the course of the eastern side of the Imperial City Wall. To see how the vast Imperial City and its once-towering walls used to look, check out the impressive diorama of the ancient complex, housed inside the free-to-enter **Imperial City Art Trading Centre** (Map p288; ⌚9am-4pm Mon-Fri), southwest of here, off Nanchizi Dajie.

[FREE] **COURTYARD GALLERY** GALLERY

Map p286 (四合院画廊; Sìhéyuàn Huàláng; 95 Donghuamen Dajie, 东华门大街95号; ⌚10am-10pm; [S]Dengshikou) Tucked away discreetly beneath its namesake restaurant, which is perched overlooking prime views of the Forbidden City moat, this basement gallery is a crisp and trendy pocket-sized space of white painted bricks and contemporary paintings.

ANCIENT OBSERVATORY OBSERVATORY

Map p286 (古观象台; Gǔ Guānxiàngtái; Jianguomen Bridge, East 2nd Ring Rd; 二环东路建国门桥; Erhuandong Lu, Jianguomen Qiao; adult ¥20; ⌚9.30am-4.30pm Tue-Sun; [S]Jianguomen) This unusual former observatory is mounted on the battlements of a watchtower lying along the line of the old Ming City Wall and originally dates back to Kublai Khan's days, when it lay north of the present site. Kublai, like later Ming and Qing emperors, relied heavily on astrologers to plan military endeavours. The present observatory – the only surviving example of several constructed during the Jin, Yuan, Ming and Qing dynasties – was built between 1437 and 1446 to facilitate both astrological predictions and seafaring navigation.

At ground level is a pleasant courtyard flanked by halls housing displays (with limited English captions). Also within the courtyard is an armillary sphere supposedly dating to 1439, supported by four dragons. At the rear is an attractive garden with grass, sundials and a further armillary sphere.

Clamber the steps to the roof of the watchtower to admire a mind-boggling array of Jesuit-designed **astronomical instruments**, embellished with sculptured bronze dragons and other Chinese flourishes – a kind of East and West astronomical fusion. The Jesuits, scholars as well as proselytisers, arrived in 1601 when Matteo Ricci and his associates were permitted to work alongside Chinese scientists. Outdoing the resident calendar-setters, they were given control of the observatory and became the Chinese court's official advisers.

POLY ART MUSEUM MUSEUM

Map p286 (保利艺术博物馆; Bǎolì Yìshù Bówùguǎn; ☎6500 8117; www.polymuseum.com; 9th fl, Poly Plaza, 14 Dongzhimen Nandajie; admission ¥20, audio guide ¥10; ⌚9.30am-4.30pm; [S]Dongsi Shitiao) This small but exquisite museum displays a glorious array of ancient bronzes from the Shang and Zhou dynasties, a magnificent high-water mark for bronze production. Check out the intricate scaling on the '*Zun* vessel in the shape of a Phoenix' (倗季凤鸟尊) or the '*You* with Divine Faces' (神面卣), with its elephant head on the side of the vessel. The detailed animist patterns on the *Gangbo You* (棡柏卣) are similarly vivid and fascinating. In an attached room are four of the Western-styled 12 bronze animals plundered with the sacking of the Old Summer Palace that have been acquired by the museum. The pig, monkey, tiger and ox peer out from glass cabinets – you can buy a model for ¥15,000. The last room is populated with a wonderful collection of standing bodhisattva statues. Resembling a semidivine race of smiling humans, most of the statues are from the Northern Qi, Northern Wei and Tang dynasties. It's a sublime presentation and some of the statues have journeyed through the centuries with pigment still attached.

Those interested in Ming-dynasty architecture should check out the nearby **Imperial Granaries** (南新仓; Map p286; Nán Xīn Cāng). Nine of the storehouses, dating from 1409, have been lovingly restored. They once contained grain and rice for Běijīng's royalty; they now house posh wine bars and members clubs.

ZHÌHUÀ TEMPLE BUDDHIST TEMPLE

Map p286 (智化寺; Zhìhuà Sì; 5 Lumicang Hutong; adult ¥20, audio guide ¥10; ⌚8.30am-4.30pm; [S]Jianguomen or Chaoyangmen) Běijīng's surviving temple brood has endured casual restoration that often buried authenticity. But this rickety non-active temple, hidden down a rarely visited *hútòng*, is thick with the flavours of old Peking, having eluded the Dulux treatment that invariably precedes entrance fee inflation and stomping tour groups. You won't find the coffered ceiling of the **Zhìhuà Hall** (it's in the USA), and the Four Heavenly Kings have vanished from Zhìhuà Gate (智化门; Zhìhuà Mén), but the **Scriptures Hall** encases a venerable Ming-dynasty wooden library topped with a seated Buddha and a magnificently unrestored ceiling. The highlight, the **Ten Thousand Buddhas Hall** (万佛殿; Wànfó Diàn), is right at the back of the complex, and is an enticing two floors of miniature niche-borne Buddhist effigies and cabinets for the storage of sutras. Unfortunately, visitors are no longer allowed to climb to the 2nd floor.

[FREE] **HÓNG LÓU** MUSEUM

Map p286 (红楼; 29 Wusi Dajie, 五四大街29号; ⌚8.30am-4.30pm; [S]National Art Museum) Built in 1918, this red-brick building was the former library and arts department of Peking University (北大; Běidà), and Mao Zedong worked here as a librarian from

BĚIJĪNG MUSEUM PASS

If you're staying in the capital for a while, the **Běijīng Museum Pass** (博物馆通票; Bówùguǎn Tōngpiào; ☎6222 3793; www.bowuguan.bj.cn; Y80) – a website and phone service in Chinese only – is a great investment that will save you both money and queuing for tickets. For ¥120 you get either complimentary access or discounted admission (typically 50%) to 65 museums, temples and tourist sights in and around Běijīng. Attractions covered include the Great Wall at Bādálǐng, Front Gate, the Drum Tower, the Bell Tower, the Confucius Temple, the Botanic Gardens, the Railway Museum, Dōngyuè Temple, Zhìhuà Temple and many others. Not all museums are worth visiting, but many are, and you only have to visit a small selection to get your money back. The pass comes in the form of a booklet (Chinese with minimal English), valid from 1 January to 31 December in any one year. The pass, which is harder to obtain as the year goes on, can be picked up from participating museums and sights, from some post offices or, most easily, from the huge bookstore known as Běijīng Books Building (p127). Go to the service desk to your far right as you enter the bookstore.

START **TIĀN'ĀNMÉN SQ**
FINISH **RAFFLES BEIJING HOTEL**
DISTANCE **2KM**
DURATION **ONE HOUR**

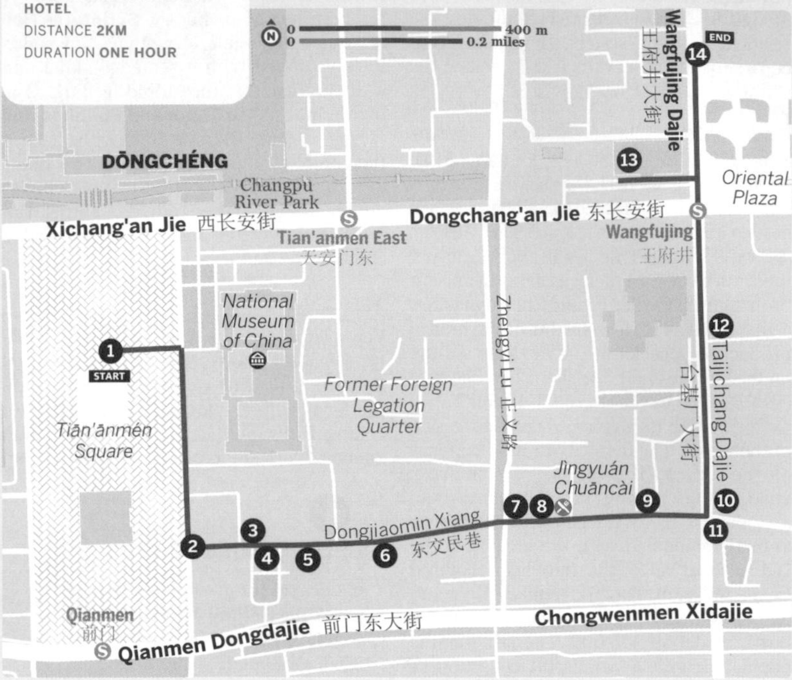

Neighbourhood Walk

Tiān'ānmén Square & Foreign Legation Quarter Walk

From [1] **Tiān'ānmén Sq**, cross the road and climb the steps into [2] **Dongjiaomin Xiang** (东交民巷). The red-brick building next to the Tiā–n'ān Hotel at No 39 was the former [3] **French Hospital**.

Through a grey-brick archway on your right, stands the elegant former [4] **Legation Quarter** of ash-grey architecture, now a collection of trendy restaurants facing onto a grass quadrangle.

Behind a wall a short walk east rises a green-roofed building at No 40, which was once the [5] **Dutch Legation**.

Further along on your right stands a building with massive pillars, the erstwhile address of the First National City Bank of New York (花旗银行; Huāqí Yínháng), now the quirky [6] **Běijīng Police Museum**.

Keep walking east to the domed building on the corner of Zhengyi Lu (正义路) and Dongjiaomin Xiang, once the [7] **Yokohama SpecieBank**.

The grey building at No 19 is the former [8] **French post office**, now Jìngyuán Chuāncài Sichuanese restaurant and ideal for lunch before you reach the former [9] **French Legation**, at No 15, with its large red entrance. The Capital Hotel on the other side is built in the former German Legation.

Backing onto a small school courtyard, the twin spires of the Gothic [10] **St Michael's Church** rise ahead at No 11, facing the green roofs and ornate red brickwork of the old [11] **Belgian Legation**.

Stroll north along Taijichang Dajie and hunt down the brick street sign embedded in the northern wall of Taijichang Toutiao (台基厂头条), carved with the old name of the road, [12] **Rue Hart**. Located along the north side of Rue Hart was the Austro-Hungarian Legation, south of which stood the Peking Club.

Reaching the north end of Taijichang Dajie, across busy Dongchang'an Jie is the [13] **Raffles Běijīng Hotel** (built 1900), which is just a stone's throw from the famous [14] **Wangfujing Dajie** shopping strip.

GROWTH OF CHRISTIANITY

Mao Zedong attempted to exorcise the nation of religious impulses, but today an estimated 400 million Chinese adhere to one faith or another. The bankruptcy of communism as a popular ideology coupled with wide-ranging social problems, from vast income disparities to a sense of powerlessness in a one-party state, has encouraged people to turn to other beliefs. And it's certainly not just the Chinese poor who are turning to religion: the drift to spiritual belief has occurred across the income spectrum.

The Chinese were traditionally either Buddhist, Taoist or Confucian; other major faiths in Běijīng are Islam and Christianity. But while religious freedom exists in China, this is freedom with Chinese characteristics. Belief systems (eg Falun Gong) can be banned overnight if Běijīng's leaders sense a threat to their political hegemony. Religious leaders of the major faiths are also cherry-picked by Běijīng. Proselytising is banned, although this is having limited effect on the spread of Christianity.

Indeed, if any religion faces a bright future in China, it is Christianity. By wiping the slate clean, Mao Zedong allowed the monotheistic religion – which had been an indecisive presence in China since the 7th century – to flourish in a land that suddenly found itself unsure what to believe in. Most Chinese Christians belong to illicit house churches, rather than the state recognised Protestant or Catholic churches, so the precise number of Christians is hard to fathom, although figures of over 100 million have been posited.

Jesus in Beijing (How Christianity Is Changing the Global Balance of Power) by David Aikman argues that China is approaching a tipping point that will transform the land into a largely Christian domain over the next 30 years. However unlikely the scenario, such an achievement would surely owe much to the communist secularisation of China, which has turned the nation's soul into a blank sheet of paper to be written upon.

1918 to 1919 before forming north China's first Communist Party here. It was also from here that he and his comrades helped launch the 1919 May Fourth Movement, after which the main road here is named; Wusi means 'five-four'. The ground floor of the main building now forms the **New Culture Movement Museum** (新文化运动纪念馆; Xīnwénhuà Yùndòng Jìniànguǎn), which commemorates the movement. The registration room contains the desk Mao used to work from, and you can also see the office of Li Dazhao, the library administrator who apparently introduced Mao to books on Marxism.

[FREE] **LAO SHE MUSEUM** HISTORIC BUILDING

Map p286 (老舍纪念馆; Lǎo Shě Jìniànguǎn; 19 Fengfu Hutong; ⏲9am-3.40pm, closed Mondays; [S]Dengshikou) Brimful of uncomplicated charm, this courtyard house off Dengshikou Xijie was the home of Lao She (1899–1966), one of Běijīng's best-loved 20th-century writers. The life of Lao She – author of *Rickshaw Boy* and *Tea House*, and former teacher at London's School of Oriental and African Studies – is detailed in a modest collection of halls, via newspaper cuttings, first-edition books, photographs and personal effects. The exhibition falls at the final hurdle, giving perfunctory mention to perhaps the most significant aspect of Lao She's life: his death by drowning in Taiping Lake on 24 August 1966 after a nasty beating by vituperative Red Guards the day before. Captions are largely in Chinese.

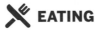

🍴 EATING

This historic part of Běijīng has a fabulous range of dining options covering every type of Chinese cuisine, as well as plenty of international places. It's also home to some of the capital's most atmospheric restaurants, from beautifully converted courtyards to the many hole-in-the-wall establishments scattered throughout the local *hútòng*. The Dōnghuámén Night Market draws tourists by the hundreds (both domestic and foreign) with its exotic insect and lizard snacks and makes for a fun evening stroll even if you don't fancy the food on offer.

TOP CHOICE ZUǑ LÍN YÒU SHÈ
CHINESE BĚIJĪNG $

Map p286 (左邻右舍褡裢火烧; 50 Meishuguan Houjie, 美术馆后街50号; dumplings per liǎng ¥4-6, dishes ¥5-20; ⊙11am-9.30pm; ⊡; ⓈNational Art Museum) This small, no-nonsense, and often raucous restaurant focuses on Běijīng cuisine. Many of the dishes in our Běijīng Menu box text can be found here, but the speciality is *dālian huǒshāo* (褡裢火烧); golden-fried finger-shaped dumplings stuffed with all manner of savoury fillings; we prefer the pork ones, but there are lamb, beef and veggie choices too. They are served by the *liǎng* (两), with one *liǎng* equal to three dumplings, and you must order at least two *liǎng* (二两; *èr liǎng*) of each filling to make it worth their while cooking a batch. Other specialities include the pickled fish (酥鲫鱼; *sū jì yú*), the spicy tofu paste (麻豆腐; *má dòufu*) and the deep-fried pork balls (干炸丸子; *gān zhá wánzi*), while filling bowls of millet porridge (小米粥; *xiǎo mǐ zhōu*) are served up for free. No English sign (look for the wooden signboard), and no English spoken, but there is an English translation of the menu available.

COURTYARD
FUSION $$$

Map p286 (四合院; Sìhéyuàn; ☏6526 8883; 95 Donghuamen Dajie, 东华门大街95号; mains ¥130-300, set menu ¥488; ⊙6-10pm; ❄; ⓈTian'anmen East or Dengshikou) Classy Courtyard enjoys a peerless location perched by the side of the moat surrounding the Forbidden City. Romantics will need to book ahead to ensure they have one of the cosy window tables that offer the best views. Forage to find the entrance (up the steps curtained by fronds of bamboo). Inside, the menu is small but sumptuous and the wine list impressive, while the basement houses a small art gallery.

CRESCENT MOON MUSLIM RESTAURANT
CHINESE XĪNJIĀNG $

Map p286 (新疆弯弯月亮维吾尔穆斯林餐厅; Xīnjiāng Wānwānyuèliàng Wéiwú'ěr Mùsīlín Cāntīng; 16 Dongsi Liutiao Hutong, 东四六条胡同16号, 东四北大街; dishes from ¥18; ⊙10am-midnight; ⊡; ⓈDongsi Shitiao) You can find a Chinese Muslim restaurant on almost every street in Běijīng. Most are run by Huí Muslims, who are Han Chinese, rather than ethnic-minority Uighurs from the remote western province of Xīnjiāng. The Crescent Moon, tucked away down a *hútòng* off Dongsi Beidajie, is the real deal – owned and staffed by Uighurs, it attracts many Běijīng-based

Uighurs and people from Central Asia, as well as a lot of Western expats. It's more expensive than most other Xīnjiāng restaurants in Běijīng, but the food is consistently good, and it has an English menu. The speciality is the leg of lamb (¥128). You can also get Xīnjiāng tea, beer (¥15) and wine (¥95), although the wine isn't the best.

HOME SWEET HOME
TAIWANESE $$

Map p286 (台湾精品料理; Táiwān Jīngpǐn Liàolǐ; 235 Chaoyangmen Nanxiaojie, 朝阳门内南小街235号; dishes from ¥25-50; ⊙11am-2pm & 5-9.30pm; ⊡❄; ⓈDengshikou) It doesn't look like much from the outside, and the interior is simple, but this friendly restaurant serves up some of the most authentic Taiwanese cuisine in town. The emphasis is on traditional Taiwanese dishes such as three-cup chicken, which comes in a clay pot, spiced with garlic and basil, as well as deep-fried pepper salt shrimp or frog and ǒ-á-chian, an oyster omelette topped with a sweet sauce that's the most popular snack in Taiwan. English menu, but no English sign.

LǍO ZHÁI YUÀN
PEKING DUCK $$

Map p286 (老宅院; 14 Liangguochang, 美术馆后街亮果厂14号, off Meishuguan Houjie; mains ¥30-50; ⊙10am-1.30pm & 4.30-8.30pm; ⊡; ⓈNational Art Museum) Good-value Běijīng roast duck in a small courtyard restaurant. The duck on the English menu costs ¥135, and is the better quality of the two types available. If you want the cheaper, but still tasty version, which costs ¥98, ask for *pǔtōng kǎo yā* (普通烤鸭; ordinary roast duck).

TEMPLE
INTERNATIONAL $$$

Map p286 (嵩祝寺餐厅; Sōngzhù Sì Cāntīng; ☏8400 2232; www.temple-restaurant.com; Sōngzhù Temple, 23 Shatanbei Jie, off Wusi Dajie, 五四大街沙滩北街23号, 嵩祝寺; mains ¥180-290; ⊙11.30am-2.30pm & 6-10pm; ❄⊡; ⓈNational Art Museum) Housed in a recently renovated 600-year-old temple and opened by celebrated chef Ignace Lecleir, this place was always going to be a bit special. It arrived on the scene, much anticipated, in 2011, and hasn't disappointed. The service is flawless, the food – salmon, lobster, pigeon, veal – is exquisite (although some moan about the small portions) and the ambience is certainly unique. It also has one of the best wine lists in town. The whole menu, including the ¥135 lunchtime set menu, can be viewed on its website. Reservations recommended.

START **BIKE BĚIJĪNG**
FINISH **BIKE BĚIJĪNG**
DISTANCE **6KM**
DURATION **1½ HOURS**

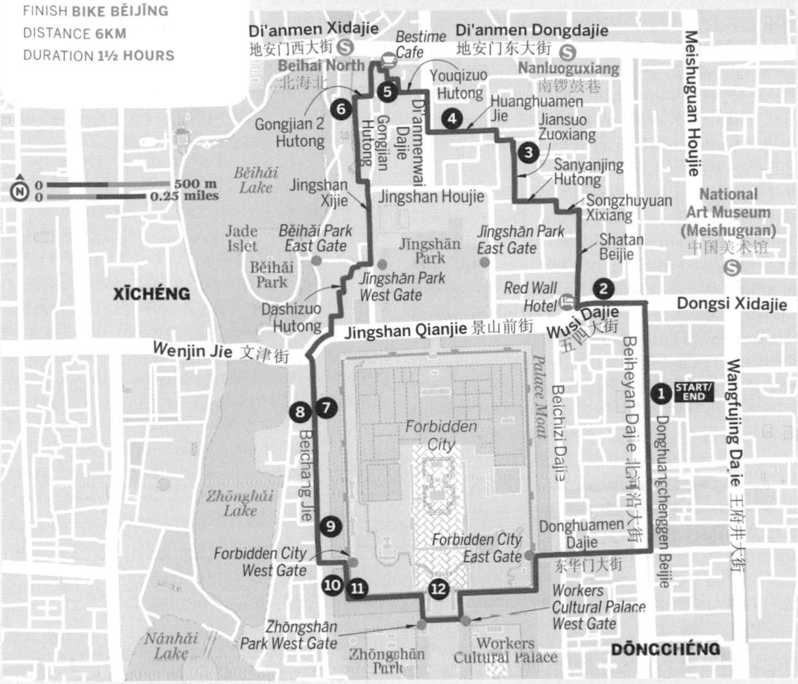

Neighbourhood Walk

Forbidden City Bike Circuit

Pick up a bike at [1] **Bike Běijīng** and head for the imperial *hútòng* east of Jǐngshān Park, passing en route the 1918 [2] **Hóng Lóu**, where Mao Zedong once worked as a librarian.

Turn right into Shatan Beijie (沙滩北街) and left into Songzhuyuan Xixiang (嵩祝院西巷). Bear right, then left into Sanyanjing Hutong (三眼井胡同). Note the elaborately carved Qing-dynasty doorway on your right, now blocked up and turned into a wall and window. Just before the end, turn right into Jiansuo Zuoxiang (吉安所左巷). No 8 was [3] **Mao Zedong's former home**.

At the end, turn left, take the second right and head towards Huanghuamen Jie (黄花门街). No 43 is the [4] **former courtyard home of imperial eunuch Li Lianyin**, a favourite of Empress Dowager Cixi.

At the end, turn right then left under an arch in part of the old imperial city wall, into Youqizuo Hutong (油漆作胡同).

Follow the wiggly [5] ***hútòng*** to Gongjian Hutong (恭俭胡同). Soon after, turn right into Gongjian 2 Hutong (恭俭二胡同), a quiet residential alleyway, which hugs the [6] **eastern wall of Běihǎi Park**.

Follow Jingshan Xijie (景山西街) to Jǐngshān Park west gate, turn right, then cycle under the car-park arch and into Dashizuo Hutong (大石作胡同), which meets Jingshan Qianjie (景山前街), where you'll see the Forbidden City moat. Follow Beichang Jie (北长街), past the now closed [7] **Fúyòu Temple** and opposite, the entrance to the small [8] **Wànshòu Xīnglóng Temple** (万寿兴隆寺).

Stop at [9] **Hángzhōu Xiǎochī** for dumplings, turn left to the west gate of the Forbidden City, and follow the [10] **Forbidden City moat** and towering [11] **palace walls** around to [12] **Meridian Gate**. Cross the square in front of the gate, and follow the moat eastward. Pass the palace's east gate before crossing onto Donghuamen Dajie (东华门大街), turning left into Donghuangchenggen Nanjie (东皇城根南街) and returning to Bike Běijīng.

CHUĀN BÀN CHINESE SÌCHUĀN $

Map p286 (川办餐厅; 28 Dongzongbu Hutong, off Chaoyangmen Nanxiaojie, 朝阳门南小街东总部胡同28号; dishes from ¥20; ⏰11am-2pm & 5-11pm Mon-Fri, 11am-11pm Sat & Sun; [E]; [S]Jianguomen) Every Chinese province has its own official building in Běijīng, complete with a restaurant for cadres and locals working in the capital who are pining for a taste of home. Often they're the most authentic places for regional cuisines. This restaurant in the Sìchuān Government Offices is always crowded and serves up just about every variety of Sìchuān food you could want. It's very much a place for fire fiends: almost every dish comes loaded with chillies and mouth-numbing Sìchuān peppercorns, whether it's bamboo shoots, Sìchuān specials such as *làzi jī* (spicy chicken), or steamed fish with pepper and taro. There's an English menu, and the helpful staff can assist you in avoiding anything too extreme. Beers are ¥10; you'll need them to restore feeling to your tongue. No English sign; it's housed in an office-block of a building, with the entrance round the back.

JÌNGYUÁN CHUĀNCÀI CHINESE SÌCHUĀN $$

Map p286 (静园川菜; 19 Dongjiaomin Xiang, 东交民巷19号; mains ¥20-50; ⏰10.30am-2pm & 4.30-9.30pm; [E]; [S]Qianmen, Tian'anmen East or Wangfujing) More expensive than other standard Sichuanese restaurants, but then other standard Sichuanese restaurants aren't housed inside the 1901 former French Post Office in the capital's former Foreign Legation Quarter. English menu with photos,

LOCAL KNOWLEDGE

BĚIJĪNG ON FOOT

The city itself may appear uncontrollably huge, but Běijīng is a city of orderly design (unlike Shànghǎi). Think of the city as one giant grid, with the Forbidden City at its centre.

Street signs in Běijīng are marked in both Chinese characters and Pinyin (romanised Chinese). Even so, understanding a little basic Chinese will help to make some sense of street names. It is also useful to refer to our detailed maps, where many roads are labelled with Chinese characters. To assist you around town, we have also frequently added road names in Chinese in the text.

The majority of Běijīng's larger streets are affixed with the word *jiē* (街), which means 'street', as in Wangfujing Dajie (Dajie here means 'big street', 'avenue' or just 'street') – 'Wangfujing St'. Occasionally the world *lù* (路) is also used, meaning 'road', as in Zhangzizhong Lu – 'Zhangzizhong Rd'. Běijīng's plentiful alleyways in the centre of town are called *hútòng* (胡同); a minority are called *xiàng* (巷), which means 'alley' or 'lane'. Another term used is *lǐ* (里), meaning 'neighbourhood'.

Many road names are also compound words that place the road in context with others in the city, by using the points of the compass. The following words are used in compound street names:

běi north 北
nán south 南
dōng east 东
xī west 西
zhōng central 中

So, Gulou Dongdajie means 'Gulou East St' and Dongdan Beidajie means 'Dongdan North St'.

However, some Běijīng street names have local idiosyncrasies. Jianguomenwai Dajie means 'the avenue outside (外; *wai*) Jianguo Gate (建国门; Jianguomen)' – that is, outside the old wall – whereas Jianguomennei Dajie (建国门内大街) means 'the avenue inside Jianguo Gate'. The gate in question no longer exists, so it survives in name alone.

Unlike countless other Chinese cities, Běijīng is one place where you won't find a Jiefang Lu (Liberation Rd), Renmin Lu (People's Rd), Zhongshan Lu (Zhongshan Rd) or a Beijing Lu (Beijing Rd). Five ring roads (环路; *huánlù*) circle the city centre in concentric rings.

LOCAL KNOWLEDGE

CYCLE-RICKSHAW PANCAKES

One of the tastiest street-food snacks to be found in Běijīng is the *jiānbing* (煎饼), a savoury pancake sprinkled with chives and spring onion and rubbed in chilli sauce before being wrapped around a crunchy slice of fried dough. They're either sold from a hole-in-the-wall stall, or simply off the back of a cycle rickshaw. Ordering is easy, as the vendor generally only sells one type; all you have to decide is whether you want chilli (*yào làjiāo*) or not (*bú yào làjiāo*), and then hand over your ¥4.

Jiānbing vendors come and go (especially those working off cycle rickshaws), but if you're stuck trying to find one, try one of these two locations:

Dongsi Shitiao Subway Station (Map p286; Dongsi Shitiao Subway Station; pancakes ¥4; ⊙7am-4pm) About 100m west of the subway station, on the south side of Dongsishitiao Lu, you'll find a woman who's been serving hungry commuters from the back of her cycle rickshaw here for years.

153 Yonghegong Dajie (Map p290; 153 Yonghegong Dajie; pancakes ¥3.5-4.5; ⊙7am-7pm) About 500m south of the Lama Temple, and operating from a hole in the wall by a restaurant called Yānlín Cāntīng (燕麟餐厅), this pancake stall is one of the few that offers a variety of pancake mixes. Choose from millet (小米; *xiǎo mǐ*), mung bean (绿豆; *lǜ dòu*), glutinous rice (糯米; *nuò mǐ*) or purple-coloured glutinous rice (紫米; *zǐ mǐ*).

---

although no English sign and not much English spoken.

BĚIJĪNG DÀDŎNG ROAST DUCK RESTAURANT   PEKING DUCK $$$

Map p286 (北京大董烤鸭店; Běijīng Dàdŏng Kăoyādiàn, ☑8522 1111; 88 Jinbao Jie, 5th fl, Jinbaohui Shopping Centre, 东城区金宝街88号 金宝汇购物中心5层; roast duck ¥238; ⊙11am-10pm; ⓢDengshikou) Ultramodern Dàdŏng sells itself on being the only restaurant that serves Běijīng roast duck with all the flavour of the classic imperial dish, but none of the fat – the leanest roast duck in the capital. For some it's hideously overpriced and far from authentic. For others it's the best roast duck restaurant in China. There are four branches: this one, by the Regent hotel, another housed in part of the former Imperial Granaries and two further east in Cháoyáng District. All are equally classy establishments.

DŌNGHUÁMÉN NIGHT MARKET   STREET FOOD $

Map p286 (东华门夜市; Dōnghuámén Yèshì; Dong'anmen Dajie, 东安门大街; snacks ¥5-15; ⊙4-10pm; ⓞ; ⓢWangfujing) A sight in itself, the bustling night market near Wangfujing Dajie is a veritable food zoo: lamb, beef and chicken skewers, corn on the cob, smelly *dòufu* (tofu), cicadas, grasshoppers, kidneys, quail eggs, snake, squid, fruit, porridge, fried pancakes, strawberry kebabs, bananas, Inner Mongolian cheese, stuffed eggplants, chicken hearts, pita bread stuffed with meat, shrimps – and that's just the start. It's not a very authentic Běijīng experience, but the vendors take great glee in persuading foreigners to try such delicacies as scorpion on a stick. Expect to pay ¥5 for a lamb skewer, far more than you would pay for the same snack from a *hútòng* vendor. More exotic skewers cost up to ¥50. Noodles or savoury pancakes (*jiānbing*) will set you back about ¥10. Prices are all marked and in English.

DŌNGZI LŰRÒU HUŎSHĀO   CHINESE HÉBĚI $

Map p286 (冬子驴肉火烧; 193 Chaoyangmen Nanxiaojie, 朝阳门南小街193号; mains ¥5-6; ⊙7am-11pm; ⓢDengshikou) This small, nononsense, but clean, restaurant serves arguably the best *lǜròu huŏshāo* (驴肉火烧; donkey-meat pastry pockets; ¥5) in Běijīng. Bowls of *xiǎomǐ zhōu* (小米粥; millet porridge; ¥2) make an ideal accompaniment, or else just grab a beer (啤酒; *píjiǔ*; ¥4). No English sign or menu, and no English spoken.

GRANDMA'S KITCHEN   AMERICAN $$

Map p286 (祖母的厨房; Zǔmǔ de Chúfáng; 47-2 Nanchizi Dajie, 南池子大街47－2号; mains ¥50-80; ⊙10am-10pm; ⓞⓞ; ⓢTian'anmen East) Handy Forbidden City branch of the popular Grandma's, serving good quality American comfort food such as burgers, pizza and sandwiches in a quaint cafe-restaurant decked out just like a country cottage.

HÁNGZHŌU XIǍOCHĪ CHINESE DUMPLINGS $

Map p286 (杭州小吃; Hángzhōu Xiǎochī; 76 Beichang Jie, 北长街76号; mains ¥5-10; ⏰5am-8pm; [S]Tian'anmen West, then Bus 5) Lao Li, the eccentric manager of What? Bar, two doors from here, swears by the boiled dumplings (蒸饺; *zhēng jiǎo*) in this simple restaurant. They come by the basket and are perfect for lining your stomach before you delve into the cheap beer at What? Bar. You can also get fluffier, steamed dumplings (小笼包; *xiǎolóng bāo*) for the same price (¥5 per basket), as well as soups (seaweed, 紫菜汤, *zǐcài tāng;* wonton, 馄沌, *hún dùn;* egg, 鸡蛋汤, *jīdàn tāng*) and noodles (beef, 牛肉面, *niúròu miàn;* spicy glass noodles, 酸辣粉, *suān là fěn*). No English sign or menu.

WÁNGFǓJǏNG SNACK STREET STREET FOOD $

Map p286 (王府井小吃街; Wángfǔjǐng Xiǎochījiē; west off Wangfujing Dajie, 王府井大街西侧; dishes/snacks ¥10; ⏰9.30am-10pm; [S]Wangfujing) Fronted by an ornate archway, this quadrant is lined with cheap-and-cheerful food stalls that are always busy. It's a good place to pick up Xīnjiāng or Muslim Uighur cuisine such as lamb skewers and flat bread. Also on offer are other dishes from all over China, including *málà tàng* (a spicy soup from Sìchuān) and *zhájiàngmiàn* (Běijīng noodles in fried bean sauce). Also being scoffed by the bowl here are Lánzhōu *lāmiàn* (Lánzhōu noodles), Shāndōng *jiānbing* (Shāndōng savoury pancake), Yúnnán *guòqiáo mǐxiàn* (Yúnnán cross-the-bridge noodles) and oodles of spicy Sìchuān food. At most outlets you have to sit outside elbow-to-elbow with other diners. You'll also find some of the more exotic skewers, such as fried scorpion, which are on offer at the nearby Dōnghuámén Night Market. Not all stalls have prices listed. As a rough guide, most things cost around ¥10 for a portion.

TEXT MESSAGE ENQUIRIES

If you want to locate or contact a tourist, entertainment, shopping or business venue in Běijīng (and 20 other cities in China) and you have a mobile phone, then text message the name of the venue to the wireless search engine GuanXi on ☎1066 9588 2929. The full name, address and directions, plus telephone number, will be immediately returned to you by SMS (¥1 to ¥2 per enquiry). The information can also be relayed in Chinese, as long as your mobile phone can support Chinese text.

TIĀNDÌ YĪJIĀ CHINESE MIXED $$$

Map p286 (天地一家; ☎8511 5556; 140 Nanchizi Dajie; 南池子大街140号; mains from ¥50; ⏰10am-2.30pm & 5-9.30pm; 🚭; [S]Tian'anmen East) Doing business from a restored building alongside Chāngpú River Park (Chāngpú Hé Gōngyuán), this refined, Chinese courtyard-style restaurant is notable for the water feature with multicoloured fish that dominates the elegant dining room. There's also a balcony overlooking the former Imperial Archives (Huángshǐ Chéng). The menu, which spans a number of provinces and styles, is strong on seafood with snob appeal – shark's fin, abalone and lobster – as well as traditional delicacies such as bird's-nest soup and local faves such as Peking duck (¥280). It also does dim sum. The wine list (from ¥450) is hugely impressive, with a number of vintage bottles. The only downside is the slightly stiff atmosphere, not helped by the black-clad waitresses, who are hardly a bundle of laughs.

DRINKING & NIGHTLIFE

If you're shopping on Wángfǔjǐng, there are four or five drinks stalls (8.30am to midnight) on the main pedestrianised shopping strip that have shaded seating areas and serve cheap soft drinks and beer (from ¥8). There are also plenty of coffee shops inside the modern shopping centre, Oriental Plaza.

ALLEY COFFEE CAFE

Map p286 (寻常巷陌咖啡厅; Xúncháng Xiàngmò Kāfēi Tīng; cnr Jingshan Dongjie & Shatan Houjie, 景山东街，沙滩后街61号; ⏰8.30am-11pm; [S]Nanluoguxiang or National Art Museum) Perfect for a coffee break after a visit to the Forbidden City or Jǐngshān Park, this cute, traveller-friendly courtyard cafe, diagonally opposite Jīngshān Park's east gate, has friendly English-speaking staff and does fresh coffee (from ¥25), cold beer and a mix of Chinese and Western food, including breakfast fry-ups (until 11am). Also rents bikes (per day ¥50, deposit ¥600) and has free wi-fi.

YǏN BAR

Map p286 (饮; 33 Qihelou Jie, 北池子大街骑河楼33号, off Beichizi Dajie; beers and cocktails from ¥50, wine from ¥250, champagne ¥400-4000; ⏰11am-2am Apr-Nov; [S]National Art Museum) Ascend the stairs of the boutique hotel the Emperor to reach this chic terrace bar, and then climb the wooden steps to their highest point for a stunning view over the rooftops of the Forbidden City. It's lovely at sunset, but the drinks aren't as special as the setting, and they certainly aren't cheap. But there's a happy hour (4pm to 10pm) on Thursdays, a DJ at weekends and a hot tub for exhibitionists.

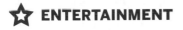

☆ ENTERTAINMENT

FORBIDDEN CITY CONCERT HALL CLASSICAL MUSIC

Map p288 (中山公园音乐堂; Zhōngshān Gōngyuán Yīnyuè Táng; ☎6559 8285; Zhongshan Park, 中山公园内; tickets ¥30-880; ⏰performances 7.30pm; [S]Tian'anmen West) Located on the eastern side of Zhōngshān Park, this is a wonderfully romantic venue for performances of classical and traditional Chinese music. It's also the best acoustically.

WHAT? BAR LIVE MUSIC

Map p286 (什么酒吧; Shénme? Jiǔbā; ☎133 4112 2757; 72 Beichang Jie, 北长街72号, 故宫西门往北; admission incl free beer ¥30; ⏰4pm-2am; [S]Tian'anmen West, then Bus 5) If you like to get up close and personal with the bands you go and see, then visit this easy-to-miss venue. That doesn't mean it is groupie heaven here; rather, it's so small that the audience might as well be on stage with the musicians. Gigs are on Fridays and Saturdays (sometimes Thursdays and Sundays too), and it's a good place to hear up-and-coming local talent. Just north of the west gate of the Forbidden City.

CHÁNG'ĀN GRAND THEATRE PEKING OPERA

Map p286 (长安大戏院; Cháng'ān Dàxìyuàn; ☎5166 4621; Chang'an Bldg, 7 Jianguomennei Dajie, 建国门内大街7号; tickets ¥80-800; ⏰performances 7.30pm; [S]Jianguomen) This theatre offers a genuine experience, with the erudite audience chatting away knowledgably among themselves during the weekly performances of Peking opera classics – this is a place for connoisseurs. There are matinees as well as evening shows, but shows are on weekends only.

CAPITAL THEATRE THEATRE

Map p286 (首都剧场; Shǒudū Jùyuàn; ☎5128 6286; 22 Wangfujing Dajie, 王府井大街22号; tickets ¥80-550; ⏰performances 7.30pm Tue-Sun; [S]Wangfujing) Located in the heart of the city on Wangfujing Dajie, the Capital has regular performances of contemporary Chinese productions and is home to a number of theatre companies, including the People's Art Experimental Theatre. Classic plays in the Chinese language often feature.

STAR CITY CINEMA

Map p286 (新世纪影城; Xīnshìjì Yǐngchéng; ☎8518 5399; 1 Dongchang'an Jie, Basement, Oriental Plaza, 东长安街1号东方广场地下一层; from ¥70; [S]Wangfujing) This six-screen cinema is one of the best places to see Western movies that get released in China. It always has one screening a day with the original, undubbed print (but that doesn't mean it

> [i]
>
> **CON 'ARTISTS'**
>
> We receive an enormous number of emails from those unfortunate enough to be scammed in Běijīng. By far the most notorious is the tea-ceremony scam, which exploits foreigners' ignorance of Chinese culture, unfamiliarity with the exchange rate and gullibility in a foreign setting; visitors are invited to drink tea at a tea house, after which the traveller is hit for a bill for hundreds of dollars. Many travellers pay up and only realise later that they have been massively conned. Foreigners at Tiān'ānmén Sq or wandering Wangfujing Dajie are also routinely hounded by pesky 'art students' either practising their English or roping visitors into going to exhibitions of overpriced art. They will try to strike up a conversation with you, but while some travellers enjoy their company, others find their attentions irritating and feel pressured into buying art. In all instances, be suspicious if you are approached by anyone who speaks good English on the street until you are sure all they want is to chat.

LOCAL KNOWLEDGE

HOW MUCH?

- *Bāozi* (steamed pork dumpling) from street stall ¥1 to ¥2
- Bus ticket ¥1
- Subway ticket ¥2
- Taxi flag-fall ¥10
- Hour in internet cafe ¥3 to ¥5
- Large bottle of local beer from a shop ¥4
- Small bottle of local beer from a bar ¥20
- Half-litre bottle of mineral water ¥1 to ¥2
- Cup of freshly ground coffee ¥20
- Local SIM card ¥100
- Lamb skewer ¥1
- Bananas from a market stall ¥4 per *jīn* (500g)
- Second-hand bicycle ¥100
- Repairing a puncture ¥2

hasn't been cut by the scissor-happy Chinese censors). It's a plush multiplex that feels no different from its equivalents in the West.

SHOPPING

Locals, out-of-towners and tourists haunt Wangfujing Dajie, a prestigious, partly pedestrianised but these days rather old-fashioned shopping street heading north on the west side of the modern shopping centre, Oriental Plaza. It boasts a solid strip of stores selling well-known midrange brands, as well as a number of tacky souvenir outlets.

ORIENTAL PLAZA SHOPPING CENTRE
Map p286 (东方广场; Dōngfāng Guǎngchǎng; ☎8518 6363; 1 Dongchang'an Jie, 东长安街1号; ⏲10am-10pm; [S]Wangfujing) Entering this vast, modern and hugely popular shopping mall is like being transported to Singapore. It's filled with midrange and high-end clothing brands from Asia and the West, plus a range of food outlets and Western coffee shops.

FOREIGN LANGUAGES BOOKSTORE BOOKS
Map p286 (外文书店; Wàiwén Shūdiàn; 235 Wangfujing Dajie, 王府井大街235号; ⏲9.30am-9.30pm; [S]Wangfujing) Stocks a decent selection of English-language novels (ground floor and 3rd floor) as well as lots of nonfiction and art, architecture and design books. The kids' section is good. It stocks hundreds of Lonely Planet guides, and this is also a good place to pick up maps of Běijīng (¥8).

ARTS & CRAFTS EMPORIUM ARTS & CRAFTS, JADE
Map p286 (工艺美术服务部; Gōngyì Měishù Fúwùbù; 200 Wangfujing Dajie, 王府井大街200号; ⏲9.30am-9.30pm; [S]Wangfujing) A souvenir market disguised as a department store, this place sells better quality goods than the big tourist markets, and in a much more stress-free environment. It's well known for its jade (with certificates of authenticity), jadeite, cloisonné vases, carpets and other Chinese arts and crafts. There's also jewellery (gold, silver, jade and pearl) on the first two floors. You'll find calligraphy, lacquerware, paintings, seals and woodcarvings on the 3rd floor. Head to the 4th floor for jade carvings. Prices are marked, but you can still bargain.

HÁOYUÁN MARKET SOUVENIRS
Map p286 (豪园市场; Háoyuán Shìchǎng; west off Wangfujing Dajie, 王府井大街西侧; [S]Wangfujing) Branching off from Wangfujing Snack St is this small, bustling souvenir market. It has lots of Mao memorabilia, pandas and Buddhas, as well as other tacky tourist tat, but if you're pushed for time and need a last-minute present, you might find something. Haggling is imperative.

TEN FU'S TEA TEA
Map p286 (天福茗茶; Tiānfú Míngchá; www.tenfu.com; 176 Wangfujing Dajie, 王府井大街176号; ⏲10am-9pm; [S]Wangfujing) With branches all across Běijīng, this Taiwanese chain is one of the easiest places to pick up tea, even if the prices are higher than at the tea shops at Mǎliándào Tea Market. It stocks top-quality loose tea from all over the country; prices start at ¥20 for a one *jīn* (500g). The staff, some of whom speak English, can arrange a free tea tasting.

NEW CHINA CHILDREN'S STORE TOYS, CLOTHING
Map p286 (新中国儿童用品商店; Xīn Zhōngguó Értóng Yòngpǐn Shāngdiàn; ☎6528 1774; 168 Wangfujing Dajie; 王府井大街168号; ⏲10am-9.30pm; [S]Wangfujing) If you need to find somewhere to occupy kids, bring them to

this maze of toys, model cars and trains, gadgets, puzzles, flashing lights and electronic noises, overseen by helpful staff. On the 2nd floor, you can find good quality children's clothing. Head to the basement for baby bottles, formula milk, nappies and pushchairs.

🏃 SPORTS & ACTIVITIES

BIKE BĚIJĪNG   CYCLING
Map p286 (康多自行车租赁; Kāngduō Zìxíngchē Zūlìn; ☎6526 5857; www.bicyclekingdom.com; 34 Donghuangchenggen Nanjie, 东皇城根南街34号; ◷9am-7pm; Ⓢ China Museum of Art) Rents a range of good quality bikes, including mountain bikes, road bikes and ordinary city bikes, and runs guided bike tours around the city and beyond, including trips to the Great Wall. Guides and shop assistants speak English. And it can also provide you with helmets (¥20), baby seats (¥50), children's trailers (¥100) and strong bike locks (free). Rental prices are ¥50 to ¥100 per day for the first day, with prices halving for any subsequent days. Deposits range from ¥600 to ¥800, depending on the bike. Alternatively, let staff scan a copy of your passport.

MÍLÚN KUNGFU SCHOOL   MARTIAL ARTS
Map p286 (北京弥纶传统武术学校; Běijīng Mílún Chuántŏng Wǔshù Xuéxiào; ☎138 1170 6568; www.kungfuinchina.com; 33 Xitangzi Hutong, 西堂子胡同33号; drop-in rate per class ¥100, 8-class card ¥600; ◷7-8.30pm Mon & Thu, 5-6.30pm Sat & Sun; Ⓢ Dengshikou) Runs classes in various forms of traditional Chinese martial arts from a historic courtyard near Wángfǔjǐng shopping district. In summer, typically in August, all classes are held in Rìtán Park. Has set-time drop-in classes, but can arrange individual schedules too. Instruction is in Chinese, but with an English translator.

JĬNGSHĀN TABLE TENNIS PARK   TABLE TENNIS
Map p286 (东城全民健身第一园; Dōngchéng Quánmín Jiànshēn Dìyī Yuán; Jingshan Houjie, 景山后街; ◷6am-10pm; Ⓢ Nanluoguxiang or Beihai North) This small exercise park has five free-to-use outdoor table tennis tables, which attract some pretty hot ping-pong. Only the tables are provided. Players need to bring their own net, bats and ball. Regulars – all too keen to show foreigners who rules the world when it comes to table tennis – will almost certainly let you join in using their equipment, but if you fancy a proper session, head to the 2nd floor of nearby Tiān Yì Goods Market (p102) to buy a cheap table-tennis set, or to Sports Masterpieces, opposite the north gate of Běihǎi Park, to buy something of better quality.

DRAGONFLY THERAPEUTIC RETREAT   MASSAGE TREATMENTS
Map p286 (悠庭保健会所; Yŏutíng Bǎojiàn Huìsuŏ; ☎6527 9368; 60 Donghuamen Dajie, 东华门大街60号; ◷10am-1am; Ⓢ Tian'anmen East) Ideal for a foot massage after hours of walking around the Forbidden City, this popular boutique has a variety of treatments designed to help you de-stress. The two-hour Hangover Relief Massage is self explanatory, but for real pampering go for the Royal Delight, in which two masseurs get to work at the same time, or the Ultimate Indulgence, an hour of full-body massage and an hour of foot reflexology. Manicures, pedicures, nails and waxing are also offered. A standard, hour-long body or foot massage costs ¥168. There is another branch in Sānlǐtún (p149)

2

3

1. Forbidden City (p52)

Spanning two dynasties and more than 500
years, the Forbidden City is an absolute
must-see for any visitor to Běijīng.

2. Tiān'ānmén Square (p60)

The world's largest public square.

3. Wángfǔjǐng Snack Street (p74)

This quadrant is lined with cheap-and-
cheerful food stalls that are always busy.

Drum Tower & Dōngchéng North

Neighbourhood Top Five

❶ Lose yourself in the maze-like network of historic **hútòng** (alleyways), or follow our *hútòng* walking tour (p89).

❷ Stroll the incense-smoke-filled halls and courtyards of the **Lama Temple** (p82), Běijīng's largest and most impressive Buddhist temple.

❸ Listen to a drumming performance inside the magnificent ancient **Drum Tower** (p84) before climbing its equally impressive neighbour, the **Bell Tower** (p85).

❹ Browse the cutesy boutique shops on **Nanluogu Xiang** (p86), before sneak-ing into a **courtyard cafe** for coffee break.

❺ Catch a local band at one of the many excellent **live-music** venues in this part of town. Jiāng Hú is a good place to start.

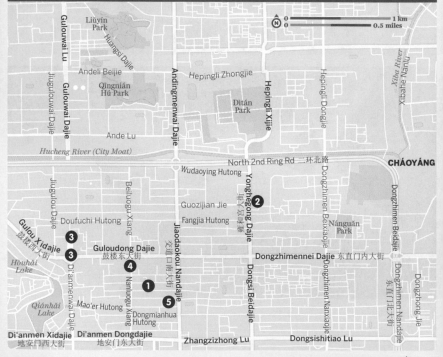

For more detail of this area see Map p290 ➡

Explore: Drum Tower & Dōngchéng North

This *hútòng*-rich neighbourhood incorporates the northern section of Běijīng's historic Dōngchéng (东城) district and is the most pleasant area in which to base yourself during your stay in the capital, although it was facing possible redevelopment as this book went to press (p99). Book yourself into a *hútòng* hostel or a beautifully converted courtyard hotel, and make this most charming of neighbourhoods your temporary home.

Whilst there are less top-name sights here than in Dōngchéng Central, there is still plenty of sightseeing to be done, although the main attraction is the chance to simply wander around the lanes getting lost.

Shop till you drop in the cute alleyway boutiques of Nanluogu Xiang before putting your feet up in a *hútòng* cafe or settling down for a meal in a converted courtyard.

At night, this neighbourhood is the city's most enjoyable place to drink. Bars here are cool rather than brash and are often tucked away in hard-to-find *hútòng* locations. Some of them double as live-music venues where you can catch the latest local bands.

Local Life

➡ **Food** To sample some authentic Běijīng grub, first check our Běijīng Menu (p91) then head to Yáojì Chǎogān (p88) for some dumplings and pig's liver stew, or to Róng Tiān (p90) for a succulent sheep-spine hotpot.

➡ **Drinking** If you prefer to hang out with young local drinkers, try If (p95) or Reef Bar (p95), or catch some live music at Jiāng Hú (p97).

➡ **Parks & Squares** Head to Dìtán Park (p86) for a spot of kite-flying. Then, come early evening, visit the public square between the Drum and Bell Towers to join in with a game of *jiànzi* (shuttlecock keepie-uppies) or some formation dancing.

Getting There & Away

➡ **Subway** Lines 8, 2 and 5 all serve this neighbourhood well.

➡ **Bus** Bus 107 links the Drum Tower with Dongzhimen Transport Hub. Bus 5 runs south from the Drum Tower, past Běihǎi and Jǐngshān Parks, along the west side of the Forbidden City and on to Qiánmén at the south end of Tiān'ānmén Square. Bus 113 runs south from Andingmennei Dajie then east to the Workers Stadium and Sānlǐtún.

Lonely Planet's Top Tip

Rent a bike while you're here, or even buy a cheap secondhand one; you can give it away when you leave. Cycling is the best way to see the city, and is especially good for exploring this area's *hútòng*.

✗ Best Places to Eat

➡ Yáojì Chǎogān (p88)
➡ Yáng Fāng Lamb Hotpot (p88)
➡ Róng Tiān Sheep Spine (p90)
➡ Bǎihé Vegetarian Restaurant (p90)
➡ Dàlǐ Courtyard (p90)

For reviews, see p88 ➡

🍷 Best Places to Drink

➡ Great Leap Brewing (p94)
➡ El Nido (p94)
➡ Reef Bar (p95)
➡ Zá Jiā (p95)
➡ Ball House (p95)
➡ Mao Mao Chong (p95)
➡ If (p95)

For reviews, see p94 ➡

◉ Best Places for Live Music

➡ Jiāng Hú (p97)
➡ Jiāng Jìn Jiǔ (p97)
➡ Yúgōng Yíshān (p97)
➡ Temple Bar (p97)
➡ Mao Livehouse (p98)

For reviews, see p97 ➡

TOP SIGHTS
LAMA TEMPLE

Běijīng's foremost Buddhist temple, the Lama Temple (雍和宫; Yōnghé Gōng) is one of the most magnificent Tibetan Buddhist temples outside Tibet itself. With three richly worked archways and five main halls (each one taller than the preceding one), revolving prayer wheels (propel them clockwise), multicoloured glaze tiles, magnificent Chinese lions, tantric statuettes and hall boards decorated with Mongolian, Manchu, Tibetan and Chinese, the sumptuous temple is a profound introduction to Tibetan Buddhist lore.

History

The temple was once the official residence of Count Yin Zhen, who became emperor in 1723 and traded up to the Forbidden City. His name changed to Yongzheng, and his former residence became Yōnghé Palace (Yōnghé Gōng). In 1744 it was converted into a lamasery (a monastery of lamas) and became home to legions of monks from Mongolia and Tibet.

In 1792 the Emperor Qianlong, having quelled an uprising in Tibet, instituted a new administrative system involving two golden vases. One was kept at the renowned Jokhang Temple in Lhasa, to be employed for determining the reincarnation of the Dalai Lama, and the other was kept at the Lama Temple for choosing the Panchen Lama. The Lama Temple thus assumed a new importance in ethnic minority control.

Premier Zhou Enlai stepped in when the Red Guards focused their iconoclastic attentions on the temple. Today the temple is an active place of worship, attracting pilgrims from across the land and thronging with worshippers, some of whom prostrate themselves at full length within its halls.

DON'T MISS
➡ 18m-tall Sandalwood Buddha
➡ Exhibition in Jiètái Lóu
➡ Exhibition in Bānchán Lóu

PRACTICALITIES
➡ 雍和宫; Yōnghé Gōng
➡ Map p290
➡ 28 Yonghegong Dajie; 雍和宫大街
➡ admission ¥25, English audioguide ¥50
➡ ◷9am-430pm
➡ Ⓢ Yonghegong-Lama Temple

Yōnghé Gate

The first hall, Yōnghé Gate (雍和门; Yōnghé Mén), houses a statue of Maitreya, the future Buddha, flanked by celestial guardians. Above it is a board inscribed with the characters 心明妙现: 'If the heart is bright, the wonderful will appear'.

In the courtyard beyond is a pond with a bronze mandala depicting Xumishan, the Buddhist paradise. In the hall on the right after Yōnghé Gate, the **Esoteric Hall** (密宗殿; Mìzōng Diàn) contains the fierce, multi-armed deity Deweidejingang. Opposite is the **Exoteric Hall** (讲经殿; Jiǎngjīng Diàn), where sutras were studied and recited.

Yōnghé Hall

With its air of peaceful reverence, the second hall, Yōnghé Hall (雍和殿; Yōnghé Diàn), contains a trinity of gilded effigies representing the past, present and future Buddhas.

Yǒngyòu Hall

The third hall, Yǒngyòu Hall (永佑殿; Yǒngyòu Diàn), contains statues of the Buddha of Longevity and the Buddha of Medicine (to the left). Peck into the **East Side Hall** (东配殿; Dōngpèi Diàn) for its esoteric gathering of cobalt-blue Buddhas and two huge dog-like creatures. Note how the tantric statues have been partially draped to disguise their couplings.

Hall of the Wheel of the Law

The fourth hall, Hall of the Wheel of the Law (法轮殿; Fǎlún Diàn), houses a statue of a benign and smiling Tsong Khapa (1357–1419), founder of the Gelukpa, or Yellow Hat, sect, robed in yellow and illuminated by the skylight. The throne seated the Dalai Lama when he lectured sutras here.

Wànfú Pavilion

The final main hall, Wànfú Pavilion (万福阁; Wànfú Gé), has a stupendous 18m-tall statue of the Maitreya Buddha in his Tibetan form, clothed in yellow satin and reputedly sculpted from a single block of sandalwood. Smoke curling up from yak-butter lamps enhances the Tibetan-like atmosphere.

Behind is the **Vault of Avalokiteshvara** (观音洞; Guānyīn Dòng), from which a small, blue-faced statue of Guanyin peeks. The pavilion is linked by an overhead walkway to the **Yánsuí Pavilion** (延绥阁; Yánsuí Gé), which encloses a huge lotus flower that revolves to reveal an effigy of the longevity Buddha.

Behind Wànfú Pavilion, worshippers gather to worship White Tara and Green Tara in the **Suíchéng Hall** (绥成殿; Suíchéng Diàn).

SIDE-HALL EXHIBITIONS

Don't miss the collection of bronze Tibetan Buddhist statues within **Jiètái Lóu** (戒台楼). Most effigies date from the Qing dynasty, from languorous renditions of Green Tara and White Tara to exotic tantric pieces (such as Samvara) and figurines of the fierce-looking Mahakala. Also peruse the collection of Tibetan Buddhist ornaments within the **Bānchán Lóu** (班禅楼): there's a fantastic array of *dorje* (Tibetan ritual sceptres), mandalas, tantric figures, and an impressive selection of ceremonial robes in silk and satin.

Photography isn't permitted inside temple buildings, although you can snap away freely around the rest of the complex. English-speaking guides (¥80) can be found in the office to the left of the entrance gate, or loitering near the entrance to the complex.

DRUM TOWER & DŌNGCHÉNG NORTH LAMA TEMPLE

TOP SIGHTS
LAMA TEMPLE

TOP SIGHTS
DRUM TOWER

Along with the older-looking Bell Tower, which stands behind it, the magnificent red-painted Drum Tower (鼓楼; Gǔ Lóu) used to be the city's official timekeeper, with drums and bells beaten and rung to mark the times of the day; effectively the Big Ben of Běijīng.

Originally built in 1272, the Drum Tower was once the heart of the Mongol capital of Dàdū, as Běijīng was then known. That structure was destroyed in a fire before a replacement was built, slightly to the east of the original location, in 1420. The current structure is a later Qing-dynasty version of that 1420 tower.

You can climb the incredibly steep inner staircase for views of the grey-tiled rooftops in the surrounding hútòng alleys. Arguably the best view of the Drum Tower is from the top of the Bell Tower. Annoyingly, though, the view isn't reciprocated because visitors aren't allowed to walk round to the north-facing side of the Drum Tower's viewing balcony.

It's still well worth climbing the tower, though, especially if you can time it to coincide with one of the regular drumming performances, which are played out on reproductions of the 25 Ming-dynasty watch drums that used to sound out across this part of the city. One of the original 25 drums – the Night Watchman's Drum (更鼓; gēnggǔ) – is on display; now dusty, battered and worn. Also on display is a replica of a Song-dynasty water clock, which was never actually used in the tower, but is interesting nonetheless.

The times of the drumming performances, which only last for a couple of minutes, are posted by the ticket office. At the time of research they were as follows: 9.30am, 10.30am, 11.30am, 1.30pm, 2.30pm, 3.30pm and 4.45pm.

DON'T MISS

➡ Drumming Performance
➡ Night Watchman's Drum

PRACTICALITIES

➡ 鼓楼; Gǔlóu
➡ Map p290
➡ Gulou Dongdajie; 鼓楼东大街
➡ admission ¥20, combined Bell Tower ticket ¥30
➡ ⊘9am-5pm, last tickets 4.40pm
➡ 🚌5, 58 or 107

TOP SIGHTS
BELL TOWER

The more modest, grey-stone structure of the Bell Tower (钟楼; Zhōng Lóu) is arguably more charming than its resplendent other half, the Drum Tower, after which this area of Běijīng is named. It also has the added advantage of being able to view its sister tower from a balcony.

Along with the drums in the Drum Tower, the bells in the Bell Tower were used as Běijīng's official timekeepers throughout the Yuan, Ming and Qing dynasties, and on until 1924. The Bell Tower looks the older of the two, perhaps because it isn't painted. In fact both are of similar age. The Bell Tower was built, like the Drum Tower, during the Mongol Yuan Dynasty, in 1272, and was rebuild in the 1440s after being destroyed in a fire. This current structure was built in 1745.

Also like the Drum Tower, the Bell Tower can be climbed up an incredibly steep inner staircase. But the views from the top are even better here, partly because the structure is set back more deeply into the surrounding *hútòng*, and partly because you can get great photos of the Drum Tower from its viewing balcony. Marvel too at the huge, 63-tonne bell suspended in the pleasantly unrestored interior. Note how Chinese bells have no clappers but are instead struck with a stout pole.

The Drum & Bell Sq, between the two towers, is a great people-watching area in which to while away some time even if you don't climb either of the two towers. There are a handful of excellent bars and cafes here too, some with rooftop views over the square. Both towers are lit up beautifully come evening.

DON'T MISS

➡ 63-tonne bell
➡ View of the Drum Tower

PRACTICALITIES

➡ 钟楼; Zhōnglóu
➡ Map p290
➡ ☎6401 2674
➡ Zhonglouwan Hutong; 钟楼湾胡同
➡ admission ¥20, combined Drum Tower ticket ¥30
➡ ⊙9am-5pm, last tickets 4.40pm
➡ ⊒5, 58 or 107

SIGHTS

LAMA TEMPLE BUDDHIST TEMPLE

See p82.

DRUM TOWER TOWER

See p84.

BELL TOWER TOWER

See p85.

CONFUCIUS TEMPLE & IMPERIAL COLLEGE CONFUCIAN TEMPLE

Map p290 (孔庙、国子监; Kǒng Miào & Guózǐjiàn; 13 Guozijian Jie; adult ¥30, audio guide ¥30; ⏲8.30am-5.30pm; [S]Yonghegong-Lama Temple) With over 30 Confucius Institutes worldwide, the Shāndōng sage is currently enjoying yet another upswing after bouts of anti-Confucian violence (the last one erupted in August 1966) singled him out for Chinese spleen. An incense stick's toss away from the Lama Temple, China's second-largest Confucian temple has had a recent refit, but the almost otherworldly sense of detachment is seemingly impossible to shift. Antediluvian *bìxì* (mythical tortoise-like dragons) glare from repainted pavilions while lumpy and ossified ancient cypresses claw stiffly at the dusty Běijīng air. A mood of impassiveness reigns and the lack of worship reinforces a sensation that time has stood still. This is made all the more palpable by the mute forest of 190 stelae recording the 13 Confucian classics in 630,000 Chinese characters at the temple rear. Also inscribed on stelae are the names of successful candidates of the highest level of the official Confucian examination system. It was the ambition of every scholar to see his name engraved here, but it wasn't easy. Each candidate was locked in one of about 8000 cubicles, measuring roughly 1.5 sq m, for a period of three days. Many died or went insane during their incarceration.

Like everywhere in town, skeletons lurk in the temple cupboard and a distasteful footnote lurks unrecorded behind the tourist blurb. Běijīng writer Lao She was dragged here in August 1966, forced to his knees in front of a bonfire of Peking opera costumes to confess his anti-Revolutionary crimes, and beaten. The much-loved writer drowned himself the next day in Taiping Lake (one of the thousands of Běijīng deaths in August and September of '66).

But in its tranquillity and reserve, the temple is a lovely sanctuary from Běijīng's often congested streets and is a true haven of peace and quiet. Some of Běijīng's last remaining *páilou* (decorated archways) bravely survive in the *hútòng* outside (Guozijian Jie) and the entire area of *hútòng* now swarms with small cafes, cutesy restaurants and boutique shops, making it an ideal place to browse in low gear. At the western end of Guozijian Jie stands a diminutive **Fire God Temple** (Huǒshén Miào; Map p290), built in 1802 and now occupied by Běijīng residents. Only the first hall – the Mountain Gate (Shān Mén) – remains recognisable and the remaining temple halls have been greatly adapted.

Next to the Confucius Temple, but within the same grounds, stands the Imperial College, where the emperor expounded the Confucian classics to an audience of thousands of kneeling students, professors and court officials – an annual rite. Built by the grandson of Kublai Khan in 1306, the former college was the supreme academy during the Yuan, Ming and Qing dynasties. On the site is a marvellous, glazed, three-gate, single-eaved decorative archway called a *liúli páifāng* (glazed archway). The Biyong Hall beyond is a twin-roofed structure with yellow tiles surrounded by a moat and topped with a gold knob, its stupendous interior housing a vermillion and gold lectern.

DÌTÁN PARK PARK

Map p290 (地坛公园; Dìtán Gōngyuán; park admission ¥2, altar ¥5; ⏲6am-9pm; [S]Yonghegong-Lama Temple) Directly north of the Lama Temple, but cosmologically juxtaposed with the **Temple of Heaven** (Tiāntán), the **Altar of the Moon** (Yuètán), the **Altar of the Sun** (Rìtán) and the **Altar to the God of the Land and the God of Grain** (Shèjìtán), Dìtán is the Temple of the Earth. The park, site of imperial sacrifices to the Earth God, lacks the splendour of Temple of Heaven Park but is certainly worth a stroll if you've just been to nearby Lama Temple. During Chinese New Year a huge temple fair is held here. The park's large **altar** *(fāngzé tán)* is square in shape, symbolising the earth.

NANLUOGU XIANG STREET

Map p290 (南锣鼓巷; [S]Nanluoguxiang) Once neglected and ramshackle, strewn with spent coal briquettes in winter and silent bar the hacking coughs of shuffling old-

CULTURAL REVOLUTION SLOGANS TOUR

As a city constantly in the throes of reinvention, Běijīng seems to change its guise almost daily. But it's all too easy to get carried away with the forward movement of Běijīng and ignore its equally relevant past. Unmarked by either a memorial or museum in Běijīng, the tragic Cultural Revolution (1966–76) is one period of history the authorities would rather just gloss over. Fortunately, faint echoes from that era still resonate in Běijīng's surviving brood of political slogans *(zhèngzhì kǒuhào)*.

Most slogans from the 1960s and 1970s have been either painted over or scrubbed clean, but some ghostly messages still haunt Běijīng. Other maxims have been exposed after layers of concrete have been stripped from walls, revealing hidden directives from the period of political fervour.

Daubed on the wall opposite **59 Nanluogu Xiang** are the characters 工业学大庆、农业学大寨、全国学解放军, which mean 'For industry study Dàqìng, for agriculture study Dàzhài, for the whole nation study the People's Liberation Army'; left of this is a much earlier slogan from the 1950s, largely obscured with grey paint. The wall opposite the Guanyue Temple at **149 Gulou Xidajie** is covered in faint, partially legible red slogans, including the characters 大立无产阶级 ('establish the proletariat') and the two characters 旧习 ('old habits').

The former Furen University (p118) has a magnificent slogan that can be seen from the road. Very indistinct characters can just be discerned under the windows of the former **Banque de L'Indo-Chine** at 34 Dongjiaomin Xiang in the Foreign Legation Quarter (p64). The **798 Art District** (p138) is heavily bedecked with slogans. One of the rarest and most enticing survives on the wall of the **Cave Café**: a personal dedication written by Lin Biao, Mao Zedong's one-time chosen successor.

The village of **Chuāndǐxià** has a generous crop of slogans. Maoist slogans can still be found on the house at **27 Yingtao Xiejie** and on the building at **65 Xidamo Changjie**, opposite the now-closed Underground City, where passers-by are again exhorted to 'study Dàqìng' (China's No 1 oilfield, whose workers were held up as exemplars of diligence) and to 'study Dàzhài' (China's model commune).

timers and the jangling of bicycle bells, the funky north–south alleyway of Nanluogu Xiang (literally 'South Gong and Drum Alley', and roughly pronounced *'nan-law-goo-syang'*) has been undergoing evolution since 1999 when **Passby Bar** first threw open its doors, and was the subject of a complete makeover in 2006. Today, the alley is an insatiably bubbly strip of bars, wi-fi cafes, restaurants, hotels and trendy shops. Don't miss exploring the quieter alleys, which fan out from the main lane and house Qing-dynasty courtyards as well as hidden cafes, restaurants and bars. Our *hútòng* walking tour can help here (p89).

WUDAOYING HUTONG — STREET

(五道营胡同; [S]Yonghegong Lama Temple) Following the huge success of the Nanluogu Xiang renovation project, Wudaoying Hutong was given a massive facelift a couple of years back, and this once residential back alley is now another wannabe trendy lane packed with wi-fi cafes, cute restaurants, boutique shops and a couple of bars. It's nowhere near as popular as Nanluogu Xiang, but there are some standout places that are well worth a visit, namely: Veggie Table (p91), Běijīng's first vegan restaurant; Natooke (p102), the capital's coolest bike shop; and Vineyard Café (p92), every expat's favourite brunch stop. There's also the unusual **Change** (交换商店; Jiāohuàn Shāngdiàn; Map p290; 67 Wudaoying Hutong, 五道营胡同67号; ⌚midday-8pm, closed Mon; [S]Yonghegong Lama Temple), a tiny second-hand 'swap shop', where you can trade in your old stuff for whatever takes your fancy. Come evening, **VA Bar** (Map p290; 67 Wudaoying Hutong, 五道营胡同67号; entrance from ¥20; ⌚2pm-late; [S]Yonghegong Lama Temple) is a popular jazz venue, with live music most nights.

MAO DUN'S FORMER RESIDENCE — HISTORIC BUILDING

Map p290 (茅盾故居; Máo Dùn Gùjū; 13 Houyuan Ensi Hutong; adult ¥5; ⌚9am-4pm Tue-Sun; [S]Beixinqiao) This small, unassuming museum off Jiaodaokou Nandajie is deep in

BARBECUE SKEWERS

The red neon 串 signs that you see hanging outside restaurants come evening, are actually shaped as the Chinese character for *chuàn* (串; skewers) and signify that the restaurant serves barbecue skewers. They are often, but not always, Muslim-food restaurants, and sometimes they are simply a hole-in-the-wall outfit, which only serves skewers. Either way, they're a favourite snack spot for locals; pull up a stool, order a bottle of local beer (啤酒; *píjiǔ*; ¥3 to ¥5) and join them for a barbecue pit-stop.

Chances are the staff won't speak a word of English, so to help you order, here's a list of the most common skewers and their usual prices:

➡ **lamb skewers** 羊肉串, *yángròu chuàn*, ¥1
➡ **steamed buns** 馒头片, *mántou piàn*, ¥1
➡ **chicken wings** 鸡翅, *jī chì*, ¥4
➡ **lamb tendon** 肉筋, *ròu jīn*, ¥1
➡ **roasted garlic** 大蒜, *dà suàn*, ¥1

the heart of the historic *hútòng* quadrant southeast of the Drum and Bell Towers. Mao Dun was the pen name of Shen Yanbing (1896–1981), who was born into an elite family in Zhèjiāng province but educated in Běijīng. In 1920 he helped found the Literary Study Society, an association promoting literary realism. Mao Dun joined the League of Left Wing Writers in 1930, becoming solidly entrenched in the bureaucracy after the communists came to power. He lay low during the Cultural Revolution, but briefly returned to writing in the 1970s. The museum is typically parsimonious and low-key.

 **EATING**

This historic part of Běijīng has a huge range of dining options covering every type of Chinese cuisine, as well as plenty of international places. It's also home to some of the capital's most atmospheric restaurants, from beautifully converted courtyards, to the many hole-in-the-wall establishments scattered throughout the local *hútòng*. Locals also head to the very popular so-called Ghost Street (簋街; Gui Jie) for hotpot and seafood at all hours.

YÁOJÌ CHǍOGĀN
CHINESE BĚIJĪNG **$**

Map p290 (姚记炒肝店; 311 Guloudong Dajie, 鼓楼东大街311号; ⊘6am-10.30pm; Ⓢ Shichahai) Proper locals' joint, serving Běijīng dishes in a noisy, no-nonsense atmosphere. The house speciality is *chǎogān*

(炒肝; pig's liver stew; ¥5 to ¥8). This is also a good place to try *zhá guànchang* (炸灌肠; garlic-topped deep-fried crackers; ¥6) and *má dòufu* (麻豆腐; spicy tofu paste; ¥10). Its steamed pork dumplings (包子; *bāozi*; per dumpling ¥1) are excellent, and are perfect for breakfast with a bowl of *xiǎomǐ zhōu* (小米粥; millet porridge; ¥2) or locals' favourite *dòuzhī* (豆汁; soy milk; ¥2). It also does a decent bowl of Běijīng's best-known noodle dish, *zhájiàng miàn* (炸酱面; ¥10). No English menu or English sign.

YÁNG FĀNG LAMB HOTPOT
MONGOLIAN HOTPOT **$**

Map p290 (羊坊涮肉; Yáng Fāng Shuàn Ròu; 270 Guloudong Dajie, 鼓楼东大街270号; broth ¥6-10, dips ¥2-4, raw ingredients ¥5-20; ⊘11am-11pm; Ⓢ Shichahai) There are two main types of hotpot in China: the ridiculously spicy one that comes from the fire-breathing southwestern city of Chóngqìng, and the milder version which is cooked in an unusual conical brass pot and which originally hails from Mongolia but has been adopted as a Běijīng speciality. Yáng Fāng is a salt-of-the-earth version of the latter, and is a real favourite with the locals round here. First order the broth you for your pot – clear (清汤锅底; *qīng tāng guōde*), or spicy (辣锅底; *là guōde*). Then choose your dipping sauce – sesame (麻酱; *má jiàng*) or chilli oil (辣椒油; *là jiāo yóu*) – before finally selecting the raw ingredients you want to cook. Our favourites include wafer-thin lamb slices (鲜羊肉; *xiān yáng ròu*), lotus root slices (藕片; *ǒu piàn*), tofu slabs (鲜豆腐; *xiān dòufu*), sweet potato (红薯;

START **NANLUOGUXIANG SUBWAY STATION**
END **DRUM & BELL TOWERS**
DISTANCE **2KM**
DURATION **ONE HOUR**

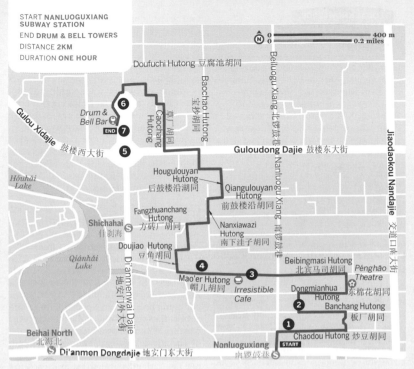

Neighbourhood Walk
Historic Hútòng around Nanluogu Xiang

➡ Běijīng's *hútòng* (p220) are the heart and soul of the city.

Exit Nanluoguxiang subway station and turn right into Chaodou Hutong (炒豆胡同). Starting at No 77, the next few courtyards once made up the ❶ **former mansion of Seng Gelinqin**, a Qing-dynasty army general. Note the enormous *bǎogǔshí* (drum stones) at the entranceway to No 77, followed by more impressive gateways at Nos 75, 69, 67 and 63. After No 53 turn left up an unmarked winding alleyway then left onto Banchang Hutong (板厂胡同).

At No 19, turn right through an unusual ❷ **hallway gate**, a connecting passageway leading to Dongmianhua Hutong (东棉花胡同). Turn right here, then left down an unnamed alley, which is signposted to Pénghāo Theatre Cafe.

Turn left onto Beibingmasi Hutong (北兵马司胡同) and cross Nanluogu Xiang into historic ❸ **Mao'er Hutong** (帽儿胡同). Stop for a drink at Irresistible Cafe, or just admire the entranceways, if the gates are open,

to the charming courtyards at Nos 5 and 11. Further on, No 37 was the ❹ **former home of Wan Rong**, who would later marry China's last emperor, Puyi.

Next, turn right down Doujiao Hutong (豆角胡同) and wind your way to Fangzhuanchang Hutong (方砖厂胡同) then Nanxiawazi Hutong (南下洼子胡同). Just before the end, turn right onto Qiangulouyan Hutong (前鼓楼沿胡同), then immediately left down Hougulouyan Hutong (后鼓楼沿胡同) and work your way north to busy Guloudong Dajie (鼓楼东大街). Turn left here and then, just before you reach the imperious red-painted ❺ **Drum Tower**, turn right into Caochang Hutong (草厂胡同). Continue down the lane beside Sea View Cafe, then take the second left: you'll see the magnificent grey-brick ❻ **Bell Tower** in front of you. Follow this wonderfully winding alley to the back of the Bell Tower then walk around the tower to ❼ **Drum & Bell Square**, a great place for people-watching. End your walk with a drink on the rooftop terrace at Drum & Bell.

TRADITIONAL BĚIJĪNG YOGHURT

On your shopping wanders through the *hútòng*, you may notice intriguing rows of little clay pots, sealed with thin, white and blue paper tops, and lined up outside small corner shops. The pots contain *lǎo Běijīng suānnǎi* (老北京酸奶), traditional Běijīng yoghurt, and make a perfect slurp-on-the-go street-side refreshment.

Prices vary slightly, but they tend to cost ¥3 if you drink them on the spot and return your pot, or ¥4 if you take them away.

hóng shǔ) and spinach (菠菜; *bō cài*). No English sign; no English menu; no English spoken.

RÓNG TIĀN SHEEP SPINE   HOTPOT $
Map p290 (容天土锅羊羯子馆; Róngtiān Tǔguō Yángjiézi Guǎn; 8 Jingtu Hutong, off Beiluogu Xiang, 北锣鼓巷净土胡同8号; sheep spine per jīn ¥29, other ingredients ¥5-10; 10.30am-10pm; Guloudajie) Rough-and-ready locals' favourite serving mouthwateringly good sheep-spine hotpot. Order your sheep-spine chunks by the *jīn* (500g). Two jins' worth (二斤; *èr jīn*) is normally about right. They will then come ready-cooked in a boiling broth – the longer you leave them to simmer, the juicier they get. You then add other raw ingredients to cook in the broth like a standard Chinese hotpot. Our favourite extras include sweet potato (红薯; *hóng shǔ*), tofu blocks (鲜豆腐; *xiān dòufu*), mushrooms (木耳; *mù'ěr*), Oriental raddish (白萝卜; *bái luóbo*) and Chinese spinach (油麦菜; *yóu mài cài*). Complimentary fresh noodles are thrown in at the end, to soak up the juices. When you're ready for them, say '*fàng miàn*' (put the noodles in). No English sign or menu, and no English spoken.

BǍIHÉ VEGETARIAN RESTAURANT   CHINESE VEGETARIAN $$
Map p290 (百合素食; Bǎihé Sùshí; 23 Caoyuan Hutong, 东直门内北小街草园胡同甲23号; dishes from ¥25; 11.30am-3pm & 5-9.30pm, tea-drinking only 2-5pm; Dongzhimen or Beixinqiao) This little gem is made up of a large courtyard that's divided into a shop selling organic coffee and tea,

and a spacious dining room. As in most Chinese vegetarian restaurants, many of the dishes masquerade as meat or fish. Here, though, they're more imaginative – think lamb kebabs, sizzling shrimp and Peking duck. With courteous service, this is one of Běijīng's more soothing dining experiences, and it's nonsmoking throughout. There's also a separate and extensive tea menu, and customers are welcome to come here just to sample the tea. To get here, walk north on Dongzhimen Beixiaojie from the junction with Ghost Street for 100m, then turn left into the first *hútòng*. The restaurant is on the right.

DÀLǏ COURTYARD   CHINESE YÚNNÁN $$$
Map p290 (大理; Dàlǐ; 8404 1430; 67 Xiaojingchang Hutong, Gulou Dongdajie, 鼓楼东大街小经厂胡同67号; set menus from ¥128; 11am-3pm & 6-11pm; Andingmen) The beautiful setting in a restored courtyard house in a *hútòng* makes this one of Běijīng's more idyllic places to eat, especially in the summer. Specialising in the subtle flavours of the cuisine of southwestern Yúnnán province, it's also one of the more creative. There's no menu. Instead, you pay ¥128, ¥200 or ¥300 per head (drinks are extra) and the chef decides what to give you, depending on what inspires him and what ingredients are fresh that day. It's the first left down Xiaojingchang Hutong; look for the red lanterns.

QÍ SHĀN MIÀN   CHINESE SHAANXI $
Map p290 (岐山面; 32 Yonghegong Dajie, 雍和宫大街32号; 10.30am-10pm; ; Yonghegong-Lama Temple) Wildly popular restaurant specialising in food from Shaanxi province. The badly translated English menu includes delicious noodle dishes – try the 'particular handmade noodle with hot oil and seasoner' or the 'Qí Shān Miàn (dry style with pork)' – as well as the house speciality: *ròujiāmò* (肉夹馍; ¥7), a baked bun filled with juicy shreds of pork, and China's answer to the burger. It's translated onto the English menu as 'Traditional Chinese pork (beef) pancake (Xi'an style)'. The bowls of hot noodle juice (面汤; *miàn tāng*) are free, and the friendly manager keeps a strict no-smoking policy; very rare for a budget restaurant in China. No English.

TÀN HUĀ LAMB BBQ
LAMB BARBECUE **$**

Map p290 (碳花烤羊腿; Tàn Huā Kǎo Yángtuǐ; 63 Beixintiao Santiao Hutong, 北新桥三条胡同 63号; lamb per jin ¥32, side dishes ¥1-12; ☺11am-midnight; Ⓢ Beixinqiao) Meat-loving Beijingers flock to this raucous joint where you roast a leg of lamb on a your own personal table-top barbecue spit before hacking away at the meatiest bits with a rudimentary, long-handled knife and fork. Tables spill out onto the lively *hútòng*, creating a party at-mosphere of multi-barbecue revelry. Order your leg of lamb (羊腿; *yáng tuǐ*) by the *jīn*. Three *jīn* (三斤; *sān jīn*) is enough for two or three people. You'll then be given a selec-tion of free cold dishes as accompaniments, plus a cumin-based dry dip to roll your lamb slices in. Other popular side dishes include barbecued naan bread (烤馕; *kǎo náng*), soy fried rice (酱油炒饭; *jiàng yóu chǎo fàn*) and noodle-drop soup (疙瘩汤; *gēda tāng*).

SOURCE
CHINESE SÌCHUĀN **$$$**

Map p290 (都江园; Dūjiāngyuán; ☑6400 3736; 14 Banchang Hutong, 板厂胡同14号; meals ¥288-488; ☺11am-2pm & 5-10pm; Ⓢ Nanluogux-iang) Swish Sìchuān with a twist, served up in a courtyard that was once the home of a famous Qing-dynasty general. Source is an amenable place to sample the delights of some of China's hottest dishes, as the chefs here tend to go easy on the chillies; they'll also adjust the temperature of the food on request. You choose from a selection of set menus (¥288/388/488), which changes every month, and there's an extensive wine list.

JĪN DǏNG XUĀN
CHINESE CANTONESE **$$**

Map p290 (金鼎轩; 77 Hepingli Xijie, 地坛南门和平里西街77号; dim sum from ¥8-20, mains ¥30-100; ☺24hr; 🅙; Ⓢ Yonghegong-Lama Tem-ple) By the south gate of Dìtán Park, this giant, busy, neon-lit, 24-hour restaurant on three floors serves up good-value dim sum, as well as a host of other mostly Cantonese dishes.

🍀 VEGGIE TABLE
INTERNATIONAL VEGAN **$$**

Map p290 (吃素的; 19 Wudaoying Hutong, 五道营胡同19号; ☺11.30am-2pm & 5.30-9.30pm; 🍃🅙; Ⓢ Yonghegong-Lama Temple) Běijīng's first fully vegan restaurant not only does

---

BĚIJĪNG MENU

The following are all classic Běijīng dishes, many of which you'll only find at places specialising in Běijīng cuisine. Try Zuǒ Lín Yòu Shè (p70), Yáojì Chǎogān (p88) or Bàodǔ Huáng (p141). Many roast duck restaurants will have some of the other Běijīng specialities as well as roast duck.

➜ **Roast Duck** (烤鸭; *kǎo yā*) Běijīng's most famous dish, the duck here is fattier but much more flavoursome than the roast duck typically served in Chinese res-taurants in the West. Like back home, though, it also comes with pancakes, cucum-ber slices and plum sauce.

➜ **Zhá Jiàng Miàn** (炸酱面) Běijīng's most famous noodle dish; thick wheat noo-dles with ground pork and cucumber shreds mixed together in a salty fermented soybean paste. Chilli oil (辣椒油; *là jiāo yóu*) is a popular optional extra.

➜ **Dàlian Huǒshāo** (褡裢火烧) Finger-shaped fried dumplings with a savoury filling.

➜ **Má Dòufu** (麻豆腐) Spicy tofu paste.

➜ **Zhá Guànchang** (炸灌肠) Deep-fried crispy crackers served with a very strong garlic dip.

➜ **Chǎo Gānr** (炒肝) Sauteed liver served in a gloopy soup.

➜ **Bào Dǔ** (爆肚) Boiled tripe, usually lamb. Sometimes served in a seasoned broth.

➜ **Yáng Zá** (羊杂) Similar to *bào dǔ*, but includes an assortment of sheep's innards, not just tripe, and is always served in a broth.

➜ **Ròu Bǐng** (肉饼) Meat patty, usually filled with pork or beef before being lightly fried.

➜ **Jiāo Quān** (焦圈) Deep-fried dough rings, usually accompanied with a cup of *dòu zhī*.

➜ **Dòu Zhī** (豆汁) Sour-tasting soy milk drink.

GHOST STREET

For a close-up look at how Beijingers treat their restaurants as party venues and not just places for a meal, take a trip to **Ghost Street** (簋街; Gui Jie; Map p290; [S]Beixinqiao).

This 1.4km strip of Dongzhimennei Dajie is home to over 150 restaurants that attract everyone from hipsters to office workers, man-bag-toting businessmen and families, as well as the odd celebrity. It never closes, making it one of Běijīng's most buzzing streets, and it's especially fun on Friday and Saturday nights. From sundown to sunrise, it's lit by hundreds of red lanterns, and traffic slows to a crawl as the restaurant workers line the side of the road trying to entice passing cars to stop at their joint. Crowds of people spill out onto the pavement waiting for a free table, while inside the packed restaurants the sweating staff rush around delivering food and beers to people celebrating the end of the week.

Most styles of Chinese cuisine are represented on Ghost Street, but it's best known for its hotpot and spicy seafood restaurants.

The giant **Xiǎo Yú Shān** (小渔山; Map p290; 195 Dongzhimennei Dajie, 东直门内大街195号; ⌚10.30am-6am) is always jammed with people cracking open crayfish and shrimp. For classic Mongolian hotpot, try **Little Sheep** (小肥羊; Xiǎo Féi Yáng; Map p290; 209 Dongzhimennei Dajie, 东直门内大街209号; ⌚9am-4am), which sources its mutton from Inner Mongolia. For the spicier, Sìchuān version of hotpot, cross the road to **Chóngqìng Kǒngliàng Huǒguō** (重庆孔亮火锅; Map p290; 218 Dongzhimennei Dajie, 东直门内大街218; pot from ¥35, dipping ingredients ¥7-20; ⌚9.30am-3am).

Ghost Street gets its English name from a mistranslation for the Chinese nickname of the street, Gui Jie (簋街). 簋 (pronounced 'guǐ') is an ancient bronze food vessel, a statue of which you can find at the far eastern end of Dongzhimennei Dajie, by the 2nd Ring Road, but it's pronounced the same as 鬼 – Chinese for ghost.

extremely healthy food, but is also environmentally sound. Not a drop of cooking oil is thrown away (instead, the leftover oil is turned into soap!), napkins and the like are made from recycled paper and the food is largely organic (it actually has a separate, 100% organic menu, although much of the main menu is organic too). The atmosphere is relaxed and friendly, and the whole restaurant is nonsmoking. Don't come here if you're in a hurry, though. Service is notoriously slow.

CAFÉ DE LA POSTE — FRENCH $$

Map p290 (云游驿; Yúnyóu Yì; 58 Yonghegong Dajie, 雍和宫大街58号; mains ¥60-80; ⌚12.30-3pm & 6pm-midnight; [S]Yonghegong-Lama Temple) Just down the street from the Lama Temple, this is the closest that Běijīng gets to an authentic French bistro. With its relaxed vibe and friendly service, it's a key meeting point for French expats. A small bar area opens into an intimate, nicely lit dining space. The food is unpretentious and hearty; the steaks (from ¥82) are impressive cuts of meat. But it does a decent Salade Lyonnais (¥38), too, while the desserts include the renowned Death by Chocolate (¥48). There's a three-course set lunch (¥78) during the week and brunch is available at weekends (¥120). The wine list starts at ¥138 a bottle. The bar stays open late, has clientele spilling out onto the pavement in the summer and is one of the cheapest places to enjoy a drink (draft beer ¥10, pastis ¥8).

VINEYARD CAFÉ — WESTERN $$

Map p290 (葡萄院儿; Pútáo Yuànr; www.vineyardcafe.cn; 31 Wudaoying Hutong, 五道营胡同31号; mains ¥70-80; set lunches ¥55-60; ⌚lunch & dinner, closed Mon; 🚭; [S]Yonghegong-Lama Temple) A huge hit with expats, this cafe-restaurant was the first place to open its doors on the now increasingly trendy lane, Wudaoying Hutong. It's a particularly popular destination for brunch or lunch, and the British owner does an excellent full English breakfast. There's a nice conservatory, a nonsmoking area and lots of sofas to sink into. In the evening, it becomes a restaurant that serves up Western standards such as mussels in white wine (¥45), as well as being a laid-back spot to relax with a drink.

Nearby, they've opened the smaller **Vine Leaf** (Map p290; 9 Jianchang Hutong, 箭厂胡同 9号; mains ¥70-80; ⊗11.30am-11.30pm, closed Mon; ⑤Andingmen), which serves authentic English pub grub in a rustic Chinese *píngfáng* (bungalow).

NOODLE IN
PAN-ASIAN $$

Map p290 (吃面; Chī Miàn; Xiaojingchang Hutong, off Guloudong Dajie, 鼓楼东大街81号小经厂胡同; mains ¥20-50; ⊗noon-10pm; 🅿; ⑤Andingmen) Run partly by members of a local punk band, this tiny place comes with retro decor, upholstered dining chairs and, as you'd expect, very cool music. The pan-Asian menu – mostly stews, curries and, of course, noodles – is quite limited, but it adds to the home-cooked feel. English spoken and English menu.

ZHĀNG MĀMA
CHINESE SICHUANESE $

Map p290 (张妈妈特色川味馆; Zhāng Māma Tèsè Chuānwèiguǎn; 4 Fensiting Hutong, off Andingmennei Dajie, 安定门内大街分司厅胡同4号; mains ¥10-20; ⊗10am-11pm; ⑤Andingmen) The speciality of this excellent-value Sichuanese restaurant is *málà xiāngguō* (麻辣香锅; ¥48 to ¥58), a fiery, chilli-laced broth that comes with either chicken (香锅鸡; *xiāngguō jī*), prawns (香锅虾; *xiāngguo xiā*) or ribs (香锅排骨; *xiāngguō páigǔ*) simmering away inside, and with a variety of vegetables added into the mix. One pot is enough to feed two or three people. Also well worth trying here is the *dàndàn miàn* (担担面; spicy dry noodles) and the rice meals; the classic being the *gōngbào jīdīng gàifàn* (宫爆鸡丁盖饭; spicy chicken with peanuts), which is lip-tinglingly delicious, thanks to the rather generous sprinkling of Sìchuān peppercorns.

BĀOZI PÙ
DUMPLINGS $

Map p290 (包子铺; 108 Guloudong Dajie, 鼓楼东大街108号; dumplings per basket ¥5, noodles ¥6-8; ⊗6am-9pm; ⑤Shichahai) A local favourite, especially for breakfast, Bāozi Pù – literally 'dumplings shop' – has been on this same corner for years. Steamed pork dumplings (包子; *bāozi*; ¥5 per basket) are the speciality – you'll see bamboo baskets of them piled up near the entrance; say '*sù bāozi*' if you want vegetable ones. The boiled dumplings (蒸饺; *zhēng jiǎo*) are also very good. Wash them down either with a traditional soy milk drink (豆浆; *dòu jiāng*) or with rice porridge (紫米粥; *zǐ mǐ zhōu*). You

could also try the knife-sliced noodles (刀削面; *dāo xiāo miàn*). There's no English sign or menu.

LǍOHÉJIĀN DONKEY-MEAT RESTAURANT
CHINESE BĚIJĪNG $

Map p290 (老河间驴肉火烧; Lǎohéjiān Lǘ Ròu Huǒshāo; 16 Guloudong Dajie, 鼓楼东大街16号; ⊗10am-midnight; ⑤Andingmen, Shichahai or Beixinqiao) All varieties of donkey dishes are served up in this diminutive little locals' favourite, but the house speciality is *lǘ ròu hǔoshāo* (驴肉火烧 ¥6), pastry pockets filled with freshly chopped donkey meat and seasoned with herbs, spices and green chillies – a perfect, if perhaps slightly unusual, takeaway snack, which is a speciality of Héběi, the largely rural province which surrounds Běijīng. If you fancy eating in, you can also get donkey-meat noodles (驴肉面; *lǘ ròu miàn*; ¥6) and donkey meat soup (驴肉汤; *lǘ ròu tāng*; ¥4) as well as all manner of donkey innards thrown into various types of broth. No English, and no English menu.

ĀN DŌNG HOTEL
DUMPLINGS $

Map p290 (安东旅社; 1-6 Anwai Dongheyan, 安外东河沿1-6号; dumplings ¥5, noodles ¥7.10; ⊗6am-9pm; ⑤Yonghegong-Lama Temple) This is a no-nonsense, hole-in-the-wall dumplings joint serving up bamboo baskets of dumplings – steamed (小笼包; *xiǎolóng bāo*) or boiled (蒸饺; *zhēng jiǎo*) – as well as decent noodles with beef (牛肉面; *niú ròu miàn*), egg (鸡蛋面; *jī dàn miàn*) and Chinese cabbage (青菜面; *qīng cài miàn*). No English.

CAFÉ SAMBAL
MALAYSIAN $$

Map p290 (☎6400 4875; 43 Doufuchi Hutong, 旧鼓楼大街豆腐池胡同43号; mains from ¥60; ⊗lunch & dinner; ⊜🅿; ⑤Guloudajie) This cool Malaysian restaurant located off Jiugulou Dajie is in a cleverly converted courtyard house at the entrance to Doufuchi Hutong. The minimalist bar opens into a narrow dining area that has a temporary roof during winter, but is open in summer so you can dine under the stars and satellites. It's a popular spot for dates. The food is classic Malaysian. Try the beef rendang (¥78), or the various sambals (from ¥90). The wine list is decent, while the barman here mixes one of the best mojitos (¥55) in town.

LOCAL KNOWLEDGE

HÚTÒNG CAFES

Cute wi-fi cafes have been all the rage in Běijīng for some time now and these days there are dozens of excellent ones, particularly in and around the *hútòng* alleys of North Dōngchéng. Some are housed in converted courtyards, most have free wi-fi, fresh coffee (from ¥20), well-priced local beer (from ¥10) and a limited choice of mostly Western food (dishes from ¥30). They are also among the cheapest places in Běijīng to sample Chinese tea (from ¥20 per cup, with unlimited refills), although their selection is usually limited to just four or five different types. Here are our current favourites:

Irresistible Cafe (诱惑咖啡厅; Yòu Huò Kāfēitīng; Map p290; 14 Mao'er Hutong, 帽儿胡同14号; ⏰11am-midnight, closed Mon & Tue; 📶) Large courtyard. Czech beers. Good, healthy food.

Cafe Confucius (秀冠咖啡; Xiù Guàn Kāfēi; Map p290; 25 Guozijian Jie, 国子监街25号; ⏰8.30am-8.30pm; 📶) Buddhist themed. Very friendly.

Zha Zha Cafe (喜鹊咖啡; Xǐque Kāfēi; Map p290; 76 Guozijian Jie, 国子监街76号; ⏰10am-10pm; 🚭📶) Wood-stripped interior. Excellent coffee.

Courtyard No 28 (28号院; Èrshíbā Hào Yuà; Map p290; Xilou Hutong, 戏楼胡同; ⏰11am-11pm; 📶) Lovely courtyard. Cheap beers.

The Other Place (Map p290; 1 Langjia Hutong, 朗家胡同1号; ⏰midday-midnight; 📶) Cool staff. Nice courtyard. No food.

Xiǎoxīn's Cafe (小新的店; Xiǎoxīnde Diàn; Map p290; 103 Nanluogu Xiang, 南锣鼓巷103号; ⏰9.30am-midnight; 📶) Quiet retreat from the Nanluogu Xiang shopping frenzy.

Sculpting in Time (雕刻时光咖啡; Diāokè Shíguāng Kāfēi; Map p290; 2 Zhongku Hutong, Drum & Bell Sq, 钟鼓楼文化广场, 钟库胡同2号; ⏰10am-10pm; 📶) Rooftop terrace with views of the Drum and Bell Towers.

DRINKING

The ancient and once quiet *hútòng* of Nanluogu Xiang, which runs north–south between Gulou Dongdajie and Di'anmen Dongdajie, has become one of Běijīng's nightlife hubs in the last few years. While the character of the *hútòng* has changed irrevocably – most of the residents have rented out their homes for bars, restaurants and shops and decamped to the suburbs – it does now feature a wide range of bars that cater to both locals and Westerners. The main strip can get quite busy, at weekends especially. For a less-hectic time, try Beiluogu Xiang, immediately to the north of Nanluogu Xiang, or the alleys around the Drum and Bell towers. Some of the coolest bars in this area have regular live-music nights (p97).

GREAT LEAP BREWING — BAR

Map p290 (大跃啤酒; Dàyuè Píjiǔ; www.greatleapbrewing.com; 6 Doujiao Hutong, 豆角胡同6号; beer per pint ¥25-50; ⏰7pm-midnight Tue-Fri, 3pm-midnight Sat, 2-9pm Sun; [S]Shichahai) A hidden gem to beat all hidden gems, this micro-brewery, run by American beer enthusiast Carl Setzer, is housed in a hard-to-find, 100-year-old Qing-dynasty courtyard and serves up a wonderful selection of unique ales made largely from locally sourced ingredients. Sip on familiar favourites such as pale ales and porters or choose from China-inspired tipples like Honey Ma, a brew made with lip-tingling Sìchuān peppercorns. From Nanluogu Xiang, walk west down Jingyang Hutong (景阳胡同), bearing right, then left, then right again before turning left down Doujiao Hutong.

EL NIDO — BAR

Map p290 (59号酒吧; Wǔshíjiǔ Hào Jiǔbā; 59 Fangjia Hutong Dongdajie, 方家胡同59号; beers from ¥10; ⏰6pm-late; [S]Andingmen) Friendly pint-sized bar, with more than 100 types of imported beer. There's no drinks menu; just dive into the fridge and pick out whichever bottles take your fancy. Prices for the foreign beers start at ¥30, while Harbin beer costs just ¥10 a bottle. There's also some imported liquor, including a number of different types of absinthe. If El Nido's is too packed (it really is tiny) then try walking up the road to **No 46**, where there's bunch of bars and cafes in a small cul-de-sac.

REEF BAR BAR

Map p290 (触礁; Chùjiāo; 14-1 Nanluogu Xiang, 南锣鼓巷14-1号; beers from ¥20, cocktails from ¥25; 🕑2pm-late; [S]Nanluoguxiang) Much more of a bar for locals than many others in the area, Reef has a friendly vibe that makes it an easy place to hang out. Located in a converted *hútòng* house, there's a small bar area, a few sofas and tables, and a wide selection of foreign beers. Run by a cheerful husband-and-wife team, it stays open into the wee hours on busy nights.

ZÁ JIĀ BAR

Map p290 (杂家; www.zajia.cc; Hóng Ēn Temple, Doufuchi Hutong, 豆腐池胡同宏恩观; 🕑1pm-2am; [S]Guloudajie) Built into the entrance gate of Hóng Ēn Guàn (宏恩观), a 600-year-old former Taoist temple – most of which is now a household goods market – beautiful Zá Jiā is a cafe by day (coffee from ¥18), bar by night (beer from ¥20). The interior is as cool as it is unique, with split-level seating reaching up into the eaves, and the atmosphere is friendly and relaxed. It sometimes holds free film screenings and art exhibitions, but if there's live music at the weekends, there's a cover charge (¥30 to ¥50).

BALL HOUSE BAR

Map p290 (波楼酒吧; Bōlóu Jiǔbā; Lǎo Mó; 40 Zhonglouwan Hutong, 钟楼湾胡同40号; 🕑2pm-late; [S]Guloudajie) A bar for those in the know, Ball House is impossible to stumble across; there's no sign and it's set back from the main *hútòng* (which circumnavigates the Bell Tower) at the end of a narrow pathway which looks like it leads to ordinary housing. There's washing hanging outside and bikes leant up against the wall, but if you push the door open at the end of the pathway, you enter an enormous, beautifully restored split-level room and one of the capital's most unusual drinking spaces. There are pool tables (¥30 per hour) and table football tables (free) dotted around the place – hence the name – but there are enough nooks and crannies to find your own quiet spot if you don't fancy the ball games. Beers from ¥15.

WEN YU'S CUSTARD SHOP CAFE

Map p290 (文宇奶酪店; Wényǔ Nǎilào Diàn; 49 Nanluoguxiang, 南锣鼓巷49号; custard drinks ¥9-12; 🕑noon until sold out) There's an obsession with yoghurt and milk custard in Běijīng, and Wen Yu's Custard Shop, on historic Nanluogu Xiang, seems to be the place everyone wants to get it from. Wen Yu is the third generation in his family carrying on the tradition of making this creamy drink, and punters queue down the lane to get their hands on a cup of it before he sells out (normally by mid-afternoon).

There are various flavours; the classic is the *yuánwèi nǎilào* (原味奶酪; original-flavour custard; ¥10). No English sign. Just follow the queue.

MAO MAO CHONG BAR BAR

Map p290 (毛毛虫; Máo Máo Chóng; 12 Banchang Hutong, 板厂胡同12号; beers from ¥25, cocktails from ¥40; 🕑7pm-midnight, closed Mon & Tue; 🚭; [S]Nanluoguxiang) This small but lively expat favourite has a rustic interior, good value cocktails and a no-smoking policy. Its pizzas also get rave reviews.

IF BAR

Map p290 (如果酒吧; Rúguǒ Jiǔbā; 67 Beiluogu Xiang, 北锣鼓巷67号; beers from ¥15; 🕑1pm-2am; [S]Guloudajie) Housed on three small levels, this quirky bar includes strange shaped furniture, cheese-like wall panelling punctured with holes, and floors with rather disconcerting glass sections that allow you to view the level below. There's a free pool table and table football (¥5) as well as a neat little roof terrace, which looks out over the *hútòng*. The basement has a small dance floor.

12SQM BAR

Map p290 (12平米; Shí'èr Píngmǐ; cnr Nanluogu Xiang & Fuxiang Hutong, 南锣鼓巷福祥胡同1号; beers from ¥20, cocktails from ¥35; 🕑noon-1am; 🚭; [S]Nanluoguxiang) Once famous for being Běijīng's smallest bar, 12SQM has grown to 45 sq m in size. Still cosy, still friendly and still completely nonsmoking.

DRUM & BELL BAR

Map p290 (鼓钟咖啡馆; Gǔzhōng Kāfēiguǎn; 41 Zhonglouwan Hutong, 钟楼湾胡同41号; beers from ¥15, cocktails from ¥35; 🕑1pm-2am; [S]Guloudajie) Located in between the Drum and Bell Towers, from whom it takes its name, the main attraction of this bar is its splendid roof terrace. It's a great spot to catch some rays on lazy Sunday afternoons, or to while away a summer evening. In winter,

LOCAL KNOWLEDGE

BĚIJĪNG'S TOP DRINKING SPOTS

Sānlǐtún Loud, brash and relatively expensive, this is where expats and Chinese partygoers come when they want to drink all night long. Here you'll find the city's best cocktail bars, biggest nightclubs, seediest dives and highest concentration of places open long into the early hours. Head to Sanlitun Lu or the Workers Stadium.

Nanluogu Xiang (p86) Far more laid back than Sānlǐtún, this historic *hútòng*, and the network of lanes branching off it, houses smaller bars – some in converted court-yards – that are better for a drink and a chat, rather than a dance. The city's coolest live-music venues are in this area too. Head to Nanluogu Xiang, Beiluogu Xiang or the square between the Drum and Bell Towers.

Hòuhǎi Lakes (p118) Neon-lit guitar bars with karaoke on tap are the speciality at this noisy but undoubtedly fun strip of bars, located attractively on the banks of Hòuhǎi and Qiánhǎi Lakes. More popular with Chinese drinkers than foreigners, and dead in winter. To enjoy a lakeside beer without the karaoke backdrop, head to the far north of Hòuhǎi Lake to the more laid-back Golden Sail Water Sports Club.

Fangjia Hutong (Map p290) No 46 is a small cul-de-sac of bars, cafes and restau-rants, although the best of the lot is El Nido, just down the alley at No 59.

Wudaoying Hutong (p87) Nanluogu Xiang's young pretender, Wudaoying has all the potential to be a popular bar street; it's just not that popular yet. Still, there are a number of cute cafes and bars to satisfy those who fancy a quiet drink in an old Běijīng back alley. And VA Bar has OK live-music nights.

Wǔdàokǒu Běijīng's prime student hangout with bars and clubs promising a cheaper alternative to Sānlǐtún. Head to Wǔdàokǒu subway station then follow the sound of revellers.

retreat downstairs, where there are comfy sofas to sink into.

MÀI
BAR

Map p290 (麦; 40 Beiluogu Xiang, 北锣鼓巷40号; cocktails from ¥45, beers from ¥25; ◷6pm-2am; ⓢGuloudajie) This area's only proper cocktail bar, Mài is funky, friendly and housed in a beautifully renovated part of an old court-yard building. Most importantly, though, the manager mixes very good cocktails.

MODERNISTA
BAR

Map p290 (老摩; Lǎo Mó; 44 Baochao Hutong, 宝钞胡同44号; ◷4pm-2am, closed Mon; ⓢGu-loudajie) Styled on a European tapas bar, this small place burst onto the scene in 2011 and continues to reel in well-dressed, artsy types with its live music (mostly jazz) and cultural events such a film screenings, dance classes and mah-jong evenings. The drinks are well priced, with beers from ¥15 and imported wines from ¥35.

SALUD
BAR

Map p290 (老伍; lǎowǔ; ☎6402 5086; 66 Nan-luogu Xiang, 南锣鼓巷66号; beers from ¥20, cocktails from ¥30; ◷3pm-late; ⓢAndingmen) The biggest and liveliest bar on Nanluogu Xiang, Salud is expat-centric, but gets very busy on weekends with a mixed crowd of locals and foreigners who party well into the early hours. Its house-special flavoured rums (¥20) come in test-tube-like vessels and are lethal.

PASSBY BAR
BAR

Map p290 (过客; Guòkè; 108 Nanluogu Xiang, 南锣鼓巷108号四合院; beers from ¥20; ◷9.30am-4am; ⓢNanluoguxiang) The first bar to open on Nanluogu Xiang, Passby is more of a restaurant these days (Western food; the pizzas are good), but the rooftop seat-ing, the long opening hours and the row of fridges stocking more than 100 types of bottled beer, are pretty tempting for late-night drinkers too. Passby is also run by travel-loving staff; friendly owner Xiao Bi-anr has made multiple cycling trips to Tibet over the years.

BED BAR
BAR

Map p290 (床吧; Chuángbā; ☎8400 1554; 17 Zhangwang Hutong, off Jiugulou Dajie, 旧鼓楼大街张旺旺胡同17号; beers from ¥25, cocktails from ¥40; ◷11am-2am; ⓢGuloudajie) One *hútòng* north of Café Sambal is this hard-to-find bar, situated in a converted courtyard. The bar area leads on to a succession of inner rooms, some with beds, and the overall ef-fect is of a place that's both intimate and spacious. It can get crowded at weekends (although it's nowhere near as popular as it once was), but there's always a spot where you can hide away. There's a DJ and small dance floor, and it does tapas-style finger food as well.

ENTERTAINMENT

[TOP CHOICE] JIĀNG HÚ LIVE MUSIC

Map p290 (江湖酒吧; Jiāng Hú Jiǔbā; 7 Dongmianhua Hutong, 东棉花胡同7号; admission from ¥30; ⏲7pm-2am; [S]Nanluoguxiang) One of the coolest places to hear Chinese indie and rock bands, Jiāng Hú, run by a trombone-playing, music-loving manager, is housed in an old courtyard and packs in the punters on a good night. Intimate, cool, and a decent spot for a drink in a courtyard, even when no bands are playing. Beers from ¥20.

[TOP CHOICE] JIĀNG JÌN JIǓ LIVE MUSIC

Map p290 (疆进酒吧; Jiāngjìnjiǔ Jiǔbā; 2 Zhongku Hutong, 钟库胡同2号(鼓楼北门; admission from ¥20; ⏲1pm-2am; [S]Guloudajie or Shichahai) This tiny, laid-back venue is the best place to hear Chinese folk music from the country's ethnic minorities, particularly Uighur and Mongolian. Live music is Thursday to Sunday only and is usually free, although there's sometimes a small cover charge on Fridays and Saturdays if a more popular act is playing. Beers from ¥15. Cocktails from ¥25.

YÚGŌNG YÍSHĀN LIVE MUSIC

Map p290 (愚公移山; ☎6404 2711; www.yugongyishan.com; 3-2 Zhangzizhong Lu, West Courtyard, 张自忠路3-2, 号段祺瑞执政府旧址西院; admission from ¥50; ⏲7pm-2am; [S]Zhangzizhonglu) Reputedly one of the most haunted places in Běijīng, this historic building has been home to Qing-dynasty royalty, warlords and the occupying Japanese army in the 1930s. You could probably hear the ghosts screaming if it wasn't for the array of local and foreign bands, solo artists and DJs who take to the stage here every week. With a very sound booking policy and a decent space to play with, this is one of the best places in town to listen to live music.

TEMPLE BAR LIVE MUSIC

Map p290 (坛酒吧; Tán Jiǔbā; Bldg B, 206 Guloudong Dajie, 鼓楼东大街206号; beers from ¥15, cocktails from ¥30; ⏲7pm-late; 🚭; [S]Shichahai) Large single-room space above a 24-hour internet cafe, with a long bar in one corner, a low stage in another and tables, chairs and sofas strewn across the rest of the floor. Three music-loving managers ensure

KTV

Karaoke, or as it's known here, KTV, is the number one leisure pastime for most Chinese people. There are hundreds of KTV venues in Běijīng and if you get the chance to go to one with some Chinese friends, take it. The enthusiasm the locals show for belting out their favourite pop classics across a small room filled with their mates is astonishing.

If you speak Mandarin, you can sing along to the latest Mando-pop hits. English speakers will have to content themselves with a smaller and older selection of tunes, but you'll always find something you can sing. At the places listed below, drinks and food are available. Prices depend on the size of the room you want and the time of day. It's always advisable to book ahead at weekends.

➡ **Tango KTV** (糖果; Tángguǒ; Map p290; ☎6428 2288; 79 Hepinglixi Jie, by south gate of Dìtán Park, 和平里西街79号, 地坛公园南门; small room (5-6 people) weekday/weekend evenings per hr ¥120/180; ⏲24hr)

➡ **Melody KTV** (麦乐迪; Màilèdí; Map p298; ☎6551 0808; A-77 Chaoyangmenwai Dajie, 朝阳门外大街A-77号; small room (5-6 people) weekday/weekend evenings per hr ¥179/229; ⏲10am-6am)

➡ **Partyworld KTV** (钱柜; Qiánguì; Map p298; ☎6588 3333; Fanli Bldg, 22 Chaoyangmenwai Dajie, accessed via Chaowaishichang Jie, 朝阳门外大街22号泛利大夏; small room (5-6 people) weekday/weekend evenings per hr ¥200/260; ⏲midday-6am)

LOCAL KNOWLEDGE

POOL HALLS

Ever since China's most successful snooker player Ding Junhui burst onto the professional scene around 10 years ago, snooker and pool have been wildly popular in China, and there are now estimated to be around 1000 pool halls in Běijīng alone, most of which are tucked away down alleys, or hidden up on the 2nd floor above shops. They're a great way of mixing with young locals in a non-touristy environment and they make for a cheap night out, as venues either sell very cheap local beer (from around ¥5) or allow you to bring your own.

The quality of the tables varies, but is generally pretty good. You tend to have to hunt around for a decent cue, though.

Expect to pay around ¥20 per hour per table; pay a ¥100 deposit when you arrive, and they'll take the hourly rate out of that.

Pool halls are very much local affairs so almost never have English signage. Instead, keep an eye out for the characters 台球 (táiqiú; pool) as you walk around the hútòng.

One of our favourite spots is **Hǎicháo Pool Hall** (海潮台球; Hǎicháo Táiqiú; Map p290; 25 Doufuchi Hutong, 豆腐池胡同25号; per hr ¥15; ⏰24hr), located above Zá Jiǎ Bar. There's no sign; look for the steps that lead up to the old arched entranceway (once the entrance to the now mostly ruined Hóng Ēn Temple) and continue up to the 2nd floor.

decent billing from local bands, and gigs are often free. No sign; walk under the decorative archway by 206 Guloudong Dajie, continue to Building B, right at the back of the small car park, then walk up the stairs to your right.

MAO LIVEHOUSE
LIVE MUSIC

Map p290 (光芒; Guāngmáng; 111 Gulou Dongdajie, 鼓楼东大街111号; admission from ¥50; ⏰8pm-late; Ⓢ Shichahai) This midsized venue, opposite the northern entrance to Nanluogu Xiang, is large enough to give the many gigs it hosts a sense of occasion, but small enough to feel intimate. The decor is functional and the sound tight. All sorts of bands play here, but if they're from overseas, the entrance price is sky-high.

PÉNGHĂO THEATRE
THEATRE

Map p290 (蓬蒿剧场; Pénghǎo Jùchǎng; ☑6400 6452; www.penghaoren.com; in an alley beside 35 Dongmianhua Hutong, 东棉花胡同35号; tickets from ¥50; Ⓢ Nanluoguxiang) Students from the nearby drama academy sometimes perform here, in this small informal nonprofit theatre, tucked away down a narrow, unnamed alleyway between Dongmianhua Hutong and Beibinmasi Hutong. The venue, which doubles as a cafe, is enchanting, and has some lovely rooftop seating areas, shaded by a 200-year-old tree which slices through part of the building. Performances are mostly modern drama, and are often held in English as well as Chinese. Its website

was down when we last checked, so try calling to see what's on. Some English spoken.

CHINA PUPPET THEATRE
THEATRE

(中国木偶剧院; Zhōngguó Mù'ǒu Jùyuàn; ☑6425 4847; www.puppetchina.com; cnr Anhua Xili & North Third Ring Road, 北三环中路安华西里; Ⓢ Hepingxiqiao, then bus 104, 101 or 特8) Popular with families, this theatre puts on shadow play, puppetry, music and dance events on Saturdays and Sundays only. There are two theatres. The larger one (大剧场; dà jùchǎng; tickets ¥180 to ¥380, shows at 10.30am and 2.30pm) hosts music and dance shows. The puppet shows are always in the small theatre (小剧场; xiǎo jùchǎng; tickets ¥100, shows at 10am, 11am, 12pm, 1.30pm and 2.30pm). No English. The theatre is less than 1km north of Liǔyìn Park. Go to Hepingxiqiao subway station, then take a west-bound bus (Nos 104, 101 or 特8) to Anzhenqiao Xi bus stop (1km) from where you'll see the fairy-tale castle-like theatre building on the other side of the ring road.

STAR LIVE
LIVE MUSIC

Map p290 (星光现场; Xīngguāng Xiànchǎng; www.clubtango.cn; 3rd fl, Tango nightclub, 79 Hepingli Xijie, 糖果3层, 和平西街79号; admission from ¥50; ⏰6.30pm-late; 🚇; Ⓢ Yonghegong-Lama Temple) It's a great space and as the only medium-sized venue in Běijīng, it hosts a fair few international bands. The venue hosts occasional dance parties, too.

SHOPPING

The wildly popular *hútòng* of Nanluogu Xiang contain an eclectic mix of clothes and gifts, sold in trendy boutique shops. It's an extremely pleasant place to shop for souvenirs, but avoid summer weekends if you can, when it gets unfeasibly busy. At its northern end, Gulou Dongdajie has become a popular place for young Beijingers to shop for vintage clothing, skater fashion and music gear.

RUÌFÚXIÁNG SILK CLOTHING

Map p290 (瑞蚨祥; Ruìfúxiáng; 50 Di'anmenwai Dajie, Dongdajie, 地安门外大街50号; ⏲10am-8.30pm; [S]Shichahai) Relatively new branch of the 150-year-old Ruìfúxiáng silk store, this place does all manner of silk items, from scarves and shawls (from ¥150) to slippers and hats (from ¥50). It's a great place to come for Chinese-style clothing (women's *qípáo* start at around ¥500), including very cute children's outfits (from ¥100). The quality is good, and the prices, which are marked, are all very reasonable considering how famous the brand is.

GRIFTED SOUVENIRS

Map p290 (贵福人地; Guìfú Tiāndì; 32 Nanluogu Xiang, 南锣鼓巷32号; ⏲10am-10pm; [S]Nanluoguxiang) A plethora of tongue-in-cheek gift options is available at this friendly shop in the heart of trendy Nanluogu Xiang. Check out the dolls of communist icons: Che Guevara, Fidel Castro, Mao, Marx and Lenin re-imagined as soft toys, and the Mao-print cushions. There are also lanterns made from recycled candy wrapping, quirky umbrellas and T-shirts. Most of the products here are made locally.

ESY DRAGON GIFT SHOP SOUVENIRS

Map p290 (石怡集; Shí Yí Jí; 19 Nanluogu Xiang, 南锣鼓巷19号; ⏲9.30am-9.30pm; [S]Nanluoguxiang) Stocks a good range of souvenirs that are of decent quality but small in size, and therefore cheap. You'll find pens, bookmarks and decorative Chinese knots for less than ¥10, while key rings emblazoned with Chinese motifs start at ¥20. Sets of coasters or Chinese cloth slippers for kids can be had for less than ¥80. If you're after something a bit fancier, there's a range of attractive hand-painted porcelain cups at the back of the shop that go for around ¥300 each.

PLASTERED 8 T-SHIRTS

Map p290 (创可贴T-恤; Chuàngkětiē Tìxù; www.plasteredtshirts.com; 61 Nanluogu Xiang, 南锣鼓巷61号; ⏲10am-10pm; [S]Nanluoguxiang) Here you'll find purveyors of ironic T-shirts (from ¥138) that are good to give as gifts or to keep as mementos of Běijīng. Opposite the entrance to the shop is a rare surviving slogan from the Cultural Revolution era, which exhorts the people to put their trust in the People's Liberation Army (PLA; China's armed forces).

C ROCK MUSIC

Map p290 (C Rock 音乐光盘店; C Rock yīnyuè guāngpán diàn; 99 Guloudong Dajie, 鼓楼东大街99号; ⏲1-11pm; [S]Andingmen) This pocket-sized shop is the best place in the area to pick up albums produced by Chinese artists. The guy who runs it speaks enough English to help you decide and is happy to let you listen to an album that takes your fancy. There's music of all types from all over China (as well as some international stuff), but the focus is on local rock bands and folk music. CDs cost between ¥25 and ¥100.

LOCAL KNOWLEDGE

DRUM TOWER DEVELOPMENT

Just as this book was going to press, controversial plans to redevelop the *hútòng*-rich area around the historic Drum and Bell Towers looked like they were back on the table. The original plans to demolish homes surrounding the two 18th-century towers, and build a complex that would be known as "Běijīng Time Cultural City", had been scrapped in 2010 after lobbying from local protestors. But after no word on the subject for almost two years, posters suddenly appeared on buildings in the area in December 2012, notifying residents that the demolition stage of the project would begin in the new year. The Drum and Bell Towers themselves won't be affected (we hope), but the face of what has for a long time been one of the most charming corners of old Běijīng will likely be changed forever.

ZHAN TIAN / GETTY IMAGES ©

1. Nanluogu Xiang (p99)
The wildly popular *hútòng* of Nanluogu Xiang are an extremely pleasant place to shop for souvenirs.

2. Lama Temple (p82)
Běijīng's foremost Buddhist temple is also one of the most magnificent Tibetan Buddhist temples outside Tibet.

3. Drum Tower (p84)
The magnificent red-painted Drum Tower used to be the city's official timekeeper, with drums beaten and bells rung to mark the times of the day.

4. Fresh Noodles
Noodles are preferred to rice in the capital.

3

MANFRED GOTTSCHALK / GETTY IMAGES ©

THE HUTONG

Hidden down a maze of narrow alleys, **The Hutong** (Map p290; ☎159 0104 6127; www.thehutong.com; 1 Jiudaowan Zhongxiang Hutong, off Shique Hutong, 北新桥石雀胡同九道弯中巷胡同1号; 🕘9am-9pm; [S]Beixinqiao) is a highly recommended Chinese-culture centre, run by a group of extremely knowledgeable expats and skilled locals. Classes are held in a peaceful converted courtyard, and focus on three main areas:

➡ **Hutong Cookery Courses** (per class ¥250; 🕘10.30am, 2.30pm & 7pm) Hugely popular, and run three times a day, the focus is on cuisine from around China, but other Asian-cuisine classes are also run. Some classes include trips to a local food market.

➡ **Hutong Chinese Tea Courses** (☎135 0112 6093; www.t-journeys.com; tea tasting/tea-market tours ¥160/250) The Hutong's 'Tea Journeys' are a wonderfully accessible way to learn about this ancient Chinese tradition. It also sells beautifully packaged own-brand teas (¥110 to ¥180).

➡ **Hutong Traditional Chinese Medicine Courses** (☎150 1151 0363; www.straightbamboo.com; 🕘8am-6pm Sun-Thu) Run by Alex Tan, an Australian-Chinese TCM expert, classes range from introductions to Qi Gong, yoga and Taoism as well as to Chinese medicine itself.

How to Find The Hutong

Come out of Exit C of Beixinqiao subway station and turn left onto Shique Hutong. Take the second right down the very narrow Jiudaowanxi Xiang (九道弯西巷), then take the first left followed by the first right and you'll see The Hutong on your right.

TIĀN YÌ GOODS MARKET MARKET

Map p290 (天意商场; Tiānyì Shāngchǎng; 158 Di'anmen Waidajie, 地安门外大街158号; 🕘9am-7.30pm; [S]Shichahai) There's little in the way of conventional souvenirs here (although there are some), but the fact that tourists don't shop here means that whatever you buy is almost bound to be a bargain. This isn't so much the place to come to buy gifts for friends back home; it's where to come for that gadget you've lost, or those pair of gloves you didn't think you'd need. Items for sale include electronics, stationery and toys (ground floor), jewellery and souvenirs (1st floor), sports equipment, including kites and table-tennis sets (2nd floor), clothing (3rd floor) and shoes, including flip-flops and old-school Chinese plimsolls (4th floor).

JH 2ND-HAND BIKE SHOP BICYCLES

Map p290 (金典新桥信托商行; Jīndiǎn Xīnqiáo Xìntuō Shànghάng; 43 Dongsibei Dajie, 东四北大街43号; 🕘9am-5pm; [S]Beixinqiao) You can pick up all sorts here, from battered old Tiānjīn-made Flying Pigeons and Shànghǎi Forevers (sometimes starting as cheap as ¥100) to lovingly restored British-made Raleighs that go for up to ¥5000. There are also some new bikes on display, but the quality of them isn't as good as at the nearby Giant shop.

GIANT BICYCLES

Map p290 (捷安特; Jié'āntè; 77 Jiaodaokoudong Dajie, 交道口东大街77号; 🕘9am-7pm; [S]Beixinqiao) One of a string of decent bike shops on this stretch of road, Giant has the biggest range of new bicycles and bike equipment, such as helmets, locks and baby seats. Bikes start at around ¥500.

SPORTS & ACTIVITIES

NATOOKE CYCLING

Map p290 (耍（自行车店）; Shuǎ (Zìxíngchē Diàn); www.natooke.com; 19-1 Wudaoying Hutong, 五道营胡同19－1号; 🕘10am-7pm; [S]Yonghegong-Lama Temple) The coolest bike shop in Běijīng, Natooke sells fixed-gear bikes (from ¥2800), but also rents a range of secondhand bikes (per day ¥50, deposit per day ¥500) including fixed-gear, road, mountain or just ordinary old Chinese town bikes.

BLACK SESAME KITCHEN COOKING CLASSES

Map p290 (☎136 9147 4408; www.blacksesamekitchen.com; 3 Heizhima Hutong, 黑芝麻胡同3号; [S]Nanluoguxiang) Runs popular cooking classes with a variety of recipes from across China; just off Nanluogu Xiang.

CHINA ACADEMY OF CHINESE MEDICAL SCIENCES
TRADITIONAL CHINESE MEDICINE

Map p290 (中国中医科学院; Zhōngguó Zhōngyī Kēxuéyuàn; ☑6401 4411; 16 Dongzhimen Nanxiaojie, 东直门南小街16号; ☉9am-5pm; Ⓢ Beixinqiao) Would-be acupuncturists and students of moxibustion can head to this large institution which has courses, run in Chinese, for greenhorn and intermediate level students of TCM. For more accessible classes, run in English, try **Straight Bamboo** (www.straightbamboo.com), which has a small centre at **The Hutong**.

CULTURE YARD
COURSES

Map p290 (天井越洋; Tiānjǐng Yuèyáng; ☑8404 4166; www.cultureyard.net; 10 Shique Hutong, 石雀胡同10号; ☉10am-7pm; Ⓢ Beixinqiao) Tucked away down a *hútòng,* this cultural centre focuses on language classes (Chinese, English, French, Spanish, Portuguese), including crash-course beginners Chinese, but also does Chinese culture workshops (tea, calligraphy, *hútòng* photography).

DÌTÁN SPORTS CENTRE
SWIMMING

Map p290 (地坛体育馆; ☑6426 4483; Andingmenwai Dajie, 安定门外大街; admission ¥30; ☉8.30am-3.30pm & 6.30-10pm Mon-Fri, noon-10pm Sat & Sun; Ⓢ Andingmen) You can find pools at some four-star and all five-star hotels, but nonguests will have to pay a fee. Outside hotels, try the pool at Dìtán Sports Centre (Dìtán Tǐyùguǎn). In summer, head to nearby **Qīngnián Hú Park** (青年湖公园; Qīngnián Hú Gōngyuán; Map p290; park entrance ¥1, pool entrance ¥30; ☉6am-9pm Jun-Aug) where there's an outdoor swimming complex with water slides and a shallow pool for young'uns. It's floodlit in the evening. You can buy swimming gear at both places.

Temple of Heaven Park & Dōngchéng South

Neighbourhood Top Five

1 Visit the unmissable **Temple of Heaven Park** (p106), where you'll find an utterly unique and simply stunning collection of halls and altars, the former site of arcane rituals. Afterwards, enjoy the park itself; one of Běijīng's most soothing experiences.

2 Scoff **Peking duck**, the capital's signature dish, in the **restaurants** (p111) where it originated.

3 Step back in time by walking along the sole remaining stretch of the old **City Walls** (p109).

4 Scavenge for pearls of all varieties in **Hóngqiáo (Pearl) Market** (p113).

5 Join the locals in one of their favourite pastimes on the restored shopping street of **Qianmen Dajie** (p110).

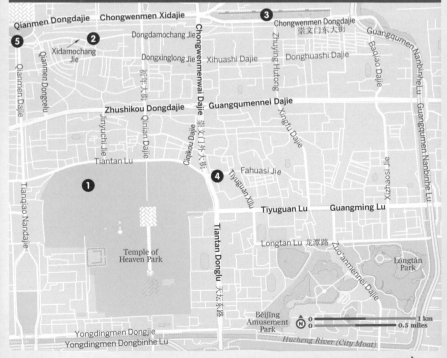

For more detail of this area see Map p292 ➡

Explore: Temple of Heaven Park & Dōngchéng South

Ranging south and southeast of the Forbidden City, and encompassing the now defunct district of Chóngwén, this neighbourhood is one of the most compact in the capital. Far less fashionable than the rest of Dōngchéng (东城) – it's something of a nightlife desert – it has always been home to the *lǎobǎixìng* (common people).

Start the day at Temple of Heaven Park. Amble through the park to the west gate and then head north to the Qiánmén area, or hit the Hóngqiáo Market, a few hundred metres north of the east gate, where five floors of pearls, jewellery, jade and more await you. Remember to ascend to the roof terrace for splendid views across the Temple of Heaven Park.

The last remaining stretch of the city walls that once enclosed Běijīng are a brief subway ride north of the Temple of Heaven. From there, wander west through the surviving *hútòng* (narrow alleyways) of the neighbourhood towards Qiánmén, where museums and the highly popular pedestrian shopping street of Qianmen Dajie await you. Nearby are some of the oldest and most traditional Peking duck restaurants of all, as well as an increasing number of Western fine dining options. Even if you don't eat there, make sure to walk through the gates of 23 Qianmen Dongdajie for a peek at some of the imposing, European-style buildings that once housed former foreign embassies.

Local Life

➡ **Hútòng** Spend some time exploring the decaying alleyways and lanes to the east of Qianmen Dajie (p110), still home to many locals.

➡ **Peking duck** If you want to eat Peking duck where the locals do, try Biànyìfāng (p112).

➡ **Park life** Serene Lóngtán Park, to the east of Temple of Heaven Park, is one of Běijīng's best-kept secrets.

Getting There & Away

➡ **Subway** Line 2 stops at Qianmen Station and Chongwenmen Station, where the north–south Line 5 intersects with it. For Temple of Heaven Park take Line 5 direct to the Tiantandongmen stop; get off at Chongwenmen for the Ming City Ruins Park and Southeast Corner Watchtower. Qianmen Station serves Qianmen Dajie and the area around it.

➡ **Bus** Bus 20 journeys from Běijīng South Train Station via the Temple of Heaven and Qianmen to Wángfǔjǐng, Dōngdān and Běijīng Train Station.

Lonely Planet's Top Tip

Do as the locals do and rise early to get to Temple of Heaven Park when it opens at sunrise. Not only will you see Běijīng's senior citizens at play – practising taichi and formation dancing – but the park is a superb, tranquil experience at this time and you'll have the jump on the crowds when the sights open at 8am.

⚒ Best Places to Eat

➡ Maison Boulud (p110)

➡ Lost Heaven (p110)

➡ Capital M (p111)

➡ Dūyīchù (p112)

For reviews, see p110 ➡

⚒ Best Peking Duck

➡ Lìqún Roast Duck Restaurant (p111)

➡ Biànyìfāng (p112)

➡ Qiánmén Quánjùdé Roast Duck Restaurant (p111)

For reviews, see p110 ➡

🔒 Best Places to Shop

➡ Hóngqiáo (Pearl) Market (p113)

➡ Qianmen Dajie (p110)

➡ Toys City (p113)

For reviews, see p113 ➡

MAREMAGNUM / GETTY IMAGES ©

TOP SIGHTS
TEMPLE OF HEAVEN PARK

The collection of halls and altars set within the delightful 276-hectare Temple of Heaven Park (天坛公园; Tiāntán Gōngyuán) is the most perfect example of Ming architectural design and absolutely extraordinary to contemplate. Each year, the Chinese emperors – the sons of heaven – came here to seek divine clearance and good harvests and to atone for the sins of their people in an esoteric ceremony of prayers and ritual sacrifices. Everything about the complex is unique, with shape, colour and sound combining to take on symbolic significance. The park itself is equally harmonious, a true oasis amid Běijīng's bedlam.

This is not so much a temple as an altar, so don't expect to see worshippers in prayer. Temple of Heaven is essentially Confucian in function and its cosmic overtones will delight numerologists, necromancers and superstitious visitors – not to mention acoustic engineers and carpenters. Seen from above the structures are round and the bases square, a pattern deriving from the ancient Chinese belief that heaven is round and earth is square. Thus the northern end of the park is semicircular and the southern end is square. Temple of the Earth, also called Dìtán, in the north of Běijīng, is on the northern compass point and Temple of Heaven is on the southern point.

There are four gates to the park, one on each point of the compass, and you can enter through any of them. The imperial approach to the temple was via **Zhāohēng Gate** (昭亨门; Zhāohēng Mén; Map p292) in the south, and that is reflected in our ordering of the principal sights below. You can enter either with just the basic park ticket (¥15), then buy a ¥20 ticket that includes

DON'T MISS

- ➡ Hall of Prayer for Good Harvests
- ➡ Echo Wall

PRACTICALITIES

- ➡ 天坛公园; Tiāntán Gōngyuán
- ➡ Map p292
- ➡ ☎6701 2483
- ➡ address: Tiantan Donglu
- ➡ admission park/through ticket (for all sights) high season ¥15/35, low season ¥10/30, audio tour ¥40 (deposit ¥100)
- ➡ 🕐park 6am-9pm; sights 8am-6pm Apr-Oct, 8am-5pm Nov-Mar
- ➡ 🚭
- ➡ [S]Tiantandongmen

each major sight later, or buy the through ticket (¥35), which gets you into the park and all the sights.

Round Altar

The 5m-high **Round Altar** (圜丘; Yuán Qiū ; Map p292) was constructed in 1530 and rebuilt in 1740. The altar once looked very different: its first incarnation was in deep-blue glazed stone before being redone in light green. The current white marble structure is arrayed in three tiers; its geometry revolves around the imperial number nine. Odd numbers were considered heavenly, and nine is the largest single-digit odd number. The top tier, thought to symbolise heaven, contains nine rings of stones. Each ring has multiples of nine stones, so that the ninth ring has 81 stones. The middle tier (earth) has the 10th to 18th rings. The bottom tier (humanity) has the 19th to 27th rings. The numbers of stairs and balustrades are also multiples of nine. If you stand in the centre of the upper terrace and say something, the sound bounces off the marble balustrades, making your voice sound louder (by nine times?).

Echo Wall

Just north of the altar, surrounding the Imperial Vault of Heaven, is **Echo Wall** (回音壁; Huíyīn Bì; Map p292), 65m in diameter. Its form has unusual acoustic properties, enabling a whisper to travel clearly from one end to the other (unless a tour group or a loudmouth with a mobile phone gets in the way). In the courtyard are the **Triple-Sounds Stones** (三音石; Sānyīn Shí). It is said that if you clap or shout while standing on the stones, the sound is echoed once from the first stone, twice from the second stone and thrice from the third stone. Queues can get long here.

Imperial Vault of Heaven

The octagonal **Imperial Vault of Heaven** (皇穹宇; Huáng Qióng Yǔ; Map p292) was built at the same time as the Round Altar, and is structured along the same lines as the older Hall of Prayer for Good Harvests. The vault once contained spirit tablets used in the winter solstice ceremony. Behind the Imperial Vault of Heaven stands the Nine Dragon Juniper, a hoary tree with a trunk of sinewy and coiling knots. Proceeding north from the Imperial Vault is a walkway called the **Red Stairway Bridge** (丹陛桥; Dānbì Qiáo; Map p292), leading to the Hall of Prayer for Good Harvests.

Hall of Prayer for Good Harvests

The crowning structure of the whole complex is the **Hall of Prayer for Good Harvests** (祈年殿; Qínián

THE WINTER SOLSTICE CEREMONY

The emperor, the Son of Heaven (天子; Tiānzǐ), visited the Temple of Heaven twice a year, but the most important ceremony was performed just before the winter solstice. The emperor and his enormous entourage passed down Qianmen Dajie in total silence to the Imperial Vault of Heaven. Commoners were not permitted to view the ceremony and remained cloistered indoors. The procession included elephant and horse chariots and long lines of lancers, nobles, officials and musicians dressed in their finest. The imperial 12m-long sedan was almost 3m wide and employed 10 bearers. The next day the emperor waited in a yellow silk tent at the southern gate while officials moved the sacred tablets to the Round Altar, where prayers and sacrificial rituals took place. It was thought that this ritual decided the nation's future; hence a hitch in any part of the proceedings was regarded as a bad omen.

The last person to attempt the ritual was Yuan Shikai, who harboured unfulfilled ambitions of becoming emperor, in 1914.

LOCATION, LOCATION, LOCATION

Building Běijīng's principal shrine in the heart of the former Chóngwén district, a traditionally down-at-heel, working-class neighbourhood outside the walls of the Imperial City, might seem unusual at first, especially as the vast majority of the capital's other major temples are located further north. But Chóngwén lies in the south, with an aspect facing the sun and indicative of *yáng* (the male and positive principle). Blessed with such positive *fēngshuǐ* (geomancy; literally 'wind and water'), it is not surprising that the Temple of Heaven was sited here.

Diàn; Map p292; admission ¥20), magnificently mounted on a three-tiered marble terrace and capped with a triple-eaved umbrella roof of purplish-blue tiles. Built in 1420, it was burnt to cinders in 1889 and heads rolled in apportioning blame (although lightning was the most likely cause). A faithful reproduction based on Ming architectural methods was erected the following year, the builders choosing Oregon fir for the support pillars, as explained by Lucian S Kirtland in *Finding the Worthwhile in the Orient* (1926):

When it was desired to rebuild the temple, and the Manchus were determined to copy in detail the building which had been destroyed, it was found that China's forests were bereft of timbers which could uphold the heavy tiled roof. After much argument with themselves, the necromancers of the court finally decided that pine logs from the forests of Oregon would constitute proper feng-shui. This decision very happily corresponded with the best engineering advice, and the New World furnished the pillars which you now see.

The four central pillars symbolise the seasons, the 12 in the next ring denote the months of the year, and the 12 outer ones represent the day, broken into 12 'watches'. Embedded in the ceiling is a carved dragon, a symbol of royalty. The patterning, carving and gilt decoration of this ceiling and its swirl of colour are a dizzying sight.

All this is made more amazing by the fact that the wooden pillars ingeniously support the ceiling without nails or cement – quite an accomplishment for a building 38m high and 30m in diameter.

Other Buildings

With a green-tiled two-tier roof, the **Animal Killing Pavilion** (Zǎishēng Tíng; Map p292) was the venue for the slaughter of sacrificial oxen, sheep, deer and other animals. Today it stands locked and passive but can be admired from the outside. Stretching out from here runs the **Long Corridor** (Cháng Láng; Map p292) where Chinese crowds sit out and deal cards, listen to the radio, play keyboards, and practise Peking opera, dance moves and hacky-sack. Sacrificial music was rehearsed at the **Divine Music Administration** (Shényuè Shǔ; Map p292) in the west of the park, while wild cats live in the dry moat of the green-tiled **Fasting Palace** (Zhāi Gōng; Map p292).

The Park

There are around 4000 ancient, knotted cypresses (some 800 years old, their branches propped up on poles) providing much-needed shade. The parkland itself is typical of Chinese parks, with the imperfections and wild irregularity of nature largely eliminated and the harmonising hand of humans accentuated in its obsessively straight lines and regular arrangements. The resulting order, balance and harmony has a haunting but slightly claustrophobic beauty.

⊙ SIGHTS

TEMPLE OF HEAVEN PARK   PARK

See p106.

BĚIJĪNG NATURAL
HISTORY MUSEUM   MUSEUM

Map p292 (北京自然博物馆; Běijīng Zìrán Bówùguǎn; ☑6702 7702; 126 Tianqiao Nandajie; admission ¥10; ◷9am-5pm Tue-Sun, last entry 4pm; ⒮Qianmen or Tiantandongmen) The main entrance to this overblown, creeper-laden museum is hung with portraits of the great natural historians, including Darwin and Linnaeus. The contents range from dinosaur fossils and skeletons, including a *Mamenchisaurus jingyanensis* (a vast sauropod that once roamed China) to creepy-crawlies, an aquarium with Nemo-esque clown fish and an exhibition on the origins of life on earth.

MING CITY WALL RUINS PARK   CITY WALLS

Map p292 (明城墙遗址公园; Míng Chéng-qiáng Yízhǐ Gōngyuán; Chongwenmen Dongdajie; ◷24hr; ⒮Chongwenmen) The city wall, levelled in the 1950s to facilitate transport and blot out the grandeur of earlier dynasties, is perhaps Běijīng's most conspicuous chunk of lost heritage. As modern-day Nánjīng in Jiāngsū province proves, modern Chinese cities can still grow without having to rip their city walls down. This last slice of the Ming Inner City Wall (originally 40km in length) has been restored and runs along the length of the northern flank of Chongwenmen Dongdajie, attached to a slender strip of park.

The wall stretches from the former site of **Chóngwén Mén** (崇文门; Chóngwén Gate), one of the nine gates of the Inner City Wall, to the Southeast Corner Watchtower and then turns north for a short distance along Jianguomen Nandajie to Beijingzhan Dongjie. Chóngwén Mén was also called Shuì Mén (税门; Tax Gate) as the capital tax bureau lay just outside the gate. You can walk the park's length, taking in its higgledy-piggledy contours and the interior layers of stone in parts of the wall that have collapsed. The restored sections run for just over 2km, rising to a height of around 15m and interrupted every 80m with buttresses extending to a maximum depth of 39m. The most interesting sections of wall are those closer to their original and more dilapidated state and some of the bricks come complete with bullet holes.

SOUTHEAST CORNER
WATCHTOWER &
RED GATE GALLERY   WATCHTOWER, GALLERY

Map p292 (东南角楼、红门画廊; Dōngnán Jiǎolóu & Hóngmén Huàláng; ☑6527 0574; adult ¥10; ◷8am-5.30pm; ⒮Jianguomen or Chongwenmen) This splendid fortification, with a green-tiled, twin-eaved roof rising up imperiously south of the Ancient Observatory, dates back to the Ming dynasty. Clamber up the steps for views alongside camera-wielding Chinese trainspotters eagerly awaiting rolling stock grinding in and out of Běijīng Train Station. As you mount the battlements, two forlorn stumps of flag abutments and a cannon or two can be seen, but really worth hunting out are the **signatures** etched in the walls by allied forces during the 1900 Boxer Rebellion (p211). You can make out the name of a certain P Foot; 'USA' is also scrawled on the brickwork. The international composition of the eight-nation force that relieved Běijīng in 1900 is noted in names such as André, Stickel and what appears to be a name in Cyrillic. One brick records the date 'Dec 16 1900'. Allied forces overwhelmed the redoubt after a lengthy engagement. Note the drainage channels poking out of the wall along its length. You can reach the watchtower from the west through the **Railway Arch**, which was built for the first railway that ran around Běijīng.

The watchtower is punctured with 144 archers' windows, and attached to it is a 100m section of the original Inner City Wall, beyond which stretches the restored **Ming City Wall**, extending all the way to Chōngwénmén and north to Beijingzhan Dongjie. Inside the highly impressive interior is some staggering carpentry: huge red pillars that are topped with solid beams surge upwards. The 1st floor is home to the **Red Gate Gallery** (Map p292; ☑6525 1005; www.redgategallery.com; admission free; ◷9am-5pm), one of Běijīng's long-established modern art galleries; the 2nd-floor gallery has a fascinating photographic exhibition on the old gates of Běijīng, while the 3rd-floor gallery contains more paintings. Say you're visiting the Red Gate Gallery and the ¥10 entry fee to the watchtower will be waived.

BĚIJĪNG RAILWAY MUSEUM   MUSEUM

Map p292 (北京铁路博物馆; Běijīng Tiělù Bówùguǎn; ☑6705 1638; 2a Qianmen Dongdajie; 前门东大街2a号; admission ¥20; ◷9am-5pm Tue-Sun; ⒮Qianmen) Located in the historic former Qiánmén Railway Station, which once connected Běijīng to Tiānjīn, this museum offers an engaging history of the development of the capital and China's railway system, with plenty of photos and models. Its size, though, means it doesn't have many actual trains. But there is a life-size model of the cab of one of China's new high-speed trains which you can clamber into (¥10). Hard-core trainspotters should make tracks for the **China Railway Museum** on the far northeastern outskirts of Běijīng, which is vast and has far more loco action.

BĚIJĪNG PLANNING EXHIBITION HALL
MUSEUM

Map p292 (北京市规划展览馆; Běijīngshì Guīhuà Zhǎnlǎnguǎn; ☑6701 7074; 20 Qianmen Dongdajie; admission ¥30; ◎9am-5pm Tue-Sun; ⑤Qianmen) It doesn't see much foot traffic, but a lot of thought has gone into making this modern museum a visitor-friendly experience. True, it strains every sinew to present Běijīng's gut-wrenching, *hútòng*-felling metamorphosis in the best possible light but the 3rd floor houses a fantastic, giant scale model of the capital mounted on a series of even bigger satellite photos; a great way to get a perspective on the city. There's also a scale model of the Forbidden City and 3-D films touting the Běijīng of the future.

LOCAL KNOWLEDGE

FROM CITY GATE TO SUBWAY STOP

The names of the subway stations of Qianmen, Chongwenmen and Jianguomen recall some of the Tartar City Wall's vast and imposing gates, which divided the Imperial City from the Chinese city beyond it. Today, Front Gate and the Southeast Corner Watchtower to the southeast are the only reminders of that wall. The road looping south from Jianguomen Station, following the line of the city moat, marks the outline of the levelled Chinese City Wall, whose gates (*mén*) survive only in street names, such as Guangqumen Nanbinhe Lu, Zuo'anmen Xibinhe Lu and Yongdingmen Dongbinhe Lu. Vestiges of this wall can still be seen at the Ming City Wall Ruins Park.

QIANMEN DAJIE
HISTORIC STREET

Map p292 (前门大街; ⑤Qianmen) Restored to resemble a late-Qing-dynasty street scene and wildly popular with domestic visitors, who come to window-shop and eat and drink at the many (overpriced) food stalls, this ancient street (once known as Zhengyangmen Dajie, or Facing the Sun Gate Street) is something of a tourist theme park now. That said, there are some silk stores worth popping into, and the rebuilt Qiánmén Decorative Arch (the original was torn down in the 1950s) looks handsome.

✖ EATING

TOP CHOICE MAISON BOULUD
FRENCH $$$

Map p292 (布鲁宫; Bùlǔ Gōng; ☑6559 9200; 23 Qianmen Dongdajie, 前门东大街23号; mains from ¥238; ◎lunch & dinner; ⊕🅿; ⑤Qianmen) Nothing symbolises the dramatic changes that Běijīng's dining scene has undergone in recent years more than this outpost of chef Daniel Boulud's empire. Located in part of the restored Legation Quarter, which was the home of embassies in pre–Cultural Revolution days, the restaurant's imposing facade gives way to a spacious, smoke-free dining room that allows for real privacy (a rarity in Běijīng restaurants) while the service is as good as it gets in the capital. The French-inspired food is predictably fine, with the menu and ingredients changing every couple of months to reflect the season. If you're not on the company credit card, the four-course lunch menu (¥198) is a very decent deal for food of this quality. Alternatively, the bar is a good place for a cocktail (from ¥70) if you just want to sample the ambience.

TOP CHOICE LOST HEAVEN
CHINESE YÚNNÁN $$$

Map p292 (花马天堂; Huāmǎ Tiāntáng; ☑8516 2698; 23 Qianmen Dongdajie, 前门东大街23号; dishes from ¥40; ◎lunch & dinner; ⊕🅿; ⑤Qianmen) The latest addition to the restaurants clustered in this former section of the Legation Quarter is the Běijīng branch of this famed Shànghǎi restaurant. It specialises in the folk cuisine of Yúnnán province and, if the spices have been toned down somewhat, then the flavours remain subtle and light and are guaranteed to transport you to China's balmy southwest. Try the Dai-style roast pork in banana leaf (¥68), or one of the many splendid salads, such as the

DUCK DEVOTION

Zhang Liqun, owner of the Lìqún Roast Duck Restaurant, is 63 years old and has spent 30 years of his life serving up duck in Běijīng.

How did you come to be a roast duck chef? Even though I'm a third-generation Beijinger, my first job was as a farmer. I left school in 1968, during the Cultural Revolution, and was sent to work on a farm in Shǎnxī. After I came back to Běijīng, I just felt an urge to cook delicious food. I had a friend who worked at Quán-jùdé Roast Duck Restaurant and he helped me get a job there in 1982.

Does it take a long time to learn how to cook Peking duck? I started at the bottom in the kitchen. First you study everything about ducks: how they should be fed and slaughtered, although cooks don't kill the ducks themselves anymore. Then you learn about all the ingredients that go into making it taste so good. Finally, you learn how to cook the bird. It takes about three years to learn how to cook it properly. It's difficult to be a good roast duck chef. You have to be very nimble with your fingers.

Why did you open your own place? By 1992 I was in charge of opening new branches of Quánjùdé and wasn't cooking anymore, so I had a lot of free time and decided to open my own restaurant. Quánjùdé didn't mind; it's a much bigger company. Back then, we sold the duck for ¥30 each and it was the same quality as it is now.

What's the secret of your restaurant's success? It's because we cook the duck in the traditional way and after 20 years we won't change that. Normally, we cook 50 ducks a day. On public holidays and at Chinese New Year, we'll go through 100 ducks in a day.

Do you still cook the duck yourself? Not unless it's a very busy time. I sometimes cook at home, but not roast duck because I see enough of that in the restaurant.

marinated beef salad and peppers or the Burmese tea leaves salad. All the dishes on the extensive menu are enticing, and there's an elegant outside area and attentive service. Book ahead.

TOP CHOICE **LÌQÚN ROAST DUCK RESTAURANT** PEKING DUCK **$$$**

Map p292 (利群烤鸭店; Lìqún Kǎoyādiàn; ☑6705 5578, 6702 5681; 11 Beixiangfeng Hutong, 前门东大街正义路南口北翔凤胡同11号; roast duck ¥220; ◷lunch & dinner; ☺⬛; Ⓢ Qianmen) Buried away in east Qiánmén, the approach to this compact courtyard restaurant is through a maze of crumbling *hútòng* that have somehow survived total demolition; look for the signs pointing the way. If that doesn't inspire confidence, reassure yourself with the thought that the delectable duck on offer here is so in demand that it's essential to call ahead to reserve both a bird and a table (otherwise, turn up off-peak and be prepared to wait an hour). Inside, it's a little tatty (no prizes for the toilets) and chaotic, but walk by the ovens with their rows of ducks on hooks, squeeze past the scurrying, harried waiters and then sit back and enjoy some of the finest duck in town.

QIÁNMÉN QUÁNJÙDÉ ROAST DUCK RESTAURANT PEKING DUCK **$$$**

Map p292 (前门全聚德烤鸭店; Qiánmén Quánjùdé Kǎoyādiàn; ☑6511 2418, 6701 1379; 30 Qianmen Dajie, 前门大街30号; roast duck ¥228; ◷lunch & dinner; ⬛; Ⓢ Qianmen) The most popular branch of Běijīng's most famous destination for duck – check out the photos of everyone from Fidel Castro to Zhang Yimou. This place is geared to the tourist hordes (both domestic and foreign). A consequence of the crowds is that service can be peremptory, while the huge two-floor venue lacks atmosphere. But the duck, while not the best in town, is pretty good, and roasted in ovens fired by fruit-tree wood. That means the birds have a unique fragrance, as well as being juicy, if slightly fatty.

CAPITAL M MEDITERRANEAN **$$$**

Map p292 (M餐厅; M Cāntīng; ☑6702 2727; 3rd fl, 2 Qianmen Dajie, 前门步行街2号; mains from ¥188; ◷lunch & dinner; ☺⬛; Ⓢ Qianmen) The terrace of this swish but relaxed restaurant, whose chef works with the cuisines of North Africa, Greece, and southern Italy and France, offers fine views over Qiánmén Gate and Tiān'ānmén Square. The large, light-filled dining room is almost as good a place to enjoy the nicely presented,

LOCAL KNOWLEDGE

THE EVOLUTION OF 23 QIANMEN DONGDAJIE

Known today for its high-class restaurants and as the site of exclusive fashion shows, 23 Qianmen Dongdajie is host to far more than just top chefs and supermodels. The elegant buildings in a neo-classical style set around a quadrangle have a unique history, having been built in 1903 to house the US embassy. The original American legation was located on Dongjiaomin Xiang and was badly damaged during the 1900 Boxer Rebellion when it, and other foreign embassies, came under siege for months.

The address stayed as the US embassy until 1949 and the communist takeover of China, when the American diplomats decamped to Taiwan. The next resident was the Dalai Lama; it was his official Běijīng home until he too fled China for India in 1959. Later, the buildings became part of the Chinese foreign ministry and were the venue for secret talks between the US and China in 1971 that led to President Nixon's historic visit to China the next year, and the beginning of the normalisation of relations between Běijīng and Washington.

unfussy menu of Mediterranean favourites. We like the tagines and king prawns done in a Catalan style with chorizo and saffron rice, but the steaks and salmon are equally enjoyable. The lunch menu is cheaper, with mains from ¥128, and there's a weekend lunch deal with two courses for ¥248. It's down the first turning on the left at the beginning of Qianmen Dajie; look for the 'M' hanging off the side of the building. It's advisable to reserve here.

BIÀNYÍFĀNG PEKING DUCK $$$

Map p292 (便宜坊烤鸭店; Biànyífāng Kǎoyādiàn; ☎6711 2244; 3rd fl, China New World Shopping Mall, 5 Chongwenmenwai Dajie, 崇文门外大街5号新世界商场二期三层; roast duck ¥198; ⏲lunch & dinner; 🚭📖; [S]Chongwenmen) Less touristy than the other duck options in the area, Biànyífāng claims to be the original Peking duck restaurant – it cites a heritage that dates back to the reign of the Qing emperor Xianfeng. The birds here are roasted in the *mènlú* style (in a closed oven, as opposed to a half-open one where the duck hangs to cook) and the meat is nice and tender. A half bird is ¥110 with all the trimmings and the menu also offers duck liver, heart and feet dishes. In fact, just about any part of the duck that is edible is available here. It's nonsmoking throughout.

DŪYĪCHÙ CHINESE DUMPLINGS $$

Map p292 (都一处; ☎6702 1555; 38 Qianmen Dajie, 前门大街38号; dishes from ¥26; ⏲9am-9pm; 📖; [S]Qianmen) Now back on the newly spiffy street where it started business during the mid-Qing dynasty, Dūyīchù specialises in the delicate dumplings called *shāomài*. The shrimp-and-leek (¥42) and veggie (¥40) ones are especially good, and are presented very nicely, but they also do a nice line in seasonal variations, such as sweet corn and bean (¥42) in the summer, or beef and yam (¥48) in the winter. There are other non-dumpling dishes on the menu too. Be prepared to queue at weekends.

WEDOMÉ CAFE $

Map p292 (味多美; Wèiduōměi; ☎6715 9205; 12 Tiyuguan Lu, 体育馆路12号; coffee & tea from ¥25; ⏲9am-10.30pm; 🚭; [S]Tiantandongmen) If you're looking for a place to rest your legs after shopping or sightseeing in the area, then retreat to the 2nd floor of this cafe opposite the east gate of the Temple of Heaven Park. It offers a wide selection of coffee, tea and juices, as well as cakes and sandwiches.

☆ ENTERTAINMENT

RED THEATRE ACROBATICS

Map p292 (红剧场; Hóng Jùchǎng; ☎6714 8691, 6714 2473; 44 Xingfu Dajie, 幸福大街44号; tickets ¥180-680; ⏲performances 5.15pm & 7.30pm; [S]Tiantandongmen) The daily show here is *The Legend of Kung Fu* and it follows one boy's journey to becoming a warrior monk. Slick, high-energy fight scenes are interspersed with more soulful dance sequences, as well as plenty of 'how do they do that' balancing on spears and other body-defying acts. It's easy to find the theatre: look for the all-red exterior set back from the road.

SHOPPING

HÓNGQIÁO (PEARL) MARKET MARKET

Map p292 (红桥市场; Hóngqiáo Shìchǎng; ☎6711 7429; 36 Hongqiao Lu, 红桥路36号; 🕑9am-7pm; [S]Tiantandongmen) Besides a cosmos of clutter (shoes, clothing, electronics and lots and lots of handbags), Hóngqiáo is home to more pearls than the South Sea. The range is huge (freshwater, seawater, white and black pearls) and prices vary incredibly depending on quality. The 3rd floor has the cheaper ones, mostly sourced from Zhèjiāng province, as well as standard jewellery. The better-quality, pricier pearls can be found on the far more hushed 4th and 5th floors, where there's a roof terrace that offers an excellent view of the Temple of Heaven. Prices are generally high, while the vendors, who all speak some English, are canny bargainers. If you have kids in tow, don't miss **Toys City** (Hóngqiáo Tiānlè Wánjù Shìchǎng; 红桥天乐玩具市场; Map p292; 🕑8.30am-7pm) in the building behind, stuffed to the gills with soft toys, cars, model kits, Wii sets, PlayStations and computer games.

SPORTS & ACTIVITIES

NTSC TENNIS CLUB TENNIS

Map p292 (国家体育总局训练局网球俱乐部; Guójiā Tǐyù Zǒngjú Xùnliànjú Wǎngqiú Jùlèbù; ☎6715 2532; 50 Tiantan Donglu, 天坛东路50号; nonmembers per hr ¥120-200; 🕑10am-10pm Mon-Fri, 8am-8pm Sat, 9am-9pm Sun; [S]Tiantandongmen) Tennis *(wǎng qiú)* is an increasingly popular sport in Běijīng, so phone in advance to book one of the inside courts here.

Běihǎi Park & Xīchéng North

Neighbourhood Top Five

❶ Once reserved for emperors only, **Běihǎi Park** (p116) is truly a park with a difference. Dominated by a large lake, dotted with temples and with a fascinating 1000-year-long history, it's one of the city's premier spots to escape the urban sprawl.

❷ Sedate during the day, raucous at night, the **Hòuhǎi lakes** (p118) are one of Běijīng's great playgrounds.

❸ Spend a morning at the impressive **Capital Museum** (p119) to understand the evolution of this great city.

❹ Enjoy a show at the **National Centre for the Performing Arts** (p123), or just stare open-mouthed at the building itself.

❺ Shop like a Beijinger at **77th Street** (p126), Xīdān's unique underground mall.

For more detail of this area see Map p294 ➡

Explore: Běihǎi Park & Xīchéng North

The majority of the Imperial City was in this part of Xīchéng (西城; literally 'West City'), lending it a regal grandeur that survives to this day. Less visited than Dōngchéng to the east, but equally impregnated with ancient temples and charming *hútòng* (narrow alleyways), it's one of the most worthwhile neighbourhoods to visit in all Běijīng.

Any tour has to start at the lakes that dominate the eastern part of the district. Take in Běihǎi Park first, perhaps spending an hour or more floating around its lake, before striking out through the park's north gate to take in the sights and *hútòng* scattered around Qiánhǎi, Hòuhǎi and Xīhǎi Lakes, collectively known as either 'Shíchàhǎi' or more commonly just 'Hòuhǎi'. Once night falls, eat at one of the many restaurants close to the lakes and then join the crowds promenading around them, stopping in for a drink at the many bars and cafes that line their shores.

A second day here is more or less an imperative. Visit the Capital Museum, Běijīng's finest, in the morning for local history and traditions. Then you're spoiled for choice. You could dive into the fascinating, still traditional *hútòng* that cut through the centre of the neighbourhood, where temples and courtyard museums await. Alternatively, peek into the grandiose Great Hall of the People or hit the busy shopping area of Xīdān. And in the evening, there's a wealth of venues to catch everything from jazz to classical music and Peking opera.

Local Life

➡ **Fly a Kite** Běihǎi Park and the neighbouring Hòuhǎi lakes are prime kite-flying territory. Visit the Three Stone Kite Shop (p126) to kit yourself out.

➡ **Hútòng** The alleyways and lanes here are far less commercial than any others in the city and a great introduction to Běijīng's tremendous street life.

➡ **Winter Sports** When winter clamps the Hòuhǎi lakes in its icy embrace, do as Beijingers do and strap on a pair of ice skates (you can hire them by the lakes).

Getting There & Away

➡ **Subway** Line 1 cuts across the south of the district, Line 2 circles it, while Line 4 runs north–south and the new Line 6 travels west–east across it.

➡ **Bus** Bus 1 runs along Xichang'an Jie, Fuxingmennei Dajie and Fuxingmenwai Dajie, taking you to Capital Museum. Bus 22 takes you from Tiān'ānmén West to Xīdān and then north to Xīnjiēkou.

Lonely Planet's Top Tip

Come nightfall, the Hòuhǎi lakes become a madhouse of milling crowds and bar touts trying to entice you into their overpriced hostelries. Avoid both by slipping down the *hútòng* that run off the lakeshore, where you'll find far more amenable bars and cafes. The lanes running west from Silver Ingot Bridge and the west shore of Qiánhǎi Lake are a good place to start.

✖ Best Places to Eat

➡ 4Corners (p121)
➡ Běipíngjū (p123)
➡ Kǒng Yǐjǐ (p121)
➡ Café Sambal (p93)
➡ Yuèlù Shānwū (p121)

For reviews, see p121 ➡

⊙ Best Places for Entertainment

➡ East Shore Jazz Café (p123)
➡ National Centre for the Performing Arts (p123)
➡ Mei Langfang Grand Theatre (p123)

For reviews, see p123 ➡

🔒 Best Places to Shop

➡ Three Stone Kite Shop (p126)
➡ 77th Street (p126)
➡ Běijīng Zoo Market (p126)

For reviews, see p126 ➡

BĚIHǍI PARK & XĪCHÉNG NORTH

TOP SIGHTS
BĚIHǍI PARK

With an extraordinary history as the former palace of the great Mongol emperor Kublai Khan, and back garden for the subsequent Yuan dynasty emperors, Běihǎi Park (北海公园) is the principal oasis for Beijingers in this part of town. With the tranquil lake of Běihǎi (literally 'North Sea') at its centre, and temples, pavilions and spirit walls scattered around it, the park offers visitors a rare chance in Běijīng to combine sightseeing with fun, whether it's mucking around in a boat, having a picnic or just watching the dancing, taichi and the parade of humanity that passes through.

You can enter the park by its southern gate on Wenjin Jie, or the northern gate on Di'anmen Xidajie. But if you're planning to move onto the Hòuhǎi lakes later, it makes sense to enter from the south and exit by the **north gate**.

Jade Islet

Made out of the heaped earth scooped out to create Běihǎi Lake itself, which some attribute to Kublai Khan, and dominated by the 36m-high **White Dagoba**, which was originally constructed in 1651 for a visit by the Dalai Lama and then rebuilt in 1741 after being destroyed in an earthquake, Jade Islet sits in the south-eastern corner of the lake. You can reach it by a land bridge close to the southern entrance, or catch a boat (¥10) from the northwestern shore if you come in by the north gate. You can also hire pedalos (¥80 per hour, ¥200 deposit) from here as well.

Yongan Temple

The principal site on **Jade Islet** is this impressive temple (included in the through ticket). Enter through the Hall of the Heavenly Kings (Tiānwáng Diàn), past the Drum and Bell Towers to the Hall of the Wheel of the Law (Fǎlún Diàn), with its central effigy of Sakya-

DON'T MISS

➡ Yongan Temple
➡ Xītiān Fànjìng

PRACTICALITIES

➡ 北海公园; Běihǎi Gōngyuán
➡ Map p294
➡ ☑ 6403 1102
➡ ticket park/through ticket Apr-Oct ¥10/20, Nov-Mar ¥5/15
➡ ⏰ 9am-9pm, sights 9am-5pm
➡ Ⓢ Xisi or Nanluogu Xiang

muni and flanked by Bodhisattvas and 18 *luóhàn* (Buddhists, especially monks, who achieved enlightenment and passed to nirvana at death). At the rear of the temple you will find a bamboo grove and quite a steep flight of steps up through a decorative archway, which is emblazoned with the characters 'Lóng Guāng' (龙光) on one side and 'Zǐzhào' (紫照) on the other side. Head up more steps to the Zhèngjué Hall (Zhèngjué Diàn), which contains a statue of Milefo and Weituo.

Pǔ'ān Hall (Pǔ'ān Diàn) the next hall, houses a statue of Tsongkhapa, who was the founder of the Yellow Hat sect of Tibetan Buddhism, flanked by statues of the fifth Dalai Lama and the Panchen Lama. Eight golden effigies on either flank include tantric statues and the goddess Heinümu, adorned with a necklace of skulls. The final flight of steep steps brings you to the **White Dagoba**.

Xītiān Fànjìng

Located on the lake's northern shore, this is one of the most interesting temples in all Běijīng (admission is included in the through ticket). The first hall, the Hall of the Heavenly Kings, takes you past Mílèfó, Weituo and the four Heavenly Kings.

The **Dàcízhēnrú Hall** (Dàcízhēnrú Diàn) dates back to the Ming dynasty and contains three huge statues of Sakyamuni, the Amithaba Buddha and Yaoshi Fo (Medicine Buddha). Sadly, the golden statue of Guanyin at the rear is not accessible. The hall is supported by huge wooden pillars (which are called *nánmù*), and you can still make out where the original stone pillars once existed. At the very rear of the temple are a glazed pavilion and a huge hall that are both unfortunately out of bounds.

The nearby **Nine Dragon Screen** (Jiǔlóng Bì; admission is included in the through ticket), a 5m-high and 27m-long spirit wall, is a glimmering stretch of coloured glazed tiles.

THE PALACE OF THE GREAT KHAN

The grandson of the even more dominant Genghis Khan, Kublai Khan conquered China and established the Yuán dynasty in 1271. He chose what is now Běihǎi Park as the site of his palace. All that remains of his former home is a large jar made of green jade dating from 1265 in the **Round City** (Tuán Chéng) near the park's southern entrance. Sadly, the Round City, which also houses the **Chéngguāng Hall** (Chéngguāng Diàn), where a white jade statue of Sakyamuni from Myanmar can be found, was closed at the time of writing. The park, though, has been associated with the centre of power of China since the 10th century, when it was laid out as an imperial garden. Even now, it remains as close to the nerve centre of the country as you are likely to get.

Less than a mile to the south is Zhōngnánhǎi, the closely guarded compound where China's president and the other most senior Chinese Communist Party (CCP) officials reside in cosy proximity to each other.

BĚIHǍI PARK & XĪCHÉNG NORTH

TOP SIGHTS
BĚIHǍI PARK

⊙ SIGHTS

BĚIHĂI PARK
PARK

See p116.

HÒUHĂI LAKES
LAKES

Map p294 (后海; Hòuhǎi; S Shichahai, Nanluogu Xiang or Jishuitan) Also known as Shíchàhǎi (什刹海) but mostly just referred to collectively as 'Hòuhǎi', the Hòuhǎi lakes are compromised of three lakes: Qiánhǎi (Front Lake), Hòuhǎi (Back Lake) and Xīhǎi (West Lake), two of which (Qiánhǎi and Hòuhǎi) are linked. Together they are one of the capital's favourite outdoor spots, heaving with locals and out-of-towners in the summer especially, and provide great people-spotting action.

During the day, senior citizens meander along, use the exercise machines scattered along the lakeshore, fish, fly kites or just sit and chew the fat. At night, the area turns into one of the more popular nightlife areas, as the restaurants, bars and cafes that surround the lakes spring into life. Many of the bars have a cookie-cutter quality though, the drinks are more expensive than elsewhere, and the lakes become a mass of pedalos circling round and round.

But it's easy enough to escape the crowds, by exploring the many *hútòng* that run both east and west of the lakes, and Hòuhǎi remains a fine spot to kick back. It's particularly good to cycle around and numerous places by the lakeshores hire out bikes by the hour (¥10 per hour, ¥200 deposit). There are many spots to rent pedalos too (¥80 per hour, ¥300 deposit), if you want to take to the water (some locals swim in the lakes, but we wouldn't advise that).

The lakes look majestic in the winter, when they freeze over and become the best place in Běijīng to ice skate. Local vendors appear magically at this time of year, with all the gear you'll need.

PRINCE GONG'S RESIDENCE
HISTORIC COURTYARD HOME

Map p294 (恭王府; Gōngwáng Fǔ; ☑8328 8149; 14 Liuyin Jie; adult ¥40, tours incl opera performance & tea ceremony ¥70; ⊙7.30am-4.30pm Mar-Oct, 8am-4pm Nov-Mar; S Ping'anli) Reputed to be the model for the mansion in Cao Xueqin's 18th-century classic *Dream of the Red Mansions,* the residence is one of Běijīng's largest private residential compounds. It remains one of the capital's more attractive retreats, decorated with rockeries, plants,

pools, pavilions and elaborately carved gateways, although it can get very crowded with tour groups. Performances of Peking opera (p233) are held in the Qing-dynasty **Grand Opera House** (Map p294; ☑6618 6628; adult Y80-120; ⊙7.30-8.40pm Mar-Oct; S Ping'anli) in the east of the grounds.

FORMER FŮRÉN UNIVERSITY
HISTORIC BUILDING

Map p294 (原辅仁大学; Yuán Fǔrén Dàxué; I Dingfu Jie; S Ping'anli) This magnificent building on Dingfu Jie, just around the corner from Prince Gong's Residence, once housed Fǔrén University, founded by the Benedictine order in 1925. Today it belongs to Běijīng Normal University. On the wall to the west of the main door is a fading quality slogan from the Cultural Revolution, which poetically intones: 伟大的领袖毛主席是我们心中最红最红的红太阳 – 'The mighty leader Chairman Mao is the reddest, reddest of red suns in our heart'. On the wall on the other side of the door is another lengthy slogan that has been largely blotted out.

SONG QINGLING FORMER RESIDENCE
MUSEUM

Map p294 (宋庆龄故居; Sòng Qìnglíng Gùjū; ☑6402 3195; 46 Beiheyan Lu; adult ¥20; ⊙9am-5pm; S Jishuitan) Madam Sòng is lovingly venerated by the Chinese as the wife of Sun Yatsen, founder of the Republic of China. Set in a lovely garden, her house, the former home of the father of Puyi (China's last emperor), is rather dormant; on display are personal items, pictures, clothing and books. But the building to the side houses a very comprehensive exhibition on Madam Sòng's fascinating life, including the car given to her by Stalin, which comes with good English captions. You can find the museum on the northern side of Hòuhǎi Lake and within reach of Prince Gong's residence.

MEI LANFANG FORMER RESIDENCE
MUSEUM

Map p294 (梅兰芳纪念馆; Méi Lánfāng Jìniàn Guǎn; ☑8322 3598; 9 Huguosi Jie; adult ¥10; ⊙9am-4pm Tue-Sun; S Ping'anli) Place of pilgrimage for Peking opera aficionados, this former *sìhéyuàn* (traditional courtyard house) of actor Mei Lanfang (1894–1961) is tucked away in a *hútòng* that's named after the nearby remains of Huguo Temple. Peking opera was popularised in the West by Mei Lanfang, who played *dàn* (female roles) and is said to have influenced Charlie

Chaplin. His former residence has been preserved as a museum, replete with costumes, furniture, opera programs and video presentations of his opera performances.

NATIONAL CENTRE FOR THE PERFORMING ARTS (NCPA) CONCERT HALL

Map p294 (国家大剧院; Guójiā Dājùyuàn; ☎6655 0000; admission ¥40; 🕘9am-5pm Tue-Sun; [S]Tian'anmen West) Critics have compared it to an egg, but it looks more like a massive mercury bead, an ultramodern missile silo or the futuristic lair of a James Bond villain. If aliens ever mustered above Běijīng, you can picture them speedily targeting the NCPA, sometimes also known as the National Grand Theatre, which rises like some huge reflective mushroom nosing up from the ground. Stand between the Great Hall of the People and the NCPA and measure, symbolically at least, how far China has come in the past 50 years. Despite protestations from designers that its round and square elements pay obeisance to traditional Chinese aesthetics, they're not fooling anyone: the NCPA is designed to embody the transglobal (transgalactic, perhaps) aspirations of contemporary China. While modernists love it to bits, traditionalists see it as a further kick in the teeth for 'old Peking'.

Examine the bulbous interior, including the titanic steel ribbing of interior bolsters (each of the 148 bolsters weighs 8 tonnes). Inside, you can tour the three halls, although individual ones are occasionally shut.

GREAT HALL OF THE PEOPLE PARLIAMENT

Map p294 (人民大会堂; Rénmín Dàhuìtáng; adult ¥30, bag deposit ¥2-5; 🕘8.30am-3pm (times vary); [S]Tian'anmen West) On the western side of Tiān'ānmén Square, on a site previously occupied by Taichang Temple, the Jinyiwei (Ming-dynasty secret service) and the Ministry of Justice, the Great Hall of the People is the venue of the legislature, the National People's Congress (NPC). The 1959 architecture is monolithic and intimidating, and a fitting symbol of China's remarkable political inertia. The tour parades visitors past a choice of 29 of its lifeless rooms named after the provinces of the Chinese universe. Also here is the banquet room where US president Richard Nixon dined in 1972, and the 10,000-seat auditorium with the familiar red star embedded in a galaxy of ceiling lights. The Great Hall of the People is closed to the public when the NPC is in session. The ticket office is down the south side of the building. Bags must be checked in but cameras are admitted.

CHINA NUMISMATIC MUSEUM MUSEUM

Map p294 (中国钱币博物馆; Zhōngguó Qiánbì Bówùguǎn; ☎6608 4178; 17 Xijiaomin Xiang; admission ¥10; 🕘9am-4pm Tue-Sun, closed when NPC in session; [S]Tian'anmen West) This intriguing three-floor museum follows the technology of money production in China, from the spade-shaped coins of the Spring and Autumn period to the coinage and paper currency of the modern day. Of particular interest are the top-floor samples of modern Chinese paper *renminbi*, from the pragmatic illustrations of the first series to the far more idealistic third series (1962) and the fourth series dating from 1987, still adorned with Mao's head.

[FREE] CAPITAL MUSEUM MUSEUM

(首都博物馆; Shǒudū Bówùguǎn; ☎6339 3339; www.capitalmuseum.org.cn; 16 Fuxingmenwai Dajie; 🕘9am-5pm Tue-Sun; [S]Muxidi) Behind the riveting good looks of the Capital Museum are some first-rate galleries, including a mesmerising collection of ancient Buddhist statues and a lavish exhibition of Chinese porcelain. There is also an interesting chronological history of Běijīng, an exhibition that is dedicated to cultural relics of Peking opera, a fascinating Běijīng Folk Customs exhibition, and displays of ancient bronzes, jade, calligraphy and paintings. Bring your passport for free entry.

WHITE CLOUD TEMPLE TAOIST TEMPLE

(白云观; Báiyún Guàn; ☎6346 3887; 9 Baiyunguan Jie; adult ¥10; 🕘8.30am-4.30pm; [S]Muxidi) White Cloud Temple, once the Taoist centre of northern China, was founded in AD 739, although most of the temple halls date from the Qing dynasty. It's a lively, huge and fascinating complex of shrines and courtyards, tended by Taoist monks with their hair gathered into topknots.

Near the temple entrance, worshippers rub a polished stone carving for good fortune. The halls at the temple, centre of operations for the Taoist Quanzhen School and abode of the China Taoist Association, are dedicated to a host of Taoist officials and marshals. The **Hall of the Jade Emperor** celebrates this most famous of Taoist deities, while Taoist housewives cluster earnestly at the **Hall to the God of Wealth** to divine their financial future. Depictions of the Taoist Hell festoon the walls of the **Shrine Hall for the Saviour Worthy**.

Drop by White Cloud Temple during the Spring Festival and you will be rewarded with the spectacle of a magnificent temple fair *(miàohuì)*. Worshippers funnel into the streets around the temple in their thousands, lured by artisans, street performers, *wǔshù* (martial arts) acts, craft workers, traders and a swarm of snack merchants.

To find the temple, walk south on Baiyun Lu, turn left into Baiyungguan Jie and it's about 50m up on the left.

XĪBIÀNMÉN WATCHTOWER — WATCHTOWER

Map p294 (西便门角楼; Xībiànmén Jiǎolóu; [S]Changchunjie) The counterpart of the Southeast Corner Watchtower, the Xibianmen Watchtower is not as impressive as its robust and better-known sibling, but you can climb up onto a section of the old city wall amid the roaring traffic.

SOUTH CATHEDRAL — CHURCH

Map p294 (南堂; Nántáng; 141 Qianmen Xidajie; 🕙Mass in Latin 6am Sun-Fri, in English 10am Sun; [S]Xuanwumen) Běijīng's South Cathedral was built on the site of the house of Jesuit missionary Matteo Ricci, who brought Catholicism to China. Since being completed in 1703, the church has been destroyed three times, including being burnt down in 1775, and endured a trashing by anti-Christian forces during the Boxer Rebellion in 1900. The church is today decorated with modern stained glass, fake marbling, red carpets, portraits of the Stations of the Cross and cream-coloured confessionals, while black bibles in Chinese lie stacked about and the occasional local nun makes an appearance. It's absolutely jammed on Christmas Eve and Good Friday.

MIÀOYĪNG TEMPLE WHITE DAGOBA — BUDDHIST TEMPLE

Map p294 (妙应寺白塔; Miàoyīng Sì Báitǎ; ☎6616 0211; 171 Fuchengmennei Dajie; adult ¥20; 🕙9am-5pm Tue-Sun; [S]Fuchengmen, then bus 13, 101, 102 or 103 to Baita Si) Towering over the surrounding *hútòng*, the Miàoyīng Temple slumbers beneath its distinctive chalk-white Yuán-dynasty pagoda, which was being refurbished at the time of writing. The highlight of a visit here is the temple's diverse collection of Buddhist statuary: pop into the Hall of the Great Enlightened One (大觉宝殿; Dàjué Bǎodiàn), which glitters splendidly with hundreds of Tibetan Buddhist effigies. In other halls resides a four-faced effigy of Guanyin (here called Parnashavari), as well as a trinity of the past, present and future Buddhas and a population of bronze *luóhàn* figures. After you finish here, exit the temple and wander the tangle of local alleyways for earthy shades of *hútòng* life.

[FREE] LU XUN MUSEUM — MUSEUM

Map p294 (鲁迅博物馆; Lǔ Xùn Bówùguǎn; ☎6616 4080; 19 Gongmenkou Ertiao; 🕙9am-4pm Tue-Sun; [S]Fuchengmen) Lu Xun (1881–1936) is often regarded as the father of modern Chinese literature. Born in Shàoxīng in Zhèjiāng province and buried in Shànghǎi, Lu Xun lived in Běijīng for over a decade. As a writer, Lu Xun, who first trained in medicine, articulated a deep yearning for reform by mercilessly exposing the foibles of the Chinese character in such tales as *Medicine* and *Diary of a Madman* (p226). The exhibits range from photos and manuscripts to personal effects.

BĚIJĪNG ZOO & BĚIJĪNG AQUARIUM — ZOO, AQUARIUM

(北京动物园、北京海洋馆; Běijīng Dòngwùyuán & Běijīng Hǎiyángguǎn; ☎6839 0274; www.bjzoo.com.cn; 137 Xizhimenwai Dajie; admission Apr-Oct ¥15, Nov-Mar ¥10, panda house ¥5 extra, zoo & aquarium adult/child ¥130/70; 🕙7.30am-6pm Apr-Oct, to 5pm Nov-Mar; [S]Běijīng Zoo) Although not as pleasant as Shànghǎi's green and wooded getaway, Běijīng Zoo is a relaxing spot for a wander among the trees, grass and willow-fringed lakes (it was once a royal garden), even if the creatures can be mere sideshows.

Zoologically speaking, the well-housed pandas are the prime diversions, especially if you are not en route to the Sìchuān wilds. The remaining menagerie remains cooped up in pitiful cages and enclosures, with the polar bears pinning their hopes on gaining admission to the excellent **Běijīng Aquarium** (☎6217 6655; adult/child ¥130/70; 🕙9am-5.30pm Apr-Oct, 10am-4.30pm Nov-Mar1) in the northeastern corner of the zoo. On view is an imaginative Amazon rainforest (complete with piranha), coral reefs, a shark aquarium and a marine mammal pavilion (which hosts lively aquatic animal displays). The ticket price to the aquarium includes entry to the zoo; you can buy this ticket at the zoo entrance.

BĚIJĪNG PLANETARIUM   PLANETARIUM

(北京天文馆; Běijīng Tiānwénguǎn; 138 Xizhimenwai Dajie; old/new bldg ¥15/10, Optical Planetarium ¥15, 4-D Theatre ¥30, Space Simulator ¥30, Digital Space Theatre ¥45; ⊙9.30am-4pm Wed-Sun; Ⓢ Běijīng Zoo) Across from the zoo, children will find something to marvel at among the telescopes, models of the planets and the solar system, and the variety of shows in the new building, even though the typical absence of thorough English captions can make full comprehension an astronomical task.

PALEOZOOLOGICAL
MUSEUM OF CHINA   MUSEUM

(中国古动物馆; Zhōngguó Gǔdòngwùguǎn; ☑8836 9210; 142 Xizhimenwai Dajie; admission ¥20; ⊙9am-4.30pm Tue-Sun; Ⓢ Běijīng Zoo) Located in a strange office block of a building (look for the dinosaur on the side), this houses the best collection of dinosaurs in Běijīng. Very few English captions, but young palaeontologists can gawp at skeletons of *Tyrannosaurus Rex* and *Tsintaosaurus* as well as *Mamenchisaurus*, Asia's biggest dino.

 **EATING**

TOP CHOICE 4CORNERS   VIETNAMESE $$

Map p294 (肆角餐吧; Sìjiǎo Cānbā; ☑6401 7797; www.these4corners.com; 27 Dashibei Hutong, 大石碑胡同27号; dishes from ¥34; ⊙11am-3am; ⊙🛜📱; Ⓢ Shichahai) A laid-back spot with a cosy outside area, 4Corners serves up a medley of zingy Vietnamese, and some Thai, dishes. The catfish in coconut (¥78) and hot and sour fish-head soup (¥45) both burst with the flavours of Southeast Asia – all lime and chilli – and there's a tremendous selection of spring rolls for those who just want to graze while imbibing one of its excellent martinis (¥40). There's live music some nights too. It's hidden down a *hútòng* just off Gulou Xidajie.

KǑNG YǏJǏ   CHINESE ZHÈJIĀNG $$

Map p294 (孔乙己酒店; ☑6618 4915; Deshengmennei Dajie, Shichahai, Hòuhǎi Nan'an, 德胜门内大街什刹海后海南岸; dishes from ¥28; ⊙lunch & dinner; Ⓢ Jishuitan) Shàoxīng

in Zhèjiāng province is famous as the birthplace of Lu Xun, the man who invented modern Chinese literature, and its eponymous, sherry-like wine. So it's entirely appropriate that this restaurant, which takes its name from an alcoholic character in one of Lu's stories, serves some dishes – such as drunken shrimp (醉虾; *zuìxiā*) and drunken chicken (醉鸡; *zuìjī*) – swimming in Shàoxīng wine. Rest assured it tastes better than *báijiǔ* (a white spirit). Also popular at this big and bustling place, with a fine outdoor area, at the northwestern edge of the Hòuhǎi lakes are the many alcohol-free pork and fish dishes, such as the very addictive *dōngpō ròu* (东坡肉). No English or picture menu; take a look at what other people are eating and point. Despite the address, the restaurant is actually by the Hòuhǎi lakeshore. To get here, turn down narrow Dongming Hútòng from Deshengmen Dajie and then right at the end of the lane.

YUÈLÙ SHĀNWŪ   CHINESE HÚNÁN $$

Map p294 (岳麓山屋; ☑6617 2696; Shichahai, 19a Qiánhǎi Xiyan, 什刹海前海西沿甲19号, 荷花市场内; dishes from ¥28; ⊙10.30am-1am; 📱; Ⓢ Guloudajie) With a wonderful view over Qiánhǎi Lake, this pretty and civilised Húnán restaurant – whose name means 'house at the foot of the mountain' – serves a range of mostly spicy but some mild dishes from the

START **YANDAI XIEJIE**
END **DI'ANMEN XIDAJIE**
DISTANCE **5KM**
DURATION **TWO HOURS**

Neighbourhood Walk
Hòuhǎi Lakes Bike Ride

This very gentle bike ride, all on the flat, whips you around the three Hòuhǎi lakes and some of the surrounding *hútòng*.

Start at the Di'anmenwai Dajie end of ❶ **Yandai Xiejie**, pedalling slowly past *name chop* (carved name seal) vendors, Tibetan silver trinket sellers, bars and cafes. Go straight on at the end of the street and you reach ❷ **Ya'er Hutong**. Cycle down it, where you'll find the Buddhist ❸ **Guanghua Temple**, which dates from the far-off Yuan dynasty. At the end of the *hútòng*, turn left into a narrow alley which will take you to Houhai Beiyan. Turn right again and almost immediately you'll pass ❹ **Dazanglonghua Temple**, built in 1719 and now a kindergarten.

Push on along Houhai Beiyan, passing the ❺ **Song Qingliang Former Residence**, once occupied by royalty. Turn left onto Houhai Xiyan and after 200m turn right onto an alley that connects with Deshengmennei Dajie. Go across that street and down the alley opposite, which leads you

to ❻ **Xīhǎi Lake**, the smallest of the three Hòuhǎi lakes but the most popular with local anglers. Circle the lake anticlockwise and return to Deshengmennei Dajie. Turn right and head down it for 200m and then turn left into ❼ **Yangfang Hutong**, home to many bars and restaurants. Follow the *hútòng* to the right and enter Liuyin Jie, which leads down to ❽ **Prince Gong's Residence**, which will be on your left.

Bear left at the end of Liuyin Jie and go onto Qianhai Xijie, which will take you to Qianhai Beiyan, the west shore of Qiánhǎi Lake. Hug the lakeshore until you reach the sharply humped ❾ **Silver Ingot Bridge**. Cross the bridge and turn sharp right. Carry along the east shore of Qiánhǎi, passing the quaint ❿ **Yinding Bridge** on your left, until you reach Di'anmen Xidajie.

province renowned for its searing flavours and for being the birthplace of Mao Zedong. It's appropriate then to try Mao's home-style pork (¥48), but it does a good boiled frog (¥78), too, as well as excellent, country-style *dòufu* (bean curd). The stewed snake with ginger is especially fiery. A bottle of *huángjiǔ* will ease it down.

HÚTÒNG PIZZA PIZZA $$

Map p294 (胡同比萨; Hútòng Bǐsà; ☎8322 8916; 9 Yindingqiao Hutong, 银锭桥胡同9号院; pizzas from ¥65; ⏲lunch & dinner; 📄; [S]Shichahai) Nestling in a *hútòng* that was one of the locations for the movie *Beijing Bicycle*, Hútòng Pizza's trademark square pizzas are some of the best in town. There's a wide selection to choose from, including veggie options, or you can build your own, and they're big: the large pizzas (from ¥105) will easily satisfy two hungry people. Salads, burgers and pasta options are available, too, as well as local and foreign beers. It gets busy, so it's advisable to book at peak times; they do deliver, though. Watch out for the mini-pond just inside the entrance; put one foot wrong and you'll be swimming with the fish.

LE PETIT SAIGON FRENCH, VIETNAMESE $$

Map p294 (西贡在巴黎; Xīgòng Zài Bālí; ☎6401 8465; 141 Jiugulou Dajie, 旧鼓楼大街141号; mains from ¥58; ⏲10.30am-11pm; 📶📄; [S]Shichahai) The menu at this stylish bistro – with a nice roof terrace in summer – is a mix of classic Vietnamese, *pho* (Vietnamese soup), lemon chicken, shrimps in tamarind sauce, and French, beef bourguignon and foie gras. The desserts are especially good. The decor and decent wine list are decidedly Gallic, making it popular with French expats and anyone in search of a proper cup of coffee (from ¥19), whether it's the European or Vietnamese variety.

BĚIPÍNGJŪ ROAST DUCK $$

Map p294 (北平居烤鸭店; 29 Di'anmenwai Dajie, 地安门外大街29号; mains ¥20-40; ⏲11am-9.30pm; 📄; [S]Shichahai) Arguably offering the best-value duck in the city, this bright, clean, family-friendly restaurant does delicious, authentic roast duck plus a small range of other Běijīng specialities, as well as dishes from other parts of China. The standard whole duck (单店烤鸭; *dāndiàn kǎoyā*) costs ¥98. You then add whatever extras you fancy: cucumber (瓜条; *guātiáo*; ¥2), spring onion (葱; *cōng*; ¥2), pancakes (鸭饼; *yābǐng*; ¥6), plum sauce (甜面酱; *tiánmiànjiàng*; ¥2). English menu with photos. Largely nonsmoking.

☆ ENTERTAINMENT

[TOP CHOICE] **EAST SHORE JAZZ CAFÉ** JAZZ

Map p294 (东岸; Dōng'àn; ☎8403 2131; 2nd floor, 2 Shichahai Nanyan, 地安门外大街 什刹海南沿2号楼2层, 地安门邮局西侧; beers from ¥35, cocktails from ¥40; ⏲3pm-2am; [S]Shichahai) Cui Jian's saxophonist, whose quartet play here, opened this chilled venue just off Di'anmenwai Dajie and next to Qiánhǎi Lake. It's a place to hear the best local jazz bands, with live performances from Wednesdays to Sundays (from 10pm), in a laid-back, comfortable atmosphere. There's a small roof terrace open in summer with a nice view of the lake and it's worth booking a table here on weekends, when it gets busy. There's no cover charge.

NATIONAL CENTRE FOR THE PERFORMING ARTS CLASSICAL MUSIC

Map p294 (国家大剧院; Guójiā Dājùyuàn; ☎6655 0000; 2 Xichang'an Jie, 西长安街2号; tickets ¥80-880; ⏲performances 7.30pm; [S]Tian'anmen West) Sometimes called the National Grand Theatre, this spectacular Paul Andreu–designed dome, known to Beijingers as the 'Alien Egg', attracts as many architectural tourists as it does music fans. But it's now *the* place to listen to classical music from home and abroad, despite the slightly dodgy acoustics and the distance of some of the seats from the stage. You can also watch ballet, opera and classical Chinese dance here. Regular mini-festivals are staged, too.

MEI LANFANG GRAND THEATRE PEKING OPERA, THEATRE

Map p294 (梅兰芳大戏院; Méi Lánfāng Dàxìyuàn; ☎5833 1288; 32 Ping'anli Xidajie, 平安里西大街32号; tickets ¥50-2080; ⏲performances 7.30pm; [S]Chegongzhuang) Named after China's most famous practitioner of Peking opera (p233), this theatre opened its doors in 2007 and has since become one of the most popular and versatile venues in town. As well as traditional opera, you can see Shakespeare productions and modern theatre. Contemporary dance companies and international ballet troupes also take to the good-sized stage on a regular basis.

TAO IMAGES LIMITED / GETTY IMAGES ©

1. Hòuhǎi Lakes (p118)
One of the capital's favourite outdoor spots, Hòuhǎi remains a fine spot to kick back.

2. Temple of Heaven Park (p106)
This park is a true oasis amid Běijīng's bedlam.

3. White Cloud Temple (p119)
Once the Taoist centre of northern China, this is a huge, lively complex of shrines and courtyards.

4. National Centre for the Performing Arts (p119)
The NCPA is designed to embody the transglobal aspirations of contemporary China.

GOING UNDERGROUND

The hordes of teens and 20-somethings who crowd out 77th St might not know it, but their favourite shopping mall was once part of what was possibly the world's largest bomb shelter. In 1969, alarmed at the prospect of possible nuclear war with either the Soviet Union or the US, Mao Zedong ordered that a huge warren of underground tunnels be burrowed underneath Běijīng. The task was completed Cultural Revolution–style – by hand – with the finishing touches made in 1979, just as the US re-opened its embassy in the capital and the Russians were marching into Afghanistan.

Legend has it that one tunnel stretched all the way to Tiānjīn (a mere 130km away), while another runs to the Summer Palace. Nowadays it is believed that some tunnels are still used for clandestine official purposes, while the rest of the underground city has been rendered unsafe by the construction boom that has gone on above it since the 1990s. But a few portions of the complex have been turned over for commercial use, such as the 77th St mall, a fitting metaphor for the way China has embraced consumerism and left Maoism far behind.

BĚIJĪNG CONCERT HALL   CLASSICAL MUSIC

Map p294 (北京音乐厅; Běijīng Yīnyuè Tīng; ✆6605 5812/7006; 1 Beixinhua Jie, 北新华街1号; tickets ¥80-880; ⏰performances 7.30pm; Ⓢ Tian'anmen West or Xīdān) The 2000-seat Běijīng Concert Hall showcases performances of classical Chinese music as well as international repertoires of Western classical music to hushed, knowledgeable audiences.

XP   LIVE MUSIC

Map p294 (小萍; Xiǎopíng; southwest cnr Di'anmennei Dajie & Di'anmenxi Dajie, 地安门内大街和地安门西大街角口; ⏰1pm-midnight, closed Mon; Ⓢ Shichahai) XP only recently opened its doors, but should prove to be a big hit, given that it's run by the same guys who were behind the hugely successful former live-music venue D22. It's a cafe and record shop by day, but transforms into a venue for experimental music by night. Usually has Slowboat Brewery beers on tap.

🛍 SHOPPING

📍 THREE STONE KITE SHOP   KITES

Map p294 (三石斋风筝; Sānshízhāi Fēngzhēng; ✆8404 4505; 25 Di'anmen Xidajie, 地安门西大街甲25号; ⏰9am-9pm; Ⓢ Nanluogu Xiang) Kites by appointment to the former Qing emperors; the great-grandfather of the owner of this friendly store used to make the kites for the Chinese royal family. There's a tremendous selection, ranging from the cheaper

and smaller ones (¥180), to huge handmade, hand-painted kites decorated with dragons and multicoloured butterflies which you can see in the air for miles around. You can also find the gear you'll need to fly your new kite here, as well as miniature framed kites, which make great gifts.

77TH STREET   SHOPPING MALL

Map p294 (77街; Qīshíqī Jiē; ✆6608 7177; B2-3F, 180 Xidan Beidajie, 西单北大街180号地下2-3层; ⏰10am-10pm; Ⓢ Xīdān) Descend the stairs into this unique underground mall and see where ordinary teenage and 20-something Beijingers go for their clothes and accessories. It opens out into a huge, circular, three-storey collection of hundreds of stores. As well as funky T-shirts, belts and bags, there are shoe shops galore and a food court. It's lots of fun, but a madhouse at weekends. To get there walk north on Xidan Beidajie from the subway and the entrance is 50m ahead – look for the 77th Street sign.

BĚIJĪNG ZOO MARKET   CLOTHES MARKET

(动物园市场; Dòngwùyuán Shìchǎng; Xizhimenwai Dajie, 西直门外大街; ⏰6am-5pm; Ⓢ Běijīng Zoo) Another key shopping spot for young Beijingers, this chaotic market sprawls across no less than seven buildings directly opposite the Běijīng Zoo (hence the name) and takes in everything from cosmetics to clothes, handbags and shoes. It's best for super-cheap T-shirts (from ¥30) and tops, knock-off jeans and other streetwear. There's no English spoken here, and sizes might be a problem for the larger traveller, but the prices are far cheaper than any other market in town and fashionistas will find a few diamonds among the dross. Kids' clothes are on the 3rd floor and the better-quality gear is on the top floors.

BĚIJĪNG BOOKS BUILDING BOOKS

Map p294 (北京图书大厦; Běijīng Túshū Dàshà; ☎6607 8477; 17 Xichang'an Jie, 西长安街17号; 🕒9am-9pm; [S]Xīdān) Massive emporium crammed with tomes of all descriptions. The ones in English, and some other foreign languages too, are in the basement. The selection of English-language fiction is ever-improving – it's not just English lit classics any more but thrillers, literary novels and chick lit too. There's a decent range of Lonely Planet guides as well.

Dashilar & Xīchéng South

Neighbourhood Top Five

1 Peruse the historic shopping street of **Dashilar** (p130), a throwback to the old imperial city that is still home to some of the oldest and most prestigious empo-riums in the city. Whether it's silk or ancient aphro-disiacs, you'll find it here.

2 Wind your way through the fascinating *hútòng* west of Meishi Jie, once infamous as old Peking's **red-light district** (p133).

3 Check out the distinctly different Muslim neigh-bourhood around **Niujie Mosque** (p130), the capital's largest.

4 Make sure to visit the **Běijīng Ancient Architec-ture Museum** (p130) to see how imperial Běijīng was built.

5 Pop into the little-vis-ited **Fǎyuán Temple** (p130), one of the city's oldest and most peaceful Buddhist shrines.

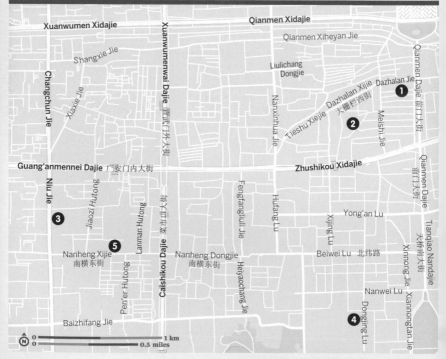

Explore: Dashilar & Xīchéng South

Divided from neighbouring Dōngchéng by Qianmen Da-jie (p110), Dashilar (大栅栏) and Xīchéng South (南西城) takes in the former district of Xuānwǔ. Its major sights are concentrated in two distinct areas: Dashilar and the surrounding alleyways, and the Muslim district around Niu Jie, with nearby *hútòng* to explore as well.

Spend a morning visiting the shops of Dashilar, before lunching at one of the small restaurants on Dazhalan Xi-jie. The *hútòng* off Dazhalan Xijie, the former red-light district of old Peking, are worth diving into.

From the western end of Dazhalan Xijie, it's a short stroll to Líulìchǎng, the capital's premier shopping street for antiques, calligraphy and traditional Chinese art, which is bisected by the busy Nanxinhua Jie. Curio-hunters will be in seventh heaven here. Round off the day by catching a show at one of the acrobatics or Peking opera theatres in the neighbourhood.

Start a second day in the area with a trip to the Běijīng Ancient Architecture Museum, a must for anyone interested in the capital's beginnings. It's a short hop by taxi, or a brisk 2km walk, northwest from there to Niu Jie, the main drag of Běijīng's Muslim Huí neighbourhood. Visit the mosque, an intriguing blend of Chinese and Arabic styles, before eating at a local Muslim restaurant. After that, backtrack to the nearby Fǎyuán Temple, a serene shrine still surrounded by *hútòng* that are good for a wander.

Local Life

➡ **Táorántíng Park** North of Běijīng South Railway Station, this is the lungs of the neighbourhood; escape here when the press of people, construction work and noise get too much.

➡ **Hútòng** Visit the alleyways sandwiched between Dazhalan Xijie and Qianmen Xidajie; they see far fewer foreigners than others in the area.

➡ **Market** Locals visit the streets around Mǎliándào Tea Market (p134) to pick up reasonably priced tea sets.

Getting There & Away

➡ **Subway** For Dashilar, get off at the Qianmen stop on Line 2. Go to Hepingmen on the same line for Líulìchǎng. Line 4 runs north–south through the neighbourhood towards Běijīng South Railway Station, with Caishikou a handy stop.

➡ **Bus** Niu Jie is connected with Wangfujing Dajie by bus 10, running through Tiān'ānmén, Xīdān and Changchun Jie.

Lonely Planet's Top Tip

Avoid the restaurants off the south end of Dashilar; many still try to charge foreigners more than locals by offering them a special English menu. Instead, head down Dazhalan Xijie for cheaper eats. Be wary too, of anyone in the Dashilar area offering to take you to a tea ceremony; it's a very expensive scam.

✗ Best Places to Eat & Drink

➡ Gǒubùlǐ (p130)
➡ Turpan Restaurant (p132)
➡ Helen's Restaurant & Bar (p132)

For reviews, see p130 ➡

◉ Best Places for Entertainment

➡ Tiānqiáo Acrobatics Theatre (p132)
➡ Húguǎng Guild Hall (p132)
➡ Lao She Teahouse (p132)

For reviews, see p132 ➡

🔒 Best Places to Shop

➡ Ruìfúxiáng (p134)
➡ Yuèhǎixuān Musical Instrument Store (p134)
➡ Mǎliándào Tea Market (p134)

For reviews, see p133 ➡

SIGHTS

DASHILAR HISTORIC SHOPPING STREET

Map p296 (大栅栏; Dàzhàlan; [S]Qianmen) Just west of Qianmen Dajie is this centuries-old shopping street, also known as Dazhalan Jie. While it has been given a makeover, which has sadly robbed it of much of its charm, many of the shops are the same ones which have been here for hundreds of years and are well worth a browse for the sometimes esoteric goods – ancient herbal remedies, handmade cloth shoes – they sell.

FǍYUÁN TEMPLE BUDDHIST TEMPLE

Map p296 (法源寺; Fǎyuán Sì; 7 Fayuansi Qianjie; adult ¥5; 🕘8.30-5pm; [S]Caishikou) Infused with an air of reverence and devotion, this lovely temple originally dates back to the 7th century. Now the **China Buddhism College**, the still active temple was built to honour Tang dynasty soldiers who had fallen during combat against the northern tribes. The temple follows the typical Buddhist layout, with drum and bell towers, but do hunt out the unusual **copper-cast Buddha** seated atop four further Buddhas, themselves ensconced atop a huge bulb of myriad effigies in the Pilu Hall (the fourth hall). Within the Guanyin Hall is a Ming-dynasty **Thousand Hand and Thousand Eye Guanyin**, while a huge supine Buddha reclines in the rear hall. From the entrance of Niujie Mosque, walk left 100m then turn left into the first *hútòng*. Follow the *hútòng* for about 10 minutes, and you'll arrive at Fǎyuán Temple.

NIÚJIĒ MOSQUE MOSQUE

(牛街礼拜寺; Niújiē Lǐbài Sì; ☎6353 2564; 88 Niu Jie; adult ¥10, admission free for Muslims; 🕘8am-sunset; [S]Caishikou) Dating back to the 10th century and lively with worshippers on Fridays (it's closed to non-Muslims at prayer times), Běijīng's largest mosque is the centre of the community for the 10,000 or so Huí Chinese Muslims who live nearby. The Chinese-styled mosque is pleasantly decorated with plants and flourishes of Arabic – look out for the main prayer hall (note that only Muslims can enter), women's quarters and the **Building for Observing the Moon** (望月楼; Wàngyuèlóu), from where the lunar calendar was calculated. Remember to dress appropriately for a mosque (no shorts or short skirts).

LOCAL KNOWLEDGE

DEATH BY A THOUSAND CUTS

The now abolished district of Xuānwǔ owed its name to the grand old gate of Xuānwǔ Mén (宣武门), long since demolished. But the irreverent locals used to call it by its more nefarious nickname, the Gate of Punishment (刑门; Xíng Mén), as it rose up near the imperial execution ground at Càishì Kǒu (菜市口), where wrongdoers endured 'slow slicing', or 'death by a thousand cuts'. Càishì Kǒu's name lives on as a subway stop on Line 4.

XIĀNNÓNG ALTAR & BĚIJĪNG ANCIENT ARCHITECTURE MUSEUM MUSEUM

Map p296 (先农坛、北京古代建筑博物馆; Xiānnóngtán & Běijīng Gǔdài Jiànzhù Bówùguǎn; ☎6304 5608; 21 Dongjing Lu; admission ¥15; 🕘9am-4pm; [S]Taoranting) This altar – to the west of the Temple of Heaven – was the site of solemn imperial ceremonies and sacrificial offerings. Glance at any pre-1949 map of Běijīng and you can gauge the massive scale of the altar, which was built in 1420. Today, many of its original structures survive, but what remains is a tranquil and little-visited constellation of relics. Located within what is called the **Hall of Jupiter** (太岁殿; Tàisuì Diàn) – the most magnificent surviving hall – is the excellent Běijīng Ancient Architecture Museum, which informatively narrates the elements of traditional Chinese building techniques. Brush up on your *dǒugǒng* (brackets) and *sǔnmǎo* (joints), get the low-down on Běijīng's courtyard houses, while eyeballing detailed models of standout temple halls and pagodas from across the land. There's a great scale model of the old walled city and English captions throughout. On Wednesdays, the first 200 visitors get in free.

EATING

GǑUBÙLǏ CHINESE DUMPLINGS $

Map p296 (狗不理; ☎6353 3338; 31 Dazhalan Jie, 大栅栏街31号; dumplings from ¥12; 🕘7.30am-10pm; [S]Qianmen) Decent, cheap eats are hard to find in this area, so this outpost of the renowned Tiānjīn restaurant will delight dumpling devotees. There are eight different types to pick from, including meat, prawn, crab and veggie options, as well as

Neighbourhood Walk
Qiánmén to Líulìchǎng Walk

➡️ Start at the ❶ **Běijīng Railway Museum**, housed in the historic Qiánmén Railway Station building. Walk south to the ❷ **Qiánmén Decorative Arch**, a rebuilt Five-Bay Decorative Arch (Wǔpáilóu) that was originally felled in the 1950s and reconstructed prior to the 2008 Olympics. The arch stands at the head of ❸ **Qianmen Dajie**, a street completely revamped in the style of old Peking. If you want, hop on a tram in a straight line all the way down to Zhushikou Xidajie (珠市口西大街).

Look at some of the ❹ **restored old shop buildings** along Qianmen Dajie, then turn right onto the historic shopping street of ❺ **Dashilar** (aka Dazhalan Jie). Down the first alley on the left is Liubiju, a traditional Běijīng *lǎozìhào* (old, established shop) famous for its pickled condiments.

Push on through the crowds on Dazhalan Jie. On your right at No 5 is ❻ **Ruìfúxiáng**, a famous old Běijīng silk store dating to 1893. Pop in and view the grey brickwork

and carved decorative flourishes of the entrance hall.

Cross Meishi Jie and enter ❼ **Dazhalan Xijie**, once known as Guanyin Temple Street. If you're peckish, stop at any of the vendors of noodles, pancakes, corn cakes or stinky tofu, then turn right at the fork with Yingtao Xiejie (樱桃斜街) to see the ❽ **plaque** marking the site of the former Guanyin Temple (Nos 6 to 8 Yingtao Xiejie) that stood here.

Continue along Yingtao Xiejie past the narrow and pinched Taitou Xiang (抬头巷; Raise Head Alley) for around 100m and examine the house at ❾ **27 Yingtao Xiejie** (also called Yingtao Hutong). The wall of the building is daubed with a largely indecipherable Cultural Revolution slogan, although the red characters 革命万岁 ('Long Live the Revolution') can be seen.

Loop round to the right and at the end of Yingtao Xiejie, turn sharp left and the road will bend round to ❿ **Liulichang Dongjie**, Běijīng's premier antique street.

THE HUÍ

China's 25 million-odd Muslims are divided into two distinct groups. One is comprised of the Uighurs, a rebellious, Turkic-speaking minority from the far west of China whose roots lie in Central Asia. The other are the Huí. You can find both in the Niu Jie area but it is predominantly a district associated with the Huí.

The descendants of Arab traders who came down the Silk Road well over a thousand years ago, the 10 million or so Huí are technically an ethnic minority. But they are spread all over China and have intermarried so much with the Han Chinese over the centuries that they are indistinguishable from them ethnically. Nor do they have their own language, speaking only Mandarin.

Yet, they are easily spotted. Many Huí women wear a headscarf, while the men sport white skullcaps. They are most associated with running restaurants; you can find a Huí eatery in even the smallest Chinese towns. Don't expect to find pork on the menu and some don't serve alcohol. Apart from the Niu Jie area, you're most likely to encounter the Huí serving up *yáng'ròu chuàn* (lamb skewers) from streetside stalls and hole-in-the-wall restaurants all over Běijīng.

plenty of cold dishes to accompany them. Picture menu.

TURPAN RESTAURANT UIGHUR $

(吐鲁番餐厅; Tǔlǔfān Cāntīng; ☑8316 4691; 6 Niu Jie, 牛街6号; kebabs from ¥10, dishes from ¥25; ☉10.30am-2.30pm, 4.30pm-8.30pm; Ⓢ Caishikou) This is a huge place, but it needs to be considering the hordes who flock here for the big, juicy and succulent lamb kebabs (nothing like the tiny skewers sold on the streets) and the array of authentic Uighur dishes, some of which are Halal, from far-off Xīnjiāng. We think the roast lamb leg is a bargain at ¥65. Picture menu.

HELEN'S RESTAURANT & BAR WESTERN $

Map p296 (海伦餐厅; Hǎilún Cāntīng; 55 Dazhalan Xijie, 大栅栏西街55号; dishes from ¥28; ☉8am-1am; 🛜🅿; Ⓢ Qianmen) With its graffiti-covered walls and lines of wooden benches, this is a backpacker hangout a (long-ish) stone's throw from Tiān'ānmén Sq. During the day it functions as a cafe serving up cheap Western eats: all-day breakfasts, sandwiches, burgers, pasta and pizza; at night the sound system gets cranked up and it all gets more raucous as those cheap beers (¥10) and buckets disappear down thirsty throats at a pace.

 **ENTERTAINMENT**

TIĀNQIÁO ACROBATICS THEATRE ACROBATICS

Map p296 (天桥杂技剧场; Tiānqiáo Zájì Jùchǎng; ☑6303 7449; 95 Tianqiao Shichang Jie, 天桥市场街95号; tickets Y180-380; ☉performances 5.30pm; Ⓢ Taranting) West of the Temple of Heaven Park, this 100-year-old theatre offers one of Běijīng's best acrobatic displays, a one-hour show performed by the Běijīng Acrobatic Troupe. Less touristy than the other venues, the high-wire display here is awesome. The entrance is down the eastern side of the building.

HÚGUǍNG GUILD HALL PEKING OPERA

Map p296 (湖广会馆; Húguǎng Huìguǎn; ☑6351 8284; 3 Hufang Lu, 虎坊桥路3号; tickets ¥180-680, opera museum ¥10; ☉performances 6.30pm, opera museum 9am-5pm; Ⓢ Caishikou) With balconies surrounding the canopied stage, the Húguǎng dates back to 1807. In 1912 the Kuomintang (KMT), led by Dr Sun Yat-sen, was founded here. The interior is magnificent, coloured in red, green and gold, and decked out with tables and a stone floor. Opposite the theatre there's a very small opera museum displaying operatic scores, old catalogues and other paraphernalia. There are also colour illustrations of the *liǎnpǔ* (types of Peking opera facial makeup) – examples include the *hóu liǎnpǔ* (monkey face) and the *chǒujué liǎnpǔ* (clown face). Shows here attract a lot of domestic tour groups. There are few English captions.

LAO SHE TEAHOUSE CHINESE PERFORMING ARTS

Map p296 (老舍茶馆; Lǎoshě Cháguǎn; ☑6303 6830; www.laosheteahouse.com; 3rd fl, 3 Qianmen Xidajie, 前门西大街3号3层; evening tickets 180-380; ☉performances 7.50pm; Ⓢ Qianmen) Lao She Teahouse, named after the celebrated writer, has daily and nightly shows, mostly in Chinese, which blend any number

LOCAL KNOWLEDGE

RED-LIGHT PEKING

These days, Dazhalan Xijie and the surrounding *hútòng* are Běijīng's backpacker central. But for hundreds of years, these innocuous-looking alleys were infamous for being old Peking's red-light district (红灯区; *hóngdēngqū*).

Centered around Bada Hutong, a collection of eight alleys, the area had already acquired a raunchy reputation in the 18th century. By the time of the fall of the Qing dynasty in 1911, there were reckoned to be over 300 brothels lining the lanes. The working girls ranged from cultivated courtesans who could recite poetry and dance gracefully and whose clients were aristocrats and court officials, to more mundane types who served the masses. It was very much an area for the locals; the small foreign community had its own little zone of brothels, dive bars and opium dens in still surviving Chuanban Hutong, close to the Chongwenmen subway stop.

Bada Hutong owed its dubious fame to the fact that it was outside the city walls (the emperors didn't want houses of ill repute close to the royal palace), yet close enough to the Imperial City for customers to get there easily. But the fall of the emperors signalled the beginning of the end of the old red-light district. Just over a month after the founding of the PRC in October 1949, soldiers marched into Bada Hutong, closed down the brothels and 'liberated' the prostitutes working there.

Many of the eight alleys that made up Bada Hutong have been demolished and/or re-built and show no sign of what went on there in the past. Shanxi Xiang, though, is still standing and the historic building that is now the hostel Leo Courtyard (p197) was once one of the most upmarket knocking shops in the capital. But it didn't do dorm beds back then.

of traditional Chinese performing arts. The evening performances of Peking opera, folk art and music, acrobatics and magic (7.50pm to 9.20pm) are the most popular. But there are also tea ceremonies, frequent folk music performances and daily shadow puppet shows. Prices depend on the type of show and your seat. Phone ahead or check the schedule online. Look for two yellow dragons on the front of the building.

LÍYUÁN THEATRE PEKING OPERA

Map p296 (梨园剧场; Líyuán Jùchǎng; ☎6301 8860, 6301 6688; Qianmen Jianguo Hotel, 175 Yong'an Lu, 永安路175号前门建国饭店; tickets without tea ¥200-280, with tea 380-580; ⏲performances 7.30pm; [S]Caishikou) This touristy theatre, in the lobby of the Qianmen Jianguo Hotel (p196), has daily performances for Peking opera newbies. If you want to, you can enjoy an overpriced tea ceremony while watching. The setting isn't traditional: it resembles a cinema auditorium (the stage facade is the only authentic touch), but it's a gentle introduction to the art form.

SHOPPING

Dashilar & Xīchéng South is one of the capital's best neighbourhoods for shopping. Apart from Dashilar (p130) itself, Liulichang (meaning 'glazed-tile factory') is Běijīng's premier antique street, even if the goods on sale are largely fake. The street is something of an oasis in the area and worth delving into for its quaint, albeit dressed-up, village-like atmosphere. Alongside ersatz Qing monochrome bowls and Cultural Revolution kitsch, you can rummage through old Chinese books, paintings, brushes, ink and paper. Prepare yourself for pushy sales staff and overly optimistic prices. If you want a name *chop* made, this is a good place to do it.

At the western end of Liulichang Xijie, a collection of more informal shops flog bric-a-brac, Buddhist statuary, Cultural Revolution pamphlets and posters, shoes for bound feet, silks, handicrafts and so on. Further west, Mǎliándào Tea Market is an essential stop for tea lovers and buyers.

[TOP CHOICE] YUÈHĂIXUĀN MUSICAL INSTRUMENT STORE — MUSICAL INSTRUMENTS

Map p296 (乐海轩门市部; Yuèhǎixuān Ménshìbù; ☎6303 1472; 97 Liliuchang Dongjie, 琉璃厂东街97号; ⏰9.30am-6pm; [S]Hepingmen) Fantastic, friendly emporium that specialises in traditional Chinese musical instruments, such as the zither-like *gǔzhēng* (some of which come with elaborate carvings on them), the *èrhú* and *bǎnhú* (two-string Chinese violins), and *gǔ* (drums). It does great gongs and has many esoteric instruments from Tibet and Mongolia, too. It's on the eastern side of Liliuchang.

RUÌFÚXIÁNG — SILK

Map p296 (瑞蚨祥丝绸店; Ruìfúxiáng Sīchóudiàn; ☎6303 5313; 5 Dazhalan Jie,大栅栏街5号; ⏰9.30am-8.30pm; [S]Qianmen) Housed in a historic building on Dashilar, this is one of the best places in town to browse for silk. There's an incredible selection of Shāndōng silk, brocade and satin-silk. The silk starts at ¥98 a metre, although most of the fabric is more expensive. Ready-made, traditional Chinese clothing is sold on the 2nd floor. Ruìfúxiáng also has an outlet at Dianmenwai Dajie (p99).

MĂLIÁNDÀO TEA MARKET — TEA

(马连道茶城; Mǎliándào Cháchéng; ☎6334 3963; 6 Maliandao Lu, 马连道路6号; ⏰9am-7pm; [S]Běijīng West Railway Station) South of Běijīng West Train Station is Mǎliándào, the largest tea market in northern China. The four-storey building is home to if not all the tea in China, then an awful lot of it. There are brews from all over the country here, including *pu'er* and *oolong*. Although it's mostly for wholesalers, the market is a great place to wander for anyone interested in tea and the vendors are normally happy to let you sample some. Maliandao Lu itself has hundreds of tea shops, where prices for tea and tea sets are lower than in the tea shops in tourist areas. To find the tea market, look for the statue of Lu Yu, the 8th-century sage who wrote the first book on growing, preparing and drinking tea, which stands outside it.

RÓNGBĂOZHĀI — CHINESE ARTWORK

Map p296 (荣宝斋; ☎6303 6090; 19 Liulichang Xijie, 琉璃厂西街19号; ⏰9am-5.30pm; [S]Hepingmen) Spread over two floors and sprawling down quite a length of the road, the scroll paintings, woodblock prints, paper, ink and brushes here are presented in a rather flat, uninspired way by bored staff – a consequence of it being state run. But it has plenty of goods on offer. Prices are generally fixed, although you can usually get 10% off.

CATHAY BOOKSHOP — BOOKS, CHINESE ARTWORK

Map p296 (中国书店; Zhōngguó Shūdiàn; ☎6303 2104; 34 Liulichang Xijie, 琉璃厂西街34号; ⏰9am-6.30pm; [S]Hepingmen) There are two branches of the Cathay Bookshop on Liulichang. This branch (Gǔjí Shūdiàn), on the south side of Liulichang Xijie opposite Róngbǎozhāi, is worth checking out for its wide variety of colour art books on Chinese painting, ceramics and furniture, and its books on religion (most books are in Chinese). Upstairs has more art books, stone rubbings and antiquarian books. The store takes MasterCard and Visa. There's another, smaller branch close by on **Liulichang**

DASHILAR – QING DYNASTY SHOPPING MALL

Shops were barred from the city centre in imperial Běijīng, so the *hútòng* south of Qiánmén served as early versions of the modern-day malls that have sprung up in the capital. Dashilar (p130) was one of the most popular and known especially for silk, although its name refers to a wicket gate that was closed at night to keep prowlers out.

Bustling markets plying specialised products thronged the surrounding alleys – lace in one, lanterns in the other, jade in the next. Now, many of the *hútòng* have been demolished and you're more likely to find someone selling fake watches than anything of real value.

For some years, there have been persistent rumours that the western end of Dashilar, Dazhalan Xijie, is next in line for a similar overhaul, one which would have a potentially dire effect on this still *hútòng*-rich neighbourhood. At the time of writing, work was going on but it was unclear if it was an updating of the street or the beginning of an attempt to transform it into something like Nanluogu Xiang. Expect some changes when you visit.

(Map p296; 18 Liulichang Xijie, 琉璃厂西街18号) that sells paper cut-outs and bookmarks, some of which feature photographs of the old Qing imperial household, including snapshots of Reginald Johnson (last emperor Puyi's Scottish tutor), Puyi practising shadow boxing, eunuchs and Cixi dressed as Avalokiteshvara (Guanyin).

TÓNGRÉNTÁNG CHINESE MEDICINE

Map p296 (同仁堂; ☎6303 1155; 24 Dazhalan Jie, 大栅栏街24号; ⏲8am-7.30pm; [S]Qianmen) This famous, now international, herbal medicine shop has been peddling pills and potions since 1669. It was a royal dispensary in the Qing dynasty and its medicines are based on secret prescriptions used by royalty. You can be cured of anything from fright to encephalitis, or so the shop claims. Traditional doctors are available on the spot for consultations. Look for the pair of *qílín* (hybrid animals that appear on earth in times of harmony) standing guard outside.

NÈILIÁNSHĒNG SHOE SHOP SHOES

Map p296 (内联升鞋店; Nèiliánshēng Xiédiàn; ☎6301 4863; 34 Dazhalan Jie, 大栅栏街34号; ⏲9am-9pm; [S]Qianmen) They say this is the oldest existing cloth shoe shop in China (it opened in 1853) and it has a factory that still employs more than 100 workers. Mao Zedong and other luminaries had their footgear made here and you too can pick up ornately embroidered shoes, or the simply styled cloth slippers frequently modelled by Běijīng's senior citizens (from ¥118). It does cute, patterned kid's slippers (from ¥58) too.

SOGO SHOPPING MALL

Map p296 (崇光百货商场; Chóngguāng Bǎihuò Shāngchǎng; ☎6310 3388; 8 Xuanwumenwai Dajie, 宣武门外大街8号; ⏲10am-10pm; [S]Caishikou) Sogo is one of Běijīng's most pleasant mall experiences. The mix of hip Japanese (Sogo is a Japanese company) and European boutiques, the convenient layout and an excellent, cheap food court on the 6th floor makes Sogo more fun than you'd expect a shopping centre to be. Add espresso bars on each floor, the impressive basement supermarket (with pharmacy) and the 6th-floor games arcade, where you can deposit kids while shopping, and you're in mall heaven.

Sānlǐtún & Cháoyáng

Neighbourhood Top Five

1 Peruse exhibitions, sip coffee and rub shoulders with China's hottest painters and sculptures at **798 Art District** (p138).

2 Hunt for treasures among hundreds of arts, crafts and antiques stalls at the wonderfully chaotic **Pānjiāyuán Market** (p148).

3 Sip **cocktails** at some of Běijīng's swankiest bars. **Apothecary** (p144) mixes the best drinks, but if you just want to pose, head to **Mesh** (p146).

4 Enjoy the best of Běijīng's **fine dining** at one of this area's numerous top-end restaurants. Try sky-high **Grill 79** (p142) for starters.

5 Muse on life's finalities in the fascinatingly morbid Taoist shrine that is **Dōngyuè Temple** (p139).

For more detail of this area see Map p298 ➡

Explore: Sānlǐtún & Cháoyáng

The only sights of interest in the spread-out district of Cháoyáng (朝阳) are Dōngyuè Temple and the pleasant Rìtán Park, although a half-day trip to 798 Arts District is recommended. After that, focus on this neighbourhood's true calling: shopping, eating and partying.

You'll find some of Běijīng's most modern and eye-catching shopping malls in Cháoyáng, and some of the best markets. Consider putting aside half a day for shopping here, including lazy brunch and lunch stops. Come evening, your choice of restaurants is staggering. Whether you fancy keeping it real with dumplings, dressing up for posh nosh or sampling international cuisine from tapas to Thai, Cháoyáng's got it covered.

Your belly full, hop in a cab to Nali Patio, the latest drinking hotspot, where you'll find fellow revellers with whom to discuss where best to dance the night away.

Local Life

➜ **Food** If you want to sidestep the expats to eat with salt-of-the-earth Beijingers, there's only one place to go. Bàodǔ Huáng is as local as local gets, so put aside your table manners and your fear of eating the unknown, and get stuck into true local cuisine.

➜ **Art** 798 Art District is well worth a trip, but for the less commercialised version head slightly further northeast to the galleries and studies at Cǎochǎngdì.

➜ **Parklife** The extremely pleasant Rìtán Park is a favourite spot for locals who come here to fly kites, play cards and do their daily exercises. Other nearby parks include Cháoyáng and Tuánjiéhú Parks, which both have popular outdoor swimming complexes.

Getting There & Away

➜ **Subway** The main bar, restaurant and clubbing areas in Sānlǐtún are between Dongsi Shitiao and Tuanjiehu stations, both of which leave you with a 10- to 15-minute walk, depending on where you're heading.

➜ **Dōngzhímén Transport Hub** The Airport Express terminates here, two subway lines meet here, and there are buses to every corner of the city, including ones to the Great Wall.

➜ **Bus** Bus 113 runs past Sānlǐtún and the Workers Stadium before turning north up Jiaodaokou Nandajie (for Nanluogu Xiang) towards Andingmen subway station. Bus 120 goes from the east gate of the Workers Stadium to Wángfǔjǐng and Qiánmén. Bus 701 runs the length of Gongrentiyuchang Beilu and continues west to Běihǎi Park.

Lonely Planet's Top Tip

The markets in this area are well accustomed to foreign tourists so prepare yourself for some seriously hard bargaining. There are no hard and fast rules as to how much to cut the starting price by. The best way to gauge how low vendors are prepared to go is simply to walk away, hopefully prompting a genuine 'last price'.

✕ Best Places to Eat

➜ Nàjiā Xiǎoguǎn (p140)
➜ Jīngzūn Peking Duck (p141)
➜ Jíxiángniǎo Xiāngcài (p141)
➜ Bàodǔ Huáng (p141)
➜ Din Tai Fung (p141)
➜ Bellagio (p141)

For reviews, see p140 ➜

🍷 Best Places to Drink

➜ Migas (p144)
➜ Apothecary (p144)
➜ Dos Kolegas (p147)
➜ Haze (p145)
➜ First Floor (p145)
➜ Saddle Cantina (p145)

For reviews, see p144 ➜

🛍 Best Places to Shop

➜ Pānjiāyuán Market (p148)
➜ Sānlǐtún Village (p148)
➜ Silk Market (p148)
➜ Sānlǐtún Yashow Clothing Market (p149)
➜ Shard Box Store (p149)

For reviews, see p148 ➜

TOP SIGHTS
798 ART DISTRICT

A vast area of disused factories built by the East Germans, 798 Art District (798艺术区; Qī Jiǔ Bā Yìshù Qū), also known as Dà Shānzi (大山子), is Běijīng's leading concentration of contemporary art galleries. The industrial complex celebrates its proletarian roots in the communist heyday of the 1950s via retouched red Maoist slogans decorating gallery interiors and statues of burly, lantern-jawed workers dotting the lanes. The voluminous factory workshops are ideally suited to art galleries that require space for multimedia installations and other ambitious projects.

Visiting

From Exit C of Dongzhimen subway station, take bus 909 (¥2) for about 6km northeast to Dashanzi Lukou Nan (大山子路口南), where you'll see the big red 798 sign. Buses run until 8.30pm. Signboards with English-language maps on them dot the lanes. Food and drink is available (p144).

Galleries

Highlights include **BTAP** (Ceramics Third Street; ⊘closed Mon), one of 798's original galleries; **UCCA** (798 Rd), a big-money gallery with exhibition halls, a funky shop and a cinema screening ¥15 films most days; **Pace** (797 Rd), a wonderfully large space holding some top-quality exhibitions; **Galleria Continua** (just south of 797 Rd), another large space below a towering, hard-to-miss brick chimney.

Cǎochǎngdì

A further extensive colony of art galleries can be found 3km northeast of 798 Art District at Cǎochǎngdì (草场地). Bus 909 continues here.

DON'T MISS

➡ UCCA
➡ Timezone 8

PRACTICALITIES

➡ 798 艺术区
➡ cnr Jiuxianqiao Lu & Jiuxianqiao Beilu; 酒仙桥路
➡ ⊘galleries 10am-6pm, some closed Mon
➡ 🚌403 or 909

SIGHTS

798 ART DISTRICT GALLERY

See p138.

DŌNGYUÈ TEMPLE TAOIST TEMPLE

Map p298 (东岳庙; Dōngyuè Miào; 141 Chaoyangmenwai Dajie; adult ¥10, with guide 40; ⏲8.30am-4.30pm Tue-Sun; [S]Chaoyangmen) Dedicated to the Eastern Peak (Tài Shān) of China's five Taoist mountains, the morbid Taoist shrine of Dōngyuè Temple is an unsettling, albeit fascinating experience. With its roots poking deep into the Yuan dynasty, what's above ground level has been revived with care and investment. Dōngyuè Temple is an active place of worship where Taoist monks attend to a world entirely at odds with the surrounding glass and steel high-rises. Note the temple's fabulous *páifāng* (memorial archway) lying to the south, divorced from its shrine by the intervention of the busy main road, Chaoyangmenwai Dajie.

Stepping through the entrance pops you into a Taoist Hades, where tormented spirits reflect on their wrongdoing and elusive atonement. You can muse on life's finalities in the **Life and Death Department** or the **Final Indictment Department**. Otherwise get spooked at the **Department for Wandering Ghosts** or the **Department for Implementing 15 Kinds of Violent Death**.

It's not all doom and gloom: the luckless can check in at the **Department for Increasing Good Fortune and Longevity**. Ornithologists will be birds of a feather with the **Flying Birds Department**, while the infirm can seek cures at the **Deep-Rooted Disease Department**. The **Animal Department** has colourful and lively fauna. English explanations detail department functions.

Other halls are no less fascinating. The huge **Dàiyuè Hall** (Dàiyuè Diàn) is consecrated to the God of Tàishān, who manages the 18 layers of hell. Visit during festival time, especially during the Chinese New Year and the Mid-Autumn Festival, and you'll see the temple at its most vibrant.

Just outside the complex, in a small car park to the east, stands the handsome, but rather lonely **Jiǔtiān Pǔhuā Gōng** (Map p298) (九天普化宫), a small temple hall which is the only remaining structure of two other Taoist temples that once also stood in this area. Built in 1647, the hall, which we think is now empty, once contained more than 70 clay and wooden statues dedicated to Léizǔ (雷祖), Taoism's God of Thunder. Unfortunately, it's not open to the public. Note the faded Cultural Revolution slogans painted on the western and northern walls, and the two impressive stone tablets that rise up from the platform at the front.

[FREE] **RÌTÁN PARK** PARK

(日坛公园; Rìtán Gōngyuán; Ritan Lu; free; ⏲6am-9pm; [S]Chaoyangmen) Meaning 'Altar of the Sun', Rìtán (pronounced 'rer-tan') is arguably the most pleasant area to spend time in this part of Běijīng. One of a set of imperial parks, which covers each compass point, Rìtán dates from 1530 and is the eastern counterpart to the likes of Temple of Heaven and Temple of Earth (Dìtán Park). The altar is now little more than a raised platform, but the surrounding park is beautifully landscaped and a popular city-centre escape. Activities include dancing, singing, kite flying, rock-climbing (¥30-50), table tennis and pond fishing (¥5 per hour). Otherwise, just stroll around and enjoy the flora, or head to one of the park's pleasant cafes; the standout one is **Stone Boat** (石舫咖啡; Shífǎng Kāfēi; Map p298; beers & coffee from ¥25, cocktails from ¥35; ⏲10am-10pm), located by a large landscaped pond.

CCTV BUILDING ARCHITECTURE

Map p298 (央视大楼; Yāngshì Dàlóu; 32 Dongsanhuan Zhonglu; [S]Jintaixizhao) Shaped like an enormous pair of trousers, and known locally as Dà Kùchǎ (大裤衩), or Big Underpants, the astonishing CCTV Tower is an architect's wet dream. Its overhang (the bum in the pants) seems to defy gravity and is made possible by an unusual engineering design which creates a three-dimensional cranked loop, supported by an irregular grid on its surface. Designed by Rem Koolhaas and Ole Scheeren of OMA, the building is an audacious statement of modernity (despite its nickname) and is a unique addition to the Běijīng skyline. In February 2008, stray fireworks from CCTV's own Lantern Festival fireworks display sent the costly Television Cultural Center in the north of the complex up in flames, burning for five hours with spectacular ferocity. CCTV famously censored its own reporting of the huge conflagration (Běijīng netizens dryly noting that CCTV created one of the year's biggest stories only to not cover it). Along with the Běijīng Mandarin Oriental,

THIS BIRD HAS FLOWN

With the spectacularly successful 2008 Olympics now a long-faded memory, the 'Bird's Nest Stadium', the iconic centrepiece of the Games, now stands forlorn and empty. Having staged just a handful of sports events since the Olympics, as well as a few music concerts, the $450 million venue is not so much a shrine to sporting excellence as a redundant symbol of the most expensive games ever staged.

While a dwindling number of mostly domestic tourists still roll up to have their photos taken on the running track, no one seems sure what to do with the innovative stadium, or how to raise the estimated $15 million a year needed to maintain it. Rumours of theme parks and shopping malls being built next door still abound. But until those plans come to fruition, the rust will continue to gather on the intricate steel structure that held the world's attention for one brief month in 2008.

The Happy Magic Water Park has at least turned the Olympic swimming venue, which stands alongside the Bird's Nest, into a popular, albeit expensive leisure facility, and the mountain biking venue and velodrome are still well used, but other less high-profile venues stand abandoned and in some cases dilapidated on the outskirts of the city. The former venues for kayaking, baseball and beach volleyball, for example, are now little more than a collection of beat-up, disused structures surrounded by overgrown patches of wasteland.

a visitor's centre and theatre were also destroyed in the blaze. Big Underpants escaped unsinged. Gardens around the complex were being landscaped at the time of research so by the time you read this you should be able to wander beneath the underbelly of this exceptional structure.

BIRD'S NEST & WATER CUBE ARCHITECTURE
(国家体育场、国家游泳中心; Guójiā Tǐyùchǎng & Guójiā Yóuyǒng Zhōngxīn; Bird's Nest ¥50, Water Cube ¥30; ⏲9am-5.30pm Nov-Feb, to 6.30pm Mar-Oct; [S]Olympic Sports Centre) After the event, walking around the Olympic Sports Centre midweek is rather like being stuck in a district of Brazilia or a soul-destroying intersection in *Gattica* or *Alphaville*. Traffic lights go red and there are no cars to stop; the green man flashes and there's no one to cross the brand-spanking-new roads. It's now hard to imagine that this was the scene of great sporting exultation in 2008, but such is the fate of most Olympics projects. Squinting in the sun, guards in ill-fitting black combat gear point the occasional group of map-clutching domestic tourists to the signature National Stadium, known colloquially as the Bird's Nest (鸟巢; Niǎocháo). Occasional events are held here, but it's generally empty. Nevertheless, it's still an iconic piece of architecture, as is the bubble-covered Water Cube next door, which now houses **Happy Magic Water Park**. The site is around 7km north of the city centre.

CHINA SCIENCE & TECHNOLOGY MUSEUM MUSEUM
(中国科技馆; Zhōngguó Kējìguǎn; 5 Beichendong Lu, 北辰东路5号; adult/child ¥30/20; ⏲9.30am-5pm Tue-Sun; South Gate of Forest Park) About 8km north of the city centre, and a big favourite with kids, this huge facility has an array of hands-on scientific exhibitions, a science playground and state-of-the-art 3D and '4D' cinemas. Walk east from South Gate of Forest Park subway station, then take the second right (10 minutes).

🍴 EATING

The presence of embassies and many foreign companies, as well as the Sānlǐtún bar and entertainment district, means this giant district has the greatest concentration of international restaurants, foreign-friendly Chinese restaurants and fine-dining options.

NÀJIĀ XIǍOGUǍN CHINESE MANCHU **$$**
Map p298 (那家小馆; ☎6567 3663; 10 Yong'an Xili, off Jianguomenwai Dajie, Chunxiu Lu, 建国门外大街永安西里10号; mains ¥40-70; ⏲11am-9.30pm; [@]; [S]Yong'anli) There's a touch of the traditional Chinese tea house to this excellent restaurant, housed in a reconstructed two-storey interior courtyard, and bubbling with old-Peking atmosphere. The menu is based on an old imperial recipe

book known as the Golden Soup Bible, and the dishes are consistently good (and well priced considering the quality). The imperial Manchu theme sounds a tad tacky, but it's carried off in a fun but tasteful way that doesn't give you the feeling you're in a tourists-only restaurant. You don't need to book (in fact, at peak times you can't), but you should be prepared to hang around for at least half an hour for a table. It's worth the wait. No English sign, and not much English spoken, but the menu is in English.

JĪNGZŪN PEKING DUCK   PEKING ROAST DUCK $$
Map p298 (京尊烤鸭; Jīngzūn Kǎoyā; ☑6417 4075; 6 Chunxiu Lu, 春秀路6号; mains ¥30-50; ☺11am-10pm; ⓓ; ⓢDongzhimen or Dongsi Shitiao) Very popular place to sample Běijīng's signature dish. Not only is the duck here extremely good value at ¥128 including all the trimmings but, unusually for a roast duck restaurant, you can also sit outside, on the wooden decking overlooking the street. The rest of the menu is a mix of Chinese cuisines, rather than Běijīng specialities, but the food here is all decent. Some English spoken. Wouldn't hurt to book, but not essential.

JÍXIÁNGNIĂO XIĀNGCÀI   CHINESE HÚNÁN $$
Map p298 (吉祥鸟湘菜; Jishikou Donglu, 吉市口东路; mains ¥20-50; ☺11am-9.30pm; ⓓ; ⓢChaoyangmen) There aren't enough places in Běijīng that serve up xiāng cài (湘菜), the name given to the notoriously spicy cuisine of Húnán province, but this large, fiery restaurant is arguably the best of them. The braised pork with brown sauce (¥38), known in China as hóngshāo ròu (红烧肉), is understandably popular – it's well known for being the favourite dish of Mao Zedong, who hailed from Húnán. But the fish head with chopped pepper (¥68) also should not be missed; nor the village style fried meat cubes (¥28). Not much English spoken here, but the menu has photos and English translations. No English sign; look for the red neon Chinese characters.

BÀODŬ HUÁNG   CHINESE BĚIJĪNG $
Map p298 (爆肚皇; 15 Dongzhimenwai Dajie, 东直门外大街15号; mains ¥10-30; ☺11am-2pm & 5-9pm; ⓢDongzhimen) In-the-know locals pile into this no-nonsense apartment-block restaurant to gobble and slurp their way through its authentic Běijīng-grub menu. The speciality is bàodŭ (爆肚; boiled lamb tripe; ¥13/25). If that's something you feel

you can't, er...stomach, then plump instead for a delicious niúròu dàcōng ròubǐng (牛肉大葱肉饼; beef and onion fried patty; ¥8). The blanched vegetables are popular side dishes; choose from chāo báicài (焯白菜; blanched cabbage; ¥4), chāo fěnsī (焯粉丝; blanched glass noodles; ¥4) or chāo dòng dòufu (焯冻豆腐; blanched tofu; ¥4). And if you haven't ordered a meat patty, grab a zhīma shāobing (芝麻烧饼; roasted sesame-seed bun; ¥1.5) instead. True Beijingers will also nibble on jiāo quān (焦圈; deep-fried dough rings; ¥1), washed down with gulps of dòu zhī (豆汁; sour soy milk). You may prefer to go for a bottle of píjiǔ (啤酒; local beer; ¥5). No English spoken, no English menu, no English sign.

DIN TAI FUNG   CHINESE DUMPLINGS $$
Map p298 (鼎泰丰; Dǐng Tài Fēng; ☑6553 1536; Gf, Shin Kong Place, 87 Jianguo Lu, 建国路87号新光天地店6楼; dumplings ¥20-70, noodles ¥30-50; ☺11.30am-9.30pm; ⓔⓓ; ⓢDawanglu) Over 20 years ago, the New York Times picked the original Taipei branch of this upmarket dumplings chain as one of the 10 best restaurants in the world. That's no longer true, but the dumplings here are certainly special. The xiǎolóngbāo – thin-skinned packages with meat or veggie fillings surrounded by a superb, scalding soup are especially fine. Din Tai Fung also does Shànghǎi hairy crabmeat jiǎozi (饺子; stuffed dumplings) and shāomài, as well as excellent soups and noodle dishes. Completely nonsmoking, it prides itself on being kid friendly and is packed out with families at weekends. It's on the top floor of the posh Shin Kong Place Mall, along with a host of other restaurants.

BELLAGIO   TAIWANESE $$
Map p298 (鹿港小镇; Lùgǎng Xiǎozhèn; ☑6551 3533; 6 Gongrentiyuchang (Gongti) Xilu, 工体西路6号; mains ¥30-60; ☺11am-5am; ⓓ; ⓢChaoyangmen) Despite the Italian name, this is a slick, late-opening Taiwanese restaurant conveniently located next to the strip of nightclubs on Gongrentiyuchang Xilu (Gongti Xilu). During the day and the evening, it attracts cashed-up locals and foreigners. After midnight, the club crowd moves in. The large menu includes Taiwanese favourites such as three cup chicken (¥46), as well as a wide range of vegetarian options. But the real reason to come here is for the wonderful puddings. The shaved-ice cream desserts are rightly renowned. Try the red beans with condensed milk on shaved ice (¥29)

and the fresh mango cubes on shaved ice (¥36). The coffee is top-notch, too.

XIĂO WÁNG'S HOME RESTAURANT
CHINESE MIXED **$$**

Map p298 (小王府; Xiǎo Wángfǔ; ☑6594 3602; 2 Guanghua Dongli, 光华东里2号; mains ¥30-50; ☺11am-10.30pm; Ⓢ Jintaixizhao) This modest, but clean, well-run restaurant has been serving customers here for almost 20 years. It's grown over time and now occupies part of three floors of an old-fashioned, low-rise housing block, and even has some neat balcony seating. The menu includes a mix of Chinese cuisine, and this is a decent place to try good-value Peking roast duck (¥128). It has an English sign, but is tucked away down an alley, so is sometimes hard to find. Best accessed from Guanghua Lu.

FÈITÁNG YÚXIĀNG
CHINESE SÌCHUĀN **$$**

Map p298 (沸腾渔乡; ☑6417 4988; Chunxiu Lu, 春秀路; mains ¥30-60; ☺11am-2pm & 5.30pm-10pm; ⓓ; Ⓢ Dongzhimen or Dongsi Shitiao) Best known for its *shuǐzhǔ yú* (水煮鱼; per *jīn* ¥50-100), a chilli-laden fish broth, translated on the menu as 'poached fish in hot chilli oil', this striking branch of the well-regarded restaurant chain does the whole range of spicy Sichuanese favourites. The fish is ordered, and priced by the *jīn* (500g). The average serving is around three *jīn* and can be shared between three or four people.

BĂOYUÁN DUMPLING RESTAURANT
CHINESE DUMPLINGS **$**

Map p298 (宝源饺子屋; Bǎoyuán Jiǎozi Wū; 6 Maizidian Jie, 麦子店街6号; mains ¥20-40, dumplings ¥10-16; ☺11.15am-10pm; ⓓ; Ⓢ Liangmaqiao or Agricultural Exhibition Centre) Fun for the kids – but also tasty enough for parents – this better-than-average dumplings restaurant dazzles diners with its multi-coloured *jiǎozi*. The dough dyes are all natural (carrots make the orange; spinach the green) and don't detract from the flavour of the fillings, which is as good as at any of Běijīng's best dumpling joints. Dumplings are ordered and priced by the *liǎng* (about 50g). One *liǎng* gets you six dumplings. Not much English spoken, but there's an English sign and menu.

DUCK DE CHINE
PEKING ROAST DUCK **$$$**

Map p298 (全鸭季; Quányáji; ☑6501 8881; Courtyard 4, 1949, near Gongrentiyuchang Beilu, 工体北路四号院; mains ¥50-150; ☺11am-2pm & 5.30-10pm; ⓓ; Ⓢ Tuanjiehu) Housed in a reconstructed industrial-style courtyard complex known as 1949, this chic restaurant incorporates both Chinese and French duck-roasting methods to produce some stand-out duck dishes, including a leaner version of the classic Peking roast duck (¥238). The pumpkin infused with sour plums is a delicious accompaniment, while the wine list is as impressive as you'd expect. Book ahead.

BĚI
EAST ASIAN **$$$**

Map p298 (北; ☑6410 5230; Opposite House Hotel, Bldg 111, Sanlitun Lu, 三里屯路11号院1号楼; mains ¥150-400; ☺6-10pm; ⓓ; Ⓢ Tuanjiehu) Located in the nightclub-like basement below ultra-trendy boutique hotel Opposite House, this achingly cool Asian restaurant specialises in Korean and Japanese cuisine. The sushi is top-notch, the tuna outstanding, and there's a strong selection of *saki* and *soju* to keep you in high spirits. Booking recommended.

BOCATA
CAFE **$**

Map p298 (3 Sanlitun Bei Lu, 三里屯北路3号; sandwiches ¥26-50; ☺11.30am-midnight; ☎; Ⓢ Tuanjiehu) Great spot for lunch, especially in summer, located slap-bang in the middle of Sānlǐtún's bar street and opposite Běijīng's trendiest shopping area. As the name suggests, there's a Mediterranean–Middle Eastern theme to the food, with decent hummus, salads (from ¥25), cold meats and cheeses (from ¥50), but most punters go for the tasty sandwiches on ciabatta. The coffee, juices and smoothies (from ¥20) go down a treat, too, and the large, tree-shaded terrace is very popular in nice weather.

CARMEN
SPANISH **$$**

Map p298 (卡门; Kǎmén; ☑6417 8038; Nali Patio north side, 81 Sanlitun Lu, 三里屯路那里花园北外1层; mains ¥30-60; ☺11.15am-10.30pm; ⓓ; Ⓢ Tuanjiehu) Arguably Běijīng's best-loved tapas joint, Carmen does a fine range of olives, cold meats, cheeses and the like, plus plenty of Mediterranean-inspired mains. The wine list is strong, and there's live music from 7.30pm every night. It's hidden round the corner from the popular terrace courtyard known as Nali Patio.

GRILL 79
INTERNATIONAL **$$$**

Map p298 (国贸79; Guómào Qīshíjiǔ; 79th fl, China World Trade Centre Phase Three, 1 Jianguomenwai Dajie, 建国门外大街1号国贸大酒店79层; mains ¥180-300; ☺midday-2pm & 6-10pm; ☺ⓓ;

(S)Guomao) Don't be put off by the name: this is so much more than a steak house. It's fine dining at its finest and, located on one of the top floors of the tallest building in the city, this is literally *the* high point of Běijīng's restaurant scene. Needless to say, the steaks (¥300 to ¥1500) are superb, but there's lobster, oysters and quality sea-fish dishes to tempt you as well, plus an extensive wine list. Lunchtime set menus start at ¥180, but the daytime views are less impressive than the evening city skyscape. Upstairs is the equally swanky cocktail bar, Atmosphere – Běijīng's highest bar.

RUMI
PERSIAN $$

Map p298 (入迷; ☑8454 3838; 1a Gongrentiyuchang Beilu, 工体北路1-1号; mains 60-150; ⊗11.30am-midnight; [₫]; (S)Tuanjiehu) Located in a strip of Middle Eastern restaurants, this is Běijīng's only Persian place. Inside, it's all cool white walls and furniture, but the food is authentic, with dishes such as *ghormeh sabzi* (a beef or vegetarian stew); fine shish kebabs (from ¥95), including a vegetarian option; and decent hummus (¥30 to ¥50). They don't serve alcohol, but you can bring your own and there's no corkage charge. Also has a large street-side terrace.

BITEAPITTA
MIDDLE EASTERN $$

Map p298 (吧嗒饼; Bāda Bǐng; Unit 201, 2nd fl, Tongli Bldg, 43 Sanlitunbei Lu, 三里屯北路43号同里花园201号; mains ¥50-100; ⊗11am-11pm; [₫]; (S)Tuanjiehu) This low-key Middle Eastern restaurant–cafe is a decent spot for lunch or a late-night filler (it stays open til 1am at weekends). Has a range of pitta-bread sandwiches (¥25 to ¥40) plus hummus, falafel, shawarma and salads. Also does a variety of kebabs (¥50 to ¥80) as well as Middle Eastern-style coffee.

NÁNJĪNG IMPRESSIONS
CHINESE NÁNJĪNG $$

Map p298 (南京大牌档; Nánjīng Dàpáidàng; 4th fl, Shimao Shopping Centre, 13 Gongrentiyuchangbei Lu, 工体北路13号世茂百货4层; mains ¥20-50; ⊗11am-2pm & 5-11pm; [₫]; (S)Tuanjiehu) This place attempts to give diners an impression of a traditional streetside Nánjīng restaurant, but this is totally fake, of course, given that it's located on the 4th floor of a modern shopping centre. But the atmosphere is fun and friendly and the food is tasty and very good value. Either tick dishes off the menu, or browse the in-restaurant snack stalls and point at what you fancy. Duck dishes are a speciality, as are the various sticky-rice dishes – try *jiāngmǐ kòuroù* (江米扣肉; a dome of sticky rice with pork belly strips; ¥32).

SĀN YÀNG CÀI
CHINESE SÌCHUĀN $$

Map p298 (三样菜; Workers Stadium North Gate, off Gongrentiyuchangbei Lu, 工人体育场北门; mains ¥40-90; ⊗11.30am-5am; [₫]; (S)Dongsi Shitiao or Tuanjiehu) The name of this place means 'three types of food', the three types being eels, frogs and loaches – three typical ingredients in Sichuanese cuisine. You can also tuck into duck neck, chicken feet and pig trotters, plus plenty of other dishes that are traditionally more palatable according to Western tastes. Whatever you order, though, expect it to be pretty spicy. The menu has English translations as well as photos, and the restaurant stays open late for munchy-driven revellers stumbling out of the nightclubs in and around the Workers Stadium.

MIDDLE 8TH
CHINESE YÚNNÁN $$

Map p298 (中8楼; Zhōng Bā Lóu; ☑6413 0629; Dongsan Jie, off Sanlitun Lu, 三里屯路东三街; mains ¥30-60; ⊗11.15am-10.30pm; [₫]; (S)Tuanjiehu) Quite how authentic the flavours

LIBRARIES CAN BE COOL

A combination of bar, cafe, restaurant and library, the **Bookworm** (书虫; Shūchóng; Map p298; ☑6586 9507; www.beijingbookworm.com; Bldg 4, Nansanlitun Lu, 南三里屯路4号楼; mains from ¥70; ⊗9am-2am; ⊜☎; (S)Tuanjiehu) is a Běijīng institution. There are 16,000-plus books you can browse while sipping your coffee or working your way through the extensive wine list. The food maintains the bookish theme, with sandwiches (¥42) and dishes named after famous authors. But the Bookworm is much more than just an upmarket cafe. It's one of the epicentres of Běijīng cultural life and hosts lectures, poetry readings, a Monday-night quiz and a very well regarded annual book festival. Any author of note passing through town gives a talk here. Check the website for upcoming events. There's a roof terrace in summer and a nonsmoking area.

are here is up for debate but the dishes are certainly full of Yúnnán character – plenty of bamboo, wild mushrooms and banana leaf–wrapped offerings – and are beautifully presented.

MÉIZHŌU
DŌNGPŌ JIŬLÓU
CHINESE SÌCHUĀN $$

Map p298 (眉州东坡酒楼 ; Chunxiu Lu, 春秀路; mains ¥15-60; ☺6.30-9am, 10.30am-2pm & 5-10pm; 🅿; SDongzhimen or Dongsi Shitiao) This good-value Sichuanese restaurant chain is one of the cheaper places to eat in this relatively expensive end of town. Despite the low prices, it still serves up good-quality, typically mouth-numbing Sìchuán dishes in a clean, comfortable setting. The menu is in English and has photos as well as very handy chilli-logo spice indicators. The only thing that's not a bargain here is the beer. The cheapest bottles cost ¥12 – a small fortune for a local beer in a Chinese restaurant.

PURPLE HAZE
THAI $$

Map p298 (紫苏庭; Zǐsū Tíng; 🕿6413 0899; 55 Xingfu Yicun, off Gongrentiyuchang Beilu, 工人体育场北路幸福一村55号; mains ¥40-70; ☺11.30am-10.30pm; 🌐; SDongsi Shitiao) The trendiest and most congenial Thai restaurant in town.

INDIAN KITCHEN
INDIAN $$

Map p298 (北京印度小厨餐厅; Běijīng Yìndù Xiǎo Chú Cāntīng; 🕿6462 7255; 2f, 2 Sanlitun Beixiaojie, 三里屯北小街2号二楼; mains ¥30-50; ☺11am-2.30pm & 5.30-11pm; SAgricultural Exhibition Center) Arguably the city's best Indian food.

ELEPHANT
RUSSIAN $$

Map p298 (大笨象; Dàbèn Xiàng; Ritan Beilu, 日坛北路; mains ¥30-60; ☺9am-4am; SChaoyangmen) Fun Russian restaurant in the heart of Běijīng's Russian district. Serves food until 1am, has cheap vodka (¥10) and has a large terrace.

798 ARTS DISTRICT
RESTAURANTS

(798艺术区; Qī Jiǔ Bā Yìshù Qū; Jiuxianqiao Lu; 酒仙桥路; 🚌909 from Dongzhimen subway station Exit C) The largely traffic-free lanes of the hip and happening 798 Arts District are dotted with pleasant cafes and restaurants. Most places have fresh coffee, free wi-fi, Western food and English menus. **At Cafe** (798 Rd; ☺10am-11pm), 798's first-ever cafe, is a popular hangout for artists. **Timezone 8** (798 Rd; ☺8.30am-8pm) is a cool cafe attached to the best art bookshop in Běijīng, while **Happy Rooster** (cnr 7 Star Rd & Ceramics First St; ☺9.30am-9pm) is 798's cheapest decent Chinese restaurant (picture menu). See p138 for more information on the arts district.

🍷 DRINKING & NIGHTLIFE

The days when Sānlǐtún was the be-all and end-all of Běijīng nightlife are long gone. These days, the main drag of Sanlitun Lu is rather tawdry – at night the touts for massage parlours and hookers emerge – and the bars are strictly for the undiscerning. But hidden within the new, ultra-modern shopping precincts of the Village is the area's latest hotspot: Nali Patio (Map p298), a small, modern courtyard space surrounded by popular bars, cafes and restaurants. Other lively areas include Courtyard 4 (just south of Gongrentiyuchangbei Lu) and the Workers Stadium, which contains most of Běijīng's busiest nightclubs. The area around Jianguomenwai Dajie is home to upmarket cocktail bars for the CBD crowd.

MIGAS BAR
BAR

Map p298 (米家思; Mǐ Jiā Sī; 6th fl, Nali Patio, 81 Sanlitunbei Lu, 三里屯北路81号那里花园6层; beer from ¥25, cocktails from ¥50, mains from ¥70; ☺midday-2.30pm & 6pm-10.30pm, bar 7.30pm-late; STuanjiehu) A good-quality Spanish restaurant, cosy indoor bar and wildly popular rooftop terrace create a three-in-one, everyone's-a-winner package at one of Sānlǐtún's most popular venues. The restaurant isn't as good value as nearby Carmen, and the service is questionable at best, but the tapas are excellent nonetheless. What most people come here for, though, is the rooftop terrace – the highest and arguably coolest spot in Sānlǐtún's Nali Patio. Good music, excellent wine and fine views.

APOTHECARY
COCKTAIL BAR

Map p298 (酒术; Jiǔ Shù; www.apothecarychina. com; 3rd fl, Nali Patio, 81 Sanlitunbei Lu, 三里屯北路81号那里花园3层; cocktails from ¥60; ☺6pm-late Tue-Sun; STuanjiehu) Widely regarded as the city's best cocktail bar, Apothecary isn't quite as swanky as some of its five-star hotel-based competitors, but it knows its drinks. Cocktails are mixed with care and attention and the classics come with their own biography on an impressive drinks menu, which also features a number of in-house creations. Also does very good food. A lot of people complain about the slow service, but for us the main sticking point here is the rather bizarre no-standing policy.

HAZE CLUB

Map p298 (A101 Guanghua Lu Soho, Guanghua Lu, 光华路光华路Soho地下1层; ¥50; ⏲11pm-6am; [S]Yong'anli) Housed in the corner of a striking Swiss-cheese lookalike tower block, this funky little basement club, with a stylish bar at ground level above it, has lively nights on Fridays, Saturdays and some Thursdays. It's mostly house, but techno and electro nights also feature, and top-name DJs are sometimes brought in. A warning: the steep, spiral staircase leading down to the club is lethal after a few drinks.

FIRST FLOOR BAR

Map p298 (壹楼; Yī Lóu; 三里屯后街同里1层, ground fl, Tongli Studios, Sanlitun Houjie; beer from ¥15, cocktails from ¥35, mains from ¥70; ⏲10am-2am; [S]Tuanjiehu) Solid bar with a pub-like vibe serving affordable drinks and pub grub. Decent size, and opens out onto the street so doesn't get as smoky as its upstairs sister bar, **Second Floor** (Map p298). Open till 4am at weekends.

SADDLE CANTINA BAR

Map p298 (West Wing, Nali Patio, 81 Sanlitun Beilu, 三里屯酒吧街81号3.3隔壁南边新白楼里边; beers from ¥20, cocktails from ¥45; ⏲10am-2am; [S]Tuanjiehu) The Mexican theme at this spacious, well-managed bar means potent margaritas (¥60) are available, as well as burritos (¥60) and fajitas (¥65 to ¥70). That is less important than the attractive 2nd-floor roof terrace, though, which overlooks popular Nali Patio and is always busy in summer. Happy hour is from 3pm to 7pm.

ATMOSPHERE COCKTAIL BAR

Map p298 (云酷酒吧; Yún Kù Jiǔbā; 80th fl, China World Summit Wing, 1 Jianguomenwai Dajie, 建国门外大街1号国贸大酒店80层; beer from ¥55, cocktails from ¥80; ⏲midday-2am; [S]Guomao) Běijīng's highest bar is perched way up on the 80th floor of the city's tallest building and is a suitably swish affair, with fine wines, excellent cocktails, Cuban cigars, live jazz and outstanding city views.

TREE BAR

Map p298 (树酒吧; Shù Jiǔbā; ☎6591 6519; 43 Sanlitun Beijie, 三里屯北街43号; beers from ¥15; ⏲11am-late Mon-Sat, 1pm-late Sun; [S]Tuanjiehu) Tucked behind a strip of largely grotty bars that get mad-busy at weekends, this low-key, long-term favourite attracts a mix of locals, expats and tourists. There's a fine selection of Belgian beers (from ¥40) and the thin-crust pizzas (from ¥50), cooked in a wood-fired oven in the bar itself, are some of the best in town. It's off the courtyard of the You Yi Youth Hostel.

NEARBY THE TREE BAR

Map p298 (树旁边酒吧; Shù Pángbiān Jiǔbā; Xingfu Sancun Yixiang, off Sanlitunbei Lu, 三里屯北路幸福三村一巷; beers from ¥10; ⏲10am-2am; [S]Tuanjiehu) Run by the same company that runs the Tree, this smaller sister bar has a cute terrace and a similarly pleasant atmosphere. It also offers some bargain drinks prices. Glasses of local lager go for just ¥10 (although admittedly they are small glasses) and during happy hour (6pm to 9pm every day) they're just ¥5!

CHOCOLATE CLUB

Map p298 (巧克力; Qiǎokèlì; 19 Ritan Beilu, 日坛北路19号; ⏲9pm-7am; [S]Chaoyangmen) There are a number of Russian-style bars around the Rìtán Park area, but with its over-the-top, gold-themed decor and cheesy floor shows, as well as a Mongolian dwarf doorman, this is the closest you will come to a genuine Moscow nightlife experience in Běijīng. Beers start at ¥30. This is a place to drink in a group, though, so do as the Russians do and order a bottle of vodka (from ¥250). It gets going after midnight.

VICS CLUB

Map p298 (威克斯; Wēikèsī; ☎5293 0333; Workers Stadium, North Gate, Gongrentiyuchang Beilu, 工人体育场北路, 工人体育场北门; Fri & Sat ¥50; ⏲7pm-late; [S]Dongsi Shitiao) Vics is not the most sophisticated nightclub. Nevertheless, it has remained a favourite with the young crowd for many years now, which makes it some sort of an institution. The tunes are mostly standard R&B and hip-hop, there's an infamous ladies night on Wednesdays (free drinks for women before midnight), and weekends see it rammed with the footloose and fancy free. If you can't score here, you should give up trying. Entry is free from Monday to Thursday; it's

LOCAL KNOWLEDGE

"GUÓ'ĀN, GUÓ'ĀN, BĚIJĪNG GUÓ'ĀN!"

Football is growing in popularity in China and although you rarely see kids playing it on the street (you're much more likely to see them playing basketball or badminton) the number of people going to watch live matches has mushroomed in recent years. Běijīng's sole professional side is **Běijīng Guó'ān** (www.fcguoan.com). They are one of China's most successful football clubs and although they lack the big money and star names of Guǎngzhōu Evergrande and Shànghǎi Shēnhuā they have a passionate core fan base, and draw large crowds for their home games at the **Workers Stadium** (工人体育场; Gongren Tiyuchang). It's not unusual for in excess of 30,000 spectators to attend big games, and going to see one before hitting the bars and clubs in the area is a decent night out for sports fans, although don't expect a particularly high standard of football.

The season runs from March until November. Match days can be Thursday, Friday, Saturday or Sunday; kick-offs are usually 7.30pm. You can find Guó'ān's fixtures in English on www.worldfootball.net. Tickets are sold online through Chinese-language websites, or over the phone (Chinese only), but are sold out so quickly it's not worth bothering trying to go through these official channels. Standard practice is to just go to the stadium an hour or so before kick-off and buy your tickets off ticket touts. Expect to pay at least double or triple the face value of the ticket, meaning you'll probably have to fork out around ¥100 to ¥150 per ticket.

If you're interested in playing football while you're in Běijīng, contact the guys who run **China ClubFootball** (www.clubfootball.com.cn).

located inside the north gate of the Workers Stadium, opposite Mix.

MIX CLUB

Map p298 (密克斯; Mìkèsī; Workers Stadium, North Gate. Gongrentiyuchang Beilu, 工人体育场北路， 工人体育场北门; ⏲8pm-late; [S]Dongsi Shitiao) Mainstream hip-hop and R&B are the drawcards at this ever-popular nightclub (admission ¥50), with big-name DJs making occasional guest appearances. A younger crowd takes to the dance floor in droves. Very similar to nearby Vics, but slightly younger clientele.

D LOUNGE BAR

Map p298 (酒术; Jiǔ Shù; Courytard 4, Gongrentiyuchangbei Lu, 工体北路4号院; cocktails from ¥50; ⏲7pm-late; [S]Tuanjiehu) High ceilings and exposed brick walls give this cool venue a converted factory feel. The bright white bar adds some futuristic flavour, while the drinks are well made and the atmosphere is trendy without being overly swanky (although some complain of slightly obnoxious staff). Popular, but hard to find because of a lack of signage; look for the lower-case 'd'.

PADDY O'SHEA'S SPORTS BAR

Map p298 (爱尔兰酒吧; Aì'érlán Jiǔbā; ☎6415 6389; 28 Dongzhimenwai Dajie, 东直门外大街28号; beers from 20; ⏲10am-2am; [S]Dongzhimen) Probably the best place in Běijīng for watching sport on TV (Premiership football especially, but also rugby and Gaelic sports), Paddy's has a large number of screens, allowing for multi-channel viewing. It's reasonably big, has a proper bar to sit at and the service is warm and efficient. The alcohol selection is sound, with Kilkenny and Guinness (¥55) on tap and lots of bottled beers. Happy hour is 3pm to 8pm Monday to Friday. Does pub grub and has a handy Indian restaurant upstairs.

DESTINATION CLUB

Map p298 (目的地; Mùdìdì; 7 Gongrentiyuchang Xilu, 工体西路7号; ¥60; ⏲8pm-late; [S]Chaoyangmen) A club for boys who like boys and girls who want a night off from them, Destination's rough-hewn, concrete-walled interior doesn't stop it being packed on weekends. But then, as Běijīng's only genuine gay club, it doesn't have to worry about any competition.

MESH COCKTAIL BAR

Map p298 (Bldg 1, Village, 11 Sanlitun Lu , 三里屯路11号院1号楼; cocktails from Y70; ⏲5pm-1am; [S]Tuanjiehu) Located inside the achingly trendy Opposite House Hotel, Mesh has been designed to within an inch of its life – white bar, mirrors, fancy light fittings and mesh screens separating its different areas – but the effect isn't overpowering and it can be fun on the right night. The lychee martinis here are rightly popular. Thursday is gay night.

XIÙ BAR

Map p298 (秀酒吧; Xiù Jiǔbā; 6th fl Park Life, Yintai Centre, 2 Jianguomenwai Dajie, 建国门外大街2银泰中心柏悦酒店6层; cocktails from ¥70; ⏲6pm-2am; [S]Guomao) With its large wood-decked open terrace and regular evening barbecues, the Park Hyatt's 6th-floor bar offers something a little different from other swish hotel bars. It's a calm, almost serene space dotted with water features and surrounding a traditional-style Chinese pavilion. The cocktails are decent without being Běijīng's best, and there's some space for dancing inside (if it's not too packed).

CARGO CLUB

Map p298 (6 Gongrentiyuchang Xilu, 工体西路6号; ¥50; ⏲8pm-late; [S]Chaoyangmen) The best of the cluster clubs located in the strip just south of the west gate of the Workers Stadium, Cargo consistently flies in some of the bigger names in dance music to play to a locals-dominated crowd. It's busier during the week than the other places nearby.

ALFA CLUB

Map p298 (阿尔法; Ā'ěrfǎ; 6 Xingfu Yicun, 幸福一村6号, 工体北门对面; beers from ¥20, cocktails from ¥35; ⏲5pm-late; [S]Dongsi Shitiao) Popular gay night on Fridays.

Q BAR BAR

Map p298 (Q吧; Top fl, Eastern Inn Hotel, Sanlitun Nanlu, 三里屯南路麦霓啤酒吧南100米; cocktails from ¥50; ⏲6pm-late; [S]Tuanjiehu) Friendly cocktail bar with large roof terrace. Accessed through Eastern Inn Hotel.

☆ ENTERTAINMENT

[TOP CHOICE] **DOS KOLEGAS** LIVE MUSIC

(两个好朋友; Liǎnggè Hǎo Péngyou; 21 Liangmaqiao Lu, 亮马桥路21号 汽车电影院内; admission ¥30, beer from ¥15; ⏲8pm-2am Mon-Sat, 10am-9pm Sun; [S]Liangmaqiao then 🚌909) Tucked away to the side of Běijīng's drive-in cinema, a couple of kilometres northeast of Sānlǐtún, this fabulously bohemian venue has a large garden with patio seating and offers evening barbecues alongside some excellent live music. This is a great place to hear local bands (punk, rock, metal), especially in the summer when the whole gig moves outdoors.

UNIVERSAL THEATRE (HEAVEN & EARTH THEATRE) ACROBATICS

Map p298 (天地剧场; Tiāndì Jùchǎng; ☎6416 0757; 10 Dongzhimen Nandajie, 东直门南大街10号; tickets ¥180-680; ⏲performance 7.15pm; [S]Dongsi Shitiao) Young performers from the China National Acrobatic Troupe perform their mind-bending, joint-popping contortions. A favourite with tour groups, so best to book ahead. Tickets are pricier the further from the stage you sit. Keep an eye out for the dismal white tower that looks like it should be in an airport – that's where you buy your tickets.

POLY PLAZA INTERNATIONAL THEATRE CLASSICAL MUSIC

Map p298 (保利大厦国际剧院, Bǎolì Dàshà Guójì Jùyuàn; ☎6506 5343, ext 5621 6500 1188; 14 Dongzhimen Nandajie, 东直门南大街14号; tickets from ¥180; ⏲performance 7.30pm; [S]Dongsi Shitiao) Right by Dongsi Shitiao subway station, this venue hosts a range of performances, including ballet, classical music, opera and traditional Chinese folk music. It also hosts an increasing number of stage plays by foreign playwrights.

CHÁOYÁNG THEATRE ACROBATICS

Map p298 (朝阳剧场; Cháoyáng Jùchǎng; ☎6507 2421; 36 Dongsanhuan Beilu, 东三环北路36号; tickets ¥180-880; ⏲performances 5.15pm & 7.15pm; [S]Hujialou) An accessible place for foreign visitors, and often bookable through your hotel, this theatre hosts visiting acrobatic troupes from around China who fill the stage with plate spinning and hoop jumping.

MEGABOX CINEMA

Map p298 (美嘉欢乐影城; Měijiā Huānlè Yǐngchéng; ☎6417 6118; B1 fl, Sanlitun Village South, 19 Sanlitun Lu, 三里屯路19号三里屯Village南区地下1层; tickets from ¥80; ⏲performances noon-midnight; [S]Tuanjiehu) Probably the easiest place in the city to watch English-language Hollywood blockbusters, MegaBox is a modern multi-screen cinema complex in the basement of the ultramodern shopping precinct **Sānlǐtún Village**. It always shows at least one or two English-language films and offers an experience that is almost identical to that found at cinemas in the West (although don't expect much English from the attendants who work here).

EAST GATE CINEMA CINEMA

Map p298 (东环影城; Dōnghuán Yǐngchéng; ☎6418 5935; Bldg B, Basement, East Gate Plaza, Dongzhong Jie, 东中街东环广场B座地下一层; admission from ¥80; [S]Dongsi Shitiao) Shows the latest big releases, both domestic and foreign. Foreign films are shown with their original soundtrack, but with Chinese subtitles.

SHOPPING

The Cháoyáng district has some of the swankiest malls in town, as well as many of the most popular markets for visitors, including the Silk Market and Yashow, two multi-floor indoor clothes and souvenir markets which are heaving at weekends. Key areas for purchases are Sānlǐtún and Guómào, but there are shops of all descriptions spread across the district. Pānjiāyuán Market is on the edge of Cháoyáng and is the city's premier souvenir market.

SĀNLǏTÚN VILLAGE SHOPPING MALL

(19 Sanlitun Lu, 三里屯路19号; ⏲10am-10pm; [S]Tuanjiehu) This ultra-modern, eye-catching collection of mid-sized malls is a shopping, and architectural highlight of this part of the city. The Village looms over what was once a seedy strip of dive bars (there are still a few of those left, mind) and has transformed the area into a hangout hotspot for locals and foreigners alike. The complex is in two sections, which book-end the slightly older 3.3 Shopping Centre. The **South Village** (Map p298) was completed a few years back and is home to Běijīng's first Apple store, the world's largest Adidas shop and a number of midrange Western clothing stores, as well as cafes, restaurants and the multi-screen cinema complex MegaBox. Nearby **North Village** (Map p298) is home to more high-end labels and local designer boutiques, including Emporio Armani, Comme des Garçons, Balenciaga and Shanghai Trio, and is set beside Běijīng's fancy-pants boutique hotel Opposite House (p197).

SILK MARKET CLOTHING & SOUVENIRS

Map p298 (秀水市场; Xiùshuǐ Shìchǎng; 14 Dongdaqiao Lu, 东大桥路14号; ⏲10am-8.30pm; [S]Yong'anli) The six-storey Silk Market continues to thrive despite some vendors being hit by lawsuits from top-name brands tired of being counterfeited on such a huge scale. Not that the legal action has stopped the coach loads of tourists who descend on this place every day. Their presence makes effective bargaining difficult. But this is a

LOCAL KNOWLEDGE

ARTS, CRAFTS & ANTIQUES

Hands down the best place in Běijīng to shop for *yìshù* (arts), *gōngyì* (crafts) and *gǔwán* (antiques) is **Pānjiāyuán Market** (潘家园古玩市场; Pānjiāyuán Gǔwán Shìchǎng; West of Panjiayuan Qiao; 潘家园桥西侧; ⏲8.30am-6pm Mon-Fri, 4.30am-6pm Sat-Sun; [S]Jinsong). Some stalls here are open every day, but the market as a whole is only at its biggest and best on weekends, when you can find everything from calligraphy, Cultural Revolution memorabilia and cigarette ad posters to Buddha heads, ceramics, Qing dynasty–style furniture and Tibetan carpets.

Pānjiāyuán hosts around 3000 dealers and up to 50,000 visitors a day, all scoping for treasures. The serious collectors are early birds, swooping here at dawn to snare precious relics. If you want to join them, an early start is essential. You might not find that rare Qianlong *dòucǎi* stem cup or late Yuán dynasty *qīnghuā* vase, but what's on view is no less than a compendium of Chinese curios and an A to Z of Middle Kingdom knick-knacks. This market is chaotic and can be difficult if you find crowds or hard bargaining intimidating. Also, ignore the 'don't pay more than half' rule here – some vendors might start at 10 times the real price. Make a few rounds to compare prices and weigh it up before forking out for something.

How to Get to Pānjiāyuán

The market is about 1km south of Jinsong subway station on Line 10. Come out of Exit D and keep walking straight. Turn right at the flyover and you'll see the market on your left. At the time of research, Line 10 was due to be extended south and will eventually include a Panjiayuan station.

good place for cashmere, T-shirts, jeans, shirts, skirts and, of course, silk, which is one of the few genuine items you will find here.

SĀNLǏTÚN YASHOW CLOTHING MARKET CLOTHING & SOUVENIRS
Map p298 (三里屯雅秀服装市场; Sānlǐtún Yǎxiù Fúzhuāng Shìchǎng; 58 Gongrentiyuchang Beilu, 工体北路58号; ⏲10am-9pm; [S]Tuanjiehu) Five floors of virtually anything you might need and a favourite with expats and visitors. Basement: shoes, handbags and suitcases. **Big Shoes** (Map p298) is useful if you're struggling to find suitably sized footwear. First floor: coats and jackets. Second floor: shirts, suits and ladies wear. Third floor: silk, clothes, carpets, fabrics and tailors to fashion your raw material into something wearable. Fourth floor: jewellery, souvenirs, toys and a beauty salon. Bargain hard here.

SHARD BOX STORE JEWELLERY
Map p298 (慎德阁; Shèndégé; ☎8561 3712; 4 Ritan Beilu, 日坛北路4号; ⏲9am-7pm; [S]Yong'anli) Using porcelain fragments from Ming and Qing dynasty vases that were destroyed during the Cultural Revolution, this fascinating family-run store creates beautiful and unique shard boxes, bottles and jewellery. The boxes range from the tiny (¥30), for storing rings or cufflinks, to the large (¥8000). It also repairs and sells jewellery, mostly from Tibet and Mongolia.

ALIEN'S STREET MARKET CLOTHING MARKET
Map p298 (老番街市场; Lǎo Fān Jiē Shìchǎng; Chaowaishichang Jie, 朝外市场街; ⏲9.30am-7pm; [S]Chaoyangmen) This somewhat cramped market, just north of Rìtán Park, is packed with a huge variety of clothing, as well as tonnes of accessories. You can find most things here and it's popular with visiting Russian traders, which means the clothes come in bigger sizes than usual and the vendors will probably greet you in Russian. Haggling is essential.

PLACE SHOPPING MALL
Map p298 (世贸天阶; Shìmào Tiānjiē; 9a Guanghua Lu, 光华路甲9号; ⏲10am-10pm; [S]Yong'anli) Dominated by its spectacular giant outdoor video screen, an object of fascination for kids, the Place has an extremely popular branch of Zara, as well as French Connection, Miss Sixty and a number of coffee shops. Also accessed from Dongdaqiao Lu and Jintong Xilu.

3.3 SHOPPING CENTRE SHOPPING MALL
Map p298 (服饰大厦; Fúshì Dàshà; 33 Sanlitun Beijie, 三里屯北街33号; ⏲11am-11pm; [S]Tuanjiehu) With its collection of trendy boutiques and accessories stores, this mall, sandwiched between the North and South blocks of the even trendier Sānlǐtún Village, caters for Běijīng's bright young things. Prices are accordingly high. But with 300 shops here, it's good window-shopping territory.

CHINA WORLD SHOPPING MALL SHOPPING MALL
Map p298 (国贸商城; Guómào Shāngchéng; 1 Jianguomenwai Dajie; 建国门外大街1号; ⏲10am-9.30pm; [S]Guomao) Adjacent to the first-rate China World Hotel, this is a popular, if soulless, mall packed with top-name brands, including Burberry, Marc Jacobs and Prada, as well as boutiques, jewellery stores and fast-food restaurants. Le Cool Ice Rink (p153) is in the basement.

BǍINǍOHUÌ COMPUTER MALL COMPUTERS & ELECTRONICS
Map p298 (百脑汇电脑市场; Bǎinǎohuì Diànnǎo Shìchǎng; 10 Chaoyangmenwai Dajie, 朝阳门外大街10号; ⏲9am-8pm; [S]Chaoyangmen or Hujialou) Four floors of gadgetry, including computers, iPods, MP3 players, blank CDs and DVDs, gaming gear, software and other accessories. The prices are fairly competitive and you can bargain here, but don't expect too much of a reduction. Next to this mall there are a number of shops that are good places to pick up mobile phones and local SIM cards. There's another Bǎinǎohuì mall across the road by Dōngyuè Temple.

SPORTS, ACTIVITIES & COURSES

There is a branch of the popular Dragonfly Therapeutic Retreat (Map p298; ☎6593 6066; ground fl, Eastern Inn Hotel, Nansanlitun Lu, Sānlǐtún; ⏲11am-1am) in Sānlǐtún.

BODHI THERAPEUTIC RETREAT MASSAGE
Map p298 (菩提会所; Pútí Huìsuǒ; ☎6417 9595; 17 Gongrentiyuchang Beilu, 工体北路17号; ⏲11am-12.30am; [S]Dongsi Shitiao) The serene setting, a blend of Thai and Chinese

1. Water Cube (p140)
This iconic piece of architecture now houses Happy Magic Water Park.

2. Dōngyuè Temple (p139)
A performance at the temple during Chinese New Year celebrations.

3. CCTV Building (p139)
Known locally as the Big Underpants, the astonishing CCTV Tower seems to defy gravity.

4. 13 Club (p164)
A dark and forbidding venue down a suitably grimy alley.

LOCAL KNOWLEDGE

TAICHI TIPS

Characterised by its lithe and graceful movements, *tàijíquán* (literally 'Fist of the Supreme Ultimate'), also known as taichi, is an ancient Chinese physical discipline practised by legions of Chinese throughout the land.

Considerable confusion exists about taichi – is it a martial art, a form of meditation, a *qìgōng* (exercise that helps channel *qì*, or energy) style or an exercise? In fact, taichi can be each and all of these, depending on what you seek from the art and how deep you dig into its mysteries.

In terms of health benefits, taichi strengthens the leg muscles, exercises the joints, gives the cardiovascular system a good workout and promotes flexibility. It also relaxes the body, dissolving stress, loosening the joints and helping to circulate *qì*.

As a system of meditation, taichi leaves practitioners feeling both centred and focused. Taichi introduces you to Taoist meditation techniques, as the art is closely allied to the philosophy of Taoism. And if you're adept at taichi, it is far easier to learn other martial arts, as you'll have learned a way of moving that is common to all of the fighting arts.

Useful Pointers

- When executing a movement, bodily motion and power are directed by the waist before moving to the hands (observe a skilled practitioner and see how the motion reaches the hands last). The hands never lead the movement.
- When performing a form (as the moving sets are called), keep your head level, neither rising nor dipping.
- Practise taichi as if suspended by an invisible thread from a point at the top of your head.
- Don't lean forward or back and keep your torso vertical.
- Relax your shoulders and let your weight sink downwards.

Where to Learn

- Běijīng Mílún School of Traditional Kung Fu (p77)
- Jīnghuá Wǔshù Association
- The Hutong (p102)

influences just moments away from the madness of Běijīng's traffic, helps you shift gears straightaway, and that's before one of the many masseurs here gets to work in a comfy, private room. Bodhi offers aromatherapy, ayurvedic, Thai- and Chinese-style massage, as well as great foot reflexology massages and a wide range of facial treatments. There's free snacks and drinks, and with TVs in all the rooms you can lie back and watch a DVD while being pummelled into shape. Prices start at ¥168 for a basic full-body massage, although Thai and ayurvedic massages cost ¥298. Massages are available for ¥128 during weekday afternoons.

YOGA YARD YOGA

Map p298 (瑜珈苑; Yújiā Yuàn; ☎6413 0774; www.yogayard.com; 6th fl, 17 Gongrentiyuchang Beilu，工体北路17号6层; [S]Dongsi Shitiao) In the same building as Bodhi Therapeutic Retreat, this friendly English-speaking centre has traditional hatha yoga classes, from beginners to advanced. Ninety-minute lessons are ¥150, but you can have a trial class for ¥75.

JĪNGHUÁ WǓSHÙ ASSOCIATION MARTIAL ARTS

Map p298 (京华武术协会; Jīnghuá Wǔshù Xiéhuì; ☎135 2228 3751; basement, Pulse Club, Kempinski Hotel, Liangmaqiao Lu, 亮马桥路凯宾斯基地下一层脉搏俱乐部; ⏲5.30-7pm Sat & Sun; [S]Liangmaqiao) Run from the gym at Pulse Club in the basement of the building next to Kempinski Hotel, classes here are held in English and are given by teachers trained in traditional Shàolín forms. *Wǔshù, qìgōng* and taichi are all taught here. Ten classes costs ¥700; there are classes for kids (five years and over), too.

HAPPY MAGIC WATER PARK   SWIMMING

(水立方嬉水乐园; Shuǐlìfāng Xīshuǐ Lèyuán; Olympic Green, off Beichen Lu, 北辰路奥林匹克公园内; water park entrance adult/child ¥200/160, swimming only ¥50; ⊙10am-9pm; Ⓢ Olympic Green) Unlike many of the 2008 Olympics venues, Běijīng's National Aquatics Centre, aka the Water Cube, has now been put to use, post Olympics. The otherworldly bubble-like structure, about 7km north of the city centre, now houses Běijīng's largest indoor water park. Inside, it's a warren of neon plastic slides, tunnels, water jets and pools, alongside elaborate, surreal underwater styling. There's a lazy river, a 40ft freefall drop inside a plastic tube, and a wave pool designed to mimic the ocean. You can pay ¥50 for a two-hour swimming session in the ordinary pool, but for full-on water-slide action you need the ¥200 ticket.

LE COOL ICE RINK   ICE SKATING

Map p298 (国贸溜冰场; Guómào Liūbīngchǎng; ✆6505 5776; Basement 2, China World Shopping Mall, 1 Jianguomenwai Dajie, 建国门外大街1号; per 90min ¥30-50; ⊙10am-10pm; Ⓢ Guomao) Like many of the rinks in Běijīng, Le Cool is not very big. But it's easily accessible and perfect for kids. Visit in the morning or evening if you want to avoid the crowds. Skate hire is included in the price, which varies depending on the time of day. Individual, 40-minute lessons are ¥100.

BERLITZ   CHINESE LANGUAGE

Map p298 (北立兹; Běilìzī; ✆6593 0478; www.berlitz.com; Room 801, Sunjoy Mansion, 6 Ritan Lu, 日坛路6号新旅大厦8层; Ⓢ Jianguomen or Yong'anli) Berlitz runs group and one-on-one classes in Chinese, but is reluctant to arrange groups for you.

BRIDGE SCHOOL   CHINESE LANGUAGE

Map p298 (桥学校; Qiáo Xuéxiào; ✆6506 4409; www.bridgeschoolchina.com; Room 903, e-Tower, Guanghua Lu, 光华路内12号楼吗01大夏9层; per hr from ¥85; Ⓢ Jintaixizhao) Similar set up to Berlitz. Group and one-on-one classes. Has set-time classes you can join at various language levels.

CHINA STUDY ABROAD   CHINESE LANGUAGE

(✆5879 4363; www.chinastudyabroad.org; 11th fl, Tower A, Bldg 1 GT International Center, Yong'an Dongli, off Jianguomenwai Dajie, 建国门外大街永安东里通用国际中心1号楼A座11层; Ⓢ Yong'anli) Professionally run organisation offering the whole spectrum of Chinese-language programs, from summer camps and private tuition to long-term university placements.

CHINA WORLD FITNESS CENTRE   FITNESS

Map p298 (中国大饭店健身中心; Zhōngguó Dàfàndiàn Jiànshēn Zhōngxīn; ✆6505 2266 ext 33; 1 Jianguomenwai Dajie, 建国门外大街1号; per day ¥200; ⊙6am-11pm; Ⓢ Guomao) A 20m pool, squash courts, steam bath and Jacuzzi are available here, as well as yoga, Pilates, ballet and Latin dance. There are posh changing rooms, too. It's in the same complex as the China World Hotel.

The Summer Palace & Hǎidiàn

Neighbourhood Top Five

1 Enjoy a taste of imperial high-life by wandering the sumptuous gardens, temples, pavilions and corridors of the glorious **Summer Palace** (p156). Take a boat across Kūnmíng Lake, or escape the crowds by walking the willow tree-lined West Causeway.

2 Commune with nature in **Fragrant Hills Park** (p161), especially beautiful in the early autumn.

3 Spend a night exploring the buzzing restaurants and clubs of **Wǔdàokǒu** (p164), Běijīng's student heartland.

4 Push through the bamboo fronds in the **Běijīng Botanic Gardens** (p160), China's top collection of flora.

5 Check out the 280,000 year-old Jīnniúshān Man at the **Arthur M Sackler Museum of Art & Archaeology** (p160) and then stroll the peaceful, leafy campus of Peking University.

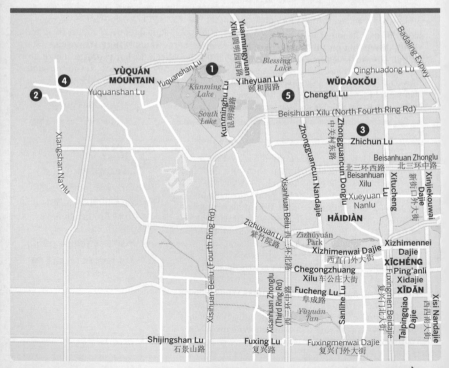

For more detail of this area see Map p297, p302 and p303 ➡

Explore: Summer Palace & Hǎidiàn

Hǎidiàn sprawls across a huge mass of west and north-west Běijīng, so you'll need to attack it in chunks, and don't expect to be able to see or do everything in one day.

Start at the Summer Palace. You could easily spend a whole day here; climb Longevity Hill for fine views over Běijīng. From there, it's a short bus ride to an amble in Fragrant Hills Park. Nature buffs will also want to visit the nearby Botanic Gardens.

In the evening head to Wǔdàokǒu. Surrounded by universities, this is one of Běijīng's most happening areas for cafes and nightlife and home to some of the best Korean and Japanese restaurants in town.

If you're on the track of temples, Hǎidiàn has some of the capital's finest examples. To temple-hop, start the day at the National Library subway stop and first take in the Indian-inspired Wǔtǎ Temple. From there, walk due west to Wànshòu Temple and then northeast towards the Great Bell Temple. You could end the day in quiet contemplation at the superb Azure Clouds Temple inside Fragrant Hills Park.

Local Life

➡ **Hangouts** Both locals and foreigners can be found at all hours in Lush (p164), a mix of cafe, bar, restaurant and nightlife venue. Bridge Café (p164) is another 24-hour hot spot.

➡ **Shopping** Wǔdàokǒu has stacks of baby boutiques, and quirky clothes shops catering for hipster students.

➡ **Parks** Hǎidiàn has many parks hidden beneath the tower blocks; retreat to them to avoid the urban sprawl, especially in the early evening.

Getting There & Away

➡ **Subway** Getting around Hǎidiàn is easy. Line 4 connects with Line 2 at Xizhimen, then runs north. Key stops include National Library, Weigongcun, Zhongguancun, East Gate of Peking University and Xiyuan (for the Summer Palace). When the Western Suburban Line is completed (after 2013), it will link the Summer Palace, Běijīng Botanic Gardens and Fragrant Hills Park to subway Line 10. For Wǔdàokǒu, and Dazhongsi, take Line 13, which connects with Line 2 at Xīzhímén. Line 10 runs east–west across the centre of Hǎidiàn, while Line 2 runs east–west across its south.

➡ **Bus** Useful buses are 331, which links Wǔdàokǒu with the Old Summer Palace and the Summer Palace, Běijīng Botanic Gardens, Sleeping Buddha Temple and Fragrant Hills Park. Bus 375 connects Wǔdàokǒu with Xīzhímén.

Lonely Planet's Top Tip

China has a special university (民族大学; Mínzú Dàxué) for its many ethnic minorities, and the area around it is where you'll find some of the most authentic restaurants serving up their local cuisines. The hub is Weigong Jie, where you can find fantastic Dǎi (a minority from the far south of Yúnnán Province) food, as well great Uighur and Mongolian eateries. To get there, jump on Line 4 to Weigongcun and then walk south 400m.

✕ Best Places to Eat

➡ Salang-Bang (p161)

➡ Lǎo Chē Jì (p164)

➡ Isshin Japanese Restaurant (p164)

For reviews, see p161 ➡

☕ Best Places to Drink

➡ Lush (p164)

➡ Bridge Café (p164)

➡ Propaganda (p164)

For reviews, see p164 ➡

◉ Best Temples

➡ Wànshòu Temple (p158)

➡ Wǔtǎ Temple (p158)

➡ Azure Clouds Temple (p161)

➡ Great Bell Temple (p160)

For reviews, see p158 ➡

TOP SIGHTS
SUMMER PALACE 颐和园

The splendid regal encampment of the Summer Palace in the northwest of town is one of Běijīng's must-see sights. This former playground for the imperial court fleeing the insufferable summer torpor of the old Imperial City is a marvel of landscaping: a wonderful, over-the-top mix of temples, gardens, pavilions, lakes, bridges, gate towers and corridors. It's a fine place just to amble around in the sunshine, but is also packed with stunning individual sights.

Hall of Benevolence & Longevity

The main building at ground level, this **hall** (Rénshòu Diàn) sits by the east gate and houses a hardwood throne. Look for the bronze animals that decorate the courtyard in front, including the mythical *qílín* (a hybrid animal that appeared on earth only at times of harmony).

Kūnmíng Lake

Three-quarters of the parkland in the palace is water, made up of Kūnmíng Lake (Kūnmíng Hú). Check out the extravagant **Marble Boat** (Map p302) moored on the northwestern shore. First built in 1755, it was restored in 1893 on the orders of Empress Cixi (using money meant to go towards building ships for the Chinese Navy). Much of it is actually wood painted to look like marble. Nearby are fine Qing-dynasty boathouses and the **Gate Tower of the Cloud-Retaining Eves** (Map p302), which once housed an ancient silver statue of Guanyu (God of War).

Boats ply the lake (¥15), running from the northern shore to South Lake Island, home to the **Dragon King**

DON'T MISS

- ➡ Longevity Hill Looming over Kūnmíng Lake and lined with superb temples and pavilions all the way to the top.
- ➡ Long Corridor Almost half a mile long with thousands of paintings covering its ceiling and beams.

PRACTICALITIES

- ➡ 颐和园; Yíhé Yuán
- ➡ 19 Xinjian Gongmen
- ➡ ticket ¥20, through ticket ¥50, audioguide ¥40, 4-/6-person pedal boat per hr ¥40/60
- ➡ 🕐8.30am-5pm, pedal boats 8.30am-4.30pm summer
- ➡ [S]Xiyuan or Beigongmen

Temple (Map p302), where royalty came to pray to the Dragon King's fearsome statue for rain in times of drought. But you can also hire your own pedalo (¥60 per hour, ¥300 deposit) or electric-powered boat (¥100 per hour, ¥400 deposit) to sail around at your own pace.

The Long Corridor

Awesome in its conception and execution, the **Long Corridor** (Cháng Láng; Map p302) is absolutely unmissable. Open at the sides but covered with a roof to shield the emperors from the elements, and with four pavilions along the way, it stretches for over 700m towards the foot of Longevity Hill. Its beams, the pavilion walls and some of the ceiling are decorated with 14,000 intricate paintings depicting scenes from Chinese history and myths, as well as classic literary texts. Your neck will ache from all that staring upwards, but the pain is worth it.

Longevity Hill

Rearing up by the side of Kūnmíng Lake and at the far end of the Long Corridor, the slopes of this 60m-high hill are covered in temples and pavilions, all arranged on a north–south axis. The most prominent and important are the **Buddhist Fragrance Pavilion** (Fóxiāng Gé; Map p302) and the **Cloud Dispelling Hall** (Páiyún Diàn; Map p302), which are connected by corridors. Awaiting you at the peak of the hill is the **Buddhist Temple of the Sea of Wisdom** (Zhìhuì Hǎi; Map p302), featuring glazed tiles (many sadly damaged) depicting Buddha. On a clear day, there are splendid views of Běijīng from here.

West Causeway

A great way to escape the crowds who converge here is to strike out along the **West Causeway** (Xīdī; Map p302) and then do a circuit of the lake by returning along the east shore. The causeway is lined with delightful willow and mulberry trees, and along the way you'll come across the grey and white marble **Jade Belt Bridge** (Map p302), which dates from the 18th century. There's also the graceful **17-Arch Bridge** (Map p302), which links the east shore to South Lake Island.

Wénchāng Gallery

South of the main entrance, come to **Wénchāng Gallery** (Map p302) to take at look at Empress Cixi's hand-writing (some of her calligraphy is on display), as well porcelain, bronzes and a jade gallery. Various other Qing-era artefacts are on show as well.

THE RISE & FALL & RISE OF THE SUMMER PALACE

It was Emperor Qianlong who created the Summer Palace, on the site of what had long been a royal garden. With the same determination he displayed in expanding China's borders, Qianlong enlisted 100,000 workers in 1749 to enlarge the gardens and deepen Kūnmíng Lake, while giving Longevity Hill its name in honour of his mother's 60th birthday. Thankfully, Qianlong was long dead by the time British and French soldiers rampaged through the palace in 1860 at the end of the Second Opium War. Apart from pillaging anything not nailed down, they trashed many of the temples and pavilions. That left Empress Cixi to restore it to its former glory, only for foreign soldiers to return in 1900 in the wake of the Boxer Rebellion. Not until after 1949 and the communist takeover was work begun to repair it.

The original name of the Summer Palace was the romantic, but not very regal, Garden of Clear Ripples. It was Empress Cixi who redubbed it in 1888.

THE SUMMER PALACE & HĂIDIÀN

TOP SIGHTS
SUMMER PALACE 颐和园

SIGHTS

SUMMER PALACE HISTORIC SITE

See p156.

WÀNSHÒU TEMPLE BUDDHIST TEMPLE

Map p297 (万寿寺; Wànshòu Sì; Suzhou Jie; adult ¥20; ⌚9am-4pm Tue-Sun; [S]National Library, or Gongzhufen, then bus 944) Ringed by a red wall on the southeastern corner of Suzhou Jie (off the Third Ring Rd), the Ming-dynasty Wànshòu Temple, or Longevity Temple, was originally consecrated for the storage of Buddhist texts. The temple's name echoes the Summer Palace's Longevity Hill (Wànshòu Shān); in fact, from Qing times the imperial entourage would put their feet up here and quaff tea en route to the palace. This temple was one of almost 50 that once lined the canal route from the western edge of the Imperial City walls (at Xīzhímén) to the Summer Palace. Now it is pretty much the only one that remains (Wǔtǎ Temple being another notable survivor). Wànshòu Temple fell into disrepair during the Republic, with the Wànshòu Hall burning down in 1937. Things went from bad to worse, and during the Cultural Revolution the temple served as an army barracks.

There's an interesting introduction to the history of the temple in the small hall (once the temple's Drum Tower) immediately to your left as you enter the complex. And as you walk through the Hall of the Deva Kings, which leads to the second courtyard, notice the illustration on your right that shows all the temples that once lined the canal. The names are in Chinese only, but see if you can spot the temple you're in (万寿寺) as well as neighbouring Yánqìng Temple (延庆寺; Yánqìng Si), nearby Dragon King Temple (龙王庙; Lóngwáng Sì) and the magnificent Wǔtǎ Temple (marked on the map with its former name, 真觉寺), all of which still stand, at least in part.

The highlight of a visit here, though, is to view the prized collection of bronze **Buddhist statuary** in the Buddhist Art Exhibition of Ming and Qing Dynasties, housed in two small halls on either side of the second courtyard. The displays guide you through the Buddhist pantheon with statues of Sakyamuni, Manjusri, Amitabha, Guanyin (in bronze and *déhuà,* or white-glazed porcelain) and exotic tantric pieces. Also look out for the *kapala* bowl made from a human skull, *dorje* and *purbhas* (Tibetan ritual daggers). Further halls contain museum exhibitions devoted to Ming and Qing porcelain and jade.

Another highlight is the Buddhist stone and clay **sculptures** housed in the large unnamed central hall at the back of the second courtyard. There are four magnificent central pieces, plus a dozen or so *arhats* (Buddhist disciples) lining the flanks. The pavilion at the rear of the whole complex once housed a 5m-high gold-lacquered brass statue that's now long gone; in its place is a miniature Ming-dynasty pagoda alloyed from gold, silver, zinc and lead.

Note that on Wednesdays the first 200 visitors get in for free.

As you exit the temple, see if you can track down the nearby remains of Yánqìng Temple and Dragon King Temple, further east along the canal. If you fancy travelling from here to the Summer Palace by boat (¥70, 20 minutes, every hour 10.30am to 4.20pm April to September), as the emperors once did, you can buy tickets at the nearby north gate of Zǐzhúyuàn Park (紫竹院公园; Zǐzhúyuàn Gōngyuán). To walk from here to Wǔtǎ Temple takes around 20 minutes.

WǓTǍ TEMPLE BUDDHIST TEMPLE

Map p297 (五塔寺; Wǔtǎ Sì; 24 Wutasi Cun, 五塔寺村24号; adult ¥20, audio guide ¥10; ⌚9am-4pm; [S]National Library, Exit C) Known previously as Zhēnjué Temple (真觉寺; Zhēnjué Sì), the distinctive Indian-styled Wǔtǎ Temple (Five Pagoda Temple) is a hugely rewarding place to visit, not only because of its unusual architectural style, but also because of the magnificent collection of stone carvings found within its grounds. The temple is topped by its five attractive namesake pagodas. The exterior of the main hall is decorated with *dorje,* hundreds of images of Buddha and legions of beasts, amid traces of red pigment. During Ming times, the temple ranged to at least six halls, all later tiled in yellow during Qing times; the terrace where the Big Treasure Hall once stood can still be seen. The temple, dating from 1473, is highly unusual for Běijīng, and well worth a visit in itself, but the highlight here is the extraordinary collection of stone carvings, some housed carefully in buildings at the back of the complex but many just scattered around the temple grounds. Pieces you might stumble across include gravestones, animal statues, carved human figures, stone stele and some enormous *bìxì* (mythical tortoiselike dragons often seen in Confucian temples). The pieces were all recovered from various places in Běijīng and put here for their protection during the latter end of the last century. Most are Qing and Ming dynasty, but there are a number of Yuán, Tang, Jin and even Eastern Han dynasty pieces, some of which are almost 2000 years old. Many, although not all, have explanatory captions in English; those captioned in Chinese only do at least have the date of origin written in numerals.

As with Wànshòu Temple, on Wednesdays the first 200 visitors get in for free here.

WORTH A DETOUR

OLD SUMMER PALACE

Located northwest of the city centre, the **Old Summer Palace** (圆明园; Yuánmíng Yuán; 28 Qinghua Xilu; adult ¥10, through ticket ¥25, map ¥6; ⏲7am-7pm; [S]Yuanmingyuan) was laid out in the 12th century. The ever-capable Jesuits were later employed by Emperor Qianlong to fashion European-style palaces for the gardens, incorporating elaborate fountains and baroque statuary. In 1860, during the Second Opium War, British and French troops torched and looted the palace, an event forever inscribed in Chinese history books as a low point in China's humiliation by foreign powers. Most of the wooden palace buildings were burned down in the process and little remains, but the hardier Jesuit-designed European Palace buildings were made of stone, and a melancholic tangle of broken columns and marble chunks survives. Note: to see these remains, you need to buy the more expensive through ticket.

The subdued marble ruins of the **Palace Buildings Scenic Area** (Xīyánglóu Jǐngqū) can be mulled over in the **Eternal Spring Garden** (Chángchūn Yuán) in the northeast of the park, near the east gate. There were once more than 10 buildings here, designed by Giuseppe Castiglione and Michael Benoist. The buildings were only partially destroyed during the 1860 Anglo-French looting (p217) and the structures apparently remained usable for quite some time afterwards. However, the ruins were gradually picked over and carted away by local people all the way up to the 1970s.

The **Great Fountain Ruins** (Dàshuǐfǎ) themselves are considered the best-preserved relics. Built in 1759, the main building was fronted by a lion-head fountain. Standing opposite is the **Guānshuǐfǎ**, five large stone screens embellished with European carvings of military flags, armour, swords and guns. The screens were discovered in the grounds of Peking University in the 1970s and later restored to their original positions. Just east of the Great Fountain Ruins stood a four-pillar archway, chunks of which remain.

West of the Great Fountain Ruins are the vestiges of the **Hǎiyàntáng Reservoir** (Hǎiyàntáng Xùshuǐchí Táijī), where the water for the impressive fountains was stored in a tower and huge water-lifting devices were employed. The metal reservoir was commonly called the Tin Sea (Xīhǎi). Also known as the Water Clock, the **Hǎiyàntáng**, where 12 bronze human statues with animal heads jetted water for two hours in a 12-hour sequence, was constructed in 1759. The 12 animal heads from this apparatus ended up in collections abroad and Běijīng is attempting to retrieve them (four can now be seen at the Poly Art Museum, p67). Just west of here is the **Fāngwàiguàn**, a building that was turned into a mosque for an imperial concubine. An artful reproduction of a former labyrinth called the **Garden of Yellow Flowers** is also nearby.

The palace gardens cover a huge area – 2.5km from east to west – so be prepared for some walking. Besides the ruins, there's the western section, the Perfection & Brightness Garden (Yuánmíng Yuán) and in the southern compound, the 10,000 Springs Garden (Wànchūn Yuán).

Bus 331 goes from the south gate (which is by Exit B of Yuanmingyuan subway station) to the east gate of the Summer Palace before continuing to the Botanic Gardens and eventually terminating at Fragrant Hills Park.

Note, you can enter the north gate of Běijīng Zoo from here. Cross the canal over the decorative arched bridge.

[FREE] **ARTHUR M SACKLER MUSEUM OF ART & ARCHAEOLOGY** MUSEUM

Map p303 (赛克勒考古与艺术博物馆; Sàikèlè Kǎogǔ Yǔ Yìshù Bówùguǎn; Peking University; ⏲9am to 4.30pm; [S]East Gate of Peking University) Excellent collection of relics brought together on the campus of Peking University (enter via west gate), although some English captions would be nice. Exhibits include the Jīnniúshān Man, a 280,000-year-old skeleton, bronze artefacts, jade pieces and a host of other relics from primordial China. Bring your passport for free entry, and afterwards make sure to wander the pleasant campus, a great way to tune out from Běijīng's frantic mayhem.

GREAT BELL TEMPLE BUDDHIST TEMPLE

Map p303 (大钟寺; Dàzhōng Sì; ☎6255 0819; 31a Beisanhuan Xilu; ticket ¥20; ⏲9am-4.30pm Tue-Sun; [S]Dazhongsi) Originally called Juéshēng Temple, this famous shrine was once a pit stop for Qing emperors who came here to pray for rain. Today the temple is named after its massive Ming-dynasty bell (6.75m tall and weighing a hefty 46.5 tonnes), which is inscribed with Buddhist sutras, comprising more than 227,000 Chinese characters, and decorated with Sanskrit incantations. The bell was cast during the reign of Emperor Yongle in 1406, with the tower built in 1733. To transport the bell from the foundry to the temple, a shallow canal was dug, and when it froze over in winter the bell was shunted across the ice by sled.

If you're bell crazy, you'll be spellbound by the exhibitions on bell casting and the collection of bells from France, Russia, Japan, Korea and other nations. Also on view are copies of the bells and chimes of the Marquis of Zeng and a collection of Buddhist and Taoist bells, including vajra bells and the wind chimes hung from temple roofs and pagodas.

[FREE] **YUÁN-DYNASTY WALLS RELICS PARK** PARK

Map p303 (元大都城垣遗址公园; Yuán Dàdū Chéngyuán Yízhǐ Gōngyuán; admission free; [S]Xitucheng) The name is an ambitious misnomer as there are not many genuine Yuán-dynasty relics here, but this slender strip of parkland, running alongside the Little Moon River (Xiǎoyuè Hé), commemorates a

WORTH A DETOUR

BĚIJĪNG BOTANIC GARDENS

Exploding with blossom in spring, the well-tended **Běijīng Botanic Gardens** (北京植物园; Běijīng Zhíwùyuán; adult ¥10, through ticket ¥45; ⏲6am-9pm summer (last entry 7pm), 7am-7pm winter (last entry 5pm); [S]Xiyuan or Yuanmingyuan, then 🚌331), set against the backdrop of the Western Hills and about 1km northeast of Fragrant Hills Park, make for a pleasant outing among bamboo fronds, pines, orchids, lilacs and China's most extensive botanic collection. Containing a rainforest house, the standout **Běijīng Botanical Gardens Conservatory** (admission with through ticket; ⏲8.30am-4pm) bursts with 3000 different varieties of plants.

About a 15-minute walk from the front gate (follow the signs), but still within the grounds of the gardens, is **Sleeping Buddha Temple** (Wòfó Sì; adult ¥5, or entry with through ticket; ⏲8am-5pm). The temple, first built during the Tang dynasty, houses a huge reclining effigy of Sakyamuni weighing 54 tonnes; it's said to have 'enslaved 7000 people' in its casting. Sakyamuni is depicted on the cusp of death, before his entry into nirvana. On each side of Buddha are arrayed some sets of gargantuan shoes, gifts to Sakyamuni from various emperors in case he went for a stroll.

On the eastern side of the gardens is the **Cáo Xuěqín Memorial** (Cáo Xuěqín Jìniànguǎn; 39 Zhengbaiqi; admission ¥10, or entry with through ticket; ⏲8.30am-4.15pm), where Cáo Xuěqín lived in his latter years. Cáo (1715–63) is credited with penning the classic *Dream of the Red Mansions*, a vast and prolix family saga set in the Qing period. Making a small buzz in the west of the gardens is the little **China Honey Bee Museum** (⏲8.30am-4.30pm Mar-Oct).

WORTH A DETOUR

FRAGRANT HILLS PARK

Easily within striking distance of the Summer Palace are Běijīng's Western Hills (西山; Xī Shān), another former villa-resort of the emperors. The part of Xī Shān closest to Běijīng is known as **Fragrant Hills Park** (香山公园; Xiāng Shān Gōngyuán; summer/winter ¥10/5; ☺6am-7.30pm; Ⓢ Xiyuan or Yuanmingyuan, then 🚌331).

Scramble up the slopes to the top of **Incense-Burner Peak** (Xiānglú Fēng), or take the **chairlift** (one way/return ¥30/50, 8.30am to 5pm). From the peak you get an all-embracing view of the countryside, and you can leave the crowds behind by hiking further into the Western Hills. Beijingers flock here in autumn when the maple leaves saturate the hillsides in great splashes of red.

Near the north gate of Fragrant Hills Park, but still within the park, is the excellent **Azure Clouds Temple** (Bìyún Sì; adult ¥10; ☺8am-5pm), which dates back to the Yuán dynasty. The **Mountain Gate Hall** contains two vast protective deities: Heng and Ha, beyond which is a small courtyard and the drum and bell towers, leading to a hall with a wonderful statue of Mílèfó – it's bronze, but coal-black with age. Only his big toe shines from numerous inquisitive fingers.

The **Sun Yatsen Memorial Hall** contains a statue and a glass coffin donated by the USSR on the death of Mr Sun (the Republic of China's first president) in 1925. At the very back is the marble **Vajra Throne Pagoda**, where Sun Yatsen was interred after he died, before his body was moved to its final resting place in Nánjīng. The **Hall of Arhats** is well worth visiting; it contains 500 *luóhàn* statues (those freed from the cycle of rebirth), each crafted with an individual personality.

Southwest of the Azure Clouds Temple is the Tibetan-style **Temple of Brilliance** (Zhāo Miào), and not far away is a glazed-tile pagoda. Both survived visits by foreign troops intent on sacking the area in 1860 and then in 1900.

There are dozens of cheap restaurants and snack stalls on the approach road to the north gate of the park, making this your best bet for lunch out of any of the sights in this part of the city.

Note that sometime after 2013, the subway will extend here via the Summer Palace and Botanic Gardens.

strip of the long-vanished Mongol city wall that it is built upon. At 9km in length, this is Běijīng's longest parkland and a relaxing place for a stroll.

MILITARY MUSEUM · MUSEUM
Map p297 (军事博物馆; Jūnshì Bówùguǎn; 9 Fuxing Lu; adult ¥20; ☺8am-5pm, last entry 4.30pm, Tue-Sun; Ⓢ Military Museum) Military enthusiasts may get a rush at this hulking monolith of a building topped with a communist star. Cold War-era F-5 fighters, the much larger F-7 and F-8, tanks and HQ-2 (Red Flag-2) surface-to-air missiles muster below, while upstairs bristles with more weaponry. For the full-on revolutionary version of China's wars, the Hall of Agrarian Revolutionary War and the Hall of the War to Resist US Aggression and Aid Korea is a tour de force of communist spin.

At the time of research, the main building was closed as part of a massive three-year renovation project, but there was still a large collection of tanks, aircraft, artillery and military vehicles on view in the forecourt, which was free to enter.

 EATING

SALANG-BANG · KOREAN $$
Map p303 (舍廊房; Shèláng Fáng; ☎8261 8201; 3rd fl, Dōngyuán Plaza, 35 Chengfu Lu, 成府路35号东源大厦3层; dishes from ¥25; ☺10.30am-3.30am; Ⓢ Wudaokou) This is one of the liveliest and most popular of the many Korean eateries in this part of town, and is always busy day and night with expat Korean students looking for a taste of home. The various hotpots, including the classic *shíguō bànfàn* (rice, vegetables, meat and an egg served in a claypot), start at ¥35, or you can grill your own meat and fish at your table. Picture menu.

CHRISTIAN KOBER / GETTY IMAGES ©

KRZYSZTOF DYDYNSKI / GETTY IMAGES ©

1. Běijīng Botanic Gardens (p160)
Goldfish pond at the Tang dynasty Sleeping Buddha Temple.

2. Summer Palace (p156)
The Summer Palace is a wonderful, over-the-top mix of temples, gardens, pavilions, lakes, bridges, gate towers and corridors.

3. Wǔtǎ Temple (p158)
This distinctive Indian-styled temple is a hugely rewarding place to visit.

WǓDÀOKǑU BEER GARDEN

When Běijīng emerges from the deep freeze of its winter, so do its residents. Come summer in Wǔdàokǒu, the area just west of the subway stop turns into a hugely popular open-air **beer garden** (Map p303). Locals congregate at the tables, supping draught beers and snacking on *shāokǎo* (barbecue) from the food stalls surrounding them. The party starts in the late afternoon and continues late, getting louder and louder as those ¥10 beers disappear down thirsty throats.

LǍO CHĒ JÌ
CHINESE SÌCHUĀN $$

Map p303 (老车记; ☑6266 6180; 5th fl, Wǔdàokǒu U-Centre, 36 Chengfu Lu, 成府路36号五道口购物中心5层; meals for 2 ¥70; ⏱10am-10pm; ⓢWudaokou) The speciality here is *málàxiāngguō* (麻辣香锅), a kind of dry hotpot where you add your own meat, fish and veggies, but it comes without the bubbling broth you get with standard hotpot. You can choose from three different levels of spice; go for the lowest if you can't handle the heat. Picture menu.

ISSHIN JAPANESE RESTAURANT
JAPANESE $

Map p303 (日本料理一心; Rìběn Liàolǐ Yī Xīn; ☑6119 3606; Room 403, West Bldg, 35 Chengfu Lu, 成府路35号院内西楼403室; sushi from ¥12; ⏱lunch & dinner; ⓘ; ⓢWudaokou) Just off an unpromising-looking road, about 50m north of the traffic lights at the intersection of Chengfu Lu and Wudaokou station, Isshin is well worth tracking down if you're in the area. With its thoughtful design, laid-back atmosphere and reasonable prices, it's a place where business types, expat Japanese and students can all feel at home. The sushi bowls (¥48), including salad, are a great deal. The extensive menu includes hotpots, udon noodles and teriyaki dishes.

BRIDGE CAFÉ
CAFE $

Map p303 (桥咖啡; Qiáo Kāfēi; ☑8286 7025; 12-8 Huaqing Jiayuan, 华清嘉园12-8; dishes from ¥32; ⏱24hr; ⓘⓘ; ⓢWudaokou) Friendly, lively and light-filled place that's a top spot for Western breakfasts, as well as home-made pasta and tasty pizzas, or coffee and drinks at any time. It's on the 2nd floor; enter through the door to the side of a gift shop and climb the stairs.

🍷 DRINKING & NIGHTLIFE

LUSH
BAR, CAFE

Map p303 (☑8286 3566; 1 Huaqing Jiayuan, Chengfu Lu, 华清嘉园1号楼2层; beers from ¥15, cocktails from ¥35; ⏱24hr; ⓐ; ⓢWudaokou) For the hordes of students in Wǔdàokǒu, both foreign and local, all roads lead to Lush. During the day it functions as a cafe with a Western menu, including breakfast (¥30), and sandwiches and salads (from ¥35). After dark, it offers something different every night, whether movie screenings, live music, a pub quiz, DJs or an open-mic night for aspiring poets and singers. There's a daily happy hour from 6pm to 10pm and it never closes. It's above the Meet Fresh Café.

PROPAGANDA
CLUB

Map p303 (☑8286 3991; Huaqing Jiayuan, 华清嘉园; ⏱8.30pm-late; ⓢWudaokou) Wǔdàokǒu's student crew are drawn to this unprepossessing but long-running club for its cheap drinks, hip-hop sounds and the chance for cultural exchange with the locals. Entry is free. It's 100m north of the east gate of Huaqing Jiayuan.

☆ ENTERTAINMENT

NATIONAL LIBRARY CONCERT HALL
CLASSICAL MUSIC

Map p297 (国家图书馆音乐厅; Guójiā Túshūguǎn Yīnyuètīng; ☑8854 5531; 33 Zhongguancun Nandajie, 中关村南大街33号; tickets ¥80-580; ⓢNational Library) Undergoing a massive refit at the time of writing, this impressive venue doesn't just put on recitals and concerts (many by overseas musicians); it's also a good place to catch Chinese classical dance, which blends martial arts styles with traditional dance choreography performances.

13 CLUB
LIVE MUSIC

Map p303 (13俱乐部; 13 Jùlèbù; ☑8668 7151; 161 Chengfu Lu, 成府路161号; admission from ¥30; ⏱6pm-late; ⓢWudaokou) A dark and forbidding venue down a suitably grimy alley. A lot of metal acts play here, so if you're a fan of guitar solos and making the sign of the horns, this is the place for you. Look for the red sign.

UME INTERNATIONAL CINEPLEX CINEMA
Map p303 (☎8211 5566; 44 Kexueyuan Nanlu, 科学院南路44号; [S]Renmin University) Posh multiplex that shows the latest movie releases, but check they haven't been dubbed into Chinese.

SHOPPING

CENTERGATE COMO ELECTRONICS
Map p303 (科贸电子城; Kēmào Diànzǐchéng; 18 Zhongguancun Dajie, 中关村大街18号; ⏲9am-7pm; [S]Zhongguancun) Zhongguancun is China's Silicon Valley and Zhongguancun Dajie and the streets around it are home to many malls selling digital and electronic products. This is one of the biggest of them, a seven-floor space full of vendors selling reasonably priced computer software and hardware, games, cell phones, MP3 players and iPods. Not all of it is the genuine article, but you can bargain here. Go to the 2nd floor for laptop repairs.

SPORTS & ACTIVITIES

FRIENDSHIP HOTEL SWIMMING
Map p303 (☎6849 8888 ext 32; 1 Zhongguancun Nandajie, 友谊宾馆 中关村南大街1号; ⏲7am-11pm; [S]Renmin University) The venerable Friendship Hotel has a great Olympic-sized pool, now sadly enclosed, costing ¥100 for a day or however long you stay.

The Great Wall

Mùtiányù 慕田峪 **p168**
Well set up for families, but with enough hiking options for an adventure.

Jiànkòu 箭扣 **p170**
Rough, rugged and unrestored. For hardcore Wall walkers only.

Huánghuā Chéng 黄花城 **p171**
Part restored, but steep in places. Good 'wild wall' hiking nearby.

Zhuàngdàokǒu 撞道口 **p172**
A short restored stretch with fabulous views, or a highly challenging off-the-beaten-track hike.

Sīmǎtái 司马台 **p173**
Exhilarating hiking options, but renovations may alter things dramatically.

Jīnshānlǐng 金山岭 **p174**
A three-hour, remote and adventurous hike from Sīmǎtái.

Bādálǐng 八达岭 **p175**
The most famous and crowded, but picture-perfect, stretch of the Wall.

Hiking the Great Wall p178
Eight hikes that will transform your trip into an unforgettable adventure.

History

The Great Wall (长城; Chángchéng), one of the most iconic monuments on earth, stands as an awe-inspiring symbol of the grandeur of China's ancient history. Dating back 2000-odd years, the Wall – or to be more accurate, Walls, for it has never been one continuous structure – snakes its way from the border with North Korea in the east to Lop Nur in the far western province of Xīnjiāng. Stretching for an estimated 8851km, it meanders its way through 17 provinces, principalities and autonomous regions. But nowhere is better than Běijīng for mounting your assault of this most famous of bastions.

The Wall has been adopted by the Chinese Communist Party (CCP), which likes to stress the unity of the Wall in its official histories. In fact, there are four distinct Walls, or five if you count the recently rebuilt sections, such as Bādálǐng. Work on the 'original' was begun during the Qin dynasty (221–207 BC), when China was unified for the first time under Emperor Qin Shihuang. Hundreds of thousands of workers, many political prisoners, laboured for 10 years to construct it. An estimated 180 million cu metres of rammed earth was used to form the core of this Wall, and legend has it that the bones of dead workers were used as building materials, too.

After the Qin fell, work on the Wall continued during the Han dynasty (206 BC–AD 220). Little more was done until almost 1000 years later during the Jin dynasty (1115–1234), when the impending threat of Genghis Khan spurred further construction. The Wall's final incarnation, and the one most visitors see today, came during the Ming dynasty (1368–1644), when it was reinforced with stone, brick and battlements over a period of 100 years and at great human cost to the two to three million people who toiled on it. During this period, it was home to around one million soldiers.

The great irony of the Wall is that it rarely stopped China's enemies from invading. It was never one continuous structure; there were inevitable gaps and it was through those that Genghis Khan rode in to take Běijīng in 1215. Perhaps the Wall's finest hour as a defensive bulwark came in 1644 at Shānhǎiguān, where the Wall meets the sea in the east, guarding the approach to Běijīng. The invading Manchus were unable to take this strip of Wall until the traitorous general Wu Sangui opened the gates, resulting in the fall of the Ming dynasty.

While the Wall was less than effective militarily, it was very useful as a kind of elevated highway for transporting people and equipment across mountainous terrain. Its beacon tower system, using smoke signals generated by burning wolves' dung, quickly transmitted news of enemy movements back to the capital. But with the Manchus installed in Běijīng as the Qing dynasty (1644–1911) and the Mongol threat long gone, there was little need to maintain the Wall, and it fell into disrepair.

Ruin & Restoration

The Wall's degeneration accelerated during the war with Japan and then the civil war that preceded the founding of the new China in 1949. Compounding the problem, the communists didn't initially have much interest in the Wall. In fact, Mao Zedong encouraged people living near it to use it as a source of free building materials, something that still goes on unofficially today. It wasn't until 1984 that Mao's successor Deng Xiaoping ordered that the Wall be restored in places and placed under government protection.

But classic postcard images of the Wall – flawlessly clad in bricks and stoutly undulating over hills into the distance – do not reflect the truth of the bastion today. While the sections closest to Běijīng and a few elsewhere have been restored to something approaching their former glory, huge parts of the Wall are either rubble or, especially in the west, simply mounds of earth that could be anything. Nevertheless, the government does a much better job of protecting the Wall than it once did, and the time when local authorities would blast sections of it into dust to make room for roads and new developments is thankfully gone.

Visiting the Wall

Bādálǐng is the most touristy part of the Wall, followed by Mùtiányù. Part-renovated and much less commercial are Sīmǎtái, Jīnshānlǐng and, to a lesser extent, Huánghuā Chéng. Unrenovated sections of 'wild wall' include Jiànkòu and Zhuàngdàokǒu, but there are many others. Most of the above can be reached using public transport. Some require a taxi or minivan ride for the last part of the journey.

Tours run by hostels, or by specialist tour companies, are far preferable to those run by ordinary hotels or general travel companies, as they tend to cater more to the needs of adventurous Western travellers and don't come with any hidden extras, such as a side trip to the Ming Tombs (a common add-on) or a tiresome diversion to a gem factory or traditional Chinese medicine centre. Almost all the hostels reviewed in this guide run Great Wall trips that we recommend. See our Sleeping chapter for details. The following reputable companies run trips to the Wall that we like:

➡ **Bespoke Běijīng** (www.bespokebeijing.com)

➡ **Dandelion Hiking** (www.chinahiking.cn)

➡ **SnapAdventures** (www.snapadventures.com)

➡ **Bike Běijīng** (p248) For cycling trips.

➡ **Běijīng Sideways** (www.beijingsideways.com) For trips in a motorbike sidecar.

Mùtiányù

Like Bādálǐng, Mùtiányù (慕田峪) is a recently renovated stretch of Wall that sees a lot of tourists and is fairly easy to reach from Běijīng. It's also well set up for families, with a cable car, a chairlift and a hugely popular toboggan ride. Far fewer tour groups come here than go to Bādálǐng, so the crowds are much more manageable, and there is the opportunity to do some good hiking.

....

Top Tip

If taking bus 916快 to Huáiróu, ignore the tout who almost always gets on this bus at Nanhua Shichang bus stop and tries to lure

The Great Wall

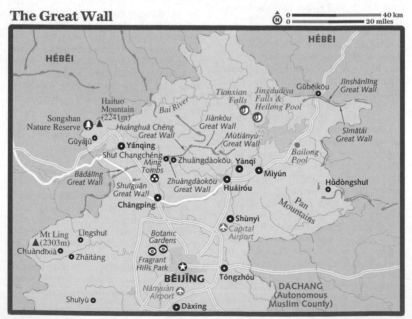

JUST HOW GREAT IS IT?

The Chinese call the Great Wall the '10,000 Lǐ Wall' (万里长城; Wànlǐ Chángchéng). With one 'Lǐ' equivalent to around 500m, this makes the Wall around 5000km long. More modern calculations, though, put the figure at far longer than that. A report by China's State Administration of Cultural Heritage in April 2009 estimated the noncontinuous length of the Ming-dynasty wall at 8851km. But the Ming dynasty was just one (albeit the most significant) of 13 dynasties to have contributed to the Wall over the course of history. A more recent, more thorough survey has calculated the total length of all fragments of the Great Wall that have ever stood, including sections that run parallel with others, and sections that have weathered away to nothing, to be 21,119km.

foreign tourists onto an expensive minibus tour to the Great Wall.

Getting There & Away

➡ **Local Bus** From Dongzhimen Wai bus stand (Map p298), bus 867 makes a special detour to Mùtiányù twice every morning (¥16, 2½ hours, 7am and 8.30am, 15 March to 15 November only) and returns from Mùtiányù twice each afternoon (2pm and 4pm). Otherwise, go via Huáiróu: from Dongzhimen Transport Hub (Dōngzhímén Shūniǔzhàn; Map p298) take bus 916快 (the character is 'kuài', and means 'fast') to Huáiróu (¥12, one hour, 6.30am to 7.30pm). Get off at Mingzhu Guangchang (明珠广场) bus stop, then take the first right to find a bunch of minivans waiting to take passengers to Mùtiányù (per person ¥15, 30 minutes). Return minivans start drying up around 6pm. The last 916快 back to Běijīng leaves Huáiróu at around 7pm. If you miss that, catch a taxi from Huáiróu to Houshayu subway station (后沙峪地铁站; Hòushāyù Dìtiě Zhàn; about ¥100), one of the most northerly subway stations on Line 15, and then take the subway back into the city centre.

➡ **Tours** Many hotels and hostels run tours to Mùtiányù.

➡ **Taxi** Around ¥500 to ¥600 return day trip from Běijīng.

Need to Know

➡ **Location** 90km from Běijīng

➡ **Price** Adult/student ¥45/25

➡ **Hours** Summer 7am-6.30pm, winter 7.30am-5.30pm

Exploring the Wall

Famed for its Ming-era guard towers and great views, this 3km-long section of wall is largely a recently restored Ming-dynasty structure that was built upon an earlier Northern Qi-dynasty edifice. With 26 watchtowers, the wall is impressive and manageable, and although it's popular, most souvenir hawking is kept to the lower levels.

From the ticket office at Mùtiányù, there are three or four stepped pathways leading up to the wall, plus a **cable car** (缆车; lǎn chē; one-way/return ¥60/80, children half-price), a **chairlift** (索道; suǒdào; one-way ¥50) and a **toboggan ride** (滑道; huá dào; adult/child ¥60/50), making this ideal for those who can't manage too many steps or who have young kids in tow.

Eating

Mùtiányù has a branch of Subway (just down from the car park). There are also lots of fruit stalls selling fresh but overpriced fruit. Up by the main entrance is **Yì Sōng Lóu Restaurant** (翼松楼餐厅; Yì Sōng Lóu Cāntīng; mains ¥20-50; 🍴), which does OK Chinese food.

SLEEPING AT MÙTIÁNYÙ

Schoolhouse (小园; Xiǎoyuán; ☑6162 6505; www.theschoolhouseatmutianyu. com; r ¥2600-5000; @ 🛜) The main building is a former primary school, about 1km down from the main car park. Accommodation is in a collection of lovingly restored buildings dotted around the area, each comprising luxury self-contained, multiroomed accommodation, which can sleep families or small groups.

Jiànkòu

For stupefying hikes along perhaps Běijīng's most incomparable section of 'wild wall', head to the rear section of the Jiànkòu Great Wall (后箭扣长城; Hòu Jiànkòu Chángchéng), accessible from the town of Huáiróu. Tantalising panoramic views of the Great Wall spread out in either direction from here, as the crumbling brickwork meanders dramatically along a mountain ridge; the setting is truly sublime. But this is completely unrestored wall, so it is both dangerous and, strictly speaking, illegal to hike along it. Make sure you wear footwear with very good grip, and never attempt to traverse this section in the rain, particularly during thunderstorms. When the weather is fine, the Jiànkòu (箭扣) area offers fabulous opportunities to hike and camp along the Wall.

Top Tip

If you don't plan on staying the night or are hiking to another section of the wall, make sure you get your taxi driver to wait for you (don't pay until afterwards!) because it's tough to find taxis at Xīzhàzi village.

Getting There & Away

➤ **Local Bus** Take bus 916快 from the Dongzhimen Transport Hub (Dōngzhímén Shūniǔzhàn; Map p298) to Huáiróu (¥12, one hour, 6.30am to 7.30pm). Get off at Mingzhu Guangchang (明珠广场) bus stop, then start negotiating for a taxi to Xīzhàzi village (西栅子村; Xīzhàzi Cūn; one-way ¥100 to ¥130, one hour).

➤ **Taxi** Around ¥500 to ¥700 return day trip from Běijīng.

Need to Know

➤ **Location** 100km from Běijīng

➤ **Price** Admission ¥20

➤ **Hours** No official opening hours

Exploring the Wall

From the drop-off at Xīzhàzi village (西栅子村; Xīzhàzi Cūn), it's a one-hour walk uphill to the wall, along a narrow dirt path which climbs through a beautiful pine forest. From here turn east (left) to hike all the way to Mùtiányù (two hours), from where you can easily pick up transport back to Huáiróu, or even to Běijīng. Note that there are different parts, or duì (队), to Xīzhàzi village. All have paths that lead up to the wall but, for the sake of ease, head to the first part of the village (一队; yī duì), which is down a lane to your left immediately after the ticket office.

THE WALL THAT DISAPPEARED

It's hard to believe that a structure that runs for 8851km (or 21,119km; see p169) could go missing, but much of the Great Wall has. The most optimistic estimates are that just one-third of the Wall is still standing. The twin culprits for this are man and nature. The cavalier official attitude that existed until very recently saw it fall prey to both individual pilferers of bricks and stone, and unscrupulous developers.

For people living close to the Wall, some of whom claim descent from the soldiers who once guarded it, all that raw building material was too tempting. Pass through villages in the Wall's vicinity and you will find everything from houses to pig pens built from stones, bricks and earth that were once part of it.

Developers and officials have destroyed whole sections of the Wall to make room for roads, luxury villas and misguided tourism projects. Official restoration work has not always been done properly; in one notorious case in Shāndōng province, bathroom tiles were used to replace the original stone.

But it is nature that poses the greatest threat to the Wall. Desertification in China started centuries ago, when imperial officials torched the forests within 95km of the Wall to deny the enemy a chance to launch surprise attacks. Now, with 400,000 hectares of grassland lost to the encroaching desert annually in China, what's left of the Wall, especially in the environmentally vulnerable northwestern provinces, faces being buried forever.

Eating

Many hikers bring a picnic for the Wall, but Jiànkòu Chángchéng Nóngjiāyuàn and Guóhuái Dàyuàn are **farmer-style courtyards** (农家院; *nóngjiāyuàn*) in the village that provide food and accommodation. Expect to pay around ¥30 for a meal. Neither has an English sign or a menu, and no English is spoken. Just look for the '农家院' signs.

Huánghuā Chéng

Less touristy than other parts of the Great Wall close to Běijīng, Huánghuā Chéng (黄花城) is an extremely rewarding, and impossibly steep, section of the Wall. Undulating across the hillsides east and west of a small reservoir and offering spectacular views of the surrounding countryside, it has undergone only partial restoration and is refreshingly free of the hawkers who can make visits to other sections a trying experience. There are good opportunities for hikes, too.

Getting There & Away

➡ **Local Bus** From Dongzhimen Transport Hub (Dōngzhímén Shūniǔzhàn; Map p298) take bus 916快 to Huáiróu (¥12, one hour, 6.30am to 7.30pm). Get off at Nanhuayuan Sanqu (南花园三区) bus stop, then walk straight ahead about 200m (crossing one road), until you get to the next bus stop, called Nanhuayuan Siqu (南花园四区). A bus to Huánghuā Chéng (¥8, one hour, until 6.30pm) stops here, but it doesn't have a number. Instead, look for a placard in the front windscreen reading: '怀柔−黄花城', which means 'Huáiróu to Huánghuā Chéng'. It only runs about once an hour, though, so if you get bored waiting hop in one of the minivans (¥10) that regularly trawl the bus stop for passengers. The last 916快 from Huáiróu back to Běijīng leaves Huáiróu at around 7pm. If you miss that, catch a taxi from Huáiróu to Houshayu subway station (后沙峪地铁站; Hòushāyù Dìtiě Zhàn; about ¥100) on Line 15.

SLEEPING AT JIÀNKÒU

Jiànkòu Chángchéng Nóngjiāyuàn (剪扣长城农家院; ☎136 9307 0117, 6161 1794; r ¥80-100; @) The first *nóngjiāyuàn* (农家院; farmer-style courtyard) you come to as you enter Xīzhàzi village. Rooms are set around a vegetable-patch courtyard, and are simple but have private bathrooms.

Guóhuái Dàyuàn (国槐大院; ☎136 2136 2662, 137 1698 220; r ¥80-120; @) Further into the village, this place has similarly clean but simple rooms. Meals cost a set-price ¥30.

➡ **Taxi** Around ¥500 to ¥600 return day trip from Běijīng.

Need to Know
➡ **Location** 77km from Běijīng
➡ **Price** No entrance fee
➡ **Hours** No official opening hours

Exploring the Wall
Strikingly free of crowds, Huánghuā Chéng allows visitors to admire this classic and well-preserved example of Ming defence, with its high and wide ramparts, intact parapets and sturdy beacon towers, in relative isolation. The patchy and periodic restoration work on the Wall here has left its crumbling nobility and striking authenticity largely intact, with the ramparts occasionally dissolving into rubble and some of the steps in ruins.

From the road, you can go either west (left) towards Zhuàngdàokǒu or east (right) up the stupidly steep section rises up from the reservoir and which eventually leads to Jiànkòu and Mùtiányù. For the eastern route, cross the small dam and follow the path that clings to the side of the Wall until it reaches the second watchtower. Then you'll have to clamber up a metal ladder to the watchtower to reach the Wall proper. From the second watchtower, the Wall climbs abruptly uphill through a series of further watchtowers before going over and dipping down the hill to continue meandering on. It is steep and, in places, the stone has been worn smooth, making it very slippery. You need shoes with very good grip. There are also no guardrails here.

SLEEPING AT HUÁNGHUĀ CHÉNG

Ténglóng Fàndiàn (滕龙饭店; ☑6165 1929; r without/with attached bathroom ¥50/80) This is one of a number of small guesthouses here. Most are on the river side of the road, but this friendly place, accessed via some steps on your left just before you reach the wall, clings to the hillside on the other side of the road and sports fine views of the Wall. Rooms are basic but clean and sleep two to three people. No English spoken.

To head west, it's easiest to climb the path that leads up to the Wall from behind Ténglóng Fàndiàn, a guesthouse up some steps from the main road. The wall on this side of the road is almost as steep and, in places, equally smooth and slippery. The views from the top here, looking down on the reservoir and at the opposite section of the Wall stretching over the mountain, are simply stunning.

Eating

There are a number of restaurants on both sides of the road, many selling grilled fish (烤鱼; *kǎoyú*). **Ténglóng Fàndiàn** (滕龙饭店; mains ¥15-35), where you can also stay the night, has an English menu and fine views of the Wall from its hillside terrace eating area.

Zhuàngdàokǒu

Zhuàngdàokǒu (撞道口), a small village just over the hill to the east of Huánghuā Chéng, has access to a rarely visited and completely unrestored section of 'wild wall'. It's also possible to hike over to Huánghuā Chéng on a restored section from here, although few people do this – surprising, considering how straightforward it is. The 'wild' section, towards the reservoir at Shuǐ Chángchéng, is crumbling away and overgrown with small trees and shrubs, but it is still possible to hike along. Just take extreme care.

Getting There & Away

➜ **Local Bus** From Dongzhimen Transport Hub (Dōngzhímén Shūniǔzhàn; Map p298) take bus 916快 to Huáiróu (¥12, one hour, 6.30am to 7.30pm). Get off at Nanhuayuan Sanqu (南花园三区) bus stop, then walk straight ahead about 200m (crossing one road), until you get to the next bus stop, which is called Nanhuayuan Siqu (南花园四区). The bus from here to Shuǐ Chángchéng (a pleasant Wall-side reservoir, but from where you cannot access the Wall) stops at Zhuàngdàokǒu (¥8, one hour, every 30 minutes until 6.30pm). It doesn't have a number. Instead look for a placard in the front windscreen reading: '怀柔—水长城', which means 'Huáiróu to Shuǐ Chángchéng'. The last 916快 bus from Huáiróu back to Běijīng leaves Huáiróu at around 7pm.

➜ **Taxi** Around ¥500 to ¥600 return day trip from Běijīng.

Need to Know

➜ **Location** 80km from Běijīng
➜ **Price** No entrance fee
➜ **Hours** No official opening hours

Exploring the Wall

The bus should drop you off at the far end of Zhuàngdàokǒu village, where the road crosses a small stream. Pick up some water and snacks at the small shop near here, then turn right and follow the lane along the stream and then up behind the houses until it meets a rocky pathway that leads up the Wall. Once at the Wall (20 minutes), turn right for a one-hour walk along a restored but very steep section of Wall, which eventually leads down to the road at Huánghuā Chéng via some fabulous viewpoints. Or turn left to commence a two-hour hike along a crumbling stretch of shrub-covered Wall towards Shuǐ Chángchéng. You'll see almost no one on this unrestored section and the going can get tricky, so take extra care here.

About 3km beyond Zhuàngdàokǒu is the **Huánghuāchéng Great Wall Lakeside Reserve** (黄花城水长城旅游区; Huánghuāchéng Shuǐchángchéng Lǚyóuqū; admission ¥25; ⊙8am-5.30pm), known simply as Shuǐ Chángchéng (水长城). You can't access the Wall here – although a path leads up to it from just before the reserve – but there are splendid vistas of crumbling sections of the Wall clinging to the surrounding hillsides. The reservoir itself is a pleasant, if unremarkable, body of water. You can get a speedboat to whisk you across it (¥15), or hire your own more-sedate boat (¥10) and paddle yourself. It takes about three hours to walk around the reservoir. The Huáiróu–Zhuàngdàokǒu bus terminates here.

Eating

On your right, just before the stream at the end of the village, is **Zǎoxiāng Tíngyuàn** (枣香庭院; mains ¥15-50), a friendly farmer-style courtyard. It's run by a welcoming couple, but they don't speak English or have an English menu. Ask for the stewed pork with roast chestnuts (栗子肉; *lìzi ròu*), the pork fried with chillies (炒肉尖椒; *chǎoròu jiānjiāo*), the braised pork belly (红烧肉; *hóng shāo ròu*), the barbecued fish (烤鱼; *kǎoyú*) or the beef and potato stew (土豆牛肉; *tǔdòu niúròu*) and you won't go wrong.

Sīmǎtái

Near the far-flung town of Gǔběikǒu and right on the border with Héběi province, the stirring remains at Sīmǎtái (司马台) make for an exhilarating Great Wall experience. Built during the reign of Ming-dynasty emperor Hongwu, the 19km stretch is characterised by watchtowers, steep plunges and scrambling ascents. It's a partly restored yet very rugged section of wall and it can be heart-thumpingly steep in places. Needless to say, the scenery out here is dramatic.

Top Tip

At the time of research, Sīmǎtái was closed for extensive renovation. The information you read here was correct up until the renovation project began several years ago. Sīmǎtái should be open again by the time you read this, but check with the China branch of Lonely Planet's Thorn Tree forum (www.lonelyplanet.com/thorntree) or at one of the hostels in Běijīng to check that the transport details here are still correct and if, post-restoration, Sīmǎtái still appeals to you.

Getting There & Away

➡ **Local Bus** Take bus 980 from Dōngzhímén Transport Hub (Dōngzhímén Shūniǔzhàn; Map p298) to Mìyún (¥15) and change to a minibus for Sīmǎtái (¥15, one hour) or a taxi (return trip ¥120).

➡ **Tours** Youth hostels used to run highly recommended early-morning trips by minibus (excluding/including admission ¥180/260) to Jīnshānlǐng for the four-hour hike to Sīmǎtái – at the time, this was the best way to visit Sīmǎtái. Buses usually left at around 6am or 7am. They would drop you at Jīnshānlǐng, then pick you up four hours later in Sīmǎtái. The entire journey from Běijīng and back would take up to 12 hours. Downtown Backpackers (p194) was planning to restart the trip once Sīmǎtái reopens. Check with staff there, or with other hostels, for details.

➡ **Taxi** Around ¥900 to ¥1000 return day trip from Běijīng.

Need to Know

➡ **Location** 135km from Běijīng
➡ **Price** Admission ¥40
➡ **Hours** 8am-5pm

Exploring the Wall

Follow the crowds to the wall (Sīmǎtái can be busy at times, but you'll soon leave the crowds behind), where you have a choice: either head west for the hike (four hours one way) to Jīnshānlǐng or walk east as far

SLEEPING AT ZHUÀNGDÀOKǑU

Zǎoxiāng Tíngyuàn (枣香庭院; ☎135 2208 3605; r ¥40-100) This modest guesthouse is housed in a 70-year-old courtyard building, which has some traditional features such as wooden window frames and paper window panes, as well as more recent add-ons such as a shower room and a dining area (you can also eat in the courtyard). A couple of rooms have TV, a couple have air-conditioning and one has a private bathroom. On your right, just before the stream at the end of the village. No English sign; no English spoken.

as you can. The hike to Jīnshānlǐng makes the long journey out here worth it, but you will need to set off early in the morning (or stay the night in Jīnshānlǐng). The Sīmǎtái section destined for Jīnshānlǐng consists of 18 watchtowers ranging north of the old vestiges of wall dating from the Northern Qi dynasty. A few slopes have 70-degree inclines and you need both hands free, so bring a day pack to hold your camera and other essentials, and take strong shoes with a good grip. One narrow section of footpath has a 500m drop, so it's no place for acrophobics. There's a cable car at both Sīmǎtái and Jīnshānlǐng, and a zip-line at Sīmǎtái too. Sīmǎtái has some unusual historic features, such as 'obstacle-walls' (walls within walls used for defending against enemies who had already scaled the Great Wall). Small cannons have been discovered in this area, as well as evidence of rocket-type weapons, such as flying knives and flying swords.

Eating

As with other remote sections of the Wall, many hikers bring a picnic, but there used to be plenty of small restaurants and snack stalls near the entrance, and there are bound to be even more once Sīmǎtái reopens.

Jīnshānlǐng

The Jīnshānlǐng (金山岭) section of the Great Wall, near the small town of Gǔběikǒu, marks the starting point of an exhilarating 7km hike to Sīmǎtái. The adventure – winding through stunningly remote mountainous terrain – takes three to four hours as the trail is steep and parts of the wall have collapsed, but it can be traversed without too much difficulty if you are reasonably fit. Note that the watchtowers are in various states of preservation and some have been stripped of their bricks. The scenery is perhaps less picturesque than at, say, Jiànkòu. Here, the landscape is drier and starker, but arguably more powerful, and it leaves you feeling that you're hiking through genuinely remote territory.

Top Tip

It can be a long trip out here so take the stress out of having to rush back the same day by arriving mid-afternoon and hunting around near the West Gate (西门; Xīmén) for lodgings. Rooms range from ¥50 to ¥100. Look for signs on buildings saying '农家院' (nóngjiāyuàn). You can then mount your assault on the Wall the next morning.

Getting There & Away

➜ **Local Bus** There are two options: the first is to catch a bus to Chéngdé (承德; ¥85, 2½ hours) from Sìhuì long-distance bus station (四惠长途汽车站; Sìhuì Chángtú Qìchēzhàn; Map p298), a 200m walk southeast of Sihui subway station, and tell the driver you want to get off at Jīnshānlǐng. You'll be dropped at a service station on the highway, about 1km from the east gate ticket office of Jīnshānlǐng (walk back under the highway and keep going). Note, you have to pay the full-price ¥85 ticket to Chéngdé, even though you'll be getting off early at Jīnshānlǐng. Your second option is to catch bus 980 from Dongzhimen Transport Hub (Dōngzhímén Shūniǔzhàn; Map p298) to Mìyún (¥15), and then take a taxi to Jīnshānlǐng (one-way ¥50). The last 980 bus back to Běijīng leaves Mìyún at 7pm. Chéngdé–Běijīng buses run along the main highway until mid-evening and usually have spare seats if you flag one down at the service station.

➜ **Tourist Bus** A special tourist bus (金山岭长城旅游班车专线; Jīnshānlǐng Chángchéng Lǚyóu bānchē zhuānxiàn; ¥120, two hours) leaves once a day for Jīnshānlǐng from Dongzhimen Wai bus stand (东直门外车站; Map p298) at 8am and returns from Jīnshānlǐng at 3pm.

➜ **Tours** Youth hostels used to run highly recommended early-morning trips by minibus (excluding/including admission ¥180/260) to Jīnshānlǐng for the four-hour hike to Sīmǎtái – at the time, this was the best way to visit Sīmǎtái. Buses usually left at around 6am or 7am. They would drop you at Jīnshānlǐng, then pick you up four hours later in Sīmǎtái. The entire journey from Běijīng and back would take up to 12 hours. Downtown Backpackers (p194) was planning to restart the trip once Sīmǎtái reopens. Check with staff there, or with other hostels, for details.

CAMPING EQUIPMENT

There are plenty of places to buy camping equipment in Běijīng, but the best place to go in terms of quality and choice is **Sanfo** (三夫户外; Sānfū Hùwài; ☎6201 1333; www.sanfo.com; 3-4 Madian Nancun, 北三环中路马甸南村4之3－4号; ◷9am-9pm). There are branches across the city, but this location on a side road of the middle section of the North 3rd Ring Rd stands out because it has three outlets side by side, as well as a few smaller cheaper camping shops next door. Walk south out of Jiandemen subway station, on Line 10, for about 800m, staying on the right-hand side of the main road, then cross under the 3rd ring road and the camping shops will be on your right.

There's a smaller, easier-to-get-to branch (Map p294) about 200m south of Fuchengmen subway station.

→ **Taxi** Around ¥900 to ¥1000 return day trip from Běijīng.

Need to Know

→ **Location** 142km from Běijīng

→ **Price** Summer/winter ¥65/55

→ **Hours** No official opening hours

Exploring the Wall

Autumn is the best season for hiking around here; in summer you'll be sweating litres, so load up with water before you go (ever-present hawkers on the wall sell pricey water for around ¥10 a bottle, or more depending on how thirsty you appear). To commence the hike to Sīmǎtái, turn left when you reach the wall and keep going. If you need it, there's a **cable car** (缆车; lǎn chē; one way/return ¥30/50) by the west gate ticket office. Arriving at Sīmǎtái you used to have to buy another ticket to cross a rope bridge (¥5), as well as the entrance ticket to the Sīmǎtái section. This may change once Sīmǎtái has been reopened after renovation.

Eating

Near the west gate entrance (西门; Xīmén) you'll find a handful of **farmer-style courtyards** (农家院; nóngjiāyuàn; r ¥80-100, meals from ¥30) which offer food and lodging. The east gate entrance (东门; Dōngmén), about 2km up from the west gate, has a hotel-lobby-like cafe, with an English menu. It's always a good idea to bring a packed lunch, though, if you're hiking for any stretch on the Wall.

Bādálǐng

The mere mention of its name sends a shudder down the spine of hardcore Wall walkers, but Bādálǐng (八达岭) is the easiest part of the Wall to get to and as such, if you are really pushed for time, this may be your only option. You'll have to put up with huge crowds of tourists, a lot of souvenir hawkers and a Wall that was completely renovated in the 1980s and so lacks a true sense of historical authenticity. The Bādálǐng Wall is highly photogenic, however, has good tourist facilities (restaurants, disabled access, cable cars etc) and can be visited on a half-day trip from Běijīng.

Top Tip

Give the despicable Bear Park a wide berth.

Getting There & Away

→ **Local Bus** The 877 (¥12, one hour, 6am to 5pm), 919 (¥12, 1½ hours, 6am to 6.30pm) and 880 (¥12, 1½ hours, 7am to 5pm) buses all leave for Bādálǐng from the northern side of the Déshèngmén gateway (德胜门; Map p294), about 500m east of Jishuitan subway station. Bus 877 goes to the east car park. The 919 and 880 buses go to the west car park. The main entrance, located beside two large archways, is between the two car parks, and uphill from both.

→ **Tour Bus** Tour buses to Bādálǐng depart from the beautifully named **Běijīng Hub of Tourist Dispatch** (北京旅游集散中心; Běijīng Lǚyóu Jísàn Zhōngxīn; ☎8353 1111), by Arrow Tower, south of Tiān'ānmén Square. Line C runs to Bādálǐng (¥120 return, includes entry to Great Wall, departs 9.30am to 11am); Line A runs to Bādálǐng

2

ILYA TERENTYEV / GETTY IMAGES ©

1. Bādálǐng (p175)

This is the easiest part of the Wall to get to.

2. Jiànkòu (p170)

For stupefying hikes along perhaps Běijīng's most incomparable section of 'wild wall'.

3. Great Wall (p166)

Restored and child-friendly or wild and dilapidated? The question isn't whether to see the Great Wall, it's how.

DAVID ALLAN BRANDT / GETTY IMAGES

and the Ming Tombs (¥180, includes entrance tickets and lunch, departs 7am to 9.30am). Plan about nine hours for the whole trip.

➡ **Train** Bādálǐng train station is a short walk down from the west car park. Morning trains (hard/soft seat ¥7/11, 75 minutes) leave from Běijīng north station (北京北站; Běijīng Běizhàn; Map p294), which is beside Xizhimen subway station, at the following times: 6.12am, 7.58am, 8.34am, 9.02am and 10.57am. Afternoon trains return at 1.02pm, 3.19pm, 3.52pm, 4.21pm, 5.33pm and 7.55pm.

➡ **Tours** All tour operators and almost all hotels run tours to Bādálǐng.

➡ **Taxi** Expect to pay around ¥400 to ¥600 for a round trip.

Need to Know

➡ **Location** 70km from Běijīng

➡ **Price** Adult/student ¥45/25

➡ **Hours** Summer 6am-7pm, winter 7am-6pm

Exploring the Wall

Běijīng's most-visited chunk of brick-clad bastion ticks all the iffy Great Wall boxes in one flourish: souvenir stalls, T-shirt flogging hawkers, restaurants, heavily restored brickwork, little authenticity, guardrails and mobs of sightseers. On the plus side, the scenery is raw and striking and the Wall, which snakes off in classic fashion into the hills, is extremely photogenic. It dates back to Ming times (1368–1644), but underwent particularly heavy restoration work during the 1950s and 1980s, when it was essentially rebuilt.

There is a **cable car** (缆车; lǎn chē; one-way/return ¥60/80; ⌚8am-4.30pm) as well as disabled access. You'll find a Bank of China ATM near the west car park.

Eating

There are dozens of restaurants on the main drags leading up to the entrance to the Wall. Most lead up from the west car park, and most are fast-food outlets or snack stalls. Give KFC and Subway a miss and go next door instead to **Yong He King** (永和大王; Yǒnghé Dàwáng; mains ¥10-20; ⌚10am-9pm; 📋) for the Chinese version of fast food: rice meals, dumplings, noodles.

Hiking the Great Wall

Běijīng is within striking distance of a number of stretches of the Great Wall and that means there are plenty of excellent hiking opportunities for would-be adventurers. Below is a list of some of our favourite Great Wall hikes near the capital. Don't take any of these lightly, though. The Wall is incredibly steep in places, crumbling away in parts, often very exposed to the elements and, at the unrestored sections, usually has no sides. Wear shoes with good grip and take a rucksack so you have both hands free for clambering. And bring plenty of water. Note, the estimated hiking times here do not include the time taken climbing up onto the Wall, which can be anything from 10 minutes to an hour.

Jīnshānlǐng to Sīmǎtái

➡ three to four hours

Very popular with youth hostel groups before Sīmǎtái closed for renovation, but will be open again by the time you read this. The three- to four-hour hike from Jīnshānlǐng is straightforward, but breathtaking. Scenery is vast, rugged and remote and the Wall is a photogenic mix of part-restored and unrestored sections. Access the Wall from the east gate at Jīnshānlǐng (a 20-minute climb up steps), then turn left when you hit the Wall.

Jīnshānlǐng West Gate to Jīnshānlǐng East Gate

➡ 90 minutes

A quicker alternative to the Sīmǎtái hike mentioned above, and one that the youth hostels were doing while Sīmǎtái was undergoing renovation. You get much of the same fabulous scenery, but only half the pain. Turn left when you hit the Wall, then climb down to your left once you reach **East Tower with Five Holes** (东五眼楼; Dōngwǔyán Lóu).

Jiànkòu to Mùtiányù

➡ two hours

Unrivalled for pure wild-wall scenery, this stretch of the Wall at Jiànkòu is very tough to negotiate, but soon links up with the easier, restored section at Mùtiányù. Access the Wall from the back of Jiànkòu Great Wall (后箭扣; Hòu Jiànkòu) at the first part of Xīzhàzi village (西栅子村一队; Xīzhàzi Cūn Yīduì). It takes an hour to reach the Wall from the village; from the sign that says 'the Great Wall here is closed', follow a narrow dirt path uphill and through a lovely pine forest. Go straight on at the abandoned wooden hut, rather than right, and when you hit the Wall, turn left.

Huánghuā Chéng to Zhuàngdàokǒu

➡ 30 minutes

A short hop rather than a hike, and on a mostly restored part of the Wall, but this comes with stunning views of the Wall by a reservoir and can be extended to take in the crumbling sections beyond Zhuàngdàokǒu. At Huánghuā Chéng, climb up the Wall to the west (left) of the road. Having scaled the Wall's high point, walk down to the lowest part of the Wall (above an archway) then climb down to your left and follow the path to Zhuàngdàokǒu village from where you can pick up a bus back to Huáiróu.

Zhuàngdàokǒu to Huánghuā Chéng

➡ one hour

It takes twice as long doing the above section in reverse, as it's mostly uphill. The best views though are from the top, so you'll be well rewarded for your exertions. Access the Wall from Zhuàngdàokǒu village; turn right at the end of the village, by the small river, then follow the river (keeping it on your left) before turning right up the hill behind the houses to climb a stony pathway. When you reach the Wall (20 minutes), turn right and keep going until you eventually descend to the main road by the reservoir. You can pick up buses to Huáiróu from here.

Zhuàngdàokǒu to Shuǐ Chángchéng

➡ two hours

Again, climb up to the Wall from Zhuàng-dàokǒu village, only this time turn left at the Wall to be rewarded with this dangerous but fabulous stretch of crumbling bastion. The Wall eventually splits at a corner tower; turn left. Then, soon after you reach another tower from where you can see the reservoir far below you, the Wall crumbles down the mountain, and is impassable. Instead of risking your life, take the path that leads down to your left, just before the tower. This path eventually links up with the Wall again, but you may as well follow it all the way down to the road from here, where you'll be able to pick up a bus back to Huáiróu from the lower one of the two large car parks.

Huánghuā Chéng to Shuǐ Chángchéng

➡ three hours

Linking two of the above hikes together, this takes in the spectacular restored section at Huánghuā Chéng, before leading to the ruined beauty of Zhuàngdàokǒu and beyond.

Mùtiányù to Shuǐ Chángchéng

➡ two to three days

For hardcore hikers only, combine four or five of the hikes mentioned here into one massive, multiday trip. Bank on at least two days, possibly three. You'll either need to camp on the Wall or find villages to stay in each evening. When you reach the wall at Mùtiányù, turn left and keep going until you reach Jiànkòu (you know when you reach this section because of the huge sweeping u-turn the Wall takes). Some time after Jiànkòu, you'll reach two forks in the Wall. At the first one, take the left fork; at the second one, the right fork, then keep hiking to Xiǎngshuǐhú (响水湖), a section of the Wall by water, which has been opened up for tourism. It's at least another day's hike from here to Huánghuā Chéng. At Huánghuā Chéng, you'll have to cross the road by the reservoir before rejoining the Wall to Zhuàngdàokǒu and Shuǐ Chángchéng, from where you can catch a bus back to Huáiróu.

Day Trips from Běijīng

Ming Tombs 十三陵 p181

Unesco-protected burial site and the final resting place for 13 of the 16 Ming-dynasty emperors.

Chuāndǐxià p182

Gorgeous, well-preserved Ming-dynasty village nestled in a remote valley.

Tánzhè Temple & Jiètái Temple 潭柘寺 & 戒台寺 p183

Two of Běijīng's oldest Buddhist temples.

Other Historic Villages p186

Skip the crowds at Chuāndǐxià and seek out some less-visited ancient settlements.

Hóngluò Temple 红螺寺 p187

Once a revered ancient temple, now a low-key, family-friendly day out.

Shídù 十渡 p187

Popular scenic valley with outdoor activities and pleasant walks.

Ming Tombs

Explore

The Unesco-protected Ming Tombs (十三陵; Shísān Líng) – Běijīng's answer to Luxor's Valley of the Kings – is the final resting place for 13 of the 16 Ming-dynasty emperors and makes a fascinating half-day trip. The scattered tombs, each a huge temple-like complex guarding an enormous burial mound at its rear, back onto the slopes of Tiānshòu Mountain. Only three tombs are open to the public, and only one has had its underground burial chambers excavated, but what you can see is impressive enough, and leaves you wondering how many priceless treasures must still be buried here.

The Best

➡ **Sights** Hall of Eminent Favours at Cháng Líng (p181), burial chambers at Dìng Líng (p182)

➡ **Best Place to Eat** Nóngjiāfàn Kuàican (p182)

Getting There & Away

➡ **Get Here** Bus 872 (¥9, one hour, 7.10am to 7.10pm) leaves from the north side of Déshèngmén gateway (德胜门; Map p204), passing all sights except Zhāo Líng, ending at Cháng Líng. Last bus back at 6pm.

➡ **Get Around** It's easy to bus-hop. Start at Cháng Líng, then take bus 872 (¥2) or 314 (¥1) to Dìng Líng. From there, bus 67 (¥1) goes to Zhāo Líng (or walk 2km). Then take bus 67 to the Hu Zhuang (胡庄) stop, from where you can walk along Spirit Way. At the end of Spirit Way is the Da Gong Men (大宫门) stop, for the 872 to Běijīng.

Need to Know

➡ **Entrance** ¥35 to ¥65
➡ **Location** 50km from Běijīng

 **SIGHTS**

CHÁNG LÍNG   TOMB
(长陵; admission ¥45, audio guide ¥50) The resting place of the first of the 13 emperors to be buried at the Ming Tombs, Cháng Líng contains the body of Emperor Yongle

Ming Tombs

⊙ 0   2 km
Ⓝ 0   1 miles

Ming Tombs

⊙ **Sights**
1 Cháng Líng B1
2 Dìng Líng A1
3 Great Palace Gate (Dàgōng Mén) A2
4 Kāng Líng A1
5 Mào Líng B1
6 Stele Pavilion A2
7 Yǒng Líng B2
8 Zhāo Líng A2

⊗ **Eating**
9 Nóngjiāfàn Kuàicān A1

⊙ **Drinking & Nightlife**
10 Cafe A2

ℹ **Transport**
11 Da Gong Men Bus Stop A3
12 Hu Zhuang Bus Stop A2
13 Terminus for Bus 67 .... A2

(1402–24), his wife and 16 concubines, and is the largest, most impressive and most important of the tombs here. Like all the tombs, it follows a standard imperial layout, a main gate (棱恩门; *língˈēn mén*) leading to the first of a series of courtyards and the main hall (棱恩殿; *língˈēn diàn*).

Beyond this lie gates leading to the Soul Tower (明楼; Míng Lóu), behind which rises the burial mound surrounded by a fortified wall (宝成; bǎo chéng). Seated upon a three-tiered marble terrace, the standout structure in this complex is the Hall of Eminent Favours (灵恩殿; Líng'ēn Diàn), containing a recent statue of Yongle, various artefacts excavated from Dìng Líng, and a breathtaking interior with vast nánmù (cedar wood) columns. As with all three tombs here, you can climb the Soul Tower at the back of the complex for views of the surrounding hills.

DÌNG LÍNG   TOMB

(定陵; admission incl museum ¥65, audio guide ¥50) Dìng Líng, the resting place of Emperor Wanli (1572–1620) and his wife and concubines, is at first sight less impressive than Cháng Líng because many of the halls and gateways have been destroyed. Many of the priceless artefacts were ruined after being left in a huge, unsealed storage room that leaked water. The treasures that were left – including the bodies of Emperor Wanli and his entourage – were looted and burned by Red Guards during the Cultural Revolution.

This is the only tomb where you can climb down into the vast burial chambers. Learn from signs around the tomb how archaeologists found their way in, following instructions they found on a carved tablet.

The small Museum of the Ming Tombs (明十三陵博物馆; Míng Shísānlíng Bówùguǎn; admission with Dìng Líng ticket), just inside the

---

EATING AT THE MING TOMBS

The grounds of the tombs are good picnic territory, and there's a **cafe** (fresh coffee and Chinese tea from ¥20; ⊘8.30am-5pm) opposite the Museum of the Ming Tombs, just inside Dìng Líng.

➡ **Nóngjiāfàn Kuàicān** (农家饭快餐; mains ¥20-40; ⊘8.30am-5.30pm) This small restaurant is in the car park at Dìng Líng (no English sign or menu). Dishes include *xīhóngshì jīdàn miàn* (西红柿鸡蛋面; egg and tomato noodles; ¥18), *zhájiàng miàn* (炸酱面; Bĕijīng-style pork noodles; ¥18), *huíguō ròu* (回锅肉; spicy cured pork; ¥28), *gōngbào jīdīng* (宫爆鸡丁; spicy chicken with peanuts; ¥22) and *yúxiāng ròusī* (鱼香肉丝; sweet and spicy shredded pork; ¥22).

Dìng Líng complex, contains a few precious remaining artefacts, plus replicas of destroyed originals.

ZHĀO LÍNG   TOMB

(昭陵; admission ¥35) With the same layout as the other two tombs, Zhāo Líng is the smallest, and many of its buildings are recent rebuilds. It's less visited than the others, so is more peaceful, and the *bǎo chéng* (宝成; fortified wall) around the burial mound is unusual in both its size and form. The tomb, resting place of Emperor Longqing (1537–72), is at the end of the village of Zhāolíng (昭陵村; Zhāolíng Cūn).

SPIRIT WAY   HISTORIC ROAD

(神道; Shéndào; admission ¥35; ⊘7am-8pm) The road to the tombs is a 7km stretch called Spirit Way. Starting from the south, with a triumphal triple archway known as the **Great Palace Gate** (Dàgōng Mén) (大宫门), the path passes through **Stele Pavilion** (Bēi Tíng) (碑亭), which contains a giant *bìxì* (mythical tortoise-like dragon) bearing the largest stele in China. A guard of 12 sets of giant stone animals and officials ensues.

Chuāndĭxià

Explore

Set in a valley 90km west of Bĕijīng and overlooked by towering peaks, the Ming-dynasty village of Chuāndĭxià is a gorgeous cluster of historic courtyard homes with old-world charm. The backdrop is lovely: terraced orchards and fields with ancient houses and alleyways rising up the hillside. Two hours is enough to wander around the village, but staying the night lets you soak up its charms without the day-trippers.

The Best...

➡ **Sight** Courtyard homes (p183)
➡ **Place to Eat** Cuan Yun Inn (p183)
➡ **Place to Drink** The terrace at Chéng Bǎo Inn (p183)

Getting There & Away

➡ **Bus** Bus 892 leaves from a stop 200m west of Pingguoyuan subway station

EATING & SLEEPING IN CHUĀNDĪXIÀ

Restaurant and guesthouse signs are clearly labelled in English, so places are easy to spot. Your best bet is to simply wander round and find what best suits you. Most restaurants have English menus. Specialities here include walnuts, apricots and roast leg of lamb.

→ **Cuan Yun Inn** (爨韵客栈; Chuànyùn Kèzhàn; 23 Chuāndīxià Village, 爨低下村23号; mains ¥20-40; ⊙6.30am-8.30pm) The best place to sample roast leg of lamb (烤羊腿; *kǎo yáng tuǐ*; ¥150). On the right of main road as you enter the village.

→ **Chéng Bǎo Inn** (城堡客栈; Chéngbǎo Kèzhàn; bed ¥20, r ¥80-100, mains ¥20-40) This 400-year-old building (which translates as Castle Inn) is perched high above much of the village and enjoys fine views from its terrace restaurant. Rooms are set around the back courtyard and are simple but charming, with bits of antique furniture. Two of the four rooms have traditional stone *kàng* beds, which can be fire-heated in winter. The shared bathroom has no shower, but you can use their neighbour's. Chéng Bǎo Inn is in the top left-hand corner of the village.

(take Exit D and turn right) and goes to Zhāitáng (斋堂; ¥16, two hours, 6.30am to 5.50pm); then take a taxi (¥20) for the last 6km to Chuāndīxià. The last bus back leaves Zhāitáng at 5pm. If you miss it, it's around ¥200 for a taxi to Pingguoyuan.

Need to Know
→ **Entrance** ¥35
→ **Opening Hours** None
→ **Location** 90km from Běijīng

◉ SIGHTS

COURTYARD HOMES
HISTORIC HOUSES

The main attraction is the courtyard homes and the steps and alleyways that link them. Great fun can be had just wandering the cobbled lanes and poking your head into whichever ancient doorways take your fancy. Many of the homes are from the Qing dynasty, while others remain from Ming times. Some have been turned into small restaurants or guesthouses, meaning you can eat, drink tea or even stay the night in a 500-year-old Chinese courtyard.

MAOIST SLOGANS
HISTORIC SLOGANS

Chuāndīxià is a museum of Maoist graffiti and slogans, especially up the incline among the better-preserved houses. Look for the very clear, red-painted slogan just past the Landlord's Courtyard (the village's principal courtyard), which reads: 用毛泽东思想武装我们的头脑 (*yòng Máozédōng sīxiǎng wǔzhuāng wǒmen de tóunǎo;* use Mao Zedong Thought to arm our minds).

TEMPLES & VIEWPOINTS
TEMPLE, VIEWPOINT

In the hills east of the village stands the small Qing-dynasty **Guāndì Temple** (关帝庙; Guāndì Miào). For panoramic bird's-eye-view photos of the village, climb the **hill** south of Chuāndīxià (to your left as you approach the village) in the direction of the Goddess Temple (娘娘庙; Niángniáng Miào).

Tánzhè Temple & Jiètái Temple

Explore
These two ancient temples, around 10km apart, make a peaceful, Buddhist-inspired city-centre escape, and can easily be visited in a half-day trip.

Getting There & Away
→ **Bus** Bus 931 (¥6, 1½ hours) goes from Pingguoyuan subway station to Tánzhè Temple – make sure you avoid the bus 931 branch line (支线; *zhīxiàn*). This bus also stops near Jiètái Temple (¥4, one hour), a 10-minute walk uphill from the bus stop.

Need to Know
→ **Entrance** ¥35 each
→ **Opening Hours** 8.30am-6pm
→ **Location** 10-20km from Běijīng

PU XIANGDONG / CORBIS ©

ZHANG SHANCHEN / CORBIS ©

Ming Tombs (p181)
ijīng's answer to Luxor's Valley of the
gs.

2. Hóngluó Temple (p187)
One of Běijīng's largest and oldest Buddhist
temples, decorated for Spring
Festival (p23).

3. Shídù (p187)
A scenic valley containing pinnacle-shaped
rock formations, pleasant rivers and
general beauty.

⊙ SIGHTS

TÁNZHÈ TEMPLE 潭柘寺 TEMPLE

(Tánzhè Sì) The largest of all Běijīng's temples, and one of the oldest, Tánzhè Temple dates from the Jin dynasty (AD 265–420) but has been modified considerably since those days.

The Buddhist temple is attractively placed amid trees in the mountains and its ascending temple grounds are overlooked by towering cypress and pine trees, many of which are so old that their gangly limbs are supported by metal props. Don't miss the small **Tǎlín Temple** (塔林寺; Tǎlín Sì) by the forecourt where you get off the bus, with its assembly of stupas. Visits to Tánzhè Temple around mid-April are recommended, as the magnolias are in bloom then.

JIÈTÁI TEMPLE 戒台寺 TEMPLE

(Jiètái Sì) About 10km southeast of Tánzhè Temple, the smaller Jiètái Temple was origi-

---

OTHER HISTORIC VILLAGES

If Chuāndǐxià is too touristy for you, these lesser-known gems might do the trick. If you fancy staying the night in Língshuǐ or Shuǐyù, look out for signs for 农家院 (nóngjiāyuàn; farmer-style courtyard). There's nowhere to stay at Gǔyájū, but some travellers have camped in the caves. This is almost certainly not allowed though, so be discreet.

Língshuǐ 灵水村

Packed with history, this alluring village is home to Běijīng's oldest temple, **Língquánchán Temple** (灵泉禅寺; Língquánchán Sì). In ruins, with the main gate pretty much all that has survived, it dates from the Han dynasty (206 BC–AD 220). Also seek out Dragon King Temple (龙王庙; Lóngwáng Miào) and the Goddess Temple (娘娘庙; Niángniáng Miào), which are joined together and complemented by a pair of ancient intertwining trees.

Língshuǐ is famed for being a village of **scholars**; 22 former residents passed the notorious imperial exams, and the village marks their achievements with annual celebrations on 6 and 7 August. Doors marked '举人' (jǔrén; graduate) show where they lived.

To get to Língshuǐ, turn right out of Exit D of Pingguoyuan subway station and walk 200m to a bus stop. Take bus 829 to Jūnxiǎng (军响; ¥12, 1½ hours, 6.30am to 5.30pm) from where you can take a taxi (¥10 to ¥20) for the final 5km.

Shuǐyù 水峪村

This is one of Běijīng's most attractive ancient villages (entrance ¥20). Head to the west side of the more modern half of town for your fix of charming cobblestone alleys and Ming- and Qing-dynasty **courtyards** (there are more than 100 old courtyards). Hunt down the weathered Goddess Temple (娘娘庙; Niángniáng Miào) – yes, this village has one too! – and keep an eye out for the numerous Qing-dynasty **millstones** dotted around the place. Try not to miss the traditional flagpole ceremony carried out each morning and afternoon by women of the village.

To get to Shuǐyù, take bus 836 from Tiānqiáo long-distance bus station (天桥长途汽车站; Tiānqiáo Chángtú Qìchēzhàn; Map p296) to Fangshan Gouwu Zhongxin bus stop (房山购物中心; ¥11, 1½ hours, 5.40am to 8pm) then cross the road to find Fangshan bus station (房山客运站; Fángshān Kèyùnzhàn) and take bus 房23 (fáng èrshísān) to Shuǐyù Cūn (水峪村; ¥11, two hours). Returning, the last 房23 bus leaves Shuǐyù at 4.20pm.

Gǔyájū 古崖居

Gǔyájū (admission ¥40) is an enigma – an ancient abandoned cave village of unknown origin that pokes out from rocks in the water-starved hills of Yánqìng District and is the stuff of storybook legends. More than a dozen cave dwellings, spanning five or six levels of an open rock face, look out over the surrounding barren landscape. Steps carved into the rock allow you to climb up and explore the pleasingly cool caves. Some of the caves on the upper levels have been cordoned off, but there's still plenty to explore. Pack some food, and picnic in one of the strangest spots in Běijīng!

To reach Gǔyájū, take bus 919 (¥12, two hours, 6am to 6pm) from Déshèngmén gateway (德胜门; Map p294) to Yánqìng Dōngguān (延庆东关) then take bus 920 (¥5, 40 minutes, 6am to 6pm) to Dōngményíng (东门营), which is about a 2km walk from Gǔyájū. The last bus 919 back to Déshèngmén leaves Yánqìng Dōngguān at 5.30pm.

SHÍDÙ

Known as the 'Guìlín of the North' and best visited during the summer rainy season, Shídù (十渡) is a scenic valley containing pinnacle-shaped rock formations, pleasant rivers and general beauty, making it a great place to hike.

Shídù means '10 crossings': before the new road and bridges were built, visitors had to cross the Jùmǎ River 10 times while travelling from Zhāngfāng (张坊) to Shídù.

As well as trekking options, there's a bundle of activities, from climbing and boating to bungee jumping (¥150 to ¥180). Some areas require tickets (¥40 to ¥90).

At Zhāngfāng Village, you can visit the **Zhāngfāng Ancient Battle Tunnel** (张坊古战到; Zhāngfāng Gǔ Zhàndào; admission ¥20), a 1000-year-old underground military facility that was discovered by chance in 1991. Bus 917 stops here before it reaches Shídù.

To visit Shídù, take bus 917 (¥22, three hours, 6am to 5pm) from Tiānqiáo bus stand (天桥汽车站; Map p296). Shídù is the last stop.

nally built in the 7th century. The main complex is dotted with ancient pine trees. One of these, **Nine Dragon Pine**, is claimed to be over 1300 years old, while the **Embracing Pagoda Pine** does just what it says.

Hóngluó Temple

Explore

Straddling the south face of Hóngluó Mountain (813m) and hidden among pine trees and bamboo, Hóngluó Temple (红螺寺; Hóngluó Sì) is one of Běijīng's largest and oldest Buddhist temples. Originally built in AD 338, all of what you see today has been rebuilt over the years, most recently in 1992. But despite the absence of genuinely old structures, a conspicuous lack of monks and a slight theme-park feel to the place (you can ride a toboggan to get to one of the temples!), the complex has a peaceful atmosphere, and the forested grounds and steep hillside climbs can make for a low-key family-friendly excursion. There are small restaurants and snack stalls close to the entrance to the complex, and some snack stalls inside, but bringing your own picnic isn't a bad option.

The Best...

➡ **Sight** Hóngluó Temple (p187)

➡ **Hike** Hóngluó Mountain summit

➡ **Quirk** 500 Arhats Garden (p187)

Getting There & Away

➡ **Bus** Bus 867 starts at Dongzhimen Wai bus stand (东直门外车站; Map p298) and ends at Hóngluó Temple (¥13, two hours, 7am to 7pm). If traffic is bad, try catching the bus from Houshayu subway station (后沙峪; ¥8, one hour) at the north end of Line 15. The last bus back is at 5pm.

Need to Know

➡ **Entrance** ¥54, audio guide ¥20

➡ **Opening Hours** 7.30am-6pm

➡ **Location** 60km from Běijīng

⊙ SIGHTS

HÓNGLUÓ TEMPLE　　　　　　　TEMPLE

(红螺寺; Hóngluó Sì) You won't see many monks, but this temple contains attractive Buddhist sculptures, particularly in **Mahavira Hall** (大雄宝殿; Dàxióng Bǎodiàn).

GUĀNYĪN TEMPLE　　　　　　　TEMPLE

(观音寺; Guānyīn Sì; toboggan one way/return ¥40/60, children half-price) From Hóngluó Temple follow a steep path to this small rebuilt temple for fabulous views. You can ride a **toboggan** (滑道; huá dào) up to or down from here. Continue 15 minutes more to Heaven Gate (天门; Tiānmén), or the **summit** (主峰; zhǔfēng; at least one hour).

500 ARHATS GARDEN　　GARDENS, MONUMENTS

(五百罗汉园; Wǔbǎi Luóhàn Yuán) To the east of the grounds, you can walk among 500 statues of *arhats* (Buddhist disciples) which are scattered, rather surreally, around the trees.

Sleeping

Běijīng's once dire hotel scene now offers something for everyone. Hostels are plentiful and offer excellent value for budget and midrange travellers, while there are plenty of five-star luxury towers that pull out all the stops. In between is Běijīng's unique collection of courtyard hotels, which allow you to soak up the irresistible charms of the city's historic hútòng (alleys).

Hostels

Many hostels are in historic buildings down Běijīng's *hútòng*, with comfortable rooms and staff tuned into foreign travellers' needs who usually speak good English. Many hostels have a homely feel, with DVD rooms, PlayStations, internet access, wi-fi, international breakfasts and other meals, libraries, laundry rooms, bicycle hire and information boards.

Courtyard Hotels

For history, try Běijīng's courtyard hotels (*sìhéyuàn bīnguǎn*), which allow you to uncover the city's *hútòng* ambience and courtyard residences. The downside are smallish rooms and a frugal range of amenities: don't expect a pool, views over town or disabled access. Courtyard hotels do, however, come with an atmosphere that is uniquely Běijīng and a charm that other hotels cannot imitate. Courtyard hotels are available for all budgets.

Luxury Hotels

Běijīng has a growing crowd of four- and five-star hotels. The best offer standards equivalent to five-star international hotels, and most big players – Hyatt, Hilton, Marriott, St Regis – are here. However, some Chinese-managed hotels can be a star lower when measured against international standards.

Standard Hotels

Midrange Chinese hotels lack character but often come with generous discounts. Expect clean (although possibly smoky) rooms with TV, kettle, internet access via cable and small attached bathrooms. Staff rarely speak much English. If you just want an unfussy, clean and comfortable room, a crowd of lower-midrange business hotel chains offer simple accommodation. Chains include **Home Inn** (www.homeinns.com), **Motel 268** (www.motel268.com), **Seven Days Inn** (www.7daysinn.cn) and **Jīnjiāng Inn** (www.jinjianginns.com).

Some ultracheap guesthouses, known as *zhāodàisuǒ* (招待所), won't take foreigners.

Homestays & Long-Term Rentals

Homestays are a great way to experience Chinese culture (and to improve your language skills). Try www.chinahomestay.org. Běijīng also has a large, fast-expanding couchsurfing community (www.couchsurfing.org).

The rental market is good value, starting at around ¥4000 for a two-bed apartment. If you speak Chinese, ask at any estate agent in your chosen part of town. If you don't, check the websites of Běijīng's expat magazines. Try **The Beijinger** (www.thebeijinger.com) or **City Weekend** (www.cityweekend.com.cn).

Websites

➜ **ctrip.com** Hotel reservations.
➜ **booking.com** Hotel reservations.
➜ **chinahomestay.org** Homestays.
➜ **couchsurfing.org** Free homestays.
➜ **airbnb.com** Short-term rentals.
➜ **thebeijinger.com** Long-term rentals.
➜ **hotels.lonelyplanet.com** Hotel reviews and reservations.

Lonely Planet's Top Choices

Aman at Summer Palace (p198) Běijīng's stand-out luxury hotel.

Peking Youth Hostel (p194) Top youth hostel; top *hútòng* location.

Courtyard 7 (p194) Beautiful courtyard hotel, oozing Qing-dynasty charm.

Red Capital Residence (p191) Compact courtyard hotel with furnishings fit for a museum.

Opposite House Hotel (p197) So trendy it hurts; the city's swankiest boutique hotel by a long way.

Schoolhouse (p169) Fabulous city retreat, just a stone's throw from The Great Wall.

Best by Budget

$

Qiánmén Hostel (p196)

Běijīng Downtown Back-packers (p194)

Three-Legged Frog Hostel (p196)

Běijīng P-Loft Youth Hostel (p194)

Red Lantern House West Yard (p195)

$$

Orchid (p194)

Emperor (p191)

Park Plaza (p191)

Jìngyuán Hotel (p191)

Bamboo Garden Hotel (p195)

$$$

DùGé (p194)

St Regis (p197)

Ritz-Carlton Běijīng, Financial Street (p195)

Côté Cour (p191)

China World Hotel (p197)

Best Courtyard Hotels

DùGé (p194)

Qiánmén Hostel (p196)

Côté Cour (p191)

Jìngyuán Hotel (p191)

Best Hútòng Hostels

Běijīng Downtown Back-packers (p194)

Three-Legged Frog Hostel (p196)

Leo Courtyard (p197)

Beijing P-Loft Youth Hostel (p194)

City Walls Courtyard (p191)

Best Luxury

St Regis (p197)

China World Hotel (p197)

Ritz-Carlton Beijing, Financial Street (p195)

Regent Běijīng (p193)

Park Hyatt (p198)

Best City Escapes

Commune by the Great Wall (p192)

Red Capital Ranch (p192)

Ténglóng Fàndiàn (p172)

Zǎoxiāng Tíngyuàn (p173)

SLEEPING NEED TO KNOW

Where to Stay

Neighbourhood	For	Against
Forbidden City & Dōngchéng Central	Hugely historic. Highest concentration of sights. Good mix of ordinary hotels and *hútòng* accommodation.	Some parts are less residential than other neighbourhoods, and so can be eerily quiet in the evenings. Slim pickings on the nightlife front.
Drum Tower & Dōngchéng North	Běijīng's most desirable neighbourhood. Perfect for delving deep into the *hútòng*. Plenty of courtyard hotels. Cafes, bars and live music on your doorstep.	Budget backpackers may be priced out. No five-star hotels.
Běihǎi Park & Xīchéng North	Plenty of *hútòng* action, and the area by the lakes sees little traffic, and so can be peaceful.	Evening karaoke bars can ruin the lakeside ambience. Choice of accommodation is limited.
Dashilar & Xīchéng South	Backpacker Central. Great choice of hostels; some historic. *Hútòng* vibe is still strong around Dashilar.	Extensive reconstruction has stolen some of the character from the area, and seen prices rise. Still relatively cheap, though.
Sānlǐtún & Cháoyáng	Great for shopping, eating and nightlife.	Area lacks character and any historical narrative.
Summer Palace & Hǎidiàn	Less touristy.	Out of the way.

🛏 Forbidden City & Dōngchéng Central

TOP CHOICE RED CAPITAL RESIDENCE
COURTYARD HOTEL $$$

(新红资客栈; Xīnhóngzī Kèzhàn; ☏8403 5308; www.redcapitalclub.com.cn; 9 Dongsi Liutiao, 东四六条9号; s/d ¥1150/1500; ❊@🖥; 🚇Zhangzizhonglu) Dressed up with Liberation-era artefacts and established in a gorgeous Qing-dynasty courtyard, this tiny but unique guesthouse – owned by American activist and author Laurence Brahm – offers a heady dose of nostalgia for a vanished age. Make your choice from four rooms decked out with paraphernalia that wouldn't look out of place in a museum: the Chairman's Residence, the two Concubine Suites or the single Author's Suite. Rooms and bathrooms arc small, but beautifully decorated. What makes this place truly unique, though, is the cigar bar: it's housed in an underground bomb shelter below the courtyard, where guests are pampered with wine, cigars and, if they like, propaganda films projected onto a pull-down screen. The shelter is reputed to have been excavated by order of Vice-Chairman Lin Biao. There's no sign on the hotel's front door, just a number. Booking is recommended, especially at weekends. Red Capital also operates a wonderfully rustic hotel (p6) by the Great Wall.

CITY WALLS COURTYARD
HÚTÒNG HOSTEL $$

(城墙旅舍; Chéngqiáng Lǚshè; ☏6402 7805; www.beijingcitywalls.com; 57 Nianzi Hutong, 碾子胡同57号; 8-/4-bed dorm ¥100/120, d ¥420; ❊@🖥; 🚇Nanluoguxiang) Expensive for a hostel, and staff could smile more often, but this is still an attractive choice because of its peaceful courtyard atmosphere and fabulous *hútòng* location – authentically hidden away in one of the city's most historic areas. The maze of alleyways can be disorientating: from Jingshan Houjie, look for the *hútòng* opening just east of Jǐngshān Table Tennis Park. Walk up the *hútòng* and follow it around to the right and then left; the hostel is on the left-hand side.

JÌNGYUÁN HOTEL
COURTYARD HOTEL $$

(婧园雅筑宾馆; Jìngyuán Yǎzhù Bīnguǎn; ☏6525 9259; jyyz2008@yahoo.com.cn; 35 Xitangzi Hutong, 西堂子胡同35号; r with shared bathroom ¥486, r ¥988-1398; ❊@🖥; 🚇Dengshikou) Once the home of the Qing-dynasty painter Pu Jin – a cousin of China's last emperor Puyi – this peaceful, good-value courtyard hotel is tucked away beside St Joseph's Church and sits next door to the courtyard HQ of Běijīng's YWCA, which owns the hotel. Rooms are fairly ordinary – like those of a standard midrange Chinese hotel – but are situated around two pleasant courtyards, and come with excellent discounts. The ones with shared bathrooms were going for around ¥298 after discounts when we were here, while those with private bathrooms could be had for ¥680. English-language skills are limited, as foreign guests are relatively rare, but staff members are friendly and unobtrusive. The lobby has a small cafe-restaurant and free wi-fi, which extends into the first courtyard.

CÔTÉ COUR
COURTYARD HOTEL $$$

(北京演乐酒店; Běijīng Yǎnyuè Jiǔdiàn; ☏6523 3958; www.hotelcotecourbj.com; 70 Yanyue Hutong, 演乐胡同70号; d ¥1150-2000; ❊@🖥; 🚇Dengshikou) With a calm, serene atmosphere and a lovely magnolia courtyard, this 14-room *hútòng* hotel makcs a charming place to rest your head. Like all courtyard hotels, rooms and bathrooms are petite, but the decor in some of them is exquisite and there's plenty of space to relax in the courtyard or on the rooftop.

EMPEROR
BOUTIQUE HOTEL $$

(皇家驿栈酒店; Huángjiā Yìzhàn Jiǔdiàn; ☏6526 5566; www.theemperor.com.cn; 33 Qihelou Jie, 北池子大街骑河楼33号, off Beichizi Dajie; r from ¥1000; ♨❊@🖥; 🚇Dengshikou) Attempting to capitalise on a majestic position just east of the Forbidden City, the Emperor's lofty ambitions were undermined by height restrictions, so upper-floor rooms merely graze the rooftops of the imperial palace. Nonetheless you can't question the excellent *fēngshuǐ* this locale brings. The unnumbered rooms are named after emperors and come with funky, albeit slightly weird, fitted furniture with lots of smooth curves and strange cubbyholes. It's quirky but cool, and the views from the rooftop bar, Yīn (p75), are simply imperial. You can get rooms here for around ¥750 if you book online through www.ctrip.com or www.booking.com.

PARK PLAZA
HOTEL $$

(北京丽亭酒店; Běijīng Lìtíng Jiǔdiàn; ☏8522 1999; www.parkplaza.com/beijingcn; 97 Jinbao Jie, 金宝街97号; d from ¥900; ♨❊@🖥;

ESCAPE TO THE GREAT WALL

As well as the accommodation options that feature in our special Great Wall section (p166), the following luxury digs offer some exclusivity beside more remote parts of China's best-known icon.

COMMUNE BY THE GREAT WALL
LUXURY HOTEL $$$

(长城脚下的公社; Chángchéng Jiǎoxià de Gōngshè; ☎8118 1888; www.communebythegreatwall.com; r from ¥2500; ✳@🔊🏊) The Commune by the Great Wall is seriously expensive but the cantilevered geometric architecture, location and superb panoramas are standouts. Positioned at the Shuǐguān Great Wall off the Badaling Hwy, the Kempinski-managed Commune may have a proletarian name but the design and presentation are purely for the affluent. Take out another mortgage and treat yourself – this is the ultimate view, with a room. There is a kids' club to boot.

RED CAPITAL RANCH
HISTORIC HOTEL $$$

(新红资避暑山庄; Xīnhóngzī Bìshǔshānzhuāng; ☎8403 5308; www.redcapitalclub.com.cn; 28 Xiaguandi Village, 怀柔县雁栖镇下关地村28号, Yanxi; r from ¥1500; ✳@🏊) Doing its own thing miles from civilisation, Red Capital Ranch is *the* Běijīng escapist option. Sooner or later, you'll want a break from the big-city cacophony. If so, why not check into one of the 10 individually styled villas at this Manchurian hunting lodge on a 20-acre estate north of town and settle down for a long, stress-free siesta. If the mountain setting – complete with Great Wall remains running through the estate – doesn't dissolve your stress, the Tibetan Tantric Space Spa will. Try to get your Běijīng sightseeing out of the way before staying here – it's quite a hike into town. Free transport is laid on daily from its city-centre sister branch, Red Capital Residence (p191).

ⓈDengshikou) A good-value riposte to the overblown top-flight hotels in the area (see the gaudy Legendale across the road for what *not* to do), the Park Plaza is a treasured find. If you can't or don't want to stretch to a five-star hotel, this friendly place has a strong location and a comfortable, modern and well-presented four-star finish. The lobby is mildly jazzy and sedate – but not subdued – with chocolate-brown leather seats, while rooms are stylish and comfortable. Not elegant, but it's modish, the living is easy and you won't be left with a gaping hole in your budget. It's hidden away behind its glitzier sister hotel, the Regent Běijīng.

HOTEL KAPOK
BOUTIQUE HOTEL $$$

(木棉花酒店; Mùmiánhuā Jiǔdiàn; ☎6525 9988; www.hotelkapok.com; 16 Donghuamen Dajie, 东华门大街16号; d from ¥1200; ✳@🔊; ⓈTiananmen East) Offering midrange cool for designer types, trendy Kapok is hidden behind a tough-to-keep-clean, all-glass-grill frontage and comes with modern rooms with plenty of glass, mirrors and white panelling, as well as free wi-fi. Even the bathrooms are glass-walled, so perhaps not a hotel to share

with your travel buddy? Discounts bring standard rooms rates down to ¥900.

RAFFLES BĚIJĪNG
HISTORICAL HOTEL $$$

(北京饭店莱佛士酒店; Běijīng Fàndiàn Láifóshì Jiǔdiàn; ☎6526 3388; www.raffles.com/beijing; 33 Dongchang'an Jie, 东长安街33号; r from ¥1800; ♿✳@🔊✳; ⓈWangfujing) Sandwiched between two drab edifices (to the east, the 1970s lines of the Běijīng Hotel; to the west, a gawky Soviet-era facade), the seven-storey Raffles oozes cachet and grandeur. The heritage building dates to 1900 when it was the Grand Hotel de Pekin, so pedigree is its middle name. Illuminated in a chandelier glow, the elegant lobby yields to a graceful staircase leading to immaculate standard doubles that are spacious and well proportioned, decked out with period-style furniture and large bathrooms. The ground floor Writers Bar offers a unique variety of stress-busting tranquillity in deluxe surroundings (with prices to match).

BĚIJĪNG SAGA INTERNATIONAL YOUTH HOSTEL
HÚTÒNG HOSTEL $

(北京实佳国际青年旅社; Běijīng Shíjiā Guójì Qīngnián Lǚshè; ☎6527 2773; sagaiyh@yahoo.cn; 9 Shijia Hutong, 史家胡同9号; dm ¥60, d without/with bathroom from ¥219/289; ❋ @ 🤶; S Dengshikou) Enjoying an interesting location on historic Shijia Hutong, this popular hostel is a grey block but the inside compensates with some character, and staff members are helpful towards travellers. Rooms are basic but well kept, and it has a refectory, a bar and, in the main lobby, a spacious seating area. The mixed dorm rooms are a decent size and include private lockers. The building is modern, but the height has advantages: head up to the huge open rooftop and directly view the Qing-dynasty-era courtyard below.

BĚIJĪNG CITY CENTRAL INTERNATIONAL YOUTH HOSTEL
HOSTEL $

(北京城市国际青年旅社; Běijīng Chéngshì Guójì Qīngnián Lǚshè; ☑8511 5050, 6525 8866; www.centralhostel.com; 1 Beijingzhan Jie, 北京站街1号; 4-8 bed dm ¥60, s/d with shared bathroom ¥128/160, d from ¥298-368; ⊜ ❋ @ 🤶; S Beijingzhan) The first youth hostel you hit after exiting Běijīng Train Station, this place is a decent choice if you can't be bothered to lug your heavy rucksack to nicer parts of the city. Rooms are pretty basic but clean and spacious enough, and there's a large bar-cafe area with free wi-fi, internet terminals, pool tables and Western food.

REGENT BĚIJĪNG
LUXURY HOTEL $$$

(北京丽晶大酒店; Běijīng Lìjīng Dàjiǔdiàn; ☑8522 1888; www.regenthotels.com; 99 Jinbao Jie, 金宝街99号; r from ¥1600; ⊜ ❋ @ 🤶 ⊠; S Dengshikou) The lavish 500-room Regent has staked out a precious plot of land on the corner of Jinbao Jie and Dongdan Bei-dajie to the east of Wangfujing Dajie. Guest rooms are good value – luxuriously styled and up to the minute. A full range of health and leisure facilities and five restaurants round off the impressive picture.

HILTON BĚIJĪNG WÁNGFǓJĪNG
LUXURY HOTEL $$$

(北京王府井希尔顿酒店; Běijīng Wángfǔjīng Xǐ'ěrdùn Jiǔdiàn; ☑5812 8888; www.wangfujing.hilton.com; Xiaowei Hutong, 王府井东大街校尉胡同, off Wangfujing Dongdajie; d ¥1550; ⊜ ❋ @ 🤶 ⊠; S Wangfujing) Modern, classy and very centrally located, this branch of the Hilton is one of Běijīng's best five-star offerings. Service is stellar and the very spacious rooms are said to be the largest in the city. The only black mark is the out-dated policy of charging guests for in-room wi-fi, at the quite frankly obscene rate of ¥120 per day! Sort it out, Hilton.

RED WALL GARDEN
COURTYARD HOTEL $$$

(红墙花园酒店; Hóngqiáng Huāyuán Jiǔdiàn; ☑5169 2222; www.rwhotel.com; 41 Shijia Hutong, 史家胡同41号; d from ¥1480; ❋ @ 🤶; S Dengshikou) Despite its old *hútòng* location, there's nothing historic about this reconstructed courtyard hotel, but it offers top-end luxury rooms, complete with very comfortable beds and some beautiful pieces of traditional Chinese wood furniture, in a two-storey complex, which surrounds two sides of a huge, nicely landscaped, central courtyard. Wi-fi and nonsmoking throughout. Small bar. Decent restaurant.

NÁNJĪNG GREAT HOTEL
HOTEL $$

(北京南京大饭店; Běijīng Nánjīng Dàfàndiàn; ☑6526 2188; 5 Xi Jie, 西街5号; s/d from ¥688/900; ❋ @ 🤶; S Wangfujing) This popular midrange hotel right in the centre of town has competitively priced and comfortable rooms. The location, a 10-minute walk east of the Forbidden City and just off Wangfujing Dajie, is a winner, although the staff's English-language skills can be rudimentary. Wi-fi in lobby only, but laptop users can get online in their rooms with a cable connection.

PENINSULA
LUXURY HOTEL

(王府饭店; Wángfǔ Fàndiàn; ☑8516 2888; www.peninsula.com; 8 Jinyu Hutong, 金鱼胡同8号; r from ¥2000; ❋ @ 🤶 ⊠; S Dengshikou) White-tile exterior looks dated these days, but the unflinchingly high standards remain.

GRAND HYATT
LUXURY HOTEL

(北京东方君悦大酒店; Běijīng Dōngfāng Jūnyuè Dàjiǔdiàn; ☑8518 1234; www.beijing.grand.hyatt.com; 1 Dongchang'an Jie, 东长安街1号; r from ¥2000; ⊜ ❋ @ 🤶 ⊠; S Wangfujing) Stylish creation lording it over Wángfǔjīng's Oriental Plaza, but loses marks for extortionate wi-fi charges (per day ¥120).

ENGLISH-LANGUAGE SKILLS

Good English-language skills among staff at Běijīng accommodation remain fitful. Youth hostels typically have excellent English-language speakers, as do five-star hotels – it's the ones in between that may not.

🛏 Drum Tower & Dōngchéng North

⭐ TOP CHOICE PEKING YOUTH HOSTEL
HÚTÒNG HOSTEL $$

(北平国际青年旅社; Běipíng Guójì Qīngnián Lǔshè; ☑8403 9098; pekinghostel@yahoo.com. cn; 113 Nanluogu Xiang, 南锣鼓巷113号; dm/ tw from ¥120/450; ❄@🛜; Ⓢ Nanluoguxiang) Fabulous, flower-filled youth hostel located on trendy Nanluogu Xiang, an historic *hútòng* that's been transformed into a lively lane of bars, cafes, restaurants and boutique shops. In keeping with its fashionable location, this is more of a boutique hostel than a backpackers' haven, with a beautifully renovated building including a quaint, country cottage–like restaurant and a wonderful rooftop cafe-bar. All the usual youth-hostel services are dished up, though, including bike hire and trips to the Great Wall.

⭐ TOP CHOICE COURTYARD 7
COURTYARD HOTEL $$$

(四合院酒店; Sìhéyuàn Jiǔdiàn; ☑6406 0777; www.courtyard7.com; 7 Qiangulou Yuan Hutong, 鼓楼东大街南锣鼓巷前鼓楼苑胡同7号, off Nanluogu Xiang; r ¥900-1500; ❄@; Ⓢ Nanluoguxiang) Immaculate rooms, decorated in traditional Chinese furniture, face onto two 300-year-old courtyards, which over the years have been home to government ministers, rich merchants and even an army general. Despite the historical narrative, rooms still come with modern comforts such as underfloor heating, broadband internet (but no wi-fi) and cable TV, and the *hútòng* location – down a quiet alley, but very close to trendy Nanluogu Xiang – is a winner. Breakfast included.

⭐ TOP CHOICE DÙGÉ
COURTYARD HOTEL $$$

(杜革四合院酒店; Dùgé Sìhéyuàn Jiǔdiàn; ☑6406 0686; www.dugecourtyard.com; 26 Qianyuan Ensi Hutong, 交道口南大街前园恩寺胡同26号; r ¥1800-2500; ❄@🛜; Ⓢ Nanluoguxiang or Beixinqiao) This 19th-century former residence was originally home to a Qing-dynasty minister but was recently converted by a Belgian-Chinese couple into an exquisite designer courtyard hotel. Each of the six rooms is decorated uniquely with modern and artistic touches blended with overall themes of traditional China. Some of the wood furniture – four-poster beds, decorative Chinese screens – is simply beautiful. Rooms are set around small romantic, bamboo-lined courtyards. The only downside is that, as with most courtyard hotels, space is at a premium, so rooms are far smaller than you'd expect from similarly priced top-end hotels.

⭐ TOP CHOICE BĚIJĪNG DOWNTOWN BACKPACKERS
HÚTÒNG HOSTEL $

(东堂客栈; Dōngtáng Kèzhàn; ☑8400 2429; www.backpackingchina.com; 85 Nanluogu Xiang, 南锣鼓巷85号; s/tw from ¥160/190, 3-/4-/8-bed dm per bed ¥85/85/75, d ¥160-210, ste ¥300; ❄@; Ⓢ Beixinqiao) A cheaper option than the excellent Peking International Youth Hostel, but still with the same wonderful *hútòng* location, Downtown Backpackers is Nanluogu Xiang's original youth hostel and it hasn't forgotten its roots. Rooms are basic, therefore cheap, but are kept clean and tidy, and staff members are fully plugged in to the needs of Western travellers. Rents bikes and runs recommended hiking trips to the Great Wall (¥280), plus a range of other city trips. Rates include breakfast.

ORCHID
COURTYARD HOTEL $$

(兰花宾馆; Lánhuā Bīnguǎn; ☑8404 4818; www.theorchidbeijing.com; 65 Baochao Hutong, 鼓楼东大街宝钞胡同65号; d ¥700-1200; ❄@🛜; Ⓢ Gulou Dajie) Opened by a Canadian guy and a Tibetan girl, this place may lack the history of other courtyard hotels, but it's been renovated into a beautiful space, with a peaceful courtyard and some rooftop seating with distant views of the Drum and Bell Towers. Rooms are doubles only and are small, but are tastefully decorated and come with Apple TV home entertainment systems. Hard to spot, the Orchid is down an unnamed, shoulder-width alleyway opposite Mr Shi's Dumplings.

BĚIJĪNG P-LOFT YOUTH HOSTEL
HÚTÒNG HOSTEL $

(跑局工厂青年旅舍; Pàojú Gōngchǎng Qīngnián Lǔshè; ☑6402 7218; ploft@yahoo.cn; 29 Paoju Toutiao, 炮局头条29号; dm/r from ¥56/195; ❄@🛜; Ⓢ Yonghegong-Lama Temple) First an 18th-century artillery factory, then a prison; now a hidden gem of a youth hostel with a distinctly urban feel to it. Embedded in a *hútòng* warren behind the Lama Temple, P Loft seems to be on the fringe of things, but it's only a short meander to the subway system. Dorms are fine, as are the private rooms with en suite, and a degree of anonymity is guaranteed by the hard-to-find location. Facilities include bar, bike hire and a roomy sports area for playing ping pong and pool.

LAMA TEMPLE YOUTH HOSTEL HÚTÒNG HOSTEL $
(北京雍和宫国际青年旅社; Běijīng Yōnghégōng Guójì Qīngnián Lǚshè; ☎6402 8663; service@lamahostel.com; 56 Beixinqiao Toutiao, 北新桥头条56号; dm/r from ¥45/220; ❄@📶; [S]Beixinqiao) The whole place lacks natural light, including the rooms, but this is a long-standing, well-run hostel with a good location. Rents bikes (per day ¥20).

Běihǎi Park & Xīchéng North

[TOP CHOICE] **RED LANTERN HOUSE WEST YARD** COURTYARD HOTEL $
(红灯笼; Hóng Dēnglóng; ☎6617 0870; 12 Xisi Beiertiao, 西四北二条12号; s ¥280, d/tw ¥360, ste ¥450; ❄@📶; [S]Xisi) The most engaging of the Red Lantern brood, West Yard is set around two lovely, quiet courtyards. The rooms are thoughtfully and comfortably furnished in an old Běijīng style – wooden beds and fittings – and the staff are efficient and unobtrusive. There's also a honeymoon suite for those in the mood for love. It's essential to book ahead. To find it, walk north on Xisi Beidajie from Xisi metro; it's two *hútòng* up on the left.

RITZ-CARLTON BEIJING, FINANCIAL STREET LUXURY HOTEL $$$
(北京金融街丽嘉酒店; Běijīng Jīnróng Jiē Lìjiā Jiǔdiàn; ☎6601 6666; www.ritzcarlton.com; 1 Jinchengfang Dongjie, 金城坊东街 1号; d ¥4500; 🚭❄@📶🏊; [S]Fuxingmen) A magnificent, modernist behemoth marooned amid the soulless towers of Běijīng's financial district, the Ritz-Carlton remains one of the city's finest hotels. Huge, comfy beds sit within luxurious and spacious rooms designed to cater for every whim of the traveller (we like the way you can charge your laptop inside the safe deposit box). The acclaimed spa and health club occupies an entire floor, while there are Chinese and Western restaurants on site. Service is predictably excellent. Discounts of 40% are available.

BAMBOO GARDEN HOTEL COURTYARD HOTEL $$
(竹园宾馆; Zhúyuán Bīnguǎn; ☎5852 0088; www.bbgh.com.cn; 24 Xiaoshiqiao Hutong, 小石桥胡同 24号; s ¥520, ste ¥990-1760, d ¥760-880; ❄@📶; [S]Gulou Dajie) The intimate, leafy courtyard at Bamboo Garden is appealing, even if the rooms, as in many of Běijīng's courtyard hotels, can't quite match the elegant, hushed atmosphere. The small singles are ordinary, so upgrading to the much more pleasant doubles and suites is recommended. The buildings date to the late Qing dynasty; its gardens once belonged to a eunuch from Empress Cixi's entourage. It's within roaming distance of the Drum and Bell Towers and the Hòuhǎi lakes.

RED LANTERN HOUSE HÚTÒNG HOSTEL
(仿古园; Fǎnggǔ Yuán; ☎8328 5771; www.redlanternhouse.com; 5 Zhengjue Hutong, 正觉胡同 5号; 4-6 bed dm ¥70, d without/with shower ¥190/290, tr ¥360; ❄@📶; [S]Jishuitan) With a charming interior, trimmed with red lanterns and opening onto an ample bar area, this is a welcoming hotel. It also has helpful staff and a winning *hútòng* location. Reserve ahead. If it's booked out, its laidback sibling, **Red Lantern House East Yard**, is a couple of minutes' walk away in an alley off Zhengjue Hutong, although that branch has no dorms.

JǏNJIĀNG INN HOTEL
(锦江之星宾馆; Jǐnjiāng Zhīxīng Bīnguǎn; ☎6405 8622; www.4008209999.com; 103 Deshengmennei Dajie, 德胜门内大街 103号; d ¥269/299; ❄@; [S]Jishuitan) There's nothing remarkable about this branch of the popular hotel chain, although the rooms are clean and modern and have broadband access. Rather, it's the fantastic location close to the border of the Hòuhǎi lakes, and within one of the most *hútòng*-rich areas of Běijīng, that makes it a great choice. Step outside and you can be lost in the surrounding labyrinth of alleys, or the bars of Hòuhǎi, in a matter of minutes.

DRUM TOWER YOUTH HOSTEL HOSTEL
(鼓韵青年旅舍; Gǔyùn Qīngnián Lǚshè; ☎8401 6565; www.24hostel.com; 51 Jiugulou Dajie, 旧鼓楼大街 51号; 6-bed dm without/with bathroom ¥60/¥80, d & tw without/with

bathroom ¥200/280 ; ❄@📶; [S]Gulou Dajie) A few years ago, this place had a deservedly bad rep among travellers. Now, it has upped its game with staff who are actually interested in helping people and clean, if uninspired, dorms and rooms. The added bonuses are a cool roof terrace and the attached next-door bar Lakers, which serves up reasonably priced Western comfort food and standard Chinese dishes. Bike hire is ¥35 a day.

BĚIJĪNG HÒUHĂI COURT YARD GUEST HOUSE HÚTÒNG HOSTEL

(三宝四合院客栈; Sānbǎo Sìhéyuàn Kèzhàn; ☎6612 8458; 14 Sanbulao Hutong, 三不老胡同14号; 4-bed dm ¥70, d & tw without/with shower ¥128/258, tr without/with shower ¥210/298; ❄@📶; [S]Pinganli) Friendly and down-to-earth family-run place that's a hop, skip and a jump from the Hòuhǎi lakes. Set around a small courtyard, the rooms and dorms are not big, but the communal bathrooms are clean and it attracts a good mix of domestic and foreign travellers. The young owner is eager to please and there's bike hire for ¥20 a day too. It's located at the Deshengmen Dajie end of Sanbulao Hutong.

BĚIJĪNG HÙGUÓSÌ HOTEL HOTEL

(护国寺宾馆; Hùguósì Bīnguǎn; ☎5933 1688; www.hgshotel.net; 125 Huguosi Jie, 护国寺街125号; d & tw ¥298-420, tr ¥480; [S]Pinganli) This place has a rather grand, faux-courtyard exterior that promises more than it delivers because the rooms and bathrooms are on the small side. But the staff are pleasant and the location is convenient: within walking distance of both Hòuhǎi and the Forbidden City. Discounts of 20% available.

GRAND MERCURE BĚIJĪNG CENTRAL LUXURY HOTEL

(美爵酒店; Měijué Jiǔdiàn; ☎6603 6688; www.grandmercure.com; 6 Xuanwumennei Dajie, 宣武门内大街 6号; d/ste ¥1177/1654; 🚭❄@📶🏊; [S]Xidan or Xuanwumen) North of the South Cathedral and formerly known as the Marco Polo, this busy four-star hotel has eager staff and is one of the best in this part of town, even if its comfortable but characterless rooms are a little overpriced. There's a tiny swimming pool, but the fitness centre is more rigorous. Discounts of 25% available.

Dashilar & Xīchéng South

[TOP CHOICE] QIÁNMÉN HOSTEL COURTYARD HOSTEL $

(前门客栈; Qiánmén Kèzhàn; ☎6313 2369, 6313 2370; www.qianmenhostel.net; 33 Meishi Jie, 煤市街 33号; 6-8 bed dm ¥60, 4-bed dm ¥70, tw without/with bathroom ¥200/240, tr 240/300; ❄@📶; [S]Qianmen) A five-minute trot southwest of Tiān'ānmén Square, this heritage hostel offers a relaxing environment with able staff. Close the door on the busy street outside and appreciate the high ceilings, original woodwork and charming antique buildings. An affable old hand, hostel owner Genghis Kane may enthusiastically show you his environmentally sound heating apparatus (fired with dried pellets of plant matter), or you can just hang out in the courtyard. The rooms are simple and not big but, like the dorms, they are clean, as are the shared bathrooms.

THREE-LEGGED FROG HOSTEL HUTÒNG HOSTEL $

(京一食青年旅舍; Jīngyī Shí Qīngnián Lǚshè; ☎6304 3721, 6304 0749; 3legs@threeleggedfroghostel.com; 27 Tieshu Xiejie, 铁树斜街 27号; 6-bed dm with bathroom ¥70, 10-bed dm ¥60, d & tw ¥220, tr ¥300, f ¥420; ❄@📶; [S]Qianmen) The name is a mystery but this is a welcome addition to the growing band of hostels along and off Dazhalan Xijie. The six-bed dorms are an excellent deal, while the rooms are compact but clean and all are set around a cute courtyard. It has a sardonic but helpful owner and a communal area out front that does Western breakfasts and evening beers.

QIÁNMÉN JIÀNGUÓ HOTEL HOTEL $$$

(前门建国饭店; Qiánmén Jiànguó Fàndiàn; ☎6301 6688; www.qianmenhotel.com; 175 Yong'an Lu, 永安路 175号; d/tw ¥1500-1800, ste ¥2200-3500; 🚭❄@📶; [S]Caishikou) Elegant in parts and popular with tour groups, this refurbished and choicely located hotel has pushed up its prices to reflect its makeover. Business is brisk, so the staff are on their toes, and the rooms are spacious, clean and bright and a decent deal with the generous discounts (up to 50% off). You can find the Líyuán Theatre to the right of the domed atrium at the rear of the hotel.

LEO COURTYARD
COURTYARD HOSTEL **$**

(上林宾馆; Shànglín Bīnguǎn; ☑6303 4609, 8316 6568; www.leohostel.com; 22 Shanxi Xiang, 陕西巷胡同 22号; 6-bed dm ¥50, tw ¥160, tr ¥270; ✿@⍨; Ⓢ Qianmen) It's a superb, historic building with a racy past featuring courtesans and the imperial elite, but the rooms themselves are a little tatty and the bathrooms nothing to write home about. Nor do the sleepy staff inspire confidence. That said, the small dorms and communal showers are clean and the attached bar-restaurant next door is a good place for a libation come sundown. It's down an alley off Dazhalan Xijie.

LEO HOSTEL
HÚTÒNG HOSTEL **$$**

(广聚园宾馆; Guǎngjùyuán Bīnguǎn; ☑6303 1595, 8660 8923; www.leohostel.com; 52 Dazhalan Xijie; 大栅栏西街 52号; 4-bed dm without/with bathroom ¥60/¥80, 8-bed dm with bathroom ¥70, 10-bed dm ¥50, d & tw ¥240; ✿@⍨; Ⓢ Qianmen) Far less atmosphere than its venerable cousin Leo Courtyard, but the dorms and rooms are more modern and frankly better, even if the overall vibe is rather sterile. But there's a fair-sized communal area which does OK food, and it's close to Tiān'ānmén Square and the surrounding sights. Always busy, it's worth booking ahead.

FAR EAST INTERNATIONAL YOUTH HOSTEL
HÚTÒNG HOSTEL **$$**

(远东国际青年旅舍; Yuǎndōng Guójì Qīngnián Lǚshè; ☑5195 8811; www.fareastyh.com; 113 Tieshu Xiejie, 铁树斜街 113号; 4-6 bed dm ¥60-65; ✿@⍨; Ⓢ Caishikou/Qianmen) This hostel is in a pretty, old courtyard opposite the **Far East Hotel** (远东饭店; Yuǎndōng Fàndiàn; d/tw Y380). If it's busy, and it mostly is, you could end up in the basement of the much less attractive hotel, although the rooms are clean with wooden floors and well-kept bunk beds. It's definitely worth booking ahead.

🛏 Sānlǐtún & Cháoyáng

TOP CHOICE OPPOSITE HOUSE
HOTEL
BOUTIQUE HOTEL **$$$**

(瑜舍; Yúshè; ☑6417 6688; www.theoppositehouse.com; 11 Sanlitun Lu, 三里屯路11号院1号楼, Bldg 1, Village; r from ¥2500; ⊖✿@⍨⊠) With see-all open-plan bathrooms, American oak bath tubs, lovely mood lighting, underfloor heating, sliding doors, complimentary beers, TVs on extendable arms and a metal basin swimming pool, this trendy Swire-owned boutique hotel is top-drawer chic. Chinese motifs are muted: this is an international hotel with prices to match. It's not the sort of place to take the kids, but couples can splash out or sip drinks in trendy Mesh (p146). The location is great for shopping, restaurants and drinking. No obvious sign, or reception area. Just walk into the striking green glass cube of a building and ask.

SĀNLǏTÚN YOUTH HOSTEL
HOSTEL **$**

(三里屯青年旅馆; Sānlǐtún Qīngnián Lǚguǎn; ☑5190 9288; www.itisbeijing.com; Chunxiu Lu, 春秀路南口往北250米路东; dm/tw from ¥60/220; ✿@⍨; Ⓢ Dongsishitiao or Dongzhimen) Sānlǐtún's only decent youth hostel, this place is very well run and extremely popular. Has added an outdoor terrace to its good-value bar-restaurant area, and still offers its usual trustworthy travel advice. Rooms are functional, but clean, and it has internet, wi-fi, a pool table, table football, bike rental (¥30) and friendly staff.

ST REGIS
LUXURY HOTEL **$$$**

(北京国际俱乐部饭店; Běijīng Guójì Jùlèbù Fàndiàn; ☑6460 6688; www.stregis.com/beijing, 21 Jianguomenwai Dajie, 建国门外大街21号; r from ¥2600; ⊖✿@⍨⊠; Ⓢ Jianguomen) Its extravagant foyer, thorough professionalism and tip-top location make the St Regis a marvellous, albeit costly, five-star choice. Sumptuous and soothing rooms ooze comfort, 24-hour butlers are at hand to fine-tune your stay and a gorgeous assortment of restaurants steers you into one of Běijīng's finest dining experiences. Shamefully, as if they weren't earning enough from their room rates, this otherwise top-class hotel charges ¥80 per day for wi-fi.

CHINA WORLD HOTEL
LUXURY HOTEL **$$$**

(中国大饭店; Zhōngguó Dàfàndiàn; ☑6505 2266; www.shangri-la.com; 1 Jianguomenwai Dajie, 建国门外大街1号; r from ¥1600; ⊖✿@⍨⊠; Ⓢ Guomao) The gorgeous five-star China World Hotel delivers an outstanding level of service to its well-dressed, largely executive travellers. The sumptuous foyer is a masterpiece of Chinese motifs, glittering chandeliers, robust columns and smooth acres of marble, an effect complemented by thoroughly modern and comfortable rooms. The amenities are extensive, dining options are first-rate and shopping needs

SLEEPING SĀNLǏTÚN & CHÁOYÁNG

are met at the adjacent China World Shopping Mall.

HOLIDAY INN EXPRESS HOTEL $$

(智选假日酒店; Zhìxuǎn Jiàrì Jiǔdiàn; ☎6416 9999; www.holidayinnexpress.com.cn; 1 Chunxiu Lu, 春秀路1号; r ¥598; ❄@📶; [S]Dongsishitiao or Dongzhimen) Brand new 350-room hotel with bright, clean, comfortable rooms (we love the big puffy pillows!) that come equipped with wide-screen TV, free wi-fi and internet access via a cable. The lobby has Apple computers for the use of guests. Staff members are friendly and speak some English.

YOYO HOTEL HOTEL $$

(优优客酒店; Yōuyōu Kèjiǔdiàn; ☎6417 3388; www.yoyohotel.cn; Bldg 10 Dongsanjie Erjie, 三里屯北路东三街二街中10楼; r from ¥310; ❄@📶; [S]Tuanjiehu) Has a modern, boutique feel to it, but rooms here are tiny. Nevertheless, they are excellent value for the location (off Sanlitun Lu) and are kept clean and tidy. Staff members speak some English and are friendly considering how rushed off their feet they usually are. There's internet via a cable inside rooms. Wi-fi is in the lobby only.

HOTEL G BOUTIQUE HOTEL $$$

(北京极栈; Běijīng Jízhàn; ☎6552 3600; www.hotel-g.com; 7a Gongrentiyuchang Xilu, 工体西路甲7号; r from ¥1250; ❄@📶) It is hard to discern the advertised '60s retro-chic style, but this snazzy boutique hotel is certainly distinctive, from its deep purples, charcoal blacks, satins, floral prints and crushed velvet to the fibre-optics by the lobby elevators. Peruse the soothing pillow menu (six varieties) to complement the gorgeously comfortable beds, snap your iPod into the docking station and Bob's your uncle. The ground-floor bar-restaurant Scarlett (open 6am to 2am) is very smart.

PARK HYATT LUXURY HOTEL $$$

(柏悦酒店; Bóyuè Jiǔdiàn; ☎8567 1234; www.beijing.park.hyatt.com; 2 Jianguomenwai Dajie, 建国门外大街2号; r from ¥2800, China Bar beer from ¥50, cocktails from ¥70; ⏰China Bar 4pm-1am; 🚭❄@📶🏊; [S]Guomao) Cool almost to the point of being unwelcoming, the beautiful Park Hyatt draws well-heeled business types and the cocktail-bar crowd, and has all the top-notch facilities you'd expect from a hotel in this location and of this standing. Reception is on the 63rd floor, while the 65th-floor China Bar has city views bettered only by nearby Atmosphere (p145).

KERRY CENTER HOTEL BUSINESS HOTEL $$$

(嘉里中心饭店; Jiālǐ Zhōngxīn Fàndiàn; ☎6561 8833; www.thekerryhotels.com; 1 Guanghua Lu, 光华路1号; r from ¥1800; 🚭❄@📶🏊; [S]Guomao) Good-quality business hotel with large gym and pool.

COMFORT INN HOTEL $$

(凯富饭店; Kǎifù Fàndiàn; ☎8523 5522; www.choicehotels.com; 6 Gongrentiyuchang Beilu, 工人体育场北路6号; r from ¥800; 🚭@📶🏊; [S]Tuanjiehu) Decent value if you don't mind a lack of pizazz.

EASTERN INN HOTEL $

(逸羽连锁酒店; Yìyǔ Liánsuǒ Jiǔdiàn; ☎6508 6611; cnr Nansanlitun Lu & Gongrentiyuchang Nanlu, 南三里屯路和工人体育场南路角口; s/d ¥299/399; ❄@; [S]Hujialou or Tuanjiehu) Clean, functional but characterless rooms with ¥50 discounts common. Not much English spoken.

Summer Palace & Hǎidiàn

[TOP CHOICE] **AMAN AT SUMMER PALACE** HERITAGE HOTEL $$$

(颐和安缦; Yíhé Ānmàn; ☎5987 9999; www.amanatsummerpalace.com; 1 Gongmen Qianjie, 宫门前街 1号; r US$650, courtyard r US$750, ste US$950; ❄@📶🏊; [S]Xiyuan) Hard to fault this exquisite hotel, a true candidate for best in Běijīng. It's located around the corner from the Summer Palace – and part of the hotel buildings date back to the 19th century and were used to house distinguished guests waiting for audiences with Empress Cixi. Superbly appointed rooms are contained in a series of picture-perfect pavilions set around courtyards, and stepping through the imposing red gates here is to enter a very different, very hushed and very privileged world. Choice restaurants, a spa, a library, a cinema, pool, squash courts and, of course, silky-smooth service round off the refined picture.

PEKING UNI INTERNATIONAL HOSTEL HOSTEL $

(未名国际青年旅舍; Wèimíng Guójì Qīngnián Lǚshè; ☎8287 1309, 6254 9667; www.pkuhostel.com; 150 Chengfu Lu, 成府路; dm ¥80, d/tw

¥278-298; [❄][@][📶]; [S]Wudaokou) Undergoing a long-overdue refit at the time of writing, this busy hostel is located in an office building and so lacks the character of many other hostels around town. It caters more for domestic travellers (and students from the surrounding universities) than it does for foreigners. But the staff members are amenable, although you won't hear much English, and the dorms and rooms, while a little cramped, are clean and sound enough. But check them before you decide, as some don't have windows.

LTH HOTEL HOTEL **$**

(兰亭汇快捷酒店; Lántínghuì Kuàijié Jiùdiàn; ☎6261 9226, 6261 8596; www.lthhotel.com; 35-5 Chengfu Lu, 成府路 35-5号; d/tw ¥268-298, tr ¥398; [❄][@]; [S]Wudaokou) Newish, modern hotel, unlike many in the area, with bright rooms (the ones with windows anyway) and a prime location close to the metro and the bar, café and club zone of Wǔdàokǒu. It's just to the side of the Dongyuan Plaza.

Understand Běijīng

Běijīng Today

Beijingers are stoic people. But even the most reserved of the city's 19 million inhabitants have been left gasping, as well as proud, at the way Běijīng has reinvented itself in recent years. As China's incoming leader Xi Jinping prepared to take charge of an increasingly influential nation, Beijingers were bracing themselves for life in the capital of a true world superpower. Rampant corruption and growing inequality are major concerns, though, and maintaining harmony could be Xi's number one challenge ahead.

Best on Film

Beijing Bicycle (2001) Lavish yet realistic film following a young and hapless Běijīng courier on the trail of his stolen mountain bike.

Lost in Beijing (2007) Close-to-the-bone, modern-day tale of a ménage-a-quatre involving a young woman, her boss, her husband and her boss's wife. Banned in China.

Cell Phone (2003) Hilarious satire of the city's rising middle classes, by Běijīng director Feng Xiaogang.

The Last Emperor (1987) Bernardo Bertolucci's multi-Oscar-winning epic, charting the life of Puyi during his accession and the ensuing disintegration of dynastic China.

Best in Print

Rickshaw Boy (Lao She, translated by Shi Xiaoqing, 1981) A masterpiece by one of Běijīng's most beloved writers about a rickshaw-puller living in early 20th-century Běijīng.

Beijing Coma (Ma Jian, 2008) Novel revolving around the democracy protests of 1989 and the political coma that ensues.

Midnight in Peking (Paul French, 2012) Gripping account of the mystery surrounding the brutal murder in 1937 of Englishwoman Pamela Werner.

Keeping the Dissidents in Check

Epitomised by the infamous and tragic crackdown on protesters in Tiān'ānmén Square in 1989, the Chinese government is known for its hard stance on dissenting voices. The personal struggles of blind civil-rights activist Chen Guangcheng made waves across the international media in 2012 when the self-trained lawyer, who had been under virtual house arrest in his home village for nearly two years, escaped and took refuge in the US embassy in Běijīng. Chen wanted to flee China, but feared for his family's safety if he did. After weeks of high-level negotiations between Běijīng and US officials, he and his family were granted US visas so that Chen could further his law studies in New York.

His case followed the high-profile arrest of dissident artist and Běijīng resident Ai Weiwei. The man who helped design the iconic National Stadium (aka the Bird's Nest) for the 2008 Olympic Games had since ruffled the feathers with his criticism of the Chinese government. He was seized at Běijīng Airport in 2011 and placed under house arrest for almost three months. Police raided his art studios just outside 798 Art District, and when eventually he was released, he faced a ¥12 million tax fine.

Political dissidents are nothing new for Běijīng, but the speed with which ideas now spread among the population is. China now has the world's highest number of netizens, and microblogging websites such as Wēibó spread news and gossip like wildfire before China's army of censors are able to muffle the messages.

Maintaining Harmony

Muzzling dissent is only part of the picture. The new government must maintain its own credibility. Two of the things Beijingers complain about most when it comes to politics are corruption among politicians and the growing inequality between rich and poor, neither of which are easy to denounce when so many of China's leaders, including Xi, are so-called 'princelings' from wealthy, privileged backgrounds. Those people hoping that Xi's new tenure might bring about political reform, though, should probably prepare to be disappointed. Xi stands amongst the more conservative ranks of the government and if anything he is likely to support stronger government controls and less transparency than before, meaning Beijingers (along with the rest of the world) will continue to be left guessing at the government's next move.

Continued Economic Growth
Of course, all these issues can be forgiven so long as the economy doesn't falter. If living standards continue to rise, people here are much more likely to remain content. But the economic slowdown in recent years, and its backdrop of continued global financial struggles, will certainly force Xi and his team to sharpen its focus. That said, more economic growth exacerbates two of the city's fundamental problems: overpopulation and pollution.

Population Pressures
Most of the workers you see on building sites across the capital are out-of-towners from the provinces. It's estimated that more than seven million Běijīng residents are migrant workers: that's a massive 36% of the city's already huge population, which is soon set to pass the 20-million mark. And ever-expanding population figures place added pressure on the environment. In fact, some analysts predict that it's the environment that will be Xi's number one concern in the coming years.

The Great Pall of China
Air pollution was brought into focus in the summer of 2012 when the government called for the US embassy to stop publishing its daily Běijīng pollution readings on its highly popular Twitter feed. The figures were wildly out of sync with official air-pollution levels published by Běijīng's Environmental Protection Bureau.

Whatever the figures, there's little doubt that Běijīng's air quality has deteriorated since the pre-Olympics clean-up, and visitors will be shocked by the pall of pollution haze that sometimes hangs over the city. There is, however, cause for optimism: Běijīng recently added 3800 natural-gas buses to its fleet – more than almost any other city in the world – and the already excellent subway system continues to be expanded. Public transport in general also remains incredibly cheap, and in a nod to the capital's rich cycling tradition, a new bike-sharing scheme was about to be unveiled as this book went to press.

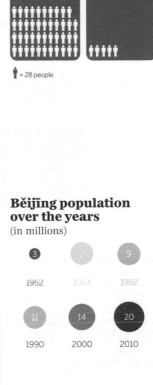

population per sq km
BEIJING · CHINA
= 28 people

Běijīng population over the years
(in millions)

3 1952 · 7 1964 · 9 1982 · 11 1990 · 14 2000 · 20 2010

if Beijing were 100 people

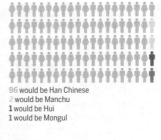

96 would be Han Chinese
2 would be Manchu
1 would be Hui
1 would be Mongul

History

Běijīng's long and colourful history goes back some 3000 years, but the city didn't become the centre of Chinese rule until 1272, when Kublai Khan made it the capital of the Mongol-led Yuan dynasty. From that time on, with the exception of two brief interludes (1368–1421 and 1928–49), Běijīng has served as the seat of power for all of China.

FROM THE BEGINNING

The Great Capital of the Mongols

The place we now call Běijīng first rose to true prominence when it was turned into a capital city by Kublai Khan (1215–94), the founder of the Mongol-ruled Yuan dynasty. The Mongols called the city Khanbalik, and it was from here that the descendants of Genghis Khan (Kublai Khan was his grandson) ruled over the largest land empire in world history. This is where Marco Polo, one of many thousands of foreigners drafted to help the Mongols govern China, came to serve as an official. Běijīng was really only the winter capital for Kublai Khan, who chose to spend the summer months at Běijīng's sister city, Xanadu, which lay to the north, 1800m up on the steppes. This was called the 'Upper Capital', or 'Shàngdū' in Chinese, while Běijīng was 'Dàdū' or 'Great Capital'.

The Mongols became the first 'barbarian' tribe to attempt to rule China. They ruled from Běijīng for just short of a century, from 1272 to 1368.

Běijīng seems a curious place to have been selected as capital of the Yuan empire, or indeed any empire. For one thing, it lacks a river or access to the sea. It is on the very outer edge of the great northern plain, and very far indeed from the rich rice granaries in the south and the source of China's lucrative exports of tea, silk and porcelain. Throughout history the Han Chinese considered this barbarian territory, home to a series of hostile predatory dynasties such as the Liao (907–1125) and the Jin (1115–1234), who also both made Běijīng their capital. To this day Chinese historians describe these peoples as primitive 'tribes' rather than nations, perhaps a prejudice from the ancient antipathy between nomadic pastoralist peoples and the sedentary farmers who are the Chinese.

TIMELINE	500,000 BC	pre–11th century BC	c 600 BC
	Peking man (*Sinanthropus pekinensis*), an example of *Homo erectus*, inhabits the region; fossils are excavated at Zhōukǒudiàn municipality from 1923 to 1927.	The first settlements in the Běijīng area are recorded (evidence suggests Paleolithic cultures living in the central areas of Běijīng).	Laotzu (Laozi), founder of Taoism, is supposedly born. Taoism goes on to coexist with later introductions such as Buddhism, a reflection of Chinese religion's syncretic nature.

Běijīng's First City Walls

Běijīng had first become a walled settlement back in AD 938 when the Khitans, one of the nomadic 'barbarian tribes', established it as an auxiliary southern capital of their Liao dynasty. When they were overthrown by Jurchens from Manchuria, the progenitors of the Manchus, it became Zhōngdū or 'Middle Capital'. Each of these three successive barbarian dynasties enlarged the walled city and built palaces and temples, especially Buddhist temples. They secured a supply of water by channelling streams from the otherwise dry limestone hills around Běijīng, and stored it in the lakes that still lie at the heart of the city.

The Lifeline of the Grand Canal

The Khitans relied on the Grand Canal to ship goods like silk, porcelain, tea and grain from the Yangzi River delta. Each successive dynasty shortened the Grand Canal. It was originally 2500km long when it was built in the 5th century by the Chinese Sui dynasty to facilitate the military conquest of northeast China and Korea. From the 10th century it was used for a different purpose: to enable these northern peoples to extract the wealth of central China. Běijīng's role was to be the terminus.

Remaining Traces

For 1000 years, half a million peasants spent six months a year hauling huge barges from Hángzhōu up the Grand Canal to Běijīng. You can still see the canal after it enters the city from Tōngzhōu, now a suburb of Běijīng, and then winds around the Second Ring Rd. The tax or tribute from central China was then stored in huge warehouses, a few of which remain. From Běijīng, the goods were carried out of the West Gate or Xīzhí Mén (where Xizhimen subway station is today), and taken up the Tánqín Gorge to Bādálǐng, which once marked the limits of the Chinese world. Beyond this pass, the caravans took the road to Zhāngjiākǒu, 6000ft above sea level where the grasslands of inner Asia begin.

End of 'Barbarian' Rule

The ultimate aim of the Khitans, Jurchens, Mongols and Manchus was to control the lucrative international trade in Chinese-made luxuries. Chinese dynasties like the Song faced the choice of paying them off or staging a bloody resistance. The Southern Song did attack and destroy Běijīng, but when it failed to defeat the Liao dynasty of the Khitans it

The Mongols referred to Zhāngjiākǒu as Kalgan, 'the Gate'. This trading route, leading to inner Asia's grasslands, was also the favourite route chosen by invaders, such as Genghis Khan.

HISTORY FROM THE BEGINNING

551 BC	5th–3rd century BC	214 BC	AD 938
The birth of Confucius. His ideas of an ethical, ordered society operating through hierarchy and self-development dominated Chinese culture until the early 20th century.	Yānjīng, capital of Yan state, is located near Běijīng. Yānjīng (which means 'Capital of Yan') was also known as Ji and moved to Xiàdū in today's Yìxiàn (in Héběi province) during the Warring States period.	Emperor Qin indentures thousands of labourers to link existing city walls into one Great Wall, made of tamped earth. The later stone-clad bastion dates from the Ming dynasty.	Běijīng is established as auxiliary capital of the Liao dynasty. Běijīng's oldest street – Sanmiao Jie, or Three Temples St – dates to this time, when it was known as Tanzhou Jie.

resorted to a strategy of 'using the barbarian to defeat the barbarian'. It made a pact with the Jurchens, and together they captured Běijīng in 1125. But instead of just helping to defeat the Khitans, the Jurchens carried on south and took the Song capital at Kāifēng. The Jurchens, however, chose not to try to govern China by themselves and instead opted to milk the Southern Song dynasty.

MING-DYNASTY BĚIJĪNG
A True Chinese City

During the time of the Khitans, Běijīng was sometimes called Yānjīng, or the 'City of Swallows'. This is still the name of a beer produced by a local brewery.

Běijīng can properly be said to have been a Chinese city only during the Ming dynasty (1368–1644), when the Emperor Yongle (whose name means perpetual happiness) used over 200,000 prisoners of war to rebuild the city, construct its massive battlements, rebuild the imperial palace and establish the magnificent Ming Tombs. He forced tens of thousands of leading Chinese families to relocate from Nánjīng, the capital founded by his father, and unwillingly settle in what they considered an alien land at the extremity of the Chinese world. Throughout the Ming dynasty, Běijīng was constantly under attack by the Mongols, and on many occasions their horsemen reached the very gates of the city. Mongol bandits roamed the countryside or hid out in the marshes south of the city, threatening communications with the empire.

Beefing Up the Great Wall

Everything needed for the gigantic enterprise of rebuilding the city – even tiles, bricks and timber – had to be shipped up the Grand Canal, but in time Běijīng grew into a city of nearly a million residents. Although farms and greenhouses sprang up around the city, it always depended on the Grand Canal as a lifeline. Most of the canal was required to ship the huge amounts of food needed to supply the garrison of more than a million men that Yongle press-ganged into building and manning the new Great Wall. The emperor was fearful of a resurgent Mongol threat. The Mongols had been pushed out of China as the Ming came to power in 1368, but they were still formidable, and by the dawn of the 15th century, they were itching to reconquer the rich lands to the south of the Great Wall. This Wall, unlike earlier walls, was clad in brick and stone, not pounded earth, and the Ming emperors kept enlarging it for the next 250 years, adding loops, spurs and watchtowers. For long stretches, the fortifications ran in two parallel bands.

1153	1215	1264	1272
Běijīng becomes capital of the Jin dynasty where it becomes known as Zhōngdū or 'Middle Capital'; the city walls are expanded and paper currency enters circulation.	The Mongols, under Genghis Khan, break through the Great Wall at several points and sack Zhōngdū, razing it to the ground and slaughtering its inhabitants.	The first Yuan emperor, Kublai Khan, sets about rebuilding the city his grandfather destroyed.	Kublai Khan renames the city Dàdū, or 'Great Capital', and officially unveils it as the capital of the Yuan dynasty. Běijīng is, for the first time, the capital of China.

The Forbidden City

Běijīng grew from a forward defence military headquarters into an administrative centre staffed by an elite corps of mandarins. They had to pass gruelling examinations that tested candidates' understanding of classical and Confucian literature. Then they were either assigned to the provinces or selected to work in the central government ministries, situated in what is now Tiān'ānmén Square, south of the Meridian Gate and the entrance to the Forbidden City. Each day the mandarins and the generals entered the 'Great Within' and kowtowed before the emperor, who lived inside, like a male version of a queen bee, served by thousands of women and eunuchs. Ming emperors were the only males permitted to live in the palace. Yongle established rigid rules and dreary rituals, and many of his successors rebelled against the constrictions.

Power of the Eunuchs

Under later Ming emperors, the eunuchs came to be more trusted and more powerful than the mandarins. There were 100,000 by the end of the Ming dynasty, more than in any other civilisation in history. A few became so powerful they virtually ruled the empire, but many died poor and destitute. Some used their wealth to build grandiose residences and tombs, or to patronise temples and monasteries located in the hills outside the walls.

A Centre for Arts & Science

Over time Běijīng became the most important religious centre in Asia, graced by more than 2000 temples and shrines. Daoists and Buddhists vied for the favour of the emperor who, as a divine being, was automatically the patron of every approved religious institution in the empire. As the residence of the emperor, Běijīng was regarded by the Chinese as the centre of the universe. The best poets and painters also flocked to Běijīng to seek court patronage. The Forbidden City required the finest porcelain, furniture and silverware, and its workshops grew in skill and design. Literature, drama, music, medicine, map-making, astrology and astronomy flourished, too, so the imperial city became a centre for arts and sciences.

Although early visitors complained about the dust and the beggars, most were awed and inspired by the city's size, magnificence and wealth. Ming culture was influential in Japan, Korea, Vietnam and with other neighbouring countries. By the close of the 15th century the Ming capital, which had started out as a remote and isolated military outpost, had become a wealthy and sophisticated Chinese city.

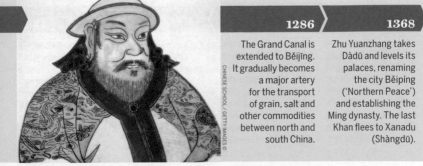

1286

The Grand Canal is extended to Běijīng. It gradually becomes a major artery for the transport of grain, salt and other commodities between north and south China.

1368

Zhu Yuanzhang takes Dàdū and levels its palaces, renaming the city Běipíng ('Northern Peace') and establishing the Ming dynasty. The last Khan flees to Xanadu (Shàngdū).

CHINESE SCHOOL / GETTY IMAGES ©

Kublai Khan

The Fall of the Ming

Despite the Great Wall, the threat from the north intensified. The Manchus (formerly the Jurchens) established a new and powerful state based in Shěnyáng (currently the capital of Liáoníng province) and watched as the Ming empire decayed. The Ming had one of the most elaborate tax codes in history, but corrupt eunuchs abused their growing power. Excessive taxation sparked a series of peasant revolts. Silver, the main form of exchange, was devalued by imported silver from the new world, leading to inflation.

One peasant rebel army, led by Li Zicheng (1606–45), actually captured Běijīng. The last Ming emperor, Chongzhen (1611–44), called on the Manchus for help and after crossing the Great Wall at Shānhǎiguān, in current-day Héběi province, they helped rout Li Zicheng's army. The Manchus then marched on Běijīng, where Emperor Chongzhen hung himself on a tree on Coal Hill, the hill in Jǐngshān Park, which overlooks the Forbidden City. Chongzhen lies buried in a Ming tomb a short distance from the grander Ming Tombs complex, and now there's a small artificial snowfield near his tomb.

The Han Chinese were forced to wear their hair in a queue (pigtail) as a symbol of their subjugation to the ruling Manchus.

QING-DYNASTY BĚIJĪNG

The Manchus Move In

The Manchus established the Qing dynasty in 1644, although it took several decades before they completed the conquest of the Ming empire. As a foreign dynasty, they took great pains to present themselves as legitimate successors to the Chinese Ming dynasty. For this reason they kept Běijīng as their capital and changed very little, effectively preserving Yongle's city. The Manchu imperial family, the Aisin Gioro Clan, moved in to the Forbidden City, and imperial princes took large courtyard palaces.

Summer Palaces

Soon the Aisin Gioro family began to feel that living inside the confines of the Forbidden City was claustrophobic. The great Emperor Kangxi (1654–1722) effectively moved the court to what is now called the Old Summer Palace, a vast parkland of lakes, canals and palaces linked to the city by the Jade Canal. The Manchus, like the Mongols, enjoyed hunting, riding, hawking, skating and archery. In summer, when Běijīng became hot and steamy, the court moved to Chéngdé (formerly Jehol or Rehol, and now in modern-day Héběi province), a week's ride to

1368–1644	1403–21	1420	1465
The great city walls are reshaped and the Great Wall is rebuilt and clad with bricks, while the basic layout of modern Běijīng is established. Běijīng becomes the world's largest city.	Emperor Yongle moves the capital south to Nánjīng ('Southern Capital'), where the imperial palace is built. Běijīng is reinstated as capital in 1421 when the Forbidden City is completed (1406–20).	The Temple of Heaven is built at the same time as the Forbidden City. The Gate of Heavenly Peace is completed and is called Chengtianmen, only to be burned down after a lightning strike in 1457.	The Gate of Heavenly Peace is rebuilt but is again torched by peasant rebels in 1644 prior to the arrival of Manchu soldiers. The reconstruction of the gate is completed in 1651.

the north. At Chéngdé the court spent three months living in felt tents (or yurts) in a walled parkland.

Bannermen

The Manchu army was divided into regiments called banners, so the troops were called Bannermen (Qírén). Each banner had a separate colour by which it was known and its troops settled in a particular residential area in Běijīng. The Embroidered Yellow Bannermen, for example, lived near the Confucius Temple, and some of their descendants remain there today. Only a minority were actually ethnic Manchus – the rest were Mongols or Han Chinese.

Policing a Divided City

Běijīng at this stage was a Manchu city and foreigners called it the 'Tartar City' ('Tartars' being the label given to any nomadic race from inner Asia). The Han Chinese lived in the 'Chinese city' to the south of Tiān'ānmén Square. This was the liveliest, most densely populated area, packed with markets, shops, theatres, brothels and hostels for provincial visitors. If Chinese people wanted to get to north Běijīng, they had to go all the way round the outside walls. The Bannermen posted at the gates prevented anyone from entering without permission. Up to 1900, the state provided all Bannermen families with clothing and free food that was shipped up the Grand Canal and stored in grain warehouses.

Fashioning Běijīng Culture

It was the Manchu Bannermen who really created a Běijīng culture. They loved Peking opera, and the city once had over 40 opera houses and many training schools. The sleeveless *qípáo* dress is really a Manchu dress. The Bannermen, who loved animals, raised songbirds and pigeons and bred exotic-looking goldfish and miniature dogs such as the Pekinese. And after the downfall of the Qing empire, they kept up traditional arts such as painting and calligraphy.

Language, Politics & Religion

Through the centuries of Qing rule, the Manchus tried to keep themselves culturally separate from the Chinese, speaking a different language, wearing different clothes and following different customs. For instance, Manchu women did not bind their feet, wore raised platform patens (shoes), and coiled their hair in distinctive and elaborate styles. All court documents were composed in the Manchu script; Manchu, Chinese and Mongolian script were used to write name signs in such places as the Forbidden City.

1644	1793	1850–68	1898
Manchu troops pour through the pass at Shānhǎiguān to impose the Qing dynasty on China. Běijīng is known in Manchu as Gemun Hecen.	British diplomat Lord Macartney visits Běijīng with British industrial products, but is told by the Qianlong emperor that China has no need of his goods.	The Taiping Rebellion blazes north and east across China, killing an estimated 20 million people. Rebels fail to reach Běijīng, but establish their 'Heavenly Capital' in Nánjīng.	Emperor Guangxu permits major reforms, including new rights for women, but is thwarted by the Dowager Empress Cixi, who has many reformers arrested and executed.

At the same time, the Qing copied the Ming's religious and bureaucratic institutions. The eight key ministries (Board of Works, Board of Revenue, Board of State Ceremonies, Board of War, Board of Rites, Board of Astronomy, Board of Medicines and Prefecture of Imperial Clan Affairs) continued to operate from the same buildings in what is now Tiān'ānmén Square. The Qing dynasty worshipped their ancestors at rites held in a temple, which is now in the Workers Cultural Palace, south of the Forbidden City. They also built a second ancestral temple devoted to the spirits of every Chinese emperor that ever ruled. For some time it was a girls' school, but it has since been turned back into a museum.

Eunuchs tended to be Buddhists (while mandarins honoured Confucius), as it gave them hope that they would return as whole men in a future reincarnation.

Buddhist Ties

The study of Confucius was encouraged in order to strengthen the loyalty of the mandarins employed by the state bureaucracy. The Manchus carried out the customary rituals at the great state temples. By inclination, however, many of the Manchu emperors were either Shamanists or followers of Tibetan Buddhism. The Shamanist shrines have disappeared, but Běijīng is full of temples and stupas connected with Tibetan Buddhism. The Emperor Qianlong considered himself the incarnation of the Bodhisattva Manjusri and cultivated strong links with various Dalai Lamas and Panchen Lamas. Many visited – a round trip usually lasted three years – and special palaces were built for them. The Manchus deliberately fostered the spread of Tibetan Buddhism among the warlike Mongols in the hope of pacifying them. Běijīng therefore developed into a holy city attracting pilgrims of all kinds.

The Dalai Lama's former Běijīng palace is now rented out by the government of the Tibet Autonomous Region.

The Jesuits

The arrival of the first Jesuits and other Christians made Běijīng an important centre of Christianity in China. Emperor Qianlong employed many Jesuits who built for him the baroque palaces that can still be seen in the ruins of the Old Summer Palace, which was burnt down by a combined force of British and French troops in 1860 during the Second Opium War.

FOREIGN POWERS & THE FALL OF THE QING

Foreign Legation Quarter

After the military defeats of the Opium Wars (1839–42 and 1856–60), the Western nations forced the Qing emperors to allow them to open formal embassies or legations in the capital. Hitherto, the emperor had

1900	1905	1908	1911
Boxer rebels commence the siege of the Foreign Legation Quarter. The Hànlín Academy is accidentally burned down by rebels trying to flush out foreigners in the British Legation.	Major reforms in the late Qing, including the abolition of the 1000-year-long tradition of examinations in the Confucian classics to enter the Chinese bureaucracy.	Two-year-old Puyi ascends the throne as China's last emperor. Local elites and new classes such as businessmen no longer support the dynasty, leading to its ultimate downfall.	The Qing dynasty collapses and the modernisation of China begins in earnest; Sun Yatsen (fundraising in America at the time) is declared president of the Republic of China.

had no equal in the world – foreign powers could only send embassies to deliver tribute, and they were housed in tributary hostels.

Boxer Rebellion

The British legation was the first to open after 1860. It lay on the east side of Tiān'ānmén Square and stayed there until the 1950s when its grounds were taken over by the Ministry of State Security. By 1900, there were a dozen legations in an odd foreign ghetto with an eclectic mixture of European architecture. The Foreign Legation Quarter never became a foreign concession like those in Shànghǎi or Tiānjīn, but it had banks, schools, shops, post offices, hospitals and military parade grounds. Much of it was reduced to rubble when the army of Boxers (a quasi-religious cult) besieged it in the summer of 1900. It was later rebuilt.

The last of the Foreign Legation Quarter's embassies left in 1967. Now most embassies are located east of the centre, in Cháoyáng District.

Empress Dowager Cixi

The Empress Dowager Cixi (1835–1908), a daughter of a Bordered Blue Bannermen, was a young concubine when the Old Summer Palace was burned down by foreign troops in 1860. Cixi allowed the palace to fall into decay, associating it with a humiliation, and instead built herself the new Summer Palace (Yíhé Yuán). She was left with a profound hatred and distrust of the Western barbarians and their ways.

Over the four decades in which Cixi ruled China 'from behind the curtain' through a series of proxy emperors, she resisted pressure to change and reform. After a naval defeat at the hands of the Japanese in 1895, young Chinese officials put forward a modernisation program. She had some of them executed outside Běijīng's walls, and imprisoned their patron and her nephew, Emperor Guangxu (1871–1908). She encouraged the Boxers to attack Westerners, especially foreign missionaries in northern China, and when Boxers besieged the Foreign Legation Quarter in 1900, Cixi stood by. When the allied forces marched into Běijīng to end the siege, she fled in disguise, an ignominious retreat that marked the final humiliation that doomed the Qing dynasty. When Cixi returned in disgrace a year later, China's modernisation had begun in earnest, but it was too late to save the Qing dynasty – it fell in 1911.

China's first (and only) parliament was established in Běijīng in what was once the imperial elephant house, now out of sight in the sprawling headquarters of Xīnhuá, the state news agency.

REPUBLICAN CHINA

After 1900, the last tribute barges arrived in Běijīng and a railway line ran along the traditional invasion route through the Jūyōng Pass to Bādálǐng. You can see the handsome clock tower and sheds of Běijīng's first railway station (Qiánmén Railway Station), recently restored as the Běijīng Railway Museum, on the southeast corner of Tiān'ānmén

1912 Yuan Shikai, leader of China's most powerful regional army, goes to the Qing court to announce that the game is up: on 12 February the last emperor, six-year-old Puyi, abdicates.

1916 Yuan Shikai dies less than a year after attempting to establish himself emperor. Yuan's monarchical claims prompted widespread resistance from Republicans.

Yuan Shikai

Square. Běijīng never became an industrial or commercial centre – that role went to nearby Tiānjīn on the coast. Yet it remained the leading political and intellectual centre of China until the late 1920s.

Hotbed of Student Activity

In the settlement imposed after 1900, China had to pay the victors heavy indemnities. Some of this money was returned to China and used to build the first modern universities, including what are now the Oxford and Cambridge of China – Qīnghuá and Peking Universities. Běijīng's university quarter was established in the Hǎidiàn district, near the Old Summer Palace (some campuses are actually in the imperial parkland). Intellectuals from all over China continued to gravitate to Běijīng, including the young Mao Zedong, who arrived to work as a librarian in 1921.

1919 May Fourth Movement

Běijīng students and professors were at the forefront of the 1919 May Fourth Movement. This was at once a student protest against the Versailles Treaty, which had awarded Germany's concessions in China to Japan, and an intellectual movement to jettison the Confucian feudal heritage and Westernise China. Mao himself declared that to modernise China it was first necessary to destroy it. China's intellectuals looked around the world for models to copy. Some went to Japan, others to the USA, Britain, Germany or, like Deng Xiaoping and Zhou Enlai, France. Many went to study Marxism in Moscow.

Modernising the City

As the warlords marched armies in and out of Běijīng, the almost medieval city began to change. Temples were closed down and turned into schools. The last emperor, Puyi, left the Forbidden City in 1924 with his eunuchs and concubines. As the Manchus adapted to the changes, they tried to assimilate and their presence faded. Western-style brick houses, shops and restaurants were built. City gates were widened and new ones added, including one at Jiànguóménwài to make way for the motorcar. Běijīng acquired nightclubs, cinemas, racecourses and a stock exchange; brothels and theatres flourished. Despite political and diplomatic crises, this was a period when people had fun and enjoyed a unique period of individual freedom.

Generalissimo Chiang Kaishek united most of the country under Chinese National Party (KMT, or Kuomintang in Chinese) rule and moved the capital to Nánjīng. Even after 1928, Běijīng's romantic air of decaying grandeur attracted Chinese and Western writers and painters trying to fuse Western and Chinese artistic traditions.

Some of 20th-century China's best literature was written in Běijīng in the 1920s and 1930s by the likes of Lao She, Lin Huiyin, Xu Zhimou, Shen Congwen and Qian Zhongshu.

1919	1927	1928	1937
Students demonstrate in Běijīng against foreign occupation of territories in China and the terms that conclude WWI. The date of the protests leads to the name of the movement.	The first shots of the Chinese Civil War are fired between the Kuomintang (KMT) and the communists. The war continues on and off until 1949.	The nationalists move the capital to Nánjīng, and Běijīng is again renamed Běipíng. This is the first time the capital of the entire nation has been in Nánjīng for almost 500 years.	The Marco Polo Bridge Incident signals the beginning of the Japanese occupation of Běijīng and the start of the Second Sino-Japanese War, which lasts until September 1945.

Japanese Occupation

It all came to end when Japan's Kwantung Army moved down from Manchuria and occupied Běijīng in 1937. By then most people who could had fled, some to Chóngqìng in Sìchuān province, which served as Chiang Kaishek's wartime capital. Others joined Mao Zedong in his communist base at Yán'ān, in Shaanxi province. Many universities established campuses in exile in Yúnnán province.

The Japanese stayed in Běijīng for eight years and, before their WWII defeat in 1945, had drawn up plans to build a new administrative capital in an area to the west of the city walls near Gōngzhǔfén. It was a miserable time for Běijīng, but the architecture was left largely untouched by the war. When the Japanese surrendered in August 1945, Běijīng was 'liberated' by US marines. The city once again became a merry place famous for its parties – the serious events took place elsewhere in China. When the civil war broke out in earnest between nationalists and communists in 1947, the worst fighting took place in the cities of Manchuria.

During the Japanese invasion, the collection of imperial treasures was secretly removed, eventually ending up in Taiwan where they can still be seen in Taipei's National Palace Museum.

HISTORY REPUBLICAN CHINA

Communist Takeover

In 1948, the Communist Eighth Route Army moved south and encircled Běijīng. General Fu Zuoyi, commander-in-chief of the nationalists' Northern China Bandit Suppression Headquarters, prepared the city for a prolonged siege. He razed private houses and built gun emplacements and dugouts along the Ming battlements. Nationalist planes dropped bags of rice and flour to relieve the shortages, some hitting skaters on frozen Běihǎi Lake. Both sides seemed reluctant to fight it out and destroy the ancient capital. The rich tried to flee on the few planes that took off from a runway constructed at Dongdan on Chang'an Dajie (Chang'an means 'Avenue of Eternal Peace'). Another airstrip was opened at Temple of Heaven Park by cutting down 20,000 trees, including 400 ancient cypresses.

On 22 January 1949 General Fu signed a surrender agreement, and on 31 January his KMT troops marched out and the People's Liberation Army (PLA) entered. A truck drove up Morrison St (now Wangfujing Dajie) blasting a continuous refrain to the residents of Běijīng (or Pěipíng as it was known then): 'Welcome to the Liberation Army on its arrival in Pěipíng! Congratulations to the people of Pěipíng on their liberation!' Behind it marched 300 soldiers in battle gear. A grand victory parade took place on 3 February with 250 assorted military vehicles, virtually all US-made and captured from the KMT over the previous two years.

1946	1949	1950s & 1960s	1956–57
Communists and the Kuomintang fail to form a coalition government, plunging China back into civil war. Communist organisation, morale and ideology all prove key to the communist victory.	With the communist victory over the KMT, Mao Zedong announces the founding of the People's Republic of China from the Gate of Heavenly Peace.	Most of Běijīng's city walls, gates and decorative arches are levelled to make way for roads. Work commences on Běijīng's labyrinthine network of underground tunnels.	The Hundred Flowers Movement promises an era of intellectual freedom, but instead leads to a purge of intellectuals, artists and thinkers who are labelled rightists and persecuted.

MAO'S BĚIJĪNG
The People Stand Up

In the spring of 1949 Mao Zedong and the communist leadership were camped in the western suburbs around Bādàchù, an area that is still the headquarters of the PLA. On 1 October 1949, Mao mounted the Gate of Heavenly Peace and declared the founding of the People's Republic of China, saying the Chinese people had stood up. He spoke only a few words in one of the very few public speeches he ever made.

Mao then moved into Zhōngnánhǎi, part of the chain of lakes and gardens immediately west of the Forbidden City and dating back to Kublai Khan. Marshal Yuan Shikai (1859–1916) had lived there too during his short-lived attempt to establish his own dynasty after 1911. Nobody is quite sure why he chose Běijīng as his capital, or why he failed to carry out his intention to raze the Forbidden City.

After 1949 many of new China's top leaders followed Mao's cue and moved their homes and offices into the old princely palaces *(wángfǔ),* thus inadvertently preserving much of the old architecture.

Mao worked as a library assistant at the former Peking University campus known as Hóng Lóu (the Red Building), now a small museum.

Industrialising

Mao wished to turn Běijīng from a 'city of consumption into a city of production'. 'Chairman Mao wants a big modern city: he expects the sky there to be filled with smokestacks,' said Peng Zhen, the first Party Secretary of Běijīng, to China's premier architectural historian, Liang Sicheng, as they stood on the Gate of Heavenly Peace looking south.

Factories Galore

Thousands of factories sprang up in Běijīng and quite a few were built in old temples. In time Běijīng developed into a centre for steel, chemicals, machine tools, engines, electricity, vinegar, beer, concrete, textiles, weapons – in fact, everything that would make it an economically self-sufficient 'production base' in case of war. By the 1970s Běijīng had become one of the most heavily polluted cities in the world.

'Communism is not love. Communism is a hammer which we use to crush the enemy.' Mao Zedong

The Great Leap Forward

The move to tear down the city's walls, widen the roads and demolish the distinctive *páilóu* (ceremonial arches) started immediately after 1949, but was fiercely contested by some intellectuals, including Liang Sicheng, who ran the architecture department of Qīnghuá University. So in the midst of the demolition of many famous landmarks, the municipal authorities earmarked numerous buildings and even old trees

1958	1966	1972	1976
The Great Leap Forward commences but plans to rapidly industrialise China result in a disastrous famine that kills millions of Chinese.	The Great Proletarian Cultural Revolution is launched by Mao Zedong in Běijīng; millions of Red Guards pack Tiān'ānmén Sq. From August to September, 1772 Beijingers are killed.	US President Richard Nixon meets with Mao Zedong in Běijīng, marking a major rapprochement during the Cold War, and the start of full diplomatic relations between the two countries.	The death of Premier Zhou Enlai sparks protests in Tiān'ānmén Sq, an event that becomes known as the Tiān'ānmén Incident. Mao Zedong dies in September.

for conservation. However, it was all to no avail – Mao's brutal political purges silenced all opposition.

The Cultural Revolution

Those intellectuals who escaped persecution in the 1950s were savagely dealt with during the Cultural Revolution (1966–76). Qīnghuá University became the birthplace of the Red Guards (a mass movement of young radicals, mobilised by Mao). In the 'bloody August' of 1966, Běijīng's middle-school students turned on their teachers, brutally murdering some of them. Some reports estimate almost 2000 people were killed in Běijīng at this time. The number excludes those beaten to death as they tried to escape Běijīng on trains – their registration as residents of Běijīng suddenly cancelled. The headquarters of the Cultural Revolution in Běijīng was in the Jiànguóménwài embassy area. It has since been demolished, and the site is now occupied by the Si-tech Department Store.

Going Underground

By 1969 Mao had fallen out with Moscow and he prepared China for a nuclear war. The city's population was turned out to build tunnels and nuclear fallout shelters. Bricks from the city walls and even the Old Summer Palace were used to build these. You can still visit the tunnels and shelters built during those years in a few places, such as Dìtán Park, where the tunnels are used as an ice rink, and at Yuètán Park, where the tunnels have been converted into a shopping arcade.

End of the Mao Era

In Mao's time the geomantic symmetry of Běijīng was radically changed. The north–south axis of the Ming city was ruined by widening Chang'an Dajie into a 10-lane, east–west highway. This was used for huge annual military parades or when visiting dignitaries arrived and the population was turned out to cheer them. In the 1950s, the centre was redesigned by Soviet architects and modelled on Moscow's Red Square. Three major gates and many other Ming buildings, including the former government ministries, were demolished, leaving the concrete expanse of Tiān'ānmén Square you see today.

Mao used the square to receive the adulation of the millions of Red Guards who flocked to Běijīng from 1966 to 1969, but after 1969 Mao exiled the Red Guards, along with 20 million 'educated youth', to the countryside. From 1976 the square became the scene of massive anti-government protests – when Premier Zhou Enlai died in 1976 the large

In the 1958 Great Leap Forward, the last qualms about preserving old Běijīng were abandoned. A new plan was approved to destroy 80% of the old capital. The walls were pulled down, but the series of ring roads planned at the time were never built.

In August and September of 1966, a total of 1772 people were killed in the capital, according to a report published by the *Beijing Daily* after 1979.

1977–79	1980
The 'Běijīng Spring' sees the first shoots of political freedom and the appearance of the short-lived 'Democracy Wall' in Xīdān. Deng Xiaoping's reformist agenda starts in 1979.	The one-child policy is enforced as a means of reducing the population; at the same time it imposes unprecedented control over the personal liberty of women.

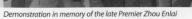

GEORGES BIANNIC / AFP / GETTY IMAGES ©

Demonstration in memory of the late Premier Zhou Enlai

and apparently spontaneous protest in the square was quelled by the police. In 1976, Mao himself died.

REFORM & PROTEST

Calls for Democracy

Deng Xiaoping (1904–97), backed by a group of veteran generals, seized power in a coup d'état and threw Mao's widow, Jiang Qing (1914–91) and her ultra-leftist cronies into the notorious Qínchéng prison outside the city, where Mao had incarcerated so many senior party veterans. This still exists not far from the Ming Tombs.

The 'Democracy Wall' in Xīdān has disappeared and been replaced by a shopping mall.

The Democracy Wall

At the third plenum of the 11th Party Congress, Deng consolidated his grip on power and launched economic reforms. At the same time thousands of people began putting up posters along a wall west of Zhōngnánhǎi, complaining of injustices under the 'Gang of Four' (Jiang Qing and her three associates) and demanding democracy. Deng initially appeared to back political reforms, but soon the activists were thrown into jail, some in the Běijīng No 1 Municipal Prison (demolished in the mid-1990s).

Rising Discontent

Contrary to popular belief, the violence that shook the city – and the watching world – during 4 June didn't take place in Tiān'ānmén Sq itself, but in the surrounding streets.

Many of the activists were former Red Guards or exiled educated youth. After 1976 they drifted back to the city, but could only find jobs in the new private sector running small market stalls, tailor shops or restaurants. After the universities opened, conditions remained poor and the intelligentsia continued to be treated with suspicion. Frustrations with the slow pace of reforms prompted fresh student protests in the winter of 1986. Peasants did well out of the first wave of reforms, but in the cities many people felt frustrated. Urban life revolved around 'work units' to which nearly everyone was assigned. The work unit distributed food, housing, bicycles, travel permits and almost everything else. Běijīng was still a rather drab, dispiriting place in the 1980s; there was much more to eat but everything else was in a lamentable state. For 30 years, there had been little investment in housing or transport.

1989 Tiān'ānmén Square Protests

In January 1987 the party's conservative gerontocrats ousted the pro-reform party chief Hu Yaobang and, when he suddenly died in the spring of 1989, Běijīng students began assembling on Tiān'ānmén Square. Of-

1987	1989	1997	2001
The Last Emperor, filmed in the Forbidden City, collects an Oscar for Best Picture, and marks a new openness in China towards the outside world.	Democracy protestors fill Tiān'ānmén Sq. Běijīng imposes martial law and on the evening of 3 June and the early hours of 4 June soldiers clear the streets, killing hundreds (perhaps thousands).	Deng Xiaoping dies before having the chance to see Hong Kong returned to Chinese rule that same year. The reconstruction of Běijīng is launched.	Work starts on the National Grand Theatre west of the Great Hall of the People, Běijīng's futuristic answer to the Shànghǎi Grand Theatre.

ficially they were mourning his passing but they began to raise slogans for political reform and against corruption. The protests snowballed as the Communist Party leadership split into rival factions, causing a rare paralysis. The police stood by as the protests spread across the country and workers, officials and ordinary citizens took to the streets. When the military tried to intervene, Beijingers surrounded the tanks.

A BEASTLY AFFAIR

In February 2009 there was an uproar in China about the sale of two bronze animal heads by the auction house Christie's. The sale was the latest twist in a saga stretching back to 1860, when the Old Summer Palace was torched by Anglo-French troops and the animal heads were presumably pilfered.

The 12 heads belonged to a dozen statues with human bodies and animal heads (representing the 12 animals of the Chinese zodiac) that jetted water from their mouths for two hours in a 12-hour sequence and formed part of a structure called the Hǎiyàntáng.

Four of the original 12 animal heads have been repatriated (by being bought at auction or donated) and can be seen at the Poly Art Museum. Of the eight still abroad, the rat and rabbit heads that appeared at Christie's became the focus of a powerful Chinese sense of injustice.

A convincing moral argument exists that the animal heads should be returned to China. However, some people have pointed to the lack of conclusive evidence that the animal heads were stolen by French or British troops; the possibility exists, they argue, that the heads were plundered by Chinese eager to get back at Manchu rule or to sell to international clients.

Although it is probable French or British troops carried off the booty, the evidence is largely circumstantial. The torching of the Old Summer Palace was a shocking act of vandalism (revenge for killing a correspondent from the London *Times*) and most of the wooden Chinese-style buildings were burned to the ground. But the Old Summer Palace's famous Jesuit-designed Western-style palaces were built of stone and far harder to destroy. It is these that can still be seen today in the jumble of ruins in the northeast corner of the palace park. Records indicate that a considerable number of these buildings survived the torching, but progressive theft by locals over the subsequent decades gradually reduced what remained.

The heads themselves are perhaps a peculiar choice of national ire for the Chinese, considering they are Western in fashion, and styled by the Jesuits. It has even been suggested that the Empress Dowager disliked the heads so much that she had them pulled down; if so, where were they stored?

What is evident is that the ruins, and the animal heads, have become symbols of China's humiliation at the hands of foreign powers, and icons that increasingly resonate as the country assumes a more central role in international affairs.

2002	2007	2008	2008
Hu Jintao becomes China's new political leader when he is appointed general secretary of the Communist Party. He governs China for the next 10 years.	After coping for nearly 40 years with two subway lines, Běijīng opens a third as part of a massive development project that expands the system to 15 lines in the next five years.	The Běijīng to Tiānjīn 'bullet train' opens for operation, reaching a top speed of 330km/h during its 29-minute journey, and setting the record for the fastest conventional train service in the world.	Běijīng hosts the Olympic Games with a dramatic opening ceremony; China tops the gold medals table; restrictions on international media are temporarily lifted.

The students set up tents on Tiān'ānmén Square and went on a hunger strike. When the premier Li Peng held a dialogue with the students that was aired live on TV, student leaders sarcastically upbraided him.

The students created the first independent student union since 1919 and celebrated the anniversary of the May Fourth Movement with a demonstration in which over a million people took to the streets. For the first time since 1949, the press threw off the shackles of state censorship and became independent. When Soviet leader Mikhail Gorbachev entered on a state visit, and was enthusiastically welcomed as a symbol of political reform, it seemed as if the Chinese Communist Party (CCP), too, would embrace political change. Party General Secretary Zhao Ziyang led the reformist faction, but the older-generation leaders, led by Deng Xiaoping, decided to arrest Zhao and retake the city with a military assault. On the night of 3 June, tens of thousands of troops backed by tanks and armoured personnel carriers entered the city from four directions, bulldozing aside the hastily erected barricades.

Many people died – some say hundreds, some thousands – and by the early hours of 4 June the troops were in control of the square. In the crackdown that followed across the country, student leaders escaped abroad while the Communist Party arrested thousands of students and their supporters, and conducted a purge of party members. Yet the 1989 protests remain the largest political demonstrations in Chinese history.

RAPID DEVELOPMENT
Economic Reform

Things began to change when Deng Xiaoping emerged from the shadows and set off in 1991 on a so-called 'southern tour', visiting his special economic zones in the south and calling for more and faster reform. Despite opposition in the party, he won the day. China began a wave of economic reforms, which transformed urban China and brought new wealth and opportunities to most urban residents, though the political system remained unchanged and some 40 million workers in state-owned factories lost their jobs. Deng's reforms pulled in a tide of foreign investment, creating two economic booms, after 1992 and 1998. Stock markets reopened, state companies were privatised and private enterprise began to flourish, especially in the service sector, which created millions of new jobs. Over 100 million peasants left the countryside to work on construction sites or in export-processing factories. The factories were moved out of Běijīng and the city once again became a 'centre of consumption'.

History Books

The City of Heavenly Tranquility: Beijing in the History of China (Jasper Becker)

The Penguin History of Modern China: The Fall and Rise of a Great Power 1850–2008 (Jonathan Fenby)

The Siege at Peking (Peter Fleming)

The Dragon Empress (Marina Warner)

2010

In a rare victory for heritage campaigners, Běijīng shelves its plans to redevelop the historic area surrounding the city's Drum and Bell Towers.

2011

Běijīng artist and political activist Ai Weiwei is placed under house arrest for almost three months. Authorities serve him with a ¥12 million tax fine.

EZRA SHAW / GETTY IMAGES ©

The National Stadium (Bird's Nest; p140)

The Heritage Protection Battle

The economy was given a huge impetus by decisions to rebuild all major cities virtually from scratch, privatise housing and sell 50- or 70-year land leases to developers. There was resistance by Party Secretary Chen Xitong to the destruction of Běijīng's centre. During the 1980s and early 1990s, Chen approved redevelopment plans that aimed to preserve and restore Běijīng's historic centre and characteristic architecture. Chen had earlier helped persuade many army and civilian work units to vacate historical sites they'd occupied during the 1970s. However, in 1995, he was ousted by Jiang Zemin, and imprisoned on corruption charges.

Rebuild & Relocate

Once the Party apparatus was under his direct control, President Jiang approved plans to completely rebuild Běijīng and relocate its inhabitants. This was part of the nationwide effort to rebuild the dilapidated and neglected infrastructure of all Chinese cities. The 'trillion-dollar' economic stimulus package was carried out with remarkable speed. In Běijīng more than a million peasants, housed in dormitories on construction sites, worked round the clock, and still do. New shopping malls, office blocks, hotels and luxury housing developments were thrown up at astonishing speed. Only a dictatorship with the vast human and industrial resources of China at its command could ever have achieved this.

Jiang wanted to turn Běijīng into another Hong Kong, with a forest of glass-and-steel skyscrapers. The new municipal leadership threw out the old zoning laws, which limited the height of buildings within the Second Ring Rd. It revoked existing land deeds by declaring old buildings to be dilapidated slums. Such regulations enabled the state to force residents to abandon their homes and move to new housing in satellite cities. Under the plan, only a fraction of the 67-sq-km Ming city was preserved.

Looking Forward Only

Some see the rebuilding as a collective punishment on Běijīng for its 1989 rebellion, but others see it as the continuing legacy of Mao's Cultural Revolution and the late Qing dynasty reformers. Many of China's recent leaders have been engineers and ex–Red Guards, including former President Hu Jintao, who graduated from Qīnghuá University during the Cultural Revolution. Běijīng's new architecture seems designed to embody their aspiration to create a new, forward-looking, hi-tech society, and mark the realisation of the goal of a new modern China.

Běijīng boasted over 3679 historic *hútòng* (narrow alleyways) in the 1980s, but only 430 were left according to a field survey in 2006 by the Běijīng Institute of Civil Engineering & Architecture.

Designs to demolish the Forbidden City and erect new party headquarters on the site were drawn up in the late 1960s but never implemented. The palace was closed for nearly 10 years and became overgrown with weeds.

HISTORY RAPID DEVELOPMENT

2011	2012	2012	2012
The high-speed rail link between Běijīng and Shànghǎi opens to the public, slashing train journey times between the two city's from 10 hours to just five.	Civil-rights activist Chen Guangcheng, held under virtual house arrest for two years, takes refuge in the US embassy in Běijīng. After long negotiations, China allows him to leave for the US.	Seventy-seven people die and more than 65,000 are evacuated from their homes after Běijīng is hit by its worst floods in 60 years.	The world holds its breath as China's new leaders are appointed at the Great Hall of the People in Tiān'ānmén Sq as part of the nation's once-in-a-decade transfer of power.

Historic Hútòng

The essence of Běijīng is its *hútòng* (胡同), the distinctive alleyways that cut across the centre of town. These enchanting passageways offer a very real glimpse of what Běijīng was like before the bulldozers and construction crews got to work, and are still home to around 20% of the residents of inner Běijīng. Immersing yourself in the *hútòng* is an essential part of any visit to the capital and by far the best way to experience Běijīng street life in all its frenetic and fascinating glory.

ORIGINS

Hútòng first appeared in Běijīng in the Yuan dynasty (1271–1368), in the wake of Genghis Khan's army. With the city, then known as Zhōngdū, reduced to rubble, it was redesigned with *hútòng* running east-west. At first, their numbers were comparatively small – there were no more than 380 by the end of the Mongol reign over Běijīng – but they began to increase during the Ming dynasty. By the Qing dynasty more than 2000 *hútòng* riddled Běijīng, giving rise to the Chinese saying, 'There are 360 *hútòng* with names and as many nameless *hútòng* as there are hairs on a cow.'

The number of alleyways peaked in the 1950s, when there were reckoned to be over 6000. In recent decades the construction of office buildings and apartment blocks, as well as the widening of roads, has resulted in the demolition of many of them. However, it's likely that somewhere between 1000 and 2000 of these beguiling lanes have avoided the bulldozers.

Venerable alleys include Zhuanta Hutong (砖塔胡同; Brick Pagoda Alley), dating from Mongol times and found west off Xisi Nandajie; and Nanluogu Xiang, which dates back 800 years and is now the best-known alley in town thanks to its emergence as a nightlife hub. Other *hútòng* survive in name only, like 900-year-old Sanmiao Jie (三庙街; Three Temple St) in Xuānwǔ District, which dates back to the Liao dynasty (907–1125). Long cited as the oldest *hútòng* of them all, little is left of the ancient alley as its courtyard houses were demolished in 2009.

Most *hútòng* lie within the loop of the Second Ring Rd. The most *hútòng*-rich neighbourhoods are in the centre and north of Dōngchéng District, closely followed by the northern part of Xīchéng District, especially the area around and to the west of Hòuhǎi Lakes. The *hútòng* here were the closest to the Forbidden City, and the nearer you lived to the imperial palace, the higher your status. For that reason, the *hútòng* immediately east and west of the Forbidden City were reserved for aristocrats and the city elite. It's in these *hútòng* that you'll find the oldest and most prestigious *sìhéyuàn* (courtyard houses), many of which are now government offices. Most date from the Qing dynasty, though many of the laneways are older.

The lanes around and close to the Forbidden City have been largely protected from the ravages of redevelopment. The houses further away were the homes of merchants and artisans, featuring more functional design with little or no ornamentation. It is these *hútòng*, especially the ones southeast and southwest of Tiān'ānmén Square, that have suffered the most from the wrecking ball.

The origins of the word '*hútòng*' are hazy. It was originally a Mongolian term, and could have referred to a passageway between *gers* (or 'yurts'), the traditional Mongol tents; or it might come from the word '*hottog*' (a well) – wherever there was water in the dry plain around Běijīng, there were inhabitants.

Walk through the once vibrant neighbourhood directly due east of Qianmen Dajie (near where Lìqún Roast Duck Restaurant is located), and you'll get a vivid impression of how many *hútòng* are clinging on for dear life in the face of property development. Nevertheless, the area around Dazahlan Xijie, itself a *hútòng*, still has many alleys left, although they lack the aesthetic value of their posh counterparts to the north.

But you can find *hútòng* of one sort of another in all Běijīng's neighbourhoods, even if some are relatively recent creations and are basically low-level housing rather than anything worthy of preservation. Wherever you choose to plunge into *hútòng* land, you'll be treading streets that have hundreds of years of history behind them.

IMPERIAL CITY HÚTÒNG

The Imperial City failed to survive the convulsions of the 20th century, but the *hútòng* that threaded through the imperial enclave remain. Many bore names denoting their former function during imperial days. Zhonggu Hutong (钟鼓胡同; Bell and Drum Alley) was responsible for the provision of bells and drums to the imperial household. Jinmaoju Hutong (巾帽局胡同; Cloth and Cap Department Alley) handled the caps and boots used by the court, while Zhiranju Hutong (织染局胡同; Weaving and Dyeing Department Alley) supplied its satins and silks. Jiucuju Hutong (酒醋局胡同; Wine and Vinegar Department Alley) managed the stock of spirits, vinegar, sugar, flour and other culinary articles.

Candles were vital items during Ming and Qing times. Supply was handled by the Làkù, which operated from Laku Hutong (蜡库胡同, Candle Storehouse). The Jade Garden Hotel sits on the former site of the Cíqìkù (Porcelain Storehouse), which kept the Forbidden City stocked with porcelain bowls, plates, wine cups and other utensils.

West of Běihǎi Park, the large road of Xishiku Dajie (西什库大街; West Ten Storehouse St) gets its name from the various storehouses scattered along its length during Ming times. Among items supplied to the Imperial City from warehouses here were paper, lacquer, oil, copper, leather and weapons, including bows, arrows and swords.

There are also *hútòng* named after the craft workers who supplied the Forbidden City with its raw materials, such as Dashizuo Hutong (大石作胡同; Big Stonemason's Alley), where stonemasons fashioned the stone lions, terraces, imperial carriageways and bridges of the Imperial City.

Now-vanished temples are also recalled in *hútòng* names, such as the Guangming Hutong (光明胡同), south of Xi'anmen Dajie, named after the huge Guāngmíng Diàn (Guāngmíng Temple) that is no more.

HÚTÒNG TODAY

Hútòng land is now a hotchpotch of the old and the new, where Qing-dynasty courtyards come complete with recently added brick outhouses and stand beneath grim apartment blocks. Adding to the lack of uniformity is the fact that many *sìhéyuàn* were subdivided in the 1960s so that they could house more people. The shortage of space, as well as the paucity of modern facilities such as heating, proper plumbing and sometimes private bathrooms and toilets, is the main reason many *hútòng* dwellers have been happy to leave the alleyways for newly built high-rise flats.

Some of the grandest *sìhéyuàn* are occupied by high-ranking CCP cadres. Mao'er Hutong off Nanluogu Xiang is known for the number of senior officials who live there, while former Premier Zhao Ziyang spent the last 15 years of his life under house arrest in a courtyard once occupied by Empress Cixi's hairdresser.

Also scattered within the Imperial City were numerous storehouses, surviving in name only in such alleys as Lianziku Hutong (帘子库胡同; Curtain Storehouse Alley), Denglongku Hutong (灯笼库胡同; Lantern Storehouse Alley) and Duanku Hutong (缎库胡同; Satin Storehouse Alley).

Hútòng

Older residents are more reluctant to abandon the *hútòng*, preferring the sense of living in a community, as opposed to a more isolated existence in the suburbs. And there are now increasing signs that many will be able to see out their days in their *hútòng* because the city authorities seem finally to have cottoned on to the worth of the *hútòng* as a principal attraction of Běijīng (although the controversial plans to relocate more than 100 households as part of a redevelopment of the historic Drum Tower area seem to buck this recent trend).

Some alleyways are now protected by law, while others have become nightlife hot spots and tourist hubs. The successful remodelling of Nanluogu Xiang has been replicated elsewhere: some of the *hútòng* behind the Drum Tower and off Gulou Dongdajie and Andingmennei Dajie have also sprouted bars, cafes and restaurants and have become almost as popular among young Beijingers as they are with visitors. The adaptation of the *hútòng* for commercial use has perhaps done more than any efforts by the central government to ensure their survival. With many *hútòng* now generating significant tax revenue for the local authority, officials have a tangible reason to shield them from redevelopment.

Best Hútòng for Eating & Drinking

Nanluogu Xiang

Beiluogu Xiang

Fangjia Hutong

Wudaoying Hutong

Beixintiao Santiao Hutong

Banchang Hutong

OLD WALLED COURTYARDS

Sìhéyuàn (四合院) are the building blocks of the *hútòng* world. Some old courtyards, such as the Lǎo Shě Museum, have been quaintly mothballed as museums, but many remain inhabited and hum with domestic activity inside and out. Doors to communal courtyards are typically left open, while from spring to autumn men collect outside their gates, drinking beer, smoking and chewing the fat. Inside, trees soar aloft, providing shade and a nesting place for birds.

Prestigious courtyards are entered by a number of gates, but the majority have just a single door. Venerable courtyards are fronted by large, thick, red doors, outside of which perch either a pair of Chinese lions or drum stones (*bǎogǔshí;* two circular stones resembling drums, each on a small plinth and occasionally topped by a miniature lion or a small dragon head). A set of square *méndāng* (wooden ornaments) above the gateway is a common sight. You may even see a set of stepping-on stones *(shàngmǎ shí)* that the owner would use for mounting his steed. The more historic courtyard gates are accessed by steps, both topped with and flanked by ornate carvings – the generosity of detail indicates the social clout of the courtyard's original inhabitants.

Many of these impressive courtyards were the residences of Běijīng's officials, wealthy families and even princes; Prince Gong's Residence on Dingfu Jie is perhaps the most celebrated example. In more recent times, many were appropriated by work units to provide housing for their workforce. Others still belong to private owners, or are used by the government or universities, but the state ultimately owns all property in China, which leaves the fate of the *hútòng* in the hands of local authorities.

Foreigners long ago cottoned on to the charm of courtyard life and breached this conservative bastion, although many are repelled by poor heating, and neighbours who can be too close for comfort by Western standards. In addition, some *hútòng* homes still lack toilets, explaining the malodorous public loos strung along many alleyways. But other homes have been thoroughly modernised and sport such features as varnished wooden floors, fully fitted kitchens and air-conditioning. Converted courtyards are prized and are much more expensive to buy or rent than even the swishest apartments.

While large numbers of old courtyard houses have been divided into smaller units, many of their historical features remain, especially their roofs. Courtyard communities are served by small shops and restaurants spread throughout the *hútòng*.

You can experience these delightful lanes to the full by spending a night in a *hútòng* courtyard hotel. There are also now a number of fine courtyard restaurants, such as Dali Courtyard or Source, which allow you to dine inside a *sìhéyuàn*.

WIND-WATER LANES

By far the majority of *hútòng* run east–west, ensuring that the main gate faces south, so satisfying *fēngshuǐ* (geomancy, literally 'wind and water') requirements. This south-facing aspect guarantees maximum sunshine and protection from negative forces prevailing from the north. This positioning mirrors the layout of all Chinese temples, which nourishes the *yáng* (the male and light aspect) while checking the *yīn* (the female and dark aspect). Less significant north–south running alleyways link the main lanes.

Some courtyards used to be further protected by rectangular stones bearing the Chinese characters for Tài Shān (Mt Tài) to vanquish bad omens. Other courtyards preserve their screen walls or spirit walls *(yǐngbì)* – *fēngshuǐ* devices erected in front of the main gate to deflect roaming spirits. Běijīng's two most impressive spirit walls are the Nine Dragon Screens at the Forbidden City and in Běihǎi Park.

Trees provide *qì* (energy) and much-needed shade in summer, and most old courtyards have a locust tree at the front, which would have been planted when the *sìhéyuàn* was constructed.

During the Cultural Revolution, selected *hútòng* were rechristened to reflect the fervour of the times. Nanxiawa Hutong was renamed Xuemaozhu Hutong, literally 'Study Mao's Writings Hutong', while Doujiao'er Hutong became Hongdaodi Hutong, or 'Red to the End Hutong'.

NAMES

Some *hútòng* are christened after families, such as Zhaotangzi Hutong (赵堂子胡同; Alley of the Zhao Family). Other *hútòng* simply took their names from historical figures, temples or local features, while a few have more mysterious associations, such as Dragon Whiskers Ditch Alley (Lóngxūgōu; 龙须沟胡同). Many reflect the merchandise that was for sale at local markets, such as Ganmian Hutong (干面胡同; Dry Flour

THE CHANGING FACE OF HÚTÒNG LAND

One by-product of the commercialisation of some *hútòng* is that they cease to be the fascinating microcosms of local life they once were. Eight years ago, Nanluogu Xiang was still full of families who had lived there for generations and was lined with *xiǎomàibù* (small general stores) and greengrocers rather than bars.

Now, virtually none of those residents remain. The vast majority have leased their courtyard homes as shops, restaurants, bars and cafes and used the sky-high rents to relocate to comfy new apartment blocks in the suburbs. Whereas once kids played in the street on summer nights, while the adults sat fanning themselves or playing Chinese chess, now young Beijingers and domestic tourists stroll up and down, shopping, eating and drinking.

This transition from living, breathing communities into something far less organic is being mimicked elsewhere, for example, at Wudaoying Hutong near the Lama Temple; while nearby Fangjia Alley is a bizarre mix of hip *hútòng* and old Běijīng, where you can sip an imported brew in a trendy bar while opposite locals sit on a doorstep and share a bottle of Yanjing beer.

The *hútòng* dwellers aren't complaining too much, though. On the contrary, it is now near impossible to buy a *sìhéyuàn* in such areas because their residents know they can guarantee their long-term future by renting them out instead. But if you're looking for a taste of truly authentic alley life, then you'll need to plunge into the *hútòng* that haven't been touched by the hand of Mammon.

Alley), while some *hútòng,* such as Gongbei Hutong (弓背胡同; Bow Back Hutong), have names derived from their shape.

Other names reflect some of the rather unusual industries that coalesced around the Forbidden City. Young Girl Lane was home to future concubines and Wet Nurse Lane was full of young mothers who breastfed the imperial offspring; they were selected from around China on scouting trips four times a year. Clothes Washing Lane was the residence of the women who did the imperial laundry. The maids, having grown old in the service of the court, were subsequently packed off to faraway places until their intimate knowledge of royal undergarments was out of date and no longer newsworthy.

Some *hútòng* names conceal their original monickers, which were considered either too unsavoury or unlucky, in homophones or similarly sounding words, or are euphemisms for what actually went on there. Guancai Hutong (棺材胡同), or 'Coffin Alley', was dropped for Guangcai Hutong (光彩胡同), which means 'Splendour Hutong'. Muzhu Hutong (母猪胡同), 'Mother Pig Hutong' or 'Sow Hutong', was elevated to the much more poetic Meizhu Hutong (梅竹胡同), or 'Plum Bamboo Hutong'. Rouge Hutong (胭脂胡同; Yanzhi Hutong) earned its name because it was the haunt of prostitutes, 'rouge' being old Běijīng slang for a working girl.

For a bird's-eye panorama of Běijīng's *hútòng* universe, view the diorama of the modern city at the Běijīng Planning Exhibition Hall. The excellent Běijīng Cultural Heritage Protection Center (www.bjchp. org) website has useful information on efforts to preserve the city's remaining *hútòng.*

DIMENSIONS

Despite an attempt at standardisation, Běijīng's alleys have their own personalities and proportions. The longest is Dongjiaomin Xiang (东交民巷), which extends for 3km, while the shortest – unsurprisingly called Yichi Dajie (一尺大街; One Foot St) – is a brief 25m. Some people contest that Guantong Hutong (贯通巷; Guantong Alley), near Yangmeizhu Xijie which is east of Liulichang Dongjie, is even shorter, at 20m.

Some *hútòng* are wide and leafy boulevards, whereas others are narrow, claustrophobic corridors. Běijīng's broadest alley is Lingjing

Hutong (灵境胡同; Fairyland Alley), with a width of 32m, but the aptly named Xiaolaba Hutong (小喇叭胡同; Little Trumpet Alley), the city's smallest, is a squeeze at 50cm.

Chubby wayfarers would struggle even more in Qianshi Hutong (钱市胡同), situated not far from Qiánmén and Dàzhàlan – its narrowest reach is a mere 44cm, although it's a pathway rather than a genuine *hútòng*. Nor do all the lanes run straight: Jiuwan Hutong (九湾胡同; Nine Bend Alley) has no less than 13 turns in it.

TOURS

Exploring Běijīng's *hútòng* is an unmissable experience. Go on a walking or cycling tour and delve deep into this alternately ramshackle and genteel, but always magical, world. Or wander off the main roads in the centre of Běijīng into the alleyways that riddle the town within the Second Ring Rd. Getting lost is part of the fun of exploring the *hútòng*, though you'll never be far from a main road.

Good places to plunge into are the alleys to the west of Hòuhǎi Lakes, the *hútòng* behind the Drum Tower, the area around Nanluogu Xiang or the roads branching west off Chaoyangmen Beixiaojie and Chaoyangmen Nanxiaojie, east of Wangfujing Dajie.

Hiring a bike is by far the best way to explore this historic world. But if you want to join a tour, the China Culture Center (Kent Center; ✏weekdays 6432 9341, weekends 6432 0141; www.chinaculturecenter.org; 29 Anjialou, Liangmaqiao Lu; Liangmaqiao) runs regular tours, or can arrange personalised tours. Call for further details, or check the website. Bike Běijīng (p248) also does guided *hútòng* tours. Many hotels run tours of the *hútòng*, or will point you in the direction of someone who does. Alternatively, any number of pedicab touts infest the roads around Hòuhǎi Lakes, offering 45-minute or one-hour tours. Such tours typically cost ¥60 to ¥120 per person.

The most significant *hútòng* have red street signs sporting the alley name. The *hútòng* name in Chinese also appears on a small metal plaque above doorways strung along each alley. A small blue plate over the doorway of a *sìhéyuàn* indicates a building protected by law.

HISTORIC HÚTÒNG TOURS

STREET SIGNS

Arts

Běijīng's arts scene has flourished over the past two decades, fuelled by China opening up to the outside world and the subsequent influx of new ideas from overseas. Virtually lobotomised during the Cultural Revolution, the capital's creative faculties have sparked into life and found some space. Visual arts in particular have prospered. From its humble beginnings in the 798 Art District, Chinese contemporary art has achieved global recognition. But Běijīng is also the unofficial capital of China's film industry, the home of its finest bands and the best place to catch the enduring vitality of the traditional Chinese performing arts. Whatever your tastes run to, you'll find it in Běijīng.

LITERATURE

In keeping with its well-read and creative reputation among ordinary and educated Chinese, Běijīng has been home to some of China's towering modern writers. The literary landscapes of Lao She, Lu Xun, Mao Dun and Guo Moruo are all forever associated with the capital. Venue of the inspirational May Fourth Movement (p212), the first stirrings of the Red Guards and the democracy protests of 1989, Běijīng's revolutionary blood has naturally seeped into its literature. Over the past century, local writers have penned their stories of sorrow, fears and aspirations amid a context of ever-changing trends and political upheaval.

The eternal Běijīng versus Shànghǎi argument occurs in the arts too. The capital is grittier and edgier than its southern counterpart, and is slightly less obsessed with making money. For those reasons, and despite its authoritarian reputation as the centre of CCP power, Běijīng attracts far more creative talent than Shànghǎi.

The Birth of Modern Chinese Literature

The publication of Lu Xun's short story *Diary of a Madman* in 1918 had the same type of effect on Chinese literature as the leather-clad Elvis Presley had on the American music scene in the early 1950s. Until Lu Xun, novels had been composed in classical Chinese *(gǔwén)*, a kind of Shakespearean language far removed from colloquial speech *(báihuà)*. That maintained the huge gulf between educated and uneducated Chinese, putting literature beyond the reach of the common person and fashioning a cliquey *lingua franca* for officials and scholars.

The opening paragraph of Lu's seminal story uses that classical language. The stultifying introduction – peppered with archaic character use and the excruciatingly pared down grammar of classical Chinese – continues as one solid block of text, without any new paragraphs or indentation. Then suddenly the passage concludes and the reader is confronted with the appearance of fluent colloquial – *spoken* – Chinese:

今天晚上, 很好的月光 *Tonight there is good moonlight*

For Lu Xun to write his short story – itself a radical fable of palpable terror – in the vernacular was dynamite. Chinese people were at last able to read language as it was spoken and the short story's influence on creative expression was electric. Lu Xun's tale records the diary entries of a man descending into paranoia and despair. Fearful that those around him are engaging in cannibalism, the man's terrifying suspicions are seen as a cri-

BĚIJĪNG BOOKSHELF

➡ *Beijing Coma* (Ma Jian, 2008) Novel revolving around protagonist Dai Wei's involvement with the pro-democracy protests of 1989 and the political coma that ensues.

➡ *Diary of a Madman and Other Stories* (Lu Xun, translated by William Lyell) Classic tale of mental disintegration and paranoia, and a critique of Confucianism in pre-revolutionary China from the father of modern Chinese literature. China's first story published in *báihuà* (colloquial speech), save the first paragraph.

➡ *Rickshaw Boy* (Lao She, translated by Shi Xiaoqing, 1981) A masterpiece by one of Běijīng's most beloved authors and playwrights about a rickshaw puller living in early-20th-century China.

➡ *Blades of Grass: The Stories of Lao She* (translated by William Lyell, 2000) This collection contains 14 stories by Lao She – poignant descriptions of people living through times of political upheaval and uncertainty.

➡ *The Maker of Heavenly Trousers* (Daniele Vare, 1935) Recently republished tale of old Běijīng with a splendid cast of dubious foreigners and plenty of insights into Chinese life in the capital in the chaotic pre-WWII days.

➡ *The Noodle Maker* (Ma Jian, translated by Flora Drew, 2004) A collection of interconnected stories as told by a state-employed writer during the aftermath of the Tiān'ānmén Square protests. Bleak, comical and unforgettable.

➡ *Midnight in Peking* (Paul French, 2012) True-life mystery of a brutal murder of an English girl in the British Legation era, with lots of juicy detail about the sinful underworld of pre-1949 Běijīng.

➡ *Black Snow* (Liu Heng, translated by Howard Goldblatt, 1993) Compelling novel about workers in Běijīng. Superbly written – a fine translation.

➡ *Peking Story: The Last Days of Old China* (David Kidd, 2003) A true story of a young man who marries the daughter of an aristocratic Chinese family in Běijīng two years before the 1949 communist revolution. The writing is simple, yet immersive.

➡ *Empress Orchid* (Anchee Min, 2004) Historical novel about Empress Cixi and her rise to empress of China during the last days of the Qing dynasty. Good historical background of Běijīng and entertaining to read.

➡ *Beijing: A Novel* (Philip Gambone, 2003) A well-written account of an American working in a medical clinic in Běijīng who falls in love with a local artist. One of the few books out there to explore in-depth the intricacies of Běijīng gay subculture.

➡ *Foreign Babes in Beijing: Behind the Scenes of a New China* (Rachel Dewoskin, 2005) An easygoing account of a young woman's five years spent in Běijīng during the mid-1990s.

tique of the self-consuming nature of feudal society. It is a haunting and powerful work, which instils doubts as to the madness of the narrator and concludes with lines that offer a glimmer of hope.

From this moment on, mainstream Chinese literature would be written as it was thought and spoken: Chinese writing had arrived in the modern age.

Pre-1989 Literature

Contemporary Chinese literature is commonly grouped into two stages: pre-1989 and post-1989. The 1949 ascendency saw literature gradually became a tool of state control and most work in this period echoed the Communist Party line, with dull, formulaic language in a socialist realist framework. Writers were required to inject their work with stock phrases and cardboard characters that embodied political ideals.

'Scar literature' – novels exploring the traumatic impact of the Cultural Revolution on Chinese society – was the most significant of all the literary movements that flowered during the late 70s and 1980s. It still flourishes today, with authors such as Yu Hua and Jiang Rong delving back into those dark days.

Inseparable from propaganda, literary production was banal and unimaginative, with creative inspiration making way for Maoist political correctness; publishing was nationalised. Literature had taken a step sideways and two steps back. The Hundred Flowers Movement (1956–57) promised a period of open criticism and debate, but instead resulted in a widespread crackdown on intellectuals, including writers. During the Cultural Revolution (1966–76), writers either toed the line or were mercilessly purged. The much-loved Běijīng writer Lao She (1899–1966) was badly beaten and humiliated by Red Guards at the Confucius Temple in August 1966 and committed suicide the next day.

After Mao's death in 1976, Chinese artists and writers threw off political constraints and began to write more freely, exploring new modes of literary expression. Western books began to appear in translation, including works by authors such as Faulkner, Woolf, Hemingway and DH Lawrence. The Chinese also developed a taste for more mainstream writers like Kurt Vonnegut and even Jackie Collins. This deluge of Western writing had a great impact on many Chinese authors who were exposed for the first time to a wide array of literary techniques and styles.

One important writer to emerge during this period was Zhang Jie, who first drew the attention of literary critics with the publication of her daring novella *Love Must Not Be Forgotten* (1979). With its intimate portrayal of a middle-aged woman and her love of a married man, the book challenged the traditional mores of marriage. The authorities disparaged the book, calling it morally corrupt, but the book was extremely popular with readers and won a national book award.

Zhang went on to write the novels *Heavy Wings* (1980) and *The Ark* (1981). *The Ark,* about three women separated from their husbands, established Zhang as China's 'first feminist author'. Shen Rong was another talented female author. Her novella *At Middle Age* (1980), tells the plight of a Chinese intellectual during the Cultural Revolution who must balance her family life with her career as a doctor.

EXILES

Chinese authors living overseas, either through choice or because of their political views, have been responsible for some of the most effective writing about China in recent years. The London-based Ma Jian left China after the Tiān'ānmén protests. His novel *Beijing Coma* (2008), which recounts the events of June 1989 from the perspective of a student left in a coma after being shot during the crackdown on the protestors, is the finest piece of fiction dealing with that momentous time.

Ma's masterpiece, though, is the remarkable *Red Dust* (2001), a memoir of the three years in the early 1980s Ma spent travelling around the remote edges of China, including Tibet, on the lam. Its opening chapters provide a fascinating snapshot of the then tiny community of bohemians in Běijīng and the suspicions they aroused among the authorities.

Native Beijinger Yiyun Li, who now lives in California, writes exquisite short stories. Both *A Thousand Years of Good Prayers* (2005) and *Gold Boy, Emerald Girl* (2010) reveal the lives of ordinary Chinese caught up in the sweeping cultural changes of the past 20 years and are told in haunting prose.

Another US-based author who writes in English is Ha Jin. His novel *Waiting* (1999) is a love story that spans two decades as its hero hangs on 18 years for official permission to get divorced so he can remarry. The harsher, more satirical *War Trash* (2004) examines the complicated web of loyalties – to family, country and political party – many Chinese struggled to reconcile in the wake of the communist takeover of China in 1949.

SEX & THE CITY

Long a taboo subject in the arts, and in Chinese society in general, sex has become one of the abiding themes of modern Chinese literature. The former poet Zhang Xianliang's *Half of Man is Woman* (1985), translated into English by Martha Avery, was a hugely controversial exploration of sexuality and marriage in contemporary China that went on to become an international bestseller. Zhang followed that with the clearly autobiographical *Getting Used to Dying* (1989), about a writer's new-found sexual freedom (also translated by Martha Avery). The novel was banned in China until 1993.

In recent years, though, it has been female authors who have most successfully mined sexuality as a theme. The provocative *Beijing Doll* (2004) by Chun Shu, translated by Howard Goldblatt, is written by a high school dropout who lives a life of casual sex, drink and drugs. The novel reveals the emergence of a shopping mall and punk-music-obsessed teenage tribe unimaginable in Běijīng even a few years before.

Annie Wang's *The People's Republic of Desire* (2006) also holds nothing back with its candid exploration of sexuality in modern Běijīng, while Anni Baobei (real name Li Jie) writes hugely popular short stories and novels, such as *Lotus* (2006), that feature alienated young women caught up in dysfunctional or abusive relationships.

Post-1989 Literature

The tragic events of 1989 inspired a more 'realist' type of literature and paved the way for a new group of writers, such as Wang Shuo and Yu Hua, to emerge. Wang, a sailor turned fiction writer, is famous for his satirical stories about China's underworld and political corruption.

Wang's stories – dark, sometimes fantastic and taking jabs at just about every aspect of contemporary Chinese society – are notable for their inventive use of Běijīng slang; his style is similar to the way the Scottish author Irvine Welsh uses the Edinburgh vernacular in novels such as *Trainspotting*. But Wang's unrelenting satirical assault has not endeared him to the Chinese authorities, who see him as a 'spiritual pollutant'.

One of Wang's most contentious novels, *Please Don't Call Me Human*, first published in 1989, was written after the Tiān'ānmén Square democracy protests and provides a mocking look at the failures of China's state security system. Wang's works appeal to a broad spectrum of Chinese society, despite being banned. He has written over 20 books as well as screenplays for TV and film. Books available in English include *Playing for Thrills* (2000) and *Please Don't Call Me Human* (1998).

Like Wang, Yu Hua grew up during the Cultural Revolution and that experience is filtered through all his work. Yu too, uses extreme situations and humour, and often violence, to illustrate his essentially absurd vision of modern-day China. But unlike Wang, Yu's novels are vast, sweeping affairs that cover decades. *To Live* (1992) follows the tribulations of one family from the founding of the new China through the Cultural Revolution.

Its impact overseas helped turn Yu into a global literary star and his subsequent novels *Chronicle of a Blood Merchant* (1995), which moves from the 1950s to the 1980s, and *Brothers* (2005), a vicious, dark satire on the rush for riches that has characterised the last two decades in China, are both available in English translation.

Mo Yan (real name Guan Moye: 'Mo Yan' is a pen-name that means 'don't speak' in Mandarin) has become a worldwide literary star since winning the Nobel Prize for Literature in 2012. His short stories and novels are less pitiless and abrasive than that of Yu Hua and Wang Shuo and, like the great Lu Xun, are essentially social commentary. Most of his work

If in town in March, get your literary fix at the International Literary Festival, held at the Bookworm. Numerous local and international authors are invited to talk, with a line-up that seems to grow more distinguished each year – another sign of Běijīng's emergence as a true world city.

is available in English. The short story collection *Shifu: You'll Do Anything for a Laugh* (2002) provides a great introduction to his writing.

By far the biggest literary hit of recent years has been Jiang Rong's *Wolf Totem* (2004), which received widespread exposure in the West after being published in English in 2008, with a Howard Goldblatt translation. Set in the grasslands of Inner Mongolia, it's a lyrical, semi-autobiographical tale of a young Běijīng student 'sent down' to live among Mongolian nomads during the Cultural Revolution and the contrasts between their lives and the one he has left behind.

The advent of the internet has spawned a whole new generation of young writers who have sprung to fame by first publishing their work online. Now, legions of wannabe authors are posting their short stories, novels and poetry on websites. At the same time, the first writers from the one-child generation (born post-1980) to attract national attention have emerged. The work of Han Han and Guo Jingming will never win any literary prizes (indeed, both authors have been accused of plagiarism, or of merely being the front for teams of ghost writers), but their tales of urban youth have made them media icons and the best-selling authors in China.

VISUAL ARTS

The founding of the new China in 1949 saw the individual artistic temperament subscripted to the service of the state. According to the communist vision, man was now the governor of his destiny and art was just another foot soldier. Chinese art consequently became art for the masses and the socialist realist style emerged dominant, with all human activity in paintings expressing the glory of the communist revolution.

Traditional precepts of Chinese classical painting were sidelined and foreign artistic techniques were imported wholesale. Washes on silk were replaced with oil on canvas while a realist attention to detail supplanted China's traditional obsession with the mysterious and ineffable. Landscapes, in which people played a minor or incidental role, were replaced with harder-edged panoramas in which humans occupied a central, commanding position. The entire course of Chinese painting – which had evolved in glacial increments over the centuries – was redirected virtually overnight.

It was only with the death of Mao Zedong in September 1976 that the shadow of the Cultural Revolution – when Chinese aesthetics were conditioned by the threat of violence – began its retreat. The individual artistic temperament was once again allowed more freedom to explore beyond propaganda. Painters such as Luo Zhongli employed the realist techniques they learned in China's art academies to portray the harsh realities etched in the faces of contemporary peasants. Others escaped the suffocating confines of socialist realism to explore new horizons, experimenting with a variety of contemporary forms.

A voracious appetite for Western art put further distance between traditional Chinese aesthetics and artistic endeavour. One group of artists, the Stars, found retrospective inspiration in Picasso and German expressionism. The ephemeral group had a lasting impact on the development of Chinese art in the 1980s and 1990s, leading the way for the New Wave movement that emerged in 1985.

New Wave artists were greatly influenced by Western art, especially the iconoclastic Marcel Duchamp, and further challenged traditional Chinese artistic norms. The New Wave artist Huang Yongping destroyed his works at exhibitions in an effort to escape from the notion of 'art'. Some New Wave artists adapted Chinese characters into abstract symbols, while others employed graphic images in a bid to shock viewers. Political realities became instant subject matter, with performance artists wrapping themselves in plastic or tape to symbolise the repressive realities of modern-day China.

Post-Tiān'ānmén

The disturbing events during and after June 1989 created artistic disillusionment with the political situation in China and hope soured into cynicism. This attitude was reflected through the 1990s in artworks permeated with feelings of loss, loneliness and social isolation. Two of the most important Běijīng artists during this period of 'cynical realism' were Yue Minjun and Fang Lijun.

Experiments with American-style pop art were another reaction to the events of 1989. Inspired by Warhol, some artists took symbols of socialist realism and transformed them into kitschy visual commentary. Images of Mao appeared against floral backgrounds and paintings of rosy-cheeked peasants and soldiers were interspersed with ads for Canon cameras and Coca-Cola. Artists were not only responding to the tragedies of the Tiān'ānmén protests but also to the rampant consumerism that was sweeping the country. Indeed, reaction to the rapid modernisation of China has been a consistent theme of much Běijīng art from the 1990s to the present day.

Throughout the 1990s, artists who felt marginalised from the cultural mainstream found escape from political scrutiny by living together in ad hoc communes and setting up their own exhibitions in non-official spaces outside of state-run institutions. Most artists relied on the financial support of foreign buyers to continue working. Despite political pressure from authorities, some artists began to receive international attention for their art, sparking the beginning of a worldwide interest in and appetite for Chinese contemporary art. A defining moment for artists was in 1999, when 20 Chinese artists were invited to participate in the Venice Biennale for the first time.

Chinese art's obsessive focus on contemporary socio-economic realities makes much creativity from this period parochial and predictable, but more universal themes have become apparent over recent years and the art climate in Běijīng has changed dramatically. Many artists who left China in the 1990s have returned, setting up private studios and galleries. Government censorship remains, but artists are branching out into other areas and moving away from overtly political content and China-specific concerns.

With scores of private and state-run galleries, Běijīng is a fantastic city to witness the changing face of contemporary Chinese art. While traditional Chinese art is still practised in the capital, Běijīng has fully surrendered to the artistic currents that sweep the international sphere. And whereas once it was foreign buyers who drove the booming art market, increasingly it is now the new local rich who are acquiring art.

Today, Běijīng is home to a vibrant community of artists practising a diverse mix of art forms, from performance art, photography, installations and video art to film, although painting remains by far the most popular visual arts medium. Běijīng artists compete internationally in art events, and joint exhibitions with European and North American artists are frequent. At the same time, numerous Western artists have flocked to Běijīng in an aesthetic *entente cordiale*.

ARTS VISUAL ARTS

Socialist realism has its roots in non-Chinese neo-classical art, the life-like canvases of Jacques Louis David and, of course, the output of Soviet Union painters. Infused with political symbolism and dripping with propaganda, it was produced on an industrial scale, with mechanical rules governing content and style.

Of all the writers to emerge via the internet, Anni Baobei is the undisputed star. Nicknamed 'Flower in the Dark' by her legions of young female fans, her intense stories about lovelorn, lonely women searching for meaning in their lives have struck a huge chord with the one-child generation.

SCISSOR-HAPPY

A walk through the thought-provoking, sometimes controversial galleries of the 798 Art District (p138), or its less commercial counterpart at Cǎochǎngdì, might make any visitor wonder why the fuss about freedom of expression and censorship in China. On the surface, at least, artists appear to be enjoying more freedom than they have since 1949 and the beginning of communist rule.

But appearances, like art itself, can be deceptive. Painters may be enjoying a relative lack of scrutiny, with the CCP having sensibly decided that no picture ever inspired a revolution (and it's no coincidence that freedom has made the visual arts by far the most vibrant of China's creative industries), but that isn't the case for other media. Cinema, TV and literature in particular remain tightly controlled and there are serious limits as to what can and can't be said. To overstep them no longer results in a prison sentence, as it does for political dissidents, but it still leads to a ban on making movies or publishing books that can last for a number of years.

Even worse than official censorship is the way 60-plus years of being constrained by the knowledge that art needs to satisfy the CCP's censors has created a culture of self-censorship. Many artists consciously, or unconsciously, hold back from doing anything that might antagonise the government. This self-suppression is in part due to the fact that children are taught the CCP's vision of the world in school and that the Chinese education system remains dominated by rote-learning. That is not well suited to nurturing creativity, out-of-the-box thinking and inventive criticism. Until this changes, the artistic ceiling in China will remain far lower than it should.

The capital hosts several art festivals, including the Dàshānzi International Arts Festival (every spring), the Affordable Art Fair (p25) in June and the Běijīng Biennale (www.biennialfoundation.org), held every two years in September/October, which attract artists, dealers and critics from around the world.

MUSIC

A key turning point for contemporary Chinese art came in February 1989 when the National Art Museum in Běijīng sponsored an exhibition devoted exclusively to Chinese avant-garde art. On the opening day, artists Tang Song and Xiao Lu fired pistol shots at their own installations and the exhibition closed.

China was a definite latecomer to pop and rock music. By the time Elvis and John Lennon were dead and punk had given way to floppy-fringed '80s new wave, Beijingers were still tapping their feet to 'The East is Red'. Like all of the arts, music was tranquilised during the Cultural Revolution as China's self-imposed isolation severed creative ties with the outside world.

It was a young, classically trained trumpet player named Cui Jian who changed all that. Cui swapped his horn for a guitar in the mid-'80s, founded a band and by 1989 was already a name to be reckoned with. But it was when his song 'Nothing to my Name' ('Yi Wo Suo You'), with its abrasive vocal style and lyrics describing feelings of loneliness and alienation, became the anthem of the 1989 Tiān'ānmén protests that he really kick-started the Chinese music scene.

Since those early days, Běijīng has always been China's rock music mecca. The masses may still prefer the saccharine confections of mainstream Cantopop and Mandopop, but the capital is home to a medley of different bands who take their sonic inspiration from punk and indie, blues, heavy metal, jazz and electronica.

Mostly, they labour in the twilight. Few local bands have record deals or are able to make any money from putting out CDs or by making music available for download. Indeed, the Chinese music industry in general suffers from widespread piracy – few young Chinese would ever consider actually buying music – and a distinctly unequal division of royalties. The upside for visitors is that bands have to rely on gigging to make a living, which means there's someone playing somewhere in Běijīng almost every night of the week.

There's an incestuous flavour to much of the scene, with frequent collaborations and musicians rotating between different groups. Some of the most popular and enduring bands are the punk outfits Brain Failure and Subs, the post-punk/new-wave-influenced Re-TROS and the noise-pop trios Hedgehog and Snapline. But there are also bands riffing on reggae, rockabilly, ska, '70s style hard rock and any number of indigenous folk styles. Jazz, too, has always been popular in China, a legacy of the foreign influence on pre-1949 Shànghǎi.

Hip-hop is in its infancy, but China has embraced electronic music in all its different glories. Club-goers can get a groove on to house, drum & bass, techno and trance every weekend. The local DJ hero is Mickey Zhang; you'll see his name on flyers all over town. Check the local listings magazines for details of upcoming gigs and club nights.

Music festivals are catching on in a big way in China, despite the authorities' automatic suspicion of any large-scale gathering of young people. In and around Běijīng, the Midi Music Festival and Strawberry are two of the best organised and showcase both local and international acts.

For classical music and opera lovers, as well as fans of classical Chinese dance, the National Centre for the Performing Arts (p123) is the hub of all activity, but there are other venues around the city too. The Běijīng Music Festival (www.bmf.org.cn), held for around 30 days during the months of October and November, features music performances by opera, jazz and classical artists from around the world, while an increasing number of orchestras and opera groups pass through town on a regular basis.

ARTS PEKING OPERA

Yue Minjun's grotesque 'laughing' portraits of himself and friends, which are designed to convey a sense of boredom and mock joviality, have become perhaps the most recognisable images of Chinese contemporary art. Yue is now a globally known artist whose individual paintings sell for in excess of US$1 million.

PEKING OPERA

Peking opera (aka Běijīng opera) is still regarded as the *crème de la crème* of all the opera styles in China and has traditionally been the opera of the masses. Intrigues, disasters or rebellions are common themes, and many opera narratives have their source in the fairy tales, stock characters and legends of classical literature.

The style of music, singing and costumes in Peking opera are products of their origins. In the past opera was performed on open-air stages in markets, streets, tea houses or temple courtyards. The orchestra had to play loudly and the performers had to develop a piercing style of singing, which could be heard over the throng. The costumes were a garish collection of sharply contrasting colours because the stages were originally lit by oil lamps.

Dance styles as far back as the Tang dynasty (618–907) employed similar movements and techniques to those used in today's opera. Provincial opera companies were characterised by their dialect and style of singing, but when these companies converged on Běijīng they started a style of musical drama called *kunqu*. This developed during the Ming dynasty, along with a more popular variety of play-acting pieces based on legends, historical events and popular novels. These styles gradually merged by the late-18th and early-19th centuries into the opera we see today.

Musicians usually sit on the stage in plain clothes and play without written scores. The *èrhú*, a two-stringed fiddle that is tuned to a low register and has a soft tone, generally supports the *húqín*, a two-stringed viola tuned to a high register. The *yuèqín*, a sort of moon-shaped four-stringed guitar, has a soft tone and is used to support the

The undisputed king of Peking opera was Mei Lanfang. Mei, who died in 1961, made his name playing female roles and introduced the outside world to China's most famous art form via overseas tours. Now, his name adorns one of Běijīng's top theatres and his former courtyard home is a museum.

èrhú. Other instruments are the *shēng* (a reed flute) and the *pípa* (lute), as well as drums, bells and cymbals. Last but not least is the *ban,* a time-clapper that virtually directs the band, beats time for the actors and gives them their cues.

Apart from the singing and the music, the opera also incorporates acrobatics and mime. Language is often archaic Chinese, music is ear-splitting (bring some cotton wool), but the costumes and make-up are magnificent. Look out for a swift battle sequence – the female warriors especially are trained acrobats who leap, twirl, twist and somersault in attack.

Few props are used in Peking opera; instead the performers substitute for them, with each move, gesture or facial expression having a symbolic meaning. A whip with silk tassels indicates an actor riding a horse, while lifting a foot means going through a doorway.

There are numerous other forms of opera. The Cantonese variety is more 'music hall', often with a 'boy meets girl' theme. Gaojia opera is one of the five local operatic forms from the Fújiàn province and is also popular in Taiwan. It has songs in the Fújiàn dialect but is influenced by the Peking-opera style.

If you get bored after the first hour or so, check out the audience antics – spitting, eating apples, plugging into a transistor radio (important sports match perhaps?) or loud tea slurping. It is lively audience entertainment fit for an emperor. Many theatres around town stage performances of Peking opera.

Traditional Chinese musical instruments include the two-stringed fiddle (*èrhú*) – famed for its desolate wail – the two-stringed viola (*húqín*), the vertical flute *(dòngxiāo)*, the horizontal flute *(dízi)*, the four-stringed lute *(pípa)* and the Chinese zither *(zhēng)*. To appreciate traditional music in Běijīng, catch performances at the Lao She Teahouse close to Tiān'ānmén Sq in the south of Xīchéng.

CINEMA

Pre-1949

Cinema in China dates back to 1896, when a Spaniard with a film projector blew the socks off a crowd in a Shànghǎi tea-house garden. Although Shànghǎi's cosmopolitan gusto would help make the city the capital of China's film industry pre-1949, China's first movie – *Conquering Jun Mountain* (an excerpt from a piece of Peking opera) – was actually filmed in Běijīng in 1905.

Like all the arts, China's film business went into a steep decline after 1949; the dark days of the Cultural Revolution (1966–76) were particularly devoid of creative output. While Taiwan's and Hong Kong's movie industries flourished, China's cinema business was coerced into satisfying political agendas, with output focused on propaganda and glorification of the Communist Party. The film industry in China has yet to recover: taboo subjects still have directors walking on egg shells and criticism of the authorities remains hazardous. Contemporary Chinese TV shows are mostly wooden and artificial, and are often costume dramas set in far-off, and politically safe, dynasties.

China is a nation in thrall to hierarchies, a legacy of Confucianism, hence film-makers are ranked by generation. The most famous of them all is the Fifth, the first generation to attend the Běijīng Film Academy after the end of the Cultural Revolution. The current generation is the Seventh.

Post-1949

Western audiences awoke to a new golden age of Chinese cinema in the 1980s and 1990s when the lush palettes and lavish tragedies of the Fifth Generation directors stimulated the right aesthetic nerves. The cinematic output of directors such as Chen Kaige and Zhang Yimou perfectly dovetailed with China's nascent opening up and escape from Mao-era constraints. Garlanded with praise, received with standing ovations and rewarded with several major film awards, rich works such as *Raise the Red Lantern* (Zhang Yimou; 1991) and *Farewell My Concubine* (Chen Kaige; 1993) redefined Chinese cinema, radiating a beauty that entranced Western cinema-goers and made their directors

BEST FILMS ABOUT BĚIJĪNG

➡ *In the Heat of the Sun* (1994) Adapted from a Wang Shuo novel, a fantastic, dream-like, highly evocative tale of Běijīng youth running wild during the latter days of the Cultural Revolution.

➡ *The Last Emperor* (1987) Bernardo Bertolucci's celebrated (seven Oscars, including best director, best costume design and best cinematography) and extravagant epic charts the life of Puyi during his accession and the ensuing disintegration of dynastic China.

➡ *Summer Palace* (2006) Unusually explicit love story between students set against the backdrop of the Tiān'ānmén Square protests that got its director Lou Ye banned from making films for five years.

➡ *Farewell My Concubine* (1993) Charting a dramatic course through 20th-century Chinese history from the 1920s to the Cultural Revolution, Chen Kaige's film is a sumptuous and stunning narrative of two friends from Peking opera school whose lives are framed against social and political turmoil.

➡ *Cell Phone* (2003) Feng Xiaogang's funniest movie, a delicious satire of Běijīng's emerging middle classes centred on two men's extramarital affairs.

➡ *Lost in Beijing* (2007) Directed by Lu Yi, China's leading female director, this banned production examines the ménage à trois between a young female worker in a massage parlour, her boss and his wife against the backdrop of a rapidly changing Běijīng.

➡ *Beijing Bicycle* (2001) Eschewing the lavish colour of Fifth Generation directors and viewing Běijīng through a realist lens, Wang Xiaoshuai's film follows young and hapless courier Guo on the trail of his stolen mountain bike.

➡ *The Gate of Heavenly Peace* (1995) Using original footage from the six weeks preceding the ending of the Tiān'ānmén protests, Richard Gordon and Carma Hinton's moving three-hour tribute to the spirit of the student movement and its demise is a must-see.

➡ *The World* (2005) Jia Zhangke's social commentary on the effects of globalisation is set in a Běijīng theme park called 'World Park', where workers and visitors play out their lives among replicas of the world's monuments.

➡ *Cala, My Dog!* (2003) Lu Xuechang's sly and subtle comedy about a Běijīng factory worker and avid gambler trying to raise the money to pay for a licence for the beloved family dog, while coping with a jealous wife and wayward teenage son.

the darlings of Cannes and other film festivals. But with many of the early Fifth Generation films banned in their home country, few Chinese cinema-goers got to admire their artistry.

Sixth Generation film directors collectively shunned the exquisite beauty of the Fifth Generation, taking the opposite tack to render the angst and grimness of modern urban Chinese life. Their independent, low-budget works, often made without official permission, put an entirely different spin on mainland Chinese film-making. Zhang Yuan set the tone with *Mama* (1990), a beautiful but disturbing film about a mother and her autistic child. This low-key film, created without government sponsorship, had a huge influence on Zhang's peers.

Other notable Sixth Generation directors include Wang Xiaoshuai, whose *Beijing Bicycle* (2001) is a tale of a Běijīng youth seeking to recover the stolen bike that he needs for his job, and Lou Ye, whose dreamy, neo-noir style displayed in films such as *Suzhou River* (2000) and *Summer Palace* (2006) mark him out from his grittier contemporaries.

But it is Jia Zhangke who is the most talented of the film-makers who emerged in the 1990s. His debut, *Pickpocket* (1997), is a remarkable portrait of a small-time criminal in a bleak provincial town, while the follow-up *Platform* (2000) was a highly ambitious tale of a changing China told through the story of a musical group who transforms from being a state-run troupe performing patriotic songs to a pop band. Subsequent movies such as *Still Life* (2006) and *24 City* (2008) have shown an increasing maturity that bodes well for the future, although like many Sixth Generation film-makers much of his early work has never been seen in Chinese cinemas.

While no Chinese directors have made the successful crossover to making western movies, Chinese actresses are increasingly in demand in Hollywood. Joan Chen was the first to make the transition after her starring role in *The Last Emperor* (1987); she has since been followed by Gong Li and Zhang Ziyi.

While the Sixth Generation were focusing on China's underbelly, a few directors have gone in the opposite direction by making unashamedly commercial movies. Native Beijinger Feng Xiaogang is the best known of them and his mix of clever comedies and action pictures, such as *Cellphone* (2003), *Assembly* (2007) and *If You Were the One* (2008) have made him China's most bankable director. Following in his footsteps is Ning Hao, whose fun crime caper *Crazy Stone* (2006) and its follow-up, *Crazy Racer* (2009), also stormed the domestic box office.

An Uncertain Future

The optimism that accompanied the rise of the Fifth and Sixth Generations has begun to dissipate in the last couple of years. Cinema-going has always been a middle-class pastime in China, with ticket prices too high for most ordinary people and industrial-scale DVD piracy further reducing the potential audience. And with more and more Hollywood productions being shown in China now, the domestic film industry is discovering, as have other film industries around the world, that it is very hard to compete with star-driven blockbuster movies.

Today, only a few directors who are able to attract domestic and overseas investment, such as Zhang Yimou and Chen Kaige, or who are seen as surefire bets, such as Feng Xiaogang, can raise significant budgets to make movies in China. Increasingly, it is historical dramas that are being shot, rather than contemporary stories. There is a real danger that the Chinese film industry will shrink into insignificance in the face of Hollywood pressure and indifference from an audience no longer satisfied by the subject-matter being approved by the CCP's censors.

A good place to see Chinese films by established and emerging directors is at the Běijīng Student Film Festival, a 20-day event held every April. Films are shown at various venues around the city – check local listing magazines for screening times.

Architecture

Whether it's the sublime Temple of Heaven or the extraordinary CCTV Building, Běijīng's shape-shifting architecture wows visitors across the generations. In the space of a few minutes, you can amble from an ancient *hútòng* (narrow alleyway) past the vermillion Forbidden City, trot alongside the mind-numbing Great Hall of the People and arrive at the vast and glittering sci-fi–style National Centre for the Performing Arts. In the process you will have spanned an architectural narrative at least six centuries long, and seen how Běijīng's buildings are as unique to the capital as the aroma of Peking duck.

TRADITIONAL ARCHITECTURE

The oldest standing structure in the Běijīng municipality is the Great Wall. Although the wall dates from the 3rd century BC, most of what you will see is the work of Ming-dynasty (1368–1644) engineers, while the tourist sections have largely been rebuilt over the past 30 years or so.

In fact, while Běijīng as we know it today dates back to the Yuan dynasty (1271–1368), nearly all traditional architecture in the capital is a legacy of the Ming and Qing dynasties (1368–1911), although most Ming-era buildings were rebuilt during the Qing dynasty. A few fitful fragments have somehow struggled through from the Mongol era, but they are rare.

Standout structures from early dynasties include the magnificent Forbidden City (the largest architectural complex in China at 72 hectares), the Summer Palace, and the remaining *hútòng* and courtyard-style homes in

---

BĚIJĪNG'S MOST NOTABLE BUILDINGS

➡ **CCTV Building** (p139) Designed by Rem Koolhaas and Ole Scheeren, this fantastic continuous loop of a building appears to defy gravity.

➡ National Centre for the **Performing Arts** (p119) Běijīng's most loved/hated building – Paul Andreu's creation is either a masterpiece or a blot on the landscape. You decide.

➡ **Forbidden City** (p52) China's incomparably majestic imperial palace.

➡ Hall of Prayer for **Good Harvests** (p108) The *ne plus ultra* of Ming-dynasty design and a feast for the eyes.

➡ **Capital Museum** (p119) Cutting-edge example of modern Chinese museum design.

➡ **Legation Quarter** (p64) A too-rare example of thoughtful and tasteful restoration.

➡ **Great Hall of the People** (p119) This monster of Soviet-inspired socialist realist design, erected during the Great Leap Forward, would look right at home in Pyongyang.

➡ **National Stadium** (p140) The 2008 Olympics may be a distant memory, but this intricate mesh of steel, still known to Beijingers as the 'Bird's Nest', remains iconic.

the centre of the city. There are also fine examples of older temple architecture at the Temple of Heaven Park and Běihǎi Park.

Most historic buildings, however, date from the Qing dynasty (1644–1911) and the latter part of the Manchu dynasty. Little survives from the Ming dynasty, although the conceptual plan of the city dates from Ming times. Old buildings were constructed with wood and paper, so fire was a perennial hazard (spot the huge bronze water vats dotted around the Forbidden City for extinguishing flames that could rapidly reduce halls to smoking mounds). Because buildings were not durable, even those that escaped fire were not expected to last long.

To see how the Ming and Qing dynasties built Běijīng visit the Běijīng Ancient Architecture Museum, which has a great scale model of the old imperial city and shows how the courtyard houses of the *hútòng* were constructed.

Home Sweet Home

Most residences in old Běijīng were once *sìhéyuàn* (p222), houses situated on four sides of a courtyard. The houses were aligned exactly – the northern house was directly opposite the southern, the eastern directly across from the western. *Sìhéyuàn* can still be found within the Second Ring Rd, and although many have disappeared, an increasing number have been transformed into hotels.

Traditionally, the Chinese followed a basic ground plan when they built their homes. In upper-class homes as well as in palaces and temples, buildings were surrounded by an exterior wall and designed on a north–south axis, with an entrance gate and a gate to block spirits that might try to enter the building. Behind the entry gates in palaces and residential buildings was a public hall and behind this were private living quarters built around a central court with a garden. The garden area of upper-class gentry and imperial families spawned an entire sub-genre of 'recreational architecture', which included gardens, pavilions, pagodas, ponds and bridges.

RELIGIOUS ARCHITECTURE

With today's religious renaissance drawing legions of Chinese to prayer, Běijīng's temples and shrines are increasingly busy places of worship, and they are also some of the finest structures in the city.

Buddhist, Taoist and Confucian temples may appear complex, but their layout and sequence of deities tend to follow quite strict schematic patterns. Temples are virtually all arranged on a north–south axis in a series of halls, with the main door of each hall facing south, as is done in courtyard houses and the halls of the Forbidden City.

Many temples have been restored to their original purpose, but others are still occupied by residents, or in the case of Dàgāoxuán Temple, by the military. Some have been converted to offices (Bǎilín Temple), while the ancient Sōngzhùyuàn Temple has found a new lease of life as one of the city's trendiest restaurants.

Chinese temples are strikingly different from Christian churches because of their open plan and succession of halls; buildings follow a hierarchy and are interspersed with breezy, open-air courtyards. This allows the weather to permeate the empty spaces, changing the mood of the temple depending on the climate. The open-air layout also allows the *qì* (flow of vital or universal energy) to circulate, dispersing stale air and allowing incense to be liberally burned.

Large numbers of Běijīng's temples, such as the Big Buddha Temple, whose memory is commemorated in the street name Dafosi Dongjie, have vanished since the Qing dynasty. Others are in the process of disappearing, such as the small Guānyīn Temple just off Dazhalan Xijie, or remain shut, such as Guǎngfúguàn Taoist Temple.

Buddhist Temples

Although there are notable exceptions, most Buddhist temples tend to follow a predictable layout. The first hall is frequently the Hall of Heavenly Kings (Tiānwáng Diàn), where a sedentary statue of the smiling and podgy Bodhisattva Maitreya (Mílèfó), also known as the Monk with the Bag or the Laughing Buddha, is flanked by the ferocious Four Heavenly Kings.

Behind is the first courtyard, where the drum and bell towers often stand, if the temple is large enough, and smoking braziers for the burning of incense may be positioned. The largest hall is usually named the Great Treasure Hall (Dàxióng Bǎodiàn), where you will often discover a golden trinity of statues, representing the historic, contemporary and future Buddhas. You can often find two rows of nine *luóhàn* (Buddhists, especially monks, who have achieved enlightenment and pass to nirvana at death) on either wall to the side. In other temples the *luóhàn* appear in a crowd of 500, housed in a separate hall; the Azure Clouds Temple in Fragrant Hills Park has an example.

A statue of Guanyin (the Goddess of Mercy) often stands at the rear of the main hall, facing north, atop a fish's head or a rocky outcrop. The goddess may also be venerated in her own hall and often has a multitude of arms. The rear hall may house Sutras (Buddhist scriptures) in a building called the Scripture Storing Hall (Cángjīnglóu).

Sometimes a pagoda *(tǎ)* may rise above the main halls or may be the last vestige of a vanished temple. These were originally built to house the remains of Buddha, and later other Buddhist relics, and were also used for storing Sutras, religious artefacts and documents. Some pagodas can still be climbed for excellent views, but many are too fragile and are out of bounds.

China's most legendary figure has endured a roller-coaster ride throughout Chinese history. These days, Confucius is enjoying an upswing with his vision of a 'harmonious society' now endorsed by the CCP. That's in marked contrast to the Cultural Revolution, when Red Guards savaged his teachings as one of the 'Four Olds'.

Taoist Temples

As Taoism predates Buddhism and connects to a more primitive and distant era, Taoist shrines are more netherworldly and project more of an atmosphere of superstition and magic. Nonetheless, in the arrangement of their halls, Taoist temples appear very similar to Buddhist temples.

You will almost certainly see the shape of the circular *bāguà* (a circular figure made up of eight possible combinations of three parallel lines) reflected in eight-sided pavilions and diagrams. The *yīn–yáng* Taiji diagram is also a common motif. Effigies of Laotzu (the Jade Emperor) and other characters popularly associated with Taoist myths, such as the Eight Immortals and the God of Wealth, are customary.

Taoist temple entrances are often guarded by Taoist door gods, similar to those in Buddhist temples, and the main hall is usually called the Hall of the Three Clear Ones (Sānqīng Diàn) and devoted to a triumvirate of Taoist deities.

Confucian Temples

Běijīng's Confucius Temple is China's second largest after the temple in Qūfù in Shāndōng, the birthplace of the sage.

Confucian temples bristle with steles celebrating local scholars, some supported on the backs of *bìxì* (mythical tortoise-like dragons). A statue of Kongzi (Confucius) usually resides in the main hall, overseeing rows of musical instruments and flanked by disciples. A mythical animal, the *qílín* (a statue exists at the Summer Palace), is commonly seen. The *qílín* was a hybrid animal that appeared on earth only in times of harmony.

REBUILDING BĚIJĪNG

For first-time visitors to Běijīng, the city can be an energising and inspiring synthesis of East and West, old and new. Yet after 1949 the characteristics of the old city of Běijīng – formidable and dwarfing city walls, vast and intimidating gates, unbroken architectural narrative and commanding sense of symmetry – were flung out the window.

Many argue (such as author Wang Jun in *Story of a City*) that the historic soul of Běijīng has been extirpated, never to return. It's a dismal irony that in its bid to resemble a Western city, Běijīng has lost a far larger proportion of historic architecture than have London, Paris or Rome.

In 1949, Mao Zedong declared that 'Forests of factory chimneys should mushroom in Běijīng'. He didn't let ancient architecture stand in the way. When the mighty Xīzhí Mén was being levelled in 1969, the Yuan-dynasty gate of Héyí Mén was discovered within the later brickwork; it disappeared too.

Going, Going, Gone

Although Běijīng has been radically altered in every decade since 1949, the current building mania really picked up pace in the 1990s, with a housing renovation policy that resulted in thousands of old-style homes and Stalinist concrete structures from the 1950s being torn down and replaced by modern apartment buildings. In the following decade, office blocks began to mushroom across the city, prompting yet more demolition.

So much of Běijīng's architectural heritage perished in the 1990s that the capital was denied a World Heritage listing in 2000 and 2001. That led the government to establish 40 protection zones throughout the older parts of the city to protect the remaining heritage buildings. But according to Unesco, more than a third of the 62-sq-km area that made up the central part of the old city has been destroyed since 2003, displacing close to 580,000 people.

One of the hardest-hit areas was the central neighbourhood of Qiánmén, once the home of scholars and opera singers. Preservationists and residents have petitioned for government protection. However, a resolution passed in 2005 to protect Běijīng's historic districts did not include many places, including Qiánmén, which had been approved for demolition before the order was passed. Road widening has bulldozed its way through the area; Qianmen Dajie itself has been restored in a mock historic style, and the Dashilar area may be the next in line for redevelopment.

While the pace of demolition has slowed, it still continues. In January 2012, the courtyard home of Liang Sicheng, known as the father of modern Chinese architecture, was pulled down despite being listed as a 'cultural relic'. Ironically, Liang had campaigned in the 1950s for the preservation of ancient Běijīng.

In with the New

Since 1949, replacing what has gone and integrating new architecture seem to have been done without much thought. The vast Legendale Hotel on Jinbao Lu is a kitsch interpretation of a Parisian apartment block curiously plonked in central Běijīng, while the glass grill exterior of the hip Hotel Kapok on Donghuamen Dajie is a jab in the eye of the staid Jade Garden Hotel next door. But it is the futuristic domelike National Centre for the Performing Arts that is perhaps Běijīng's most controversial building, thanks to its location so close to the Forbidden City.

The eventual consequences of this great urban reshaping cannot be estimated. The growing self-respect and self-belief among ordinary Chinese has initiated a movement to reinstate traditional Chinese architectural aesthetics. The rebuilding of Yǒngdìng Mén (Yǒngdìng Gate) and the decorative arches of Qiánmén and Xīdān indicate this process is under way.

Survival Guide

Transport

GETTING TO BĚIJĪNG

Air

Most international travellers will fly into Běijīng, although there are international train routes to and from Russia, Mongolia and Vietnam, as well as trains to and from Lhasa and Hong Kong. Average flight times include: London (10 hours), New York (14 hours) and Sydney (12 hours). Běijīng's international airport is Běijīng Capital International Airport (PEK). If arriving from elsewhere in China, you may also fly into the small Nányuàn Airport (NAY).

You can book flights, tours and rail tickets online at www.lonelyplanet.com/bookings. You can also purchase tickets in person at the **Civil Aviation Administration of China** (中国民航; CAAC; Zhōngguó Mínháng; Aviation Bldg; 民航营业大厦; Mínháng Yíngyè Dàshà; ☑6656 9118, domestic 6601 3336, international 6601 6667; 15 Xichang'an Jie; ☺7am-midnight).

For good deals on flights to and from Běijīng, check the following websites:

C-trip (www.ctrip.com)

eLong (www.elong.net)

Travel Zen (www.travelzen.com)

eBookers (www.ebookers.com)

Expedia (www.expedia.com)

Běijīng Capital International Airport

Currently the world's second busiest airport, **Běijīng Capital International Airport** (北京首都国际机场; Běijīng Shǒudū Guójì Jīchǎng; PEK; ☑6454 1100) has three terminals. The beautifully designed **Terminal 3** (三号航站楼; sān hào hángzhànlóu) deals with most long-haul flights, although international flights also use **Terminal 2** (二号航站楼; èr hào hángzhànlóu). Both are connected to the slick Airport Express, which links up with Běijīng's subway system. The smaller **Terminal 1** (一号航站楼; yī hào hángzhànlóu) is a 10-minute walk from Terminal 2. Free 24-hour shuttle buses connect all three terminals.

FACILITIES

All terminals have ATMs, money-changing facilities, information desks with English-speaking staff, booths selling local SIM cards, plenty of eating options and shops galore (although much less so at Terminal 1).

SLEEPING

If you need to stay by the airport, **Langham Place** (北京首都机场朗豪酒店; Lǎngháo Jiǔdiàn; ☑6457 5555; www.beijingairport.langhamplacehotels.com; 1 Erjing Lu, Terminal 3; 北京首都机场三号航站二径路1号; r from ¥1260; ❋@◎⬚) lays on a free shuttle bus and is well regarded.

AIRPORT EXPRESS

The **Airport Express** (机场快轨; jīchǎng kuàiguǐ; one way ¥25; ☺30min), also written as ABC (Airport Běijīng City), is quick and convenient and links Terminals 2 and 3 to Běijīng's subway system at Sanyuanqiao station (Line 10) and Dongzhimen station (Lines 2 and 13). Trains times are as follows: Terminal 3 (6.21am to 10.51pm); Terminal 2 (6.35am to 11.10pm); Dongzhimen (6am to 10.30pm).

BUS

There are 10 different routes for the airport **shuttle bus** (机场巴士; jīchǎng bāshì; one way ¥16), including those listed here. They all leave from all three terminals and run from around 5am to midnight.

Line 1 To Fāngzhuāng (方庄), via Dàběiyáo (大北窑) for the CBD (国贸; guó mào)

Line 2 To Xīdàn (西单)

Line 3 To Běijīng Train Station (北京站; Běijīng Zhàn), via Dōngzhímén (东直门), Dōngsìshítiáo (东四十条) and Cháoyángmén (朝阳门)

Line 7 To Běijīng West Train Station (西站; xī zhàn)

Line 10 To Běijīng South Train Station (南站; nán zhàn)

Coach service to Tiānjīn (天津, ¥80, 2½ hours, 8am to 10pm hourly)

TAXI

A taxi (using its meter) should cost ¥80 to ¥100 from the airport to the city centre, including the ¥15 airport expressway toll; bank on 30 minutes to one hour to get into town. Join the taxi ranks and ignore approaches from drivers. When you get into the taxi, make sure the driver uses the meter (打表; dǎ biǎo). It is also useful to have the name of your hotel written down in Chinese to show the driver. Very few drivers speak any English.

CAR
The **Vehicle Administration Office** (车管所; chēguǎnsuǒ; ☑6453 0010; ⊙9am-6pm) on the 1st floor of Terminal 3 – look for the 'Traffic Police' sign – issues temporary driving licences for use in Běijīng municipality. Applicants must be between the ages of 18 and 70 and must hold a temporary Chinese visa (three months or less). The straightforward process involves checking out your driving license and undergoing a simple medical test (including an eye-sight test). You'll also need three passport photos and copies and translations of your documents, although it can arrange this for you at the office. The whole procedure takes about 30 minutes and costs ¥10. Once you have the license, you can hire a car from **Hertz** (www.hertzchina.com), which has an office just along the corridor. Self-drive hire cars (自驾; zìjià) start from ¥230 per day (up to 150km per day), with a ¥20,000 deposit. A car-with-driver service (代驾; dàijià)

is also available (from ¥660 per day).

ROAD RULES
Cars in China drive on the right-hand side of the road. Even skilled drivers will be unprepared for China's roads: in cities like Běijīng, cars lunge from all angles and chaos abounds.

Nányuàn Airport
The very small **Nányuàn Airport** (南苑机场; Nányuàn Jīchǎng; NAY; ☑6797 8899) feels more like a provincial bus station than an airport, but it does service quite a few domestic routes. Airport facilities are limited to a few shops and snack stalls, and English-language skills are minimal.

BUS
The shuttle bus (机场巴士; jīchǎng bāshì) goes to Xīdān (西单; ¥16, two hours, 11.15am to 12.50am), from where you can pick up the subway.

TAXI
Around ¥60 to the Tiān'ānmén Sq area. Ignore drivers who approach you. Use the taxi queue. And make sure the driver uses the meter (打表; dǎ biǎo).

Train
Běijīng has three major train stations for long-distance travel (Běijīng Station, Běijīng West Station and Běijīng South Station. Běijīng

North Station is used much less.

Train Ticket Types
It is possible to upgrade (补票; bǔpiào) your ticket once aboard your train. If you have a standing ticket, for example, find the conductor and upgrade to a hard-seat, soft-seat, hard-sleeper or soft-sleeper (if there are any available).

SOFT-SLEEPER
Soft-sleepers (软卧; ruǎn wò) are very comfortable, with four air-conditioned bunks in a closed compartment. They tend to cost as much as discounted airfares to the same destination.

All Z-class trains are soft-sleeper trains, with very comfortable, up-to-date berths. A few T-class trains also offer two-berth compartments, with their own toilet. Tickets on upper

CLIMATE CHANGE & TRAVEL
Every form of transport that relies on carbon-based fuel generates CO_2, the main cause of human-induced climate change. Modern travel is dependent on aeroplanes, which might use less fuel per kilometre per person than most cars but travel much greater distances. The altitude at which aircraft emit gases (including CO_2) and particles also contributes to their climate change impact. Many websites offer 'carbon calculators' that allow people to estimate the carbon emissions generated by their journey and, for those who wish to do so, to offset the impact of the greenhouse gases emitted with contributions to portfolios of climate-friendly initiatives throughout the world. Lonely Planet offsets the carbon footprint of all staff and author travel.

LEFT LUGGAGE

Left-luggage counters (行李寄存; *xíngli jìcún*) and lockers can be found at all the main Běijīng train stations. Prices are ¥5 to ¥10 per bag per day. They tend to be open from around 6am to 11pm.

berths are slightly cheaper than lower berths.

HARD-SLEEPER
Just over half the price of soft-sleepers, hard-sleepers (硬卧; *yìng wò*) are the golden ticket that everyone wants. They tend to be comprised of six air-conditioned bunks in an open-ended doorless compartment. There is less room than in soft-sleeper, but they are still comfortable (clean bedding is still provided), and they are much more social affairs, offering a better chance to meet people than the rather sterile environment of a soft-sleeper. There is a small price difference between berths, with the lowest bunk (下铺; *xiàpù*) the most expensive, then the middle (中铺; *zhōngpù*), then the highest bunk (上铺; *shàngpù*).

As with all other classes, smoking is prohibited. Lights and speakers go out at around 10pm. Each compartment is equipped with its own hot-water flask, filled by an attendant. Hard-sleeper tickets are the most difficult of all to buy; you almost always need to buy these a few days in advance.

SEATS
Soft-seat class (软座; *ruǎn zuò*) is more comfortable but not nearly as common as hard-seat class. First-class (一等; *yīděng*) and 2nd-class (二等; *èrděng*) soft-seats are available in D-, C- and G-series high-speed trains. First class comes with TVs, mobile phone and laptop charging points, and seats arranged two abreast.

Second-class soft-seats are also very comfortable; staff are very courteous throughout. Overcrowding is not permitted. On older trains, soft-seat carriages are often double-decker, and are not as plush as on the faster and more modern high-speed express trains.

Hard-seat class (硬座; *yìng zuò*) is not available on the faster and plusher C-, D- and G-series trains, and is only found on T-, K- and N-series trains, and trains without a number prefix; a handful of Z-series trains have hard-seat. Hard-seat class generally has padded seats, but it's hard on your sanity; often unclean and noisy, and painful on the long haul. Since hard-seat is the only class most locals can afford, it's packed to the gills.

You should get a ticket with an assigned seat number, but if seats have sold out, ask for a standing ticket (无座、站票; *wúzuò* or *zhànpiào*), which gets you on the train, where you may find a seat or can upgrade; otherwise you will have to stand in the carriage or between carriages (with the smokers). Hard-seat sections on newer trains are air-conditioned and less crowded.

Buying Train Tickets

TICKET COUNTERS
There are no longer dedicated ticket offices for foreigners at the main stations in Běijīng, although there is sometimes a ticket window with a temporary 'for foreigners' sign attached to it. Look out for this. Otherwise, join any queue, but arm yourself with a few key Chinese phrases, or better still have a Chinese person write down what you want so you can show the ticket seller. Increasingly, ticket sellers at the three main stations speak a bit of English, but don't bank on it.

PLANNING AHEAD
Never aim to get a hard-sleeper (or, increasingly, soft-sleeper) ticket on the day of travel – plan ahead. Most tickets can be booked in advance between two and 10 days prior to your intended date of departure. Buying hard-seat tickets at short notice is usually no hassle, but it may be a standing ticket rather than a numbered seat. Tickets can only be purchased with cash, and you will need to show your passport to get them.

RETURN TICKETS
Tickets are one-way only. If you want to buy tickets for a train between two destinations beyond the city you are buying your ticket in, it is often better to go to an in-

TRAIN CATEGORIES

CATEGORY	MEANING	TYPE
C	*chengji gāosù* (城际高速)	ultra-high-speed express
D	*dòngchē, héxiè hào* (动车和谐号)	high-speed express
G	*gāotiě* (高铁)	high-speed
K	*kuàisù* (快速)	fast train
T	*tèkuài* (特快)	express
Z	*zhídá tèkuài* (直达特快)	direct express (overnight)

dependent ticket office that charges a commission.

BUSY PERIODS

As with air travel, buying tickets around the Chinese New Year and during the 1 May and 1 October holiday periods ranges from very hard to impossible. Particularly at those times, touts swarm around train stations (especially Běijīng Train Station and Běijīng West) selling black-market tickets; this can be a way of getting scarce tickets, but foreigners frequently get ripped off. You're better off trying one of the many independent train ticket offices dotted around the city – they charge a ¥10 mark-up per ticket. Or else ask at your hotel or hostel – they will usually take a mark-up of around ¥50 per ticket.

ONLINE BOOKINGS

Tickets can be bought online at **China Trip Advisor** (www.chinatripadvisor.com) or **China Train Timetable** (www.china-train-ticket.com), but they charge a huge commission (typically 50%). For trains from Hong Kong to Běijīng, tickets can be ordered online at no mark-up from **KCRC** (www.mtr.com.hk).

BULLET TRAIN TO TIĀNJĪN

You can't book tickets in advance for the C-class 'bullet train' from Běijīng South to Tiānjīn; they just put you on the next available train, but you rarely have to wait more than half an hour (except during public holidays).

Běijīng Train Station

The most central of Běijīng's four main train stations, **Běijīng Train Station** (北京站; Běijīng Zhàn), which is linked to the subway system, is mainly for T-class trains (tèkuài), slow trains and trains bound for the northeast; most fast trains heading south now depart from Běijīng South Train Station and Běijīng West Train

Station. Slower trains to Shànghǎi also go from here.

Approximate travel times and typical train fares (hard-sleeper unless indicated):

Dàlián 大连 Z-series train, soft-sleeper ¥390, 10½ hours (8.46pm)

Dàlián 大连 T- and K-series, ¥260, 12 hours (6.07pm and 8.06pm)

Dàtóng 大同 K-series, ¥108, six hours (regular)

Hā'ěrbīn 哈尔滨 D-series, soft-seat ¥267, 10 hours (7.13am, 1.51pm and 2.18am)

Hā'ěrbīn 哈尔滨 T-series ¥281, 12 hours (4.50pm and 9.26pm)

Jílín 吉林 T-series, ¥263, 12 hours (7.10pm)

Shànghǎi 上海 T-series, soft-sleeper ¥327, 14 hours (4.56pm and 7.28pm)

Běijīng West Train Station

The gargantuan **Běijīng West Train Station** (西站; Xī Zhàn) accommodates fast Z-series trains, such as the following (fares are soft-sleeper unless indicated):

Chángshā 长沙 ¥529, 13 hours (6.16pm)

Fúzhōu 福州 ¥458, 20 hours (3.08pm)

Hànkǒu (Wǔhàn) 汉口 ¥429, 10 hours (8.54pm and 9.12pm)

Kowloon (Hong Kong) 九龙 ¥488, 24 hours (train Q97, 1.08pm)

Lánzhōu 兰州 Z- and T-series, hard-sleeper ¥345, 17 hours (2.31pm and 8.09pm)

Nánchāng 南昌 Hard-sleeper ¥319, 11½ hours (7.45pm, 8pm and 8.06pm)

Wǔchāng (Wǔhàn) 武昌 Hard-sleeper ¥281, 10 hours (9pm and 9.06pm)

Xī'ān 西安 Hard-sleeper ¥270 to ¥290, 11 to 12 hours (8.03pm and 8.48pm)

Other typical train fares for hard-sleeper tickets, and approximate travel times:

Chángshā 长沙 T- and K-series, ¥345, 14 hours (regular)

Chéngdū 成都 T- and K-series, ¥418 to ¥469, 26 to 31 hours (9am, 11.08am, 6.29pm and 9.52pm)

Chóngqìng 重庆 T- and K-class trains, ¥409 to ¥458, 25 to 30 hours (five daily)

Guǎngzhōu 广州 T- and K-class trains, ¥458, 21 hours (five daily)

Guìyáng 贵阳 T-series, ¥490, 29 hours (3.58pm and 4.57pm)

Kūnmíng 昆明 T-series, ¥578, 38 hours (4.37pm)

Shēnzhèn 深圳 T and K-series, ¥467, 24-29 hours (8.12pm and 11.45pm)

Shíjiāzhuāng 石家庄 D-series, second-class seat, ¥82, two hours (regular)

Ürümqi 乌鲁木齐 T-series, ¥569, 34 hours (10.08am)

Xī'ān 西安 T-series, ¥274, 13 to 14 hours (regular from 2pm onwards)

Xīníng 西宁 T-series, ¥379-430, 20-24 hours (1.59pm and 8.09pm)

Yíchāng 宜昌 K-series, ¥319-333, 21½ hours (1.35pm and 11.11pm)

TIBET

For **Lhasa** (拉萨; Lāsà) in Tibet (西藏; Xīzàng), the T27 (hard-seat/hard-sleeper/soft-sleeper ¥389/766/1189, 44 hours) leaves Běijīng West at 8.09pm, taking just under two days. In the return direction, the T28 departs Lhasa at 1.45pm and arrives at Běijīng West at 8.07am.

SUBWAY

At the time of research, Běijīng West was on the disconnected subway Line 9, so it was better to use Military Museum subway station on Line 1; turn left out of Exit D of the subway station, then left again and keep walking (15 minutes).

INTERNATIONAL TRAINS

Mongolia

Two, sometimes three direct weekly trains leave from Běijīng Train Station to the Mongolian capital of Ulaanbaatar (乌兰巴托; Wūlánbātuō): the **Trans-Mongolian Railway train (K3)** (hard-sleeper/soft-sleeper/delux ¥1430/2056/2241; ☻7.45am, 30hr) goes via Ulaanbaatar en route to Moscow, and leaves every Wednesday. Meanwhile the **K23** service has a train which leaves on Tuesdays (¥1430/2056/2241, ☻8.05am, 30hr) plus one which leaves on Saturdays (¥1472/2056/2202, ☻8.05am, 30hr). In the summer, both trains usually run, but at other times of the year it is only one or the other. Double check at the CITS office.

In the other direction, the **K4** leaves Ulaanbaatar at 7.15am on Tuesday and arrives in Běijīng at 2.04pm on Wednesday. The **K24** departs from Ulaanbaatar at 8.05am on either Thursday, Friday or both days, and reaches Běijīng the following day at 2.04pm.

Russia

The Trans-Siberian Railway runs from Běijīng to Moscow (莫斯科; Mòsīkē) via two routes: the aforementioned **Trans-Mongolian Railway train (K3)** (hard-sleeper/soft-sleeper/delux ¥4049/5962/6527) and the **Trans-Manchurian Railway train (K19)** (hard-sleeper/delux ¥4473/6953). The K19 leaves Běijīng Train Station every Saturday at 11pm. It arrives in Moscow on Friday at 5.58pm. The return **K20** leaves Moscow at 11.55pm on Saturday and arrives in Běijīng on Friday at 5.32am.

Vietnam

There are two weekly trains from Běijīng to Hanoi (河内; Hénèi). The **T5** (M2 in Vietnam) leaves Běijīng West Train Station at 3.45pm on Thursday and Sunday, arriving in Hanoi at 8.10am on Saturday and Wednesday.

In the other direction, the **T6** (M1 in Vietnam) leaves Hanoi at 6.30pm on Tuesday and Friday and arrives at Běijīng West at 12.07pm on Friday and Monday. Only soft-sleeper tickets (¥2390) are available.

By the time you read this, though, Line 9 should be connected to the rest of the subway network.

BUS

Public buses leave from the right of the station as you exit. Useful **Bus 52** heads east past Xīdàn, Běijīng Train Station and Jiànguómén.

TAXI

Use the official taxi rank (underneath North Plaza) or walk a block away from the station and hail a cab on the street. Ignore drivers who approach you. Insist drivers use the meter (打表; dǎbiǎo).

Běijīng South Train Station

The ultra-modern **Běijīng South Station** (南站; Nán Zhàn), which is linked to the subway system on Line 4, accommodates very high speed 'bullet' trains to destinations such as Tiānjīn, Shànghǎi, Hángzhōu and Qīngdǎo.

Fúzhōu 福州 D-series, second-class seat ¥676, 15 hours (7.50am)

Hángzhōu 杭州 G-series, second-class seat ¥631, six hours (regular)

Jǐ'nán 济南 G-series, second-class seat ¥185, 1½ hours (regular)

Nánjīng 南京 G-series, second-class seat ¥445, four hours (regular)

Qīngdǎo 青岛 G- and D-series, second-class seat ¥250 to ¥315, five hours (regular)

Shànghǎi (Hóngqiáo station) 上海虹桥 G-class trains, second-class seat, ¥555, 5½ hours (regular)

Sūzhōu 苏州 G-series, second-class seat ¥525, five hours (regular)

Tiānjīn 天津 C-series, ¥55, 30 minutes (regular)

Běijīng North Train Station

The smaller **Běijīng North Station** (北站; Běi Zhàn) is a short walk north of Xizhimen subway station.

Hohhot 呼和浩特 K-series, hard-sleeper ¥137, nine hours (11.47pm)

Bādǎlǐng Great Wall 八达岭 Hard-/soft-seat ¥7/10, 75 minutes (regular)

Bus

There are numerous long-distance bus stations, but no international bus routes to Běijīng.

North Korea

There are four weekly services to Pyongyang (平壤; Píngrǎng; hard-sleeper ¥1164 to ¥1214, soft-sleeper ¥1692 to ¥1737). The **K27** and **K28** both leave twice a week from Běijīng Train Station, meaning there's a train on Monday, Wednesday, Thursday and Saturday. Each train leaves at 5.30pm and arrives the following day at 7.30pm.

Return trains leave from Pyongyang at 10.10am on Monday, Wednesday, Thursday and Saturday and arrive the following day in Běijīng at 8.31am.

Visas, Tickets & Tours

Visas aren't available at these border crossings. Ensure you arrange yours beforehand. You can't buy international tickets at train stations in Běijīng. You'll have to go through a travel agency. For Mongolia, Russia and Vietnam, buy tickets at the helpful office of the state-owned **CITS** (China International Travel Service; Zhōngguó Guójì Lǚxíngshè; ✆6512 0507; 9 Jianguomennei Dajie, Běijīng International Hotel, Dōngchéng; ◷9am-noon & 1.30pm-5pm Mon-Fri, 9am-noon Sat-Sun), housed round the back of the left-hand side of the lobby of the Běijīng International Hotel (北京国际饭店; Běijīng Guójì Fàndiàn), one block north of Běijīng Train Station.

Trans-Siberian/Mongolian/Manchurian tickets can be bought from home, using **Intourist Travel** (www.intourist.com), which has branches in the UK, the USA, Canada, Finland and Poland.

For North Korea, buy tickets at the office of **CRTS** (China Railway Travel Service; 中国铁道旅行社; Zhōngguó Tiědào Lǚxíngshè; ✆5182 6541; 20 Beifengwo Lu, 北蜂窝路20号; ◷9am-4pm). There's no English sign, but it's opposite the easy-to-spot Tiānyòu Hotel (天佑大厦; Tiānyòu Dàxià). Walk straight out of Exit C1 of Military Museum subway station, take the first right and CRTS will be on your left (10 minutes).

For help with booking a tour to North Korea, Běijīng's leading tour company to the area is **Koryo Tours** (www.koryogroup.com).

Bāwángfén Long-distance Bus Station

Bāwángfén Long-distance Bus Station (八王坟长途客运站; Bāwángfén Chángtú Kèyùnzhàn; 17 Xidawang Lu) is in the east of town, 500m south of Dawanglu subway station. Destinations include the following:

Bāotóu 包头 Sleeper ¥181, 12 hours, one daily (6pm)

Chángchūn 长春 ¥320, 12 hours, one daily (6pm)

Dàlián 大连 ¥326, 8½ hours, two daily (noon and 10pm)

Hā'ěrbīn 哈尔滨 ¥301, 14 hours, once daily but only if enough passengers (5.30pm)

Shěnyáng 沈阳 ¥165, nine hours, regular (8am to 10pm)

Tiānjīn 天津 ¥35, two hours, regular (9.30am to 6.30pm)

Sìhuì Long-distance Bus Station

Sìhuì Long-distance Bus Station (六里桥长途站; Liùlǐqiáo Chángtúzhàn; 四惠长途汽车站; Sìhuì Chángtú Qìchēzhàn; Jianguo Lu) is in the east of town, 200m east of Sihui subway station. Destinations include the following:

Bāotóu 包头 ¥180, 12 hours, one daily (10.30am)

Chéngdé 承德 ¥85, four hours, regular (7am to 4pm)

Dāndōng 丹东 ¥220, 12 hours, one daily (4pm)

Jìxiàn 蓟县 ¥30, two hours, regular (6.40am to 7.20pm)

Liùlǐqiáo Long-distance Bus Station

Liùlǐqiáo Long-distance Bus Station (六里桥长途站; Liùlǐqiáo Chángtúzhàn) is in the southwest of town, one subway stop from Běijīng West Train Station. Destinations include the following:

Dàtóng 大同 ¥133, 4½ hours, regular (7.10am to 6pm)

Héféi 合肥 ¥380, 13 hours, one daily (1.45pm)

Luòyáng 洛阳 ¥148, 10 hours, one daily (7.30pm)

Shíjiāzhuāng 石家庄 ¥83, 3½ hours, two daily (8am and 5.30pm)

Xiàmén 厦门 ¥580, 30 hours, every other day (11am)

Xī'ān 西安 ¥298, 12 hours, one daily (5.45pm)

Zhèngzhōu 郑州 Seat/sleeper ¥128/158, 8½ hours, seat 8.30am, sleeper 7pm and 9pm

Liánhuāchí Long-distance Bus Station

Liánhuāchí Long-distance Bus Station (莲花池长途汽车站; Liánhuāchí Chángtú Qìchēzhàn) is a short walk north of Liùlǐqiáo Long-distance Bus Station. Destinations include the following:

Ānyáng 安阳 ¥120, 6½ hours, 8am to 7pm (regular)

Luòyáng 洛阳 ¥150, 11 hours, one daily (6.30pm)

Yán'ān 延安 ¥251, 14 hours, one daily (2.30pm)

Zhàogōngkǒu Long-distance Bus Station

Zhàogōngkǒu Long-distance Bus Station (赵公口汽车站; Zhàogōngkǒu Qìchēzhàn) is in the south, 10 minutes walk west of Liujiayao subway station. Destinations include the following:

Tiānjīn 天津 ¥30-35, two hours, regular (7am-6pm)

Shànghǎi 上海 ¥340, 16 hours (4.30pm)

Jǐnán 济南 ¥129, 5½ hours four daily (6am, 8am, 11am and 12.40pm)

Ferry

Tánggū Port

The nearest major port is **Tánggū Port** (塘沽港; Tánggū Gǎng), 160km from Běijīng. Take an express train from Běijīng South Train Station to Tánggū (2nd-/1st-/deluxe-class seat ¥66/80/112, 55 minutes, hourly from 7.20am to 8.20pm), then bus 102 to the port. There's a weekly ferry to **Kōbe** (神户; Shénhù; from ¥1700, 52 hours, 8pm Friday) in Japan, (日本; Rìběn) and two weekly ferries to **Incheon** (仁川; Rénchuān; from ¥1300, 27 hours, 11am Thursday and Sunday) in South Korea (韩国; Hánguó). There's also a daily overnight ferry to Dàlián (大连; ¥308 to ¥1280, 12 hours, 7pm) in China's Liáoníng province.

GETTING AROUND BĚIJĪNG

Bicycle

Cycling is the most enjoyable way of getting round Běijīng. The city is as flat as a mah jong table and almost every road has a bike lane. The quiet, tree-lined *hútòng* (alleys) are particularly conducive to cycling.

Bike Rental

The following are good options for renting bicycles (租自行车; *zū zìxíngchē*):

Bike Běijīng (康多自行车租赁; Kāngduō Zìxíngchē Zūlìn; ☎6526 5857; www.bicyclekingdom.com; 34 Donghuangchenggen Nanjie, 东皇城根南街34号; ⏲9am-7pm; [S]China Museum of Art)

Natooke (耍（自行车店）; Shuǎ (Zìxíngchē Diàn); www.natooke.com; 19-1 Wudaoying Hutong, 五道营胡同19－1号; ⏲10am-7pm; [S]Yonghegong-Lama Temple)

Bike repair stands around the Hòuhǎi lakes also rent bikes (per hour ¥10). Hostels typically charge ¥30 per day for a standard town bike.

Buying a Bike

Giant (捷安特; Jié'āntè; 77 Jiaodaokoudong Dajie, 交道口东大街77号; ⏲9am-7pm; [S]Beixinqiao) For new bikes and equipment.

JH 2nd-hand Bike Shop (金典新桥信托商行; Jīndiǎn Xīnqiáo Xìntuō Shàngháng; 43 Dongsibei Dajie, 东四北大街43号; ⏲9am-5pm; [S]Beixinqiao) For classic old bone-rattlers.

Bike-Sharing Scheme

Běijīng's new bike-sharing scheme was just being unveiled at the time of research. Initially open only to Chinese nationals, there were plans to open it to foreigners at a later date, so check once you arrive here. To use the bikes, you must have an ordinary Běijīng **travel card** (交通一卡通; jiāotōng yīkǎtōng; refundable deposit ¥20) that is activated for bike-rental use.

At the time of research the two most convenient places in which to get your travel card activated were at subway stations. One was by Exit A2 of Tiantan Dongmen subway station. The other was by Exit A of Dongzhimen subway station. Both desks were only open Monday to Friday from 9.30am to 11.30am and from 2pm to 4pm, but once you had a card activated you could use the bikes any time.

You need to pay a ¥400 deposit to activate the card for bike use, and then ensure it has at least ¥30 on it.

Bike-sharing kiosks are dotted around the city. Simply swipe your card at one of them to get a bike; then swipe again when you put it back. Bike use is free for the first hour, so if you use them cleverly, swapping bikes at another kiosk before you hour is up, it means free bikes! After the first hour, it's ¥1 per hour to begin with, rising in price to ¥2, ¥3 or ¥4 per hour, depending on how long you keep the bike for.

Subway

Massive, and growing, the **Běijīng subway system** (地铁; dìtiě; www.bjsubway.com; per trip ¥2; ⏲6am-11pm) is modern, easy to use and cheap. Get a **travel card** (交通一卡通; jiāotōng yīkǎtōng; refundable deposit ¥20) if you don't fancy queuing for tickets for each trip. The card won't make trips any cheaper, but it will get you a 60% discount on all bus journeys within Běijīng.

To recognise a subway station (地铁站; *dì tiě zhàn*) look for the subway symbol, which is a blue English capital 'D' with a circle around it.

There's a pull-out subway map at the back of this book.

Taxi

Taxis (出租车; *chūzūchē*) are everywhere, although finding one can be a problem during rush hour and rainstorms, and between around 8pm and 10pm – prime time for people heading home after eating out at a restaurant.

Flag fall is ¥10, and lasts for three kilometres. After that it's ¥2 per kilometre. Drivers also add a small flat-rate fuel surcharge (usually ¥3). Rates increase slightly at night.

Drivers rarely speak any English so it's important to have the name and address of where you want to go written down in Chinese characters. And always remember to keep your hotel's business card on you so you can get home at the end of the night.

By law, taxi drivers must use the meter (打表; dǎbiǎo). If they refuse, get out and find another cab. The exception is for long, out-of-town trips to, say, the Great Wall, where prices are agreed (but not paid for!) beforehand.

Taxi Drivers & Companies

Miles Meng (☑137 1786 1403; www.beijingtourvan.blog.sohu.com) Friendly, reliable, English-speaking driver with various decent vehicles. Prices for day-long trips to the Great Wall start at ¥600 per vehicle (for the Mùtiányù Great Wall area), and he can drop you at one part of the Wall and pick you up at another to allow for hikes. See his blog for more prices.

Mr Sun (孙先生; Sūn Xiānsheng; ☑136 5109 3753) Only speaks Chinese but is very reliable and can find other drivers if he's busy. Does round trips to the Wall from ¥600.

Xīn Lǔchéng (新旅程; ☑6235 5003) Local taxi company. Does round trips to the Great Wall for around ¥500. No English spoken.

Shǒuqì Jítuán (☑139 1137 3093) Local taxi company. Does round trips to the Great Wall for around ¥700. No English spoken.

Bus

Běijīng's buses (公共汽车; gōnggòng qìchē) have always been numerous and dirt cheap (from ¥1), but they're now becoming easier to use for non-Chinese-speaking visitors, with swipe cards, announcements in English, and bus stop signs written in Pīnyīn as well as Chinese characters. Nevertheless, it's still a challenge to get from A to B successfully, and the buses are still as packed as ever, so you rarely see foreigners climbing onboard.

If you use a travel card (p248), you get 60% discount on all journeys. Useful routes:

1 Runs along Chang'an Jie, Jianguomenwai Dajie and Jianguomennei Dajie: Sihuizhan, Bawangfen, Yong'anli, Dongdan, Xidan, Muxidi, Junshi Bowuguan, Gongzhufen, Maguanying

4 Runs along Chang'an Jie, Jianguomenwai Dajie and Jianguomennei Dajie: Gongzhufen, Junshi Bowuguan, Muxidi, Xidan, Tiananmen West, Dongdan, Yong'anli, Bawangfen, Sihuizhan

5 Deshengmen, Di'anmen, Beihai Park, Xihuamen, Zhongshan Park, Qianmen

15 Běijīng Zoo, Fuxingmen, Xidan, Hepingmen, Liulichang, Tianqiao

20 Běijīng South Train Station, Tianqiao, Dashilar, Tiananmen Sq, Wangfujing, Dongdan, Běijīng Train Station

44 outer ring Xinjiekou, Xizhimen, Fuchengmen, Fuxingmen, Changchunjie, Xuanwumen, Qianmen, Taijichang, Chongwenmen, Dongbianmen, Chaoyangmen, Dongzhimen, Andingmen, Deshengmen, Xinjiekou

52 Běijīng West Train Station, Muxidi, Fuxingmen, Xidan, Gate of Heavenly Peace, Dongdan, Běijīng Train Station, Jianguomen

103 Běijīng Train Station, Dengshikou, China Art Gallery, Forbidden City (north entrance), Beihai Park, Fuchengmen, Běijīng Zoo

332 Běijīng Zoo, Weigongcun, Renmin Daxue, Zhongguancun, Haidian, Běijīng University, Summer Palace

These double-decker routes may also be useful:

2 Qianmen, north on Dongdan Beidajie, Dongsi Nandajie, Dongsi Beidajie, Lama Temple, Zhonghua Minzu Yuan (Ethnic Minorities Park), Asian Games Village

3 Jijia Miao (the southwest extremity of the Third Ring Rd), Grand View Garden, Leyou Hotel, Jingguang New World Hotel, Tuanjiehu Park, Agricultural Exhibition Center, Lufthansa Center

4 Běijīng Zoo, Exhibition Center, Second Ring Rd, Holiday Inn Downtown, Yuetan Park, Fuxingmen Dajie flyover, Qianmen Xidajie, Qianmen

Rickshaw

Rickshaws (三轮车; sānlúnchē) are now less common, particularly in the city centre, but you'll still see them (both cycle-powered and motorised) around major tourist sights. They're fun, but they're generally more expensive than taxis, and for eign tourists are often heavily overcharged. If you do take one, make sure you are clear about the pre-agreed price (writing it down is a good idea), and about which currency you are negotiating in.

Hútòng Tours

Rickshaw tours (45 minutes, per person ¥60) can be taken around the Hòuhǎi Lakes and around the alleys by the Drum Tower, but they're really aimed at tour groups and riders don't speak English.

Directory A–Z

Business Hours

China officially has a five-day working week. Saturday and Sunday are both holidays, but much remains open at weekends.

Banks Banks, offices and government departments are normally open Monday to Friday, roughly from 9am until 5pm or 6pm (some closing for two hours in the middle of the day). Some banks have branches that are open at weekends as well. Bank of China branches are generally open weekdays from 9am to noon and 2pm to 4.30pm. Foreign-card-friendly ATMs are plentiful. Travel agencies, foreign-exchange counters in tourist hotels and some of the local branches of the Bank of China have similar opening hours, but are generally open on weekends as well, at least in the morning.

Museums & Parks Most Běijīng museums stay open on weekends and close on one weekday (usually Monday). Museums tend to stop selling tickets half an hour before they close.

Parks are generally open from 6am to around 9pm or later, although they can open later and shut earlier in winter. Opening hours for sights are listed under each entry in the Neighbourhoods chapter.

Shops & Restaurants Shops are generally open from 10am to 9pm, seven days a week, while restaurants tend to run from 11am to 11pm, although some shut in the afternoon between the hours of 2pm and 5.30pm. Some restaurants open specifically for breakfast too (typically from 6am to 8.30am) The only time some restaurants might completely close is for the week around Chinese New Year.

Internet Cafes Usually 24/7.

Bars Běijīng's entertainment sector is working increasingly long hours, and it's possible to find something to eat and somewhere to drink at any hour of the day. Some smaller bars may stay closed on Mondays.

Customs Regulations

Chinese customs generally pay tourists little attention. There are clearly marked 'green channels' (nothing to declare) and 'red channels' (something to declare) at the airport.

Duty Free You're allowed to import up to 400 cigarettes or the equivalent in tobacco products, 1.5L of alcohol and 50g of gold or silver. Importation of fresh fruit and meat is prohibited. There are no restrictions on the importation of foreign currency; however, you should declare any cash that exceeds US$5000 (or its equivalent in another currency).

DVDs Pirated DVDs and CDs are illegal exports from China as well as illegal imports into most other countries. If they are found by the authorities, they will be confiscated.

Antiques Objects considered to be antiques require a certificate and red seal to clear customs. To get the proper certificate and seal, your antiques must be inspected by the **Relics Bureau** (Wénwù Jiàndìng; ☑6401 4608), where no English is spoken. Anything made before 1949 is considered an antique and needs a certificate, and if it was made before 1795 it cannot legally be taken out of the country.

Discount Cards

Student Cards An International Student Identity Card (ISIC; www.isiccard.com) may be useful as you could get half-price entry to some sights. Chinese signs at most sights clearly indicate that students pay half price – so push the point. If you are studying in China, your school will issue you with a student card, which is more useful for discounts on admission charges.

Seniors People over the age of 65 are frequently eligible for a discount, so make sure you take your passport with you as proof of age when visiting sights.

Free Sights Tickets must be purchased for most sights in Běijīng and beyond, although more and more museums now carry free entrance (you will need to show your passport, though), and places like parks are so cheap they are as good as free.

Museum Pass The annual ¥120 Běijīng Museum Pass is a good investment if you're staying awhile.

Travel Card It's also worth getting hold of a free travel card (¥20 deposit) at any subway station or large bus station. It makes subway travel more convenient (although not any cheaper) and gives you 60% off all bus rides you take, including those out to the Great Wall.

Electricity

220V/50Hz

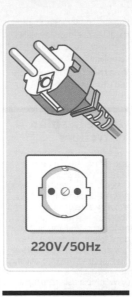

220V/50Hz

Embassies & Consulates

Embassies (大使馆; *dàshǐguǎn*) in Běijīng are open from 9am to noon and from 1.30pm to 4pm Monday to Friday, but visa departments, which are often in separate office blocks these days (check the embassy website), are sometimes only open in the morning. There are three main embassy areas: Jiànguóménwài, Sānlǐtún and Liàngmǎqiáo.

Note, it has become increasingly common in recent years for embassies to turn down visa applications from foreigners who do not live in China. It's always preferable to arrange visas from your home country, if at all possible.

Jiànguóménwài Area

Indian Embassy (印度大使馆; ☑8531 2500; www.indianembassy.org.cn; Ritan Donglu; 日坛东路)

Irish Embassy (爱尔兰大使馆; ☑6532 2691; www.embassyofireland.cn; 3 Ritan Donglu, 日坛东路3号)

Mongolian Embassy (蒙古大使馆; ☑6532 1203; www.mongolembassychina.org; 2 Xiushui Beijie, 建国门外大街秀水北街2号) Near Jianguomenwai Dajie.

New Zealand Embassy (新西兰大使馆; ☑8532 7000; www.nzembassy.com/china; 1 Ritan Dong'erjie, 日坛北路日坛东二街1号, off Ritandong Lu)

Singapore Embassy (新加坡大使馆; ☑6532 1115; www.mfa.gov.sg/beijing; 1 Xiushui Beijie, 建国门外大街秀水北街1号) Near Jianguomenwai Dajie

Thai Embassy (泰国大使馆; ☑6532 1749; www.thaiembassy.org; 40 Guanghua Lu, 光华路40号)

UK Embassy Consular Section (英国大使馆; ☑8529 6083; 21st fl, Kerry Center, 1 Guanghua Lu, 光华路1号家里中心21层)

Vietnamese Embassy (越南大使馆; ☑6532 1155; 32 Guanghua Lu, 光华路32号)

Sānlǐtún Area

Australian Embassy (澳大利亚大使馆; ☑5140 4111; www.austemb.org.cn; 21 Dongzhimenwai Dajie, 东直门外大街21号)

Cambodian Embassy (柬埔寨大使馆; ☑6532 1889; 9 Dongzhimenwai Dajie, 东直门外大街9号)

Canadian Embassy (加拿大大使馆; ☑5139 4000; www.beijing.gc.ca; 19 Dongzhimenwai Dajie, 东直门外大街19号)

German Embassy (德国大使馆; ☑8532 9000; www.china.diplo.de; 17 Dongzhimenwai Dajie, 东直门外大街17号)

Italian Embassy (意大利大使馆; ☑8532 7600; www.ambpechino.esteri.it; 2 Sanlitun Dong'erjie, 三里屯东二街)

Laotian Embassy (老挝大使馆; ☑6532 1224; 11 Sanlitun Dongsijie, 三里屯东四街11号)

Nepalese Embassy (尼泊尔大使馆; ☑6532 1795; www.nepalembassy.org.cn; 1 Sanlitun Xiliujie, 三里屯西六街)

Netherlands Embassy (荷兰大使馆; ☑8532 0200; www.hollandinchina.org; 4 Liangmahe Nanlu, 亮马河南路4号)

South African Embassy (南非洲大使馆; ☑8532 0000; www.saembassy.org.cn; 5 Dongzhimenwai Dajie, 东直门外大街5号)

Liàngmǎqiáo Area

Japanese Embassy (日本大使馆; ☑8531 9800; www.cn.emb-japan.go.jp; 1 Liangmaqiaodong Jie, 亮马桥东街1号)

South Korean Embassy (韩国大使馆; ☑8351 0700; www.china.koreanembassy.cn; 20 Dongfang Donglu, 亮马桥第三使馆区东方东路, off Liangmaqiao Lu)

US Embassy (美国大使馆; ☑Consular 8531 3300, Embassy 8531 3000; http://beijing.usembassy-china.org.cn; 55 Anjialou Lu, 亮马桥安家楼路55号, off Liangmaqiao Lu)

Other Areas

Russian Embassy (俄罗斯大使馆; ☑6532 1381; www.russia.org.cn; 4 Dongzhimen Beizhongjie, 东直门内大街东直门北中街4号, off Dongzhimennei Dajie)

Emergency

Important telephone numbers in Běijīng include the following:

Ambulance (☑120)
Directory Inquiries (☑114)
Fire (☑119)
International Directory Inquiries (☑115)
Police (☑110)
Public Security Bureau (☑foreigners' section 8402 0101)
Běijīng Tourism Hotline (☑6513 0828, press 1 for English; ☉24hr) Has English-speaking operators available to answer questions and hear complaints.

Weather (☑121) In English and Chinese.

Gay & Lesbian Travellers

Even though the Chinese authorities take a dim view of homosexuality, which was officially classified as a mental disorder until 2001, a low-profile gay and lesbian scene exists in Běijīng. For an informative and up-to-date lowdown on the latest gay and lesbian hotspots in Běijīng (and the rest of China) have a look at the **Utopia** (www.utopia-asia.com/tipschin.htm) site or invest in a copy of the *Utopia Guide to China*. Another useful publication is the **Spartacus International Gay Guide** (Bruno Gmunder Verlag), a best-selling guide for gay travellers.

Health

Except for the thick layer of air pollution that sometimes blankets the city, Běijīng is a reasonably healthy city and you needn't fear tropical diseases such as malaria. Do, though, bear in mind more immediate dangers – the greatest safety issue you will probably face is crossing the road.

It's worth taking your own medicine kit so you have remedies at hand. It is advisable to take your own prescription drugs with you because they could be more expensive or hard to find in the capital. Until recently, antibiotics (kàngjūnsù), sleeping pills (ānmiányào), antidepressants and other medications could be picked up prescription-free from many chemists in Běijīng, but this is no longer the case. If you require a specific type of drug, ensure you take an adequate supply. When looking for medications in Běijīng, make sure you take along the brand and the generic name so that pharmacy staff can locate it for you.

Vaccinations

Proof of vaccination for Yellow Fever is required if entering China within six days of visiting an infected country. If you are travelling to China from Africa or South America, check with a travel medicine clinic about whether you need the vaccine.

The following vaccinations are recommended for those travelling to China:

Adult diphtheria/tetanus (ADT) A booster is recommended if it is more than 10 years since your last shot. Side effects include a sore arm and fever.

Hepatitis A One shot provides almost 100% protection for up to a year; a booster after 12 months provides another 20 years' protection. Mild side effects include a sore arm, fever and headaches.

Hepatitis B Now considered a routine vaccination for most travellers. Given as three shots over six months, this vaccine can be combined with Hepatitis A (Twinrix). In most people the course gives lifetime protection. Mild side effects include a sore arm and headaches.

Measles/mumps/rubella (MMR) Two lifetime doses of MMR are recommended unless you have had the diseases. Many adults under the age of 35 require a booster. Occasionally a rash and flu-like illness occur about a week after vaccination.

Typhoid Needed if spending more than two weeks in China. A single injection provides around 70% protection for two to three years.

Varicella (chickenpox) If you haven't had chickenpox,

discuss this vaccine with your doctor. Chickenpox can be a serious disease in adults and has such complications as pneumonia and encephalitis.

Under certain circumstances, or for those at special risk, the following vaccinations are recommended. Discuss these with a doctor who specialises in travel medicine.

Influenza If you are over 50 years of age or have a chronic medical condition such as diabetes, lung disease or heart disease, you should have an influenza shot annually.

Japanese encephalitis There is risk only in the rural areas of China. Recommended if travelling to rural areas for more than a month during summer.

Pneumonia (Pneumococcal) This vaccine is recommended for travellers over 65 or those with chronic lung or heart disease. A single shot is given, with a booster in five years.

Rabies Recommended if spending more than three months in China. Three injections given over a one-month period are required.

If you are pregnant or breastfeeding, consult a doctor who specialises in travel medicine before having any vaccines.

Diseases

BIRD FLU
'Bird flu' or Influenza A (H5N1) is a subtype of the type A influenza virus. This virus typically infects birds and not humans; however, in 1997 the first documented case of bird-to-human transmission was recorded in Hong Kong. The virus has been eliminated from most of the 63 countries infected at its peak in 2006, which saw 4,000 outbreaks across the globe, but it remains endemic in Bangladesh, China, Egypt, India, Indonesia and Vietnam.

Very close contact with dead or sick birds is the principal source of infection and bird-to-human transmission does not easily occur.

Symptoms include high fever and typical influenza-like symptoms with rapid deterioration, leading to respiratory failure and often death. It is not recommended for travellers to carry antiviral drugs such as Tamiflu; rather, immediate medical care should be sought if bird flu is suspected.

There is currently no vaccine available to prevent bird flu. For up-to-date information, check the websites www.who.int/en.

HEPATITIS A
This virus is transmitted through contaminated food and water, and infects the liver, causing jaundice (yellow skin and eyes), nausea and extreme tiredness. There is no specific treatment available; you just need to allow time for the liver to heal, which might take many weeks.

HEPATITIS B
This disease is common in China and is transmitted via infected body fluids, including through sexual contact. The long-term consequences can include liver cancer and cirrhosis.

HIV & SEXUALLY TRANSMITTED INFECTIONS
The Chinese government is taking HIV seriously, and overall HIV prevalence is low in the country. However, among certain high risk groups – gay men, sex workers, people who inject

drugs – prevalence of HIV and other sexually transmitted infections is comparatively high, reaching 20% among some groups in some areas. Consistently using condoms during any sexual encounter is an effective way to protect yourself from becoming infected and you should obviously never share needles.

If you have engaged in any risky behaviour while travelling, including unprotected sex or injecting drugs, you should get a check-up immediately. You can do this at most major Chinese hospitals or at any Centre for Disease Control (疾控中心; jíkòng zhōngxīn). There's one in every district of the city, including this one just off Nanluogu Xiang: **Dōngchéng Disease Prevention & Control Centre** (东城疾控中心; Dōngchéng Jíkòng Zhōngxīn; ☑6404 0807; 5 Beibingmasi Hutong, 东城区交道口南大街北兵马司胡同5号, off Nanluoguxiang).

For up-to-date information on HIV in China, visit the website of **UNAIDS China** (www.unaids.org.cn).

INFLUENZA
Flu is common in Běijīng in winter. This virus gives you high fevers, body aches and general symptoms, such as a cough, runny nose and sore throat. Antibiotics won't help unless you develop a complication, such as pneumonia. Anyone travelling in winter could think about vaccination, but it is particularly recommended for the elderly or those with underlying medical conditions.

TRAVELLER'S DIARRHOEA

This is the most common problem faced by travellers in Asia. Most traveller's diarrhoea is caused by bacteria and thus responds rapidly to a short course of appropriate antibiotics. How soon you treat your diarrhoea will depend on individual circumstances, but it is a good idea to carry treatment in your medical kit.

TUBERCULOSIS (TB)

This is a rare disease in travellers that's contracted after prolonged close exposure to a person with an active TB infection. Symptoms include a cough, weight loss, night sweats and fevers. Children under the age of five spending more than six months in China should receive BCG (Bacillus Calmette-Guérin) vaccination. Adults are rarely immunised.

TYPHOID

This serious bacterial infection is contracted from contaminated food and water. Symptoms include high fever, headache, a cough and lethargy. The diagnosis is made via blood tests, and treatment is with specific antibiotics.

Environmental Hazards

AIR POLLUTION

Běijīng is one of the most polluted cities in the world. Although the government improved the situation prior to the 2008 Olympics and kept certain measures in place after the games (eg restricting car use), those with chronic respiratory conditions should ensure they have adequate personal medication with them in case symptoms worsen.

WATER

Don't drink the tap water or eat ice. Bottled water (but check the seal is not broken on the cap), soft drinks, alcohol and drinks made from boiled water (tea, coffee) are fine.

Internet Access

Hotels Most midrange and top-end hotels provide broadband internet access as standard for travellers who have brought laptops with them (although some charge a daily rate); many also have wi-fi areas, which are usually free of charge. Most youth hostels have computer terminals, but levy a small internet charge (around ¥10 per hour). Often they offer free access for a limited period (usually 30 minutes). Almost all hostels have free wi-fi.

Internet Cafes Internet cafes (网吧; wǎngbā) are generally easy to find, although some are tucked away down side streets and above shops. They are generally open 24 hours. Standard rates are ¥3 to ¥5 per hour, although there are usually different priced zones within each internet cafe – the common area (pǔtōng qū) is the cheapest. Rates can also vary depending on what time you go online. Smoking is often tolerated in internet cafes. Many internet cafes do not allow the use of a USB stick. The neighbourhood maps in this guidebook have handily located internet cafes marked on them with the @ icon.

Internet Cafes: procedure Internet cafes are required to see your passport before allowing you to go online, and a record of your visit may be made. You will be filmed or digitally photographed at reception by a rectangular metal box that sits on the counter of each licensed internet cafe in town. Usually you will then be given a card with a number (zhèngjiànhào) and password (mìmǎ or kǒulìng) to enter into the on-screen box before you can start.

Wi-fi Cafes It is increasingly common for Western-style bars and cafes to offer free wi-fi. Be prepared for occasionally slow connections and the sudden disappearance of sites for periods of time.

Censorship Some politically sensitive websites and some of the more popular social media websites, such as Twitter, Facebook and YouTube are blocked in China. To access such websites whilst here you will need to run your laptop or smartphone through a VPN (virtual private network).

Legal Matters

Drugs China's laws against the use of illegal drugs are harsh, and foreign nationals have been executed for drug offences (trafficking in more than 50g of heroin can result in the death penalty).

Judicial System The Chinese criminal justice system does not ensure a fair trial, and defendants are not presumed innocent until proven guilty. China conducts more judicial executions than the rest of the world combined; up to 10,000 per year (27 per day), according to some estimates. If arrested, most foreign citizens have the right to contact their embassy.

Medical Services

As the national capital, Běijīng naturally sports some of China's best medical facilities and services.

Clinics

A consultation with a doctor in a private clinic will cost between ¥200 and ¥800, depending on where you go.

It will cost ¥10 to ¥50 in a state hospital.

Bayley & Jackson Medical Center (庇利积臣医疗中心; Bìlì Jīchén Yīliáo Zhōngxīn; ☑8562 9998; www. bjhealthcare.com; 7 Ritan Donglu, Cháoyáng; ☺dental 9am-4pm Mon-Fri, medical 8.30am-6pm Mon-Sat) Full range of medical and dental services; attractively located in a courtyard next to Ritan Park. Dental check up, ¥456; medical consultation, ¥500.

Běijīng Union Hospital (协和医院; Xiéhé Yīyuàn; ☑6529 6114, emergency 6529 5284; 53 Dongdan Beidajie, Dōngchéng; ☺24hr) A recommended hospital, open 24 hours and with a full range of facilities for inpatient and outpatient care, plus a pharmacy. Head for **International Medical Services** (国际医疗部; Guójì Yīliáo Bù; ☑6529 5284, 6915 4270), a wing reserved for foreigners, which has English-speaking staff and telephone receptionists.

Běijīng United Family Hospital (和睦家医疗; Hémùjiā Yīliáo; ☑6433 3960, 24hr emergency hotline 6433 2345; www.unitedfamily hospitals.com; 2 Jiangtai Lu, Cháoyáng; ☺24hr) Can provide alternative medical treatments, along with a comprehensive range of inpatient and outpatient care. There is a critical care unit. Emergency room staffed by expat physicians.

Hong Kong International Medical Clinic (北京香港国际医务诊所; Běijīng Xiānggǎng Guójì Yīwù Zhěnsuǒ; ☑6553 2288; www.hkclinic.com; 9th fl, Office Tower, Hong Kong Macau Center, Swissôtel, 2 Chaoyangmen Beidajie, Cháoyáng; ☺9am-9pm, dental 9am-7pm) Well-trusted dental and medical clinic with English-speaking staff. Includes obstetric and gynaecological services and facilities for ultrasonic scanning. Immunisations can also be performed. Prices are more reasonable than at International SOS. Full medical check-ups start from ¥2500 for men, ¥3000 for women and ¥1000 for children. Dental check-up: ¥300; medical consultation: ¥680. Has night staff on duty too, so you can call for advice round the clock.

International SOS (国际 SOS医务诊所; Guójì SOS Yīwù Zhěnsuǒ; ☑24hr alarm centre ☑6462 9100, clinic appointments ☑6462 9199, dental appointments ☑6462 0333; www.internationalsos.com; Suite 105, Wing 1, Kunsha Bldg, 16 Xinyuanli, off Xin Donglu, Cháoyáng; ☺9am-8pm Mon-Fri, 9am-6pm Sat & Sun) Offering 24-hour emergency medical care, with a high-quality clinic with English-speaking staff. Dental check up: ¥900; medical consultation: ¥1160.

Pharmacies

Pharmacies (药店; yàodiàn) are identified by a green cross. Several sizeable pharmacies on Wangfujing Dajie stock both Chinese (zhōngyào) and Western medicine (xīyào). As with many large shops in Běijīng, once you have chosen your item you are issued with a receipt that you take to the till counter (shōuyíntái) where you pay, then you return to the counter where you chose your medicine to collect your purchase. Note that many chemists are effectively open 24 hours and have a small window or slit through which you can pay for and collect medicines through the night.

Watson's (屈臣氏; Qūchénshì; CC17 Oriental Plaza, 1 Dongchang'an Jie, Dōngchéng) Has many branches and is geared towards selling cosmetics, sunscreens, deodorants and the like.

Běijīng Wángfǔjīng Pharmaceutical Store (北京王府井医药商店; Běijīng Wángfǔjīng Yīyào Shāngdiàn; ☑6524 0122; 267 Wangfujing Dajie, Dōngchéng; ☺8.30am-9pm) For a large range of Western and Chinese drugs.

Money

Rénmínbì (RMB), or 'people's money', is issued by the Bank of China. The basic unit of Chinese currency is the yuán, designated in this book by a '¥', but usually written in shops and on signs with its Chinese character (元). Yuán is also referred to colloquially as kuài or kuàiqián. There are also smaller denominations of jiǎo and fēn. Ten jiǎo – in spoken Chinese, it's known as máo – make up one yuán. Ten fēn make up one jiǎo, but these days fēn are rare because they are worth next to nothing.

ATMs

Most ATMs (取款机; qǔkuǎnjī) in Běijīng now accept foreign credit cards and bank cards connected to Plus, Cirrus, Visa, MasterCard and Amex; there could be a small withdrawal charge levied by your bank (or the local bank).

The following banks have extensive ATM networks:

Bank of China (中国银行; Zhōngguó Yínháng)

Industrial and Commercial Bank of China (ICBC) (工商银行; Gōngshāng Yínháng)

China Construction Bank (中国建设银行; Zhōngguó Jiànshè Yínháng)

Agricultural Bank of China (ABC) (中国农业银行; Zhōngguó Nóngyè Yínháng)

ATM screens almost always offer the choice of English or Chinese operation. There are ATMs in the arrivals hall at Capital Airport, and in many large department stores and hotels. We've marked some handy ATMs on our maps.

Banks

Bank of China (中国银行; Zhōngguó Yínháng; ☎6513 2214; 19 Dong'anmen Dajie, 东城区东安门大街19号, Dōngchéng District) By the Dōnghuámén Night Market, this is one of dozens of branches around Běijīng with money-changing facilities.

HSBC (汇丰银行; Huìfēng Yínháng; ☎6526 0668, nation-wide 800 820 8878; www.hsbc.com.cn; 1st fl, Block A, COFCO Plaza, 8 Jianguomennei Dajie, Dōngchéng; ☺9am-5pm Mon-Fri, 10am-6pm Sat) One of four branches in the capital.

Changing Money

Foreign currency can be changed at large branches of banks, such as the Bank of China, CITIC Industrial Bank, ICBC and the China Construction Bank, at the airport, money-changing counters of hotels and at several department stores, as long as you have your passport. You should be able to change foreign currency into rénmínbì at foreign-exchange outlets and banks at large international airports outside China, but rates may be poor. Hotels usually give the official rate, but some will add a small commission. Some upmarket hotels will change money for their own guests only.

Keep at least a few ex-change receipts if you want to change any remaining rénmínbì back into another currency at the end of your trip.

Counterfeit Bills

Counterfeit notes are a problem across China, Běijīng in-cluded. Very few shopkeep-ers will accept a ¥50 or ¥100 note without first running it under an ultraviolet light.

Credit Cards

Credit is not big in China. The older generation doesn't like debt, however short-term. Although it is increasingly fashionable for young Chinese to use credit cards, numbers remain low compared to the West. Banks like Bank of China, ICBC, China Construction Bank and Zhaoshang Bank all issue credit cards and are trying to encourage the Chinese to spend. In Běijīng, credit cards are relatively straightforward to use, but don't expect to be able to use them everywhere, and always carry enough cash. Where they are accepted, credit cards often deliver a slightly better exchange rate than in banks. Money can also be withdrawn at most ATMs on credit cards such as Visa, MasterCard and Amex. Credit cards generally can't be used to buy train tickets, but Civil Aviation Administration of China (CAAC; 中国民航; Zhōngguó Mínháng) offices readily ac-cept international Visa cards for buying air tickets.

Money Transfers

If you need cash in a dash, **Western Union** (☎800 820 8668; www.westernunion.com) arrange money transfers that arrive in just 15 minutes. Counters can be found all over town at branches of China Post and the Agricul-tural Bank of China.

Tipping

Almost no one in Běijīng asks for tips. Tipping used to be refused in restaurants, but nowadays many midrange and top-end eateries include their own (often huge) service charge; cheap res-taurants do not expect a tip. Taxi drivers do not ask for or expect tips.

Travellers Cheques

Travellers cheques cannot be used everywhere; as with credit cards, always ensure you carry enough ready cash. You should have no problem cashing them at top-end tourist hotels, but they are of little use in budget hotels and restau-rants. Bear in mind that most hotels will only cash the cheques of guests. If cash-ing them at banks, aim for the larger banks such as the Bank of China or ICBC. Some banks won't change travel-lers cheques at the weekend.

Sticking to the major companies such as Thomas Cook, Amex and Visa is advisable, particularly if you plan to travel outside Běijīng. Keep your exchange receipts so you can change your money back to its original currency when you leave.

Post

Large post offices are gen-erally open daily between 8.30am and 6pm. We've marked some on our maps. You can also post letters via your hotel reception desk, or at green post boxes around town.

Letters and parcels marked 'Poste Restante, Běijīng Main Post Office' will arrive at the **International Post Office** (国际邮电局; Guójì Yóudiàn Jú; ☎6512 8114; Jianguomen Beidajie, Cháoyáng; ☺8.30am-6pm), 200m north of Jianguomen Station. Outsized parcels going overseas should be sent from here (parcels can be bought at the post of-fice); smaller parcels (up to around 20kg) can go from smaller post offices. Both outgoing and incoming packages will be opened and inspected. If you're send-ing a parcel, don't seal the package until you've had it inspected.

Letters take around a week to reach most overseas destinations. China charges extra for registered mail, but offers cheaper postal rates for printed matter, small packets, parcels, bulk mail-ings and so on.

Express Mail Service

(EMS; 快递; *kuàidì*) is available for registered deliveries to domestic and international destinations from most post offices around town. Prices are very reasonable.

Courier Companies

Several private couriers in Běijīng offer international express posting of documents and parcels, and have reliable pick-up services as well as drop-off centres:

DHL (敦豪快递; Dūnháo Kuàidì; ☑800 810 8000, ☑5790 5288; www.cn.dhl.com; Unit C18, 9 Jiuxianqiao Beilu, Cháoyáng, 朝阳区酒仙桥北路9号) This branch, beside Běijīng's 798 Art District is one of five, all on the outskirts of town.

FedEx (Federal Express; 联邦快递; Liánbāng Kuàidì; ☑6438 5560, toll free landline ☑800 988 1888, toll free mobile phones ☑400 886 1888; www.fedex.com/cn; Room 101, Tower C, Lonsdale Center, 5 Wanhong Lu, Cháoyáng, 朝阳区万红路5号蓝涛中心C座101; ☺9am-9pm Mon-Sat) One of four branches in Běijīng. FedEx also has self-service counters in Kodak Express shops around town.

United Parcel Service (UPS快递; UPS Kuàidì; ☑800 820 8388, ☑6505 5005; www.ups.com; Room 1822, China World Tower 1,1 Jianguomenwai Dajie, Cháoyáng, 朝阳区建国门外大街1号国际贸易中心1座1822室; ☺9am-6pm Mon-Fri) One of 11 branches in Běijīng.

Public Holidays

China has 11 national holidays:

New Year's Day 1 January
Chinese New Year 10 February 2013, 31 January 2014
International Women's Day 8 March

Tomb Sweeping Festival 5 April
International Labour Day 1 May
Youth Day 4 May
International Children's Day 1 June
Birthday of the Chinese Communist Party 1 July
Anniversary of the Founding of the People's Liberation Army 1 August
Moon Festival end of September
National Day 1 October

Many of the above are nominal holidays that do not result in leave. The 1 May holiday is a three-day holiday, while National Day marks a week-long holiday from 1 October; the Chinese New Year is also a week-long holiday for many. It's not a great idea to arrive in China or go travelling during these holidays as things tend to grind to a halt. Hotel prices all over China rapidly shoot up during the May and October holiday periods.

Relocating

The following international companies can help you move house in Běijīng. Rates are typically around US$500 to US$1000 per cubic metre:

Asian Express (亚洲捷运国际货运代理; Yàzhōu Jiéyùn; ☑8580 1473, ☑8580 1472, ☑8580 1471; www.aemovers.com.hk; Room 1612, Tower D, SOHO New Town, 88 Jianguo Lu, Cháoyáng)

Crown Worldwide (Crown 国际货运代理; Crown Guójì Huòyùndàilǐ; ☑5801 8088; www.crownworldwide.com; 16 Xingmao Yijie, Tōngzhōu Logistics Park, Tōngzhōu District, 通州区马驹桥兴贸一街16号) Southeast Běijīng.

Safe Travel

Generally speaking, Běijīng is a very safe city compared to other similarly sized cities around the world. Serious crime against foreigners is rare, although on the rise.

Crime Guard against pickpockets, especially on public transport and crowded places such as train stations. A money belt is the safest way to carry valuables, particularly when travelling on buses and trains. Hotels are usually safe places to leave your stuff and older establishments may have an attendant watching who goes in and out on each floor. Staying in dormitories carries its own set of risks, and while there have been a few reports of thefts by staff, the culprits are more likely to be other guests. Use lockers as much as possible.

Loss Reports If something of yours is stolen, report it immediately to the nearest Foreign Affairs Branch of the Public Security Bureau (PSB). Staff will ask you to fill in a loss report before investigating the case. If you have travel insurance it is essential to obtain a loss report so you can claim compensation. Be prepared to spend many hours, perhaps even several days, organising it. Make a copy of your passport in case of loss or theft.

Road Safety The greatest hazard may well be crossing the road, a manoeuvre that requires alertness and dexterity. It often seems like a mad scramble on the streets as vehicles squeeze into every available space. Traffic often comes from all directions (bikes, in particular, often ride the wrong way down streets), and a seeming reluctance to give way holds sway. If right of way is uncertain, drivers tend to dig in their heels. Ignore zebra crossings; cars are not obliged to stop at them, and never do. And take care at traffic light crossings; the green 'cross now' light doesn't necessarily mean that traffic won't run you down, as cars can still turn on red lights and bicycles, electric bikes and motor bikes rarely stop at red lights.

Scams

Tea Houses Be wary of anyone luring you to cafes, tea houses or art galleries on Wangfujing Dajie, Tiān'ānmén Sq and other popular tourist areas. Foreigners have been scammed by English-speaking people who invite them to vastly overpriced tea ceremonies or art shows.

Taxis At Capital Airport never take a taxi from touts inside the arrivals halls, where a well-established illegal taxi operation attempts to lure weary travellers into a ¥300-plus ride to the city (one man acts as a taxi pimp for a squad of drivers). Also beware of fraudsters trying to sell you departure tax (now included in the price of your ticket) at Capital Airport.

Rickshaws Whenever taking a ride in a rickshaw, ask the driver to write the amount down on a piece of paper first (have a pen and paper ready), so there is no ambiguity about how much the trip will cost, otherwise you could be ripped off. And be clear as to which currency you are negotiating in.

Taxes

Four- and five-star hotels add a service charge of 15%, and smarter restaurants levy a service charge of 10%. With the exception of some top-end establishments, tipping is not expected anywhere or in any situation.

Telephone

International and domestic calls can be made easily from your hotel room or from public telephones, which are plentiful. Local calls from hotel-room phones are usually free, while international calls are expensive. If making a domestic phone call, public phones at newspaper stands (报刊亭; *bàokāntíng*) and hole-in-the-wall shops (小卖部; *xiǎomàibù*) are useful; make your call and pay the owner (a local call is around five *jiǎo*). Most public phones take IC cards (p259).

When making domestic long-distance or international calls in China, it's cheapest to use an IP card (p259). Domestic long-distance and international phone calls can also be made from main telecommunications offices or 'phone bars' (*huàbā*).

The country code to use to access China is ✆86; the code for Hong Kong is ✆852 and Macau is ✆853. To call a number in Běijīng from abroad, dial the international access code (✆00 in the UK, ✆011 in the USA and so on), dial the country code (✆86) and then the area code for Běijīng (✆010), dropping the first zero, and then dial the local number. For telephone calls within the same city, drop the area code (*qūhào*).

Important city area codes within China include the following:

CITY	AREA CODE
Běijīng	010
Chéngdū	028
Chóngqìng	023
Guǎngzhōu	020
Hángzhōu	0571
Haěrbi	0451
Hong Kong	852
Jǐnán	0531
Kūnmíng	0871
Nánjīng	025
Qīngdǎo	0532
Shànghǎi	021
Shíjiāzhuāng	0311
Tiānjīn	022
Xiàmén	0592

Mobile Phones

Mobile phone shops (手机店; *shǒujīdiàn*) such as China Mobile and China Unicom sell SIM cards, which cost from ¥60 to ¥100 and include ¥50 of credit. Note that numbers containing 4s are avoided by the Chinese, making them cheaper. You can top up credit with ¥20 to ¥100 credit-charging cards (充值卡; *chōngzhí kǎ*). Cards are available from the ubiquitous newspaper kiosks and corner shops displaying the China Mobile sign.

The mobile phone you use in your home country should work (as long as it has not been locked by your network – check with your phone company before you go) or you can buy a pay-as-you-go phone locally (from ¥300). China Mobile's local, non-roaming city call charge is seven *jiǎo* per minute if calling a landline and 1.50 *jiǎo* per minute if calling another mobile phone. Receiving calls on your mobile is free from mobile phones and seven *jiǎo* from landline phones. Roaming charges cost an additional two *jiǎo* per minute and the call receiving charge is the same. Overseas calls can be made for ¥4.80 per minute plus the local charge per minute by dialling ✆17951 – then follow the instructions and add 00 before the country code. Otherwise you will be charged the International Dialling Code call charge plus seven *jiǎo* per minute.

If you have an English-speaking Chinese contact, mobile phones can be particularly useful for communicating a message to non-English speakers. Just phone your friend, tell him/

her what you want to say and hand the phone over to whoever you are trying to communicate with. Surprisingly, random strangers are rarely fazed by this.

Phonecards

For domestic calls, IC (Integrated Circuit; *IC kǎ*) cards, available from kiosks, hole-in-the-wall shops, internet cafes and China Telecom offices, are prepaid cards in a variety of denominations that can be used in most public telephones. Note that some IC cards can only be used locally while other cards can be used in phones throughout China, so check this when you purchase one.

For international calls on a mobile phone or hotel phone and for long-distance domestic calls buy an IP (Internet Phone; *IP kǎ*) card. International calls on IP cards are ¥1.80 per minute to the USA or Canada, ¥1.50 per minute to Hong Kong, Macau and Taiwan, and ¥3.20 to all other countries; domestic long-distance calls are ¥0.30 per minute. Follow the instructions on the reverse; English-language service is usually available. IP cards come in various denominations, typically with a big discount (a ¥100 card should cost around ¥40). IP cards can be found at the same places as IC cards. Again, some IP cards can only be used locally, while others can be used nationwide, so it is important to buy the right card (and check the expiry date).

Time

All of China runs on the same time as Běijīng, which is set eight hours ahead of GMT/UTC (there's no daylight saving time during summer). When it's noon in Běijīng it's 4am the same day in London; 5am in Frankfurt, Paris and Rome; noon in Hong Kong; 2pm in Melbourne; 4pm in Wellington; and, on the previous day, 8pm in Los Angeles and 11pm in Montreal and New York.

Toilets

Over the last decade the capital has made its toilets less of an assault course of foul smells and primitive appliances, but many remain pungent. Make a beeline for fast-food outlets, top-end hotels and department stores for more hygienic alternatives. Toilet paper is rarely provided in streetside public toilets so keep a stash with you. Toilets are often squat versions, although most public toilets will have one sit-down toilet for disabled users (and inflexible Westerners). As a general rule, if you see a wastebasket next to the toilet, that's where you should throw the toilet paper; otherwise the loo could choke up and flood.

Remember that the symbol for men is 男 (*nán*) and women is 女 (*nǔ*).

Tourist Information

Staff at the chain of **Běijīng Tourist Information Centers** (北京旅游咨询; Běijīng Lǚyóu Zīxún Fúwù Zhōngxīn; ⊙9am-5pm) generally have limited English-language skills and are not always helpful, but you can grab a free tourist map of town, nab handfuls of free literature and, at some branches, rustle up train tickets. Useful branches include the following:

Běijīng Train Station (☑6528 4848; 16 Laoqianju Hutong)

Capital Airport (☑6459 8148; Terminal 3, Capital Airport)

Hòuhǎi Lakes (49 Di'anmenxi Dajie, 地安门西大街49号, Hòuhǎi Lakes) Has an excellent, very detailed free map of all the hùtòng alleys surrounding the lakes of Hòuhǎi. Can also arrange rickshaw tours of the hùtòng with English-speaking riders.

Wángfǔjǐng (269 Wangfujing Dajie, 王府井大街269号, Wángfǔjǐng; ⊙9am-9pm) On the main shopping strip.

The **Běijīng Tourism Hotline** (☑6513 0828, press 1 for English; ⊙24hr) has English-speaking operators available to answer questions and hear complaints.

CITS (China International Travel Service; ☑8511 8522; www.cits.com.cn; Room 1212, CITS Bldg, 1 Dongdan Beidajie, Dōngchéng; ⊙9am-7pm) is more useful for booking tours, China-wide.

Hotels can offer you advice or connect you with a suitable tour, and some have useful tourist information desks that can point you in the right direction.

The best travel advice for independent travellers is usually dished out at youth hostels, although be aware that they will sometimes try to get you to sign up to one of their tours rather than give you impartial advice. Tours run by youth hostels are generally pretty good, though.

Travellers with Disabilities

If you are wheelchair bound or have a mobility disability, Běijīng can unfortunately be a major obstacle course. Pavements are often crowded and in a dangerous condition, with high curbs often preventing wheelchair access. Many streets can be crossed only via underground or overhead walkways with steps. You will also have to stick to the main roads, as parked cars and bicycles often occupy the pavements of smaller alleys and lanes, forcing others on to the road. Escalators in subways normally only go up, but wheelchair lifts have been installed in numerous stations (although you may have to send someone down to find a member of staff to operate them). Getting around temples and big sights such as the Forbidden City and the Summer Palace can be trying for those in wheelchairs. It is recommended that you take a lightweight chair so you can collapse it easily when necessary, such as to load it into the back of a taxi. Most, but not all, hotels will have lifts, and while many top-end hotels do have rooms for those with disabilities as well as good wheelchair access, hotel restaurants may not.

Those with sight, hearing or mobility disabilities must be extremely cautious of the traffic, which almost never yields to pedestrians.

Visas

Applying for Visas

Apart from citizens of Japan, Singapore and Brunei, all visitors to China require a visa, which covers the whole of China, although there remain restricted areas that require an additional permit from the PSB. Permits are also required for travel to Tibet, a region that the authorities can suddenly bar foreigners from entering.

Your passport must be valid for at least six months after the expiry date of your visa and you'll need at least one entire blank page in your passport for the visa.

At the time of writing, prices for a single-entry 30-day visa were as follows:
➡ £30 for UK citizens
➡ US$140 for US citizens
➡ US$30 for all other nationals
Double-entry visas:
➡ £45 for UK citizens
➡ US$140 for US citizens
➡ US$45 for all other nationals

Six-month multiple-entry visas:
➡ £90 for UK citizens
➡ US$140 for US citizens
➡ US$60 for all other nationals
A standard 30-day single-entry visa can be issued from most Chinese embassies abroad in three to five working days. Express visas cost twice the usual fee. In some countries (eg the UK and the US), the visa service has been outsourced from the Chinese embassy to a Chinese Visa Application Service Centre, which levies an extra administration fee. In the case of the UK, a single-entry visa costs £30, but the standard administration charge levied by the centre is a further £35.25, making visa applications expensive.

A standard 30-day visa is activated on the date you enter China, and must be used within three months of the date of issue. Sixty-day and 90-day travel visas are harder to get, but are still given. To stay longer, you can extend your visa in China at least once, sometimes twice.

Visa applications require a completed application form (available at the embassy or downloaded from its website) and at least one photo (51mm x 51mm). You normally pay when you collect your visa. A visa mailed to you takes up to three weeks. In the US and Canada, mailed applications have to go via a visa agent, at extra cost. In the US, many people use the **China Visa Service Center** (☑in the USA 800 799 6560; www.mychina visa.com), which offers prompt service. It takes 10 to 14 days.

Hong Kong is a good place to pick up a China visa. China Travel Service (CTS) can obtain one for you, or you can apply directly to the **Visa Office of the People's Republic of China** (☑3413 2300; 26 Harbour Rd, 7th fl, Lower Block, China Resources Centre, Wan Chai; ☺9am-noon & 2-5pm Mon-Fri). Visas processed here in one/two/three days cost HK$400/300/150.

Double-entry visas are HK$220, while six-month/one-year multiple-entry visas are HK$400/600 (plus HK$150/250 for express/urgent service). American and UK passport holders pay considerably more for their visas. You need two photos.

Note that political events can suddenly make visas more difficult to get or renew.

When asked about your itinerary on the application form, list standard tourist destinations; if you are considering going to Tibet or western Xīnjiāng, just leave it off the form. The list you give isn't binding. Those working in media or journalism may want to profess a different occupation; otherwise, a visa may be refused or may be of a shorter length than requested. There are eight visa categories (for most travellers, an L visa will be issued):

TYPE	ENGLISH NAME	CHINESE NAME
C	flight attendant	chéngwù 乘务
D	resident	dìngjū 定居
F	business or student	fǎngwèn 访问
G	transit	guòjìng 过境
J	journalist	jìzhě 记者
L	travel	lǚxíng 旅行
X	long-term student	liúxué 留学
Z	working	gōngzuò 工作

Visa Extensions

The Foreign Affairs Branch of the local PSB – the police force – handles visa extensions. The visa office at the **PSB main office** (北京公安局出入境管理处, Běijīngshì Gōng'ānjú Chūrùjìng Guǎnlǐchù; ☑8401 5292, ☑8402 0101; 2 Andingmen Dongdajie, Dōngchéng;

8.30am-4.30pm Mon-Sat) is on the 2nd floor, accessed from the north second ring road. You can also apply for a residence permit here.

First-time extensions of 30 days are usually easy to obtain on single-entry tourist visas; further extensions are harder to get, and may only give you another week. Travellers report generous extensions in provincial towns, but don't bank on this. Popping south to Hong Kong to apply for a new tourist visa is another option.

Extensions to single-entry visas vary in price, depending on your nationality. At the time of writing, US travellers paid ¥185, Canadians ¥165, UK citizens ¥160 and Australians ¥100. Expect to wait up to five days for your visa extension to be processed.

The penalty for overstaying your visa in China is up to ¥500 per day. Some travellers have reported having trouble with officials who read the 'valid until' date on their visa incorrectly. For a one-month travel (L) visa, the 'valid until' date is the date by which you must enter the country (within three months of the date the visa was issued), not the date upon which your visa expires.

Residence Permits

The 'green card' is a residence permit, issued to English teachers, foreign expats and long-term students who live in China. Green cards are issued for a period of six months to one year and must be renewed annually. Besides needing all the right paperwork, you must also pass a health exam, for which there is a charge. Families are automatically included once the permit is issued, but there is a fee for each family member. If you lose your card, you'll pay a hefty fee to have it replaced.

Passports

Chinese law requires foreign visitors to carry their passport with them at all times; it is the most basic travel document and all hotels (and, these days, internet cafes too) will insist on seeing it. You also often need it to buy train tickets or to get into some tourist sights, particularly those which are free. The Chinese government requires that your passport be valid for at least six months after the expiry date of your visa. You will need at least one entire blank page in your passport for the visa.

It's also a good idea to bring an ID card with your photo in case you lose your passport. Even better, make photocopies, or take digital photos of your passport – your embassy may need these before issuing a new one. You should also report the loss to the local PSB. Be careful who you pass your passport to, as you may never see it again.

Women Travellers

Women travellers generally feel safe in Běijīng. Chinese men are not macho and respect for women is deeply ingrained in Chinese culture.

As with anywhere else, you will be taking a risk if you travel alone. If you are concerned, a self-defence course can equip you with extra physical skills and boost your confidence before your trip. A whistle or small alarm can be a useful defence against an unpleasant encounter. If travelling to towns outside Běijīng, stick to hotels near the town centre. For further tips, consult www.oculartravel. com, which has a very useful section for women travellers. Another handy website is www.journeywoman.com.

Tampons (*wèishēng miántiáo*) can be found almost everywhere. It may be advisable to take supplies of the pill (*bìyùnyào*), although you will find brands like Marvelon at local pharmacies.

Work

Over the past decade it has become easier for foreigners to find work in Běijīng, although having Chinese-language skills is becoming increasingly important.

Teaching jobs that pay by the hour are usually quite lucrative. If you have recognised ELT qualifications, such as TEFL and/ or experience, teaching can be a rewarding and profitable way to earn a living in Běijīng. International schools offer salaries in the region of ¥6000 to ¥10,000 per month to qualified teachers, with accommodation often provided. More basic (and plentiful) teaching positions will offer upwards of around ¥100 per hour. Schools regularly advertise in Expat magazines, such as *The Beijinger*; you can visit its classified pages online at www. thebeijinger.com. Also hunt for teaching jobs on www. teachabroad.com. You could also try approaching organisations such as the **British Council** (www.britishcouncil. org) which runs teacher placement programmes in Běijīng and beyond.

There are also opportunities in translation, freelance writing, editing, proofreading, the hotel industry, acting, modelling, photography, bar work, sales and marketing, and beyond. Most people find jobs in Běijīng through word of mouth, so networking is the key.

Doing Business

Difficulties for foreigners attempting to do business have eased up, but the China work environment can still be frustrating. Renting properties, getting licences, hiring employees and paying taxes can generate mind-boggling quantities of red tape. Many foreign businesspeople who have worked in China say that success is usually the result of dogged persistence and finding cooperative officials.

If you are considering doing business in China, plenty of preliminary research is recommended. In particular, talk to other foreigners who are already working here. Alternatively, approach a firm of business consultants for advice, or approach one of the following Běijīng business associations:

American Chamber of Commerce (中国美国商会; Zhōngguó Měiguó Shānghuì; ☑8519 0800; www.amcham -china.org.cn; The Office Park, Tower AB, 6th fl, 10 Jintongxi Lu, Cháoyáng, 朝阳区金桐西路10号远洋光华国际AB座6层)

British Chamber of Commerce (中国英国商会; Zhōngguó Yīngguó Shānghuì; ☑8525 1111; www.britishcham ber.cn; Room 1001, China Life Tower, 16 Chaoyangmenwai Dajie, Cháoyáng, , 朝阳门外大街16号中国人寿大厦1001室)

Canada-China Business Council (加中贸易理事会; Jiāzhōng Màoyì Lǐshìhuì; ☑8526 1820; www.ccbc.com; Suite 11A16, Tower A, Hanwei Plaza, 7 Guanghua Road, Cháoyáng, 朝阳区光华路7号汉威大厦A座)

China-Australia Chamber of Commerce (中国澳大利亚商会; Zhōngguó Àodàlìyà Shānghuì; ☑6595 9252; www. austcham.org; 910, Tower

A, U-Town Office Building, 1 Sanfengbeili, Cháoyáng, 朝阳区三丰北里1号 悠唐写字楼A座910室)

China Britain Business Council (CBBC; 英中贸易协会; Yīngzhōng Màoyì Xiéhuì; ☑8525 1111; www.cbbc.org; Room 1001, China Life Tower, 16 Chaoyangmenwai Dajie, Cháoyáng, 朝阳区朝阳门外大街16号, 中国人寿大厦1001室)

European Union Chamber of Commerce in China (中国欧盟商会; Zhōngguó Ōuméng Shànghuì; ☑6462 2066; www.european chamber.com.cn; Room C-412, Lufthansa Center, 50 Liangma-qiao Lu, Cháoyáng, 朝阳区亮马桥路50号, 燕莎中心写字楼C-412室)

French Chamber of Commerce & Industry (中国法国工商会; Zhōngguó Fǎguó Gōngshānghuì; ☑6461 0260; www.ccifc.org; Room C-712, 7th fl, Office Building Lufthansa Center, 50 Liangmaqiao Lu, Cháoyáng, 朝阳区亮马桥路50号, 燕莎中心写字楼C-712室)

US-China Business Council (美中贸易全国委员会; Měizhōng Màoyì Quánguó Wěiyuánhuì; ☑6592 0727; www.uschina.org; ITIC Bldg, Suite 10-01, 19 Jianguomenwai Dajie, Cháoyáng, 朝阳区建国门外大街19号, 国际大厦10-01室)

Business Cards

Business cards are essential in China. Cards are exchanged much in the same way as handshakes are in the West. To be caught without a card in a business setting is like attending an official function in jeans and trainers. Try to get your name translated into (simplified) Chinese and have it printed on the reverse of the card. You can get name cards made cheaply at local printers, but it's better to have some made before you arrive (try your local Chinatown). When proffering and receiving business cards, emulate the Chinese method of respectfully using the thumb and forefinger of both hands.

Volunteering

Large numbers of Westerners work in China with international development charities such as:

VSO (www.vso.org.uk) VSO, which can provide you with useful experience and the chance to learn Chinese.

Global Vision International (GVI; www.gvi.co.uk) Teaching in China.

Global Volunteer Network (www.globalvolunteer network.org) Connecting people with communities in need.

Joy in Action (JIA; www. jia-workcamp.org) Establishing work camps in places in need in south China.

World Teach (www. worldteach.org) Volunteer teachers.

Language

Discounting its many ethnic minority languages, China has eight major dialect groups: Pǔtōnghuà (Mandarin), Yue (Cantonese), Wu (Shanghainese), Mǐnbei (Fuzhou), Mǐnnan (Hokkien-Taiwanese), Xiang, Gan and Hakka. These dialects also divide into subdialects.

It's the language spoken in Běijīng which is considered the official language of China. It's usually referred to as Mandarin, but the Chinese themselves call it Pǔtōnghuà (meaning 'common speech'). Pǔtōnghuà is variously referred to as Hànyǔ (the Han language), Guóyǔ (the national language) or Zhōngwén or Zhōngguóhuà (Chinese). You'll find that knowing a few basics in Mandarin will not only come in handy in Běijīng, but also in many other parts of the country (although it may be spoken there with a regional accent).

Writing

Chinese is often referred to as a language of pictographs. Many of the basic Chinese characters are highly stylised pictures of what they represent, but around 90% are compounds of a 'meaning' element and a 'sound' element.

A well-educated, contemporary Chinese speaker might use between 6000 and 8000 characters. To read a Chinese newspaper you need to know 2000 to 3000 characters, but 1200 to 1500 would be enough to get the gist.

Theoretically, all Chinese dialects share the same written system. In practice, Cantonese adds about 3000 specialised characters of its own and many of the dialects don't have a written form at all.

WANT MORE?

For in-depth language information and handy phrases, check out Lonely Planet's *Mandarin Phrasebook*. You'll find it at **shop.lonelyplanet.com**, or you can buy Lonely Planet's iPhone phrasebooks at the Apple App Store.

Pinyin & Pronunciation

In 1958 the Chinese adopted Pinyin, a system of writing their language using the Roman alphabet. The original idea was to eventually do away with Chinese characters. However, tradition dies hard, and the idea was abandoned.

Pinyin is often used on shop fronts, street signs and advertising billboards. However, in the countryside and the smaller towns you may not see a single Pinyin sign anywhere, so unless you speak Chinese you'll need a phrasebook with Chinese characters.

In this chapter we've provided Pinyin alongside the Mandarin script. Below is a brief guide to the pronunciation of Pinyin letters.

Vowels

a	as in 'father'
ai	as in 'aisle'
ao	as the 'ow' in 'cow'
e	as in 'her' (without 'r' sound)
ei	as in 'weigh'
i	as the 'ee' in 'meet' (or like a light 'r' as in 'Grrr!' after c, ch, r, s, sh, z or zh)
ian	as the word 'yen'
ie	as the English word 'yeah'
o	as in 'or' (without 'r' sound)
ou	as the 'oa' in 'boat'
u	as in 'flute'
ui	as the word 'way'
uo	like a 'w' followed by 'o'
yu/ü	like 'ee' with lips pursed

Consonants

c	as the 'ts' in 'bits'
ch	as in 'chop', with the tongue curled up and back
h	as in 'hay', articulated from further back in the throat
q	as the 'ch' in 'cheese'
sh	as in 'ship', with the tongue curled up and back
x	as the 'sh' in 'ship'
z	as the 'ds' in 'suds'
zh	as the 'j' in 'judge', with the tongue curled up and back

The only consonants that occur at the end of a syllable are n, ng and r.

In Pinyin, apostrophes are occasionally used to separate syllables in order to prevent ambiguity, eg the word píng'ān can be written with an apostrophe after the 'g' to prevent it being pronounced as pín'gān.

Tones

Mandarin is a language with a large number of words with the same pronunciation but a different meaning. What distinguishes these homophones (as these words are called) is their 'tonal' quality – the raising and the lowering of pitch on certain syllables. Mandarin has four tones – high, rising, falling-rising and falling, plus a fifth 'neutral' tone that you can all but ignore. Tones are important for distinguishing meaning of words – eg the word ma has four different meanings according to tone: mā (mother), má (hemp, numb), mǎ (horse), mà (scold, swear). Tones are indicated in Pinyin by the following accent marks on vowels: ā (high), á (rising), ǎ (falling-rising) and à (falling).

Basics

When asking a question it is polite to start with qǐng wèn – literally, 'May I ask?'.

Hello.	你好。	Nǐhǎo.
Goodbye.	再见。	Zàijiàn.
How are you?	你好吗？	Nǐhǎo ma?
Fine. And you?	好。你呢？	Hǎo. Nǐ ne?
Excuse me.		
(to get attention)	劳驾。	Láojià.
(to get past)	借光。	Jièguāng.
Sorry.	对不起。	Duìbùqǐ.
Yes./No.	是。/不是。	Shì./Bùshì.
Please ...	请……	Qǐng ...
Thank you.	谢谢你。	Xièxie nǐ.
You're welcome.	不客气。	Bù kèqi.

What's your name?
你叫什么名字？　　Nǐ jiào shénme míngzi?

My name is ...
我叫……　　Wǒ jiào ...

Do you speak English?
你会说英文吗？　　Nǐ huìshuō Yīngwén ma?

I don't understand.
我不明白。　　Wǒ bù míngbái.

Accommodation

Do you have a single/double room?
有没有(单人/　　Yǒuméiyǒu (dānrén/
套)房？　　tào) fáng?

To get by in Mandarin, mix and match these simple patterns with words of your choice:

How much is (the deposit)?
(押金)多少？　　(Yājīn) duōshǎo?

Do you have (a room)?
有没有(房)？　　Yǒuméiyǒu (fáng)?

Is there (heating)?
有(暖气)吗？　　Yóu (nuǎnqì) ma?

I'd like (that one).
我要(那个)。　　Wǒ yào (nàge).

Please give me (the menu).
请给我(菜单)。　　Qǐng gěiwǒ (càidān).

Can I (sit here)?
我能(坐这儿)吗？　　Wǒ néng (zuòzhèr) ma?

I need (a can opener).
我想要(一个　　Wǒ xiǎngyào (yīge
开罐器)。　　kāiguàn qì).

Do we need (a guide)?
需要(向导)吗？　　Xūyào (xiàngdǎo) ma?

I have (a reservation).
我有(预订)。　　Wǒ yǒu (yùdìng).

I'm (a doctor).
我(是医生)。　　Wǒ (shì yīshēng).

How much is it per night/person?
每天/人多少钱？　　Měi tiān/rén duōshǎo qián?

air-con	空调	kōngtiáo
bathroom	浴室	yùshì
bed	床	chuáng
campsite	露营地	lùyíngdì
cot	张婴儿床	zhāng yīng'ér chuáng
guesthouse	宾馆	bīnguǎn
hostel	招待所	zhāodàisuǒ
hotel	酒店	jiǔdiàn
window	窗	chuāng

Directions

Where's a (bank)?
(银行)在哪儿？　　(Yínháng) zài nǎr?

What's the address?
地址在哪儿？　　Dìzhǐ zài nǎr?

Could you write the address, please?
能不能请你　　Néngbúnéng qǐng nǐ
把地址写下来？　　bǎ dìzhǐ xiě xiàlái?

Can you show me where it is on the map?
请帮我找它在　　Qǐng bāngwǒ zhǎo tā zài
地图上的位置。　　dìtú shàng de wèizhi.

Go straight ahead.		
一直走。		Yìzhí zǒu.
at the traffic lights		
在红绿灯		zài hónglǜdēng
behind	背面	bèimiàn
far	远	yuǎn
in front of ...	……的前面	... de qiánmian
near	近	jìn
next to	旁边	pángbiān
on the corner	拐角	guǎijiǎo
opposite	对面	duìmiàn
Turn left.	左转。	Zuǒ zhuǎn.
Turn right.	右转。	Yòu zhuǎn.

Eating & Drinking

What would you recommend?
有什么菜可以
推荐的? — Yǒu shénme cài kěyǐ tuījiàn de?

What's in that dish?
这道菜用什么
东西做的? — Zhèdào cài yòng shénme dōngxi zuòde?

That was delicious.
真好吃。 — Zhēn hǎochī.

The bill, please!
买单! — Mǎidān!

Cheers!
干杯! — Gānbēi!

I'd like to	我想预订	Wǒ xiǎng yùdìng
reserve	一张……	yìzhāng ...
a table for ...	的桌子。	de zhuōzi.
(eight) o'clock	（八）点钟	(bā) diǎn zhōng
(two) people	（两个）人	(liǎngge) rén
I don't eat ...	我不吃……	Wǒ bùchī ...
fish	鱼	yú
nuts	果仁	guǒrén
poultry	家禽	jiāqín
red meat	牛羊肉	niúyángròu

Key Words

bar	酒吧	jiǔbā
bottle	瓶子	píngzi
bowl	碗	wǎn
breakfast	早饭	zǎofàn
cafe	咖啡屋	kāfēiwū
chidren's menu	儿童菜单	értóng càidān
(too) cold	（太）凉	(tài) liáng
dinner	晚饭	wǎnfàn
food	食品	shípǐn
fork	叉子	chāzi
glass	杯子	bēizi
highchair	高凳	gāodèng
hot (warm)	热	rè
knife	刀	dāo
local specialties	地方小吃	dìfāng xiǎochī
lunch	午饭	wǔfàn
market	菜市	càishì
menu	（英文）	(Yīngwén)
(in English)	菜单	càidān
plate	碟子	diézi
restaurant	餐馆	cānguǎn
(too) spicy	（太）辣	(tài) là
spoon	勺	sháo
vegetarian food	素食食品	sùshí shípǐn

Meat & Fish

beef	牛肉	niúròu
chicken	鸡肉	jīròu
duck	鸭	yā
fish	鱼	yú
lamb	羊肉	yángròu
pork	猪肉	zhūròu
seafood	海鲜	hǎixiān

Fruit & Vegetables

apple	苹果	píngguǒ
banana	香蕉	xiāngjiāo
carrot	胡萝卜	húluóbo
celery	芹菜	qíncài
cucumber	黄瓜	huángguā
fruit	水果	shuǐguǒ
grape	葡萄	pútáo
green beans	扁豆	biǎndòu
mango	芒果	mángguǒ
mushroom	蘑菇	mógū

Signs

入口	Rùkǒu	**Entrance**
出口	Chūkǒu	**Exit**
问讯处	Wènxùnchù	**Information**
开	Kāi	**Open**
关	Guān	**Closed**
禁止	Jìnzhǐ	**Prohibited**
厕所	Cèsuǒ	**Toilets**
男	Nán	**Men**
女	Nǚ	**Women**

onion	洋葱	yáng cōng
orange	橙子	chéngzi
pear	梨	lí
pineapple	凤梨	fènglí
plum	梅子	méizi
potato	土豆	tǔdòu
radish	萝卜	luóbo
spring onion	小葱	xiǎo cōng
sweet potato	地瓜	dìguā
vegetable	蔬菜	shūcài
watermelon	西瓜	xīguā

Other

bread	面包	miànbāo
butter	黄油	huángyóu
egg	蛋	dàn
herbs/spices	香料	xiāngliào
pepper	胡椒粉	hújiāo fěn
salt	盐	yán
soy sauce	酱油	jiàngyóu
sugar	砂糖	shātáng
tofu	豆腐	dòufu
vinegar	醋	cù
vegetable oil	菜油	càiyóu

Drinks

beer	啤酒	píjiǔ
coffee	咖啡	kāfēi
(orange) juice	(橙)汁	(chéng) zhī
milk	牛奶	niúnǎi
mineral water	矿泉水	kuàngquán shuǐ
red wine	红葡萄酒	hóng pútáo jiǔ
rice wine	米酒	mǐjiǔ
soft drink	汽水	qìshuǐ
tea	茶	chá
(boiled) water	(开)水	(kāi) shuǐ
white wine	白葡萄酒	bái pútáo jiǔ
yoghurt	酸奶	suānnǎi

Question Words

How?	怎么？	Zěnme?
What?	什么？	Shénme?
When?	什么时候	Shénme shíhòu?
Where?	哪儿	Nǎr?
Which?	哪个	Nǎge?
Who?	谁？	Shuí?
Why?	为什么？	Wèishénme?

Emergencies

Help!	救命！	Jiùmìng!
I'm lost.	我迷路了。	Wǒ mílù le.
Go away!	走开！	Zǒukāi!

Call a doctor!		
请叫医生来！		Qǐng jiào yīshēng lái!
Call the police!		
请叫警察！		Qǐng jiào jǐngchá!
I'm ill.		
我生病了。		Wǒ shēngbìng le.
It hurts here.		
这里痛。		Zhèlǐ tòng.
Where are the toilets?		
厕所在哪儿？		Cèsuǒ zài nǎr?

Shopping & Services

I'd like to buy ...		
我想买……		Wǒ xiǎng mǎi ...
I'm just looking.		
我先看看。		Wǒ xiān kànkan.
Can I look at it?		
我能看看吗？		Wǒ néng kànkan ma?
I don't like it.		
我不喜欢。		Wǒ bù xǐhuan.
How much is it?		
多少钱？		Duōshǎo qián?
That's too expensive.		
太贵了。		Tàiguì le.
Can you lower the price?		
能便宜一点吗？		Néng piányi yīdiǎn ma?
There's a mistake in the bill.		
帐单上有问题。		Zhàngdān shàng yǒu wèntí.

ATM	自动取款机	zìdòng qǔkuǎn jī
credit card	信用卡	xìnyòng kǎ
internet cafe	网吧	wǎngbā
post office	邮局	yóujú
tourist office	旅行店	lǚxíng diàn

Time & Dates

What time is it?		
现在几点钟？		Xiànzài jǐdiǎn zhōng?
It's (10) o'clock.		
(十)点钟。		(Shí) diǎn zhōng.
Half past (10).		
(十)点三十分。		(Shí) diǎn sānshífēn.

Numbers

1	一	yī
2	二/两	èr/liǎng
3	三	sān
4	四	sì
5	五	wǔ
6	六	liù
7	七	qī
8	八	bā
9	九	jiǔ
10	十	shí
20	二十	èrshí
30	三十	sānshí
40	四十	sìshí
50	五十	wǔshí
60	六十	liùshí
70	七十	qīshí
80	八十	bāshí
90	九十	jiǔshí
100	一百	yībǎi
1000	一千	yīqiān

morning	早上	zǎoshàng
afternoon	下午	xiàwǔ
evening	晚上	wǎnshàng
yesterday	昨天	zuótiān
today	今天	jīntiān
tomorrow	明天	míngtiān
Monday	星期一	xīngqī yī
Tuesday	星期二	xīngqī èr
Wednesday	星期三	xīngqī sān
Thursday	星期四	xīngqī sì
Friday	星期五	xīngqī wǔ
Saturday	星期六	xīngqī liù
Sunday	星期天	xīngqī tiān

Transport

boat	船	chuán
bus (city)	大巴	dàbā
bus (intercity)	长途车	chángtú chē
plane	飞机	fēijī
taxi	出租车	chūzū chē
train	火车	huǒchē
tram	电车	diànchē

I want to go to ...
我要去…… — Wǒ yào qù …

Does it stop at ...?
在……能下车吗? — Zài ... néng xià chē ma?

At what time does it leave?
几点钟出发? — Jǐdiǎnzhōng chūfā?

At what time does it get to ...?
几点钟到……? — Jǐdiǎnzhōng dào ...?

I want to get off here.
我想这儿下车。 — Wǒ xiǎng zhèr xiàchē.

When's the first/last (bus)?
首趟/末趟(车)几点走? — Shǒutàng/Mòtàng (chē) jǐdiǎn zǒu?

A ... ticket to (Dàlián).	一张到 (大连)的 ……票。	Yīzhāng dào (Dàlián) de ... piào.
1st-class	头等	tóuděng
2nd-class	二等	èrděng
one-way	单程	dānchéng
return	双程	shuāngchéng

aisle seat	走廊的 座位	zǒuláng de zuòwèi
ticket office	售票处	shòupiàochù
timetable	时刻表	shíkè biǎo
window seat	窗户的 座位	chuānghu de zuòwèi

bicycle pump	打气筒	dǎqìtóng
child seat	婴儿座	yīng'érzuò
helmet	头盔	tóukuī
mechanic	机修工	jīxiūgōng
petrol	汽油	qìyóu
service station	加油站	jiāyóu zhàn

I'd like to hire a ...	我要租 一辆……	Wǒ yào zū yīliàng ...
4WD	四轮驱动	sìlún qūdòng
bicycle	自行车	zìxíngchē
car	汽车	qìchē
motorcycle	摩托车	mótuōchē

Does this road lead to ...?
这条路到……吗? — Zhè tiáo lù dào ... ma?

How long can I park here?
这儿可以停多久? — Zhèr kěyi tíng duōjiǔ?

The car has broken down.
汽车是坏的。 — Qìchē shì huài de.

I have a flat tyre.
轮胎瘪了。 — Lúntāi biě le.

GLOSSARY

arhat – Buddhist, especially a monk, who has achieved enlightenment and passes to nirvana at death

běi – north; the other points of the compass are *nán* (south), *dōng* (east) and *xī* (west)

bīnguǎn – tourist hotel

bìxì – mythical tortoise-like dragons often depicted in Confucian temples

bodhisattva – one worthy of nirvana but who remains on earth to help others attain enlightenment

bówùguǎn – museum

bǔpiào – upgrade

cāntīng – restaurant

CCP – Chinese Communist Party, founded in Shànghǎi in 1921

Chángchéng – the Great Wall

chop – see *name chop*

CITS – China International Travel Service; the organisation deals with China's foreign tourists

dàfàndiàn – large hotel

dàjiē – avenue

dàshà – hotel, building

dàxué – university

dìtiě – subway

dōng – east; the other points of the compass are *běi* (north), *nán* (south) and *xī* (west)

dòngwùyuán – zoo

fàndiàn – hotel or restaurant

fēngshuǐ – geomancy, literally 'wind and water', the art of using ancient principles to maximise the flow of *qì*, or vital energy

gé – pavilion, temple (Taoist)

gōng – palace, temple

gōngyuán – park

gùjū – house, home, residence

hé – river

hú – lake

Huí – ethnic Chinese Muslims

hútòng – a narrow alleyway

jiāng – river

jiǎo – see *máo*

jiē – street

jié – festival

jīn – unit of measurement equal to 500g

jiǔdiàn – hotel

kǎoyādiàn – roast duck restaurant

kuài – colloquial term for the currency, *yuán*

Kuomintang – Chiang Kaishek's Nationalist Party, the dominant political force after the fall of the Qing dynasty

líng – tomb

lóu – tower

lù – road

luóhàn – see *arhat*

máo – colloquial term for *jiǎo*, 10 of which equal one *kuài*

mén – gate

miào – temple

name chop – a carved name seal that acts as a signature

nán – south; the other points of the compass are *běi* (north), *dōng* (east) and *xī* (west)

páilou – decorated archway

Pinyin – the official system for transliterating Chinese script into the Roman alphabet

PLA – People's Liberation Army

PRC – People's Republic of China

PSB – Public Security Bureau; the arm of the police force set up to deal with foreigners

qì – flow of vital or universal energy

qì gōng – exercise that channels *qì*

qiáo – bridge

qílín – a hybrid animal that only appeared on earth in times of harmony

rénmín – people, people's

renminbi – literally 'people's money', the formal name for the currency of China; shortened to RMB

shān – hill, mountain

shāngdiàn – shop, store

shìchǎng – market

sì – temple, monastery

sìhéyuàn – courtyard house

tíng – pavilion

wǔshù – martial arts

xī – west; the other points of the compass are *běi* (north), *nán* (south) and *dōng* (east)

yáng – positive, bright and masculine; the complementary principle to *yīn*

yīn – negative, dark and feminine; the complementary principle to *yáng*

yuán – the Chinese unit of currency; also referred to as RMB (see also *renminbi*)

zhōng – middle, centre

Behind the Scenes

SEND US YOUR FEEDBACK

We love to hear from travellers – your comments keep us on our toes and help make our books better. Our well-travelled team reads every word on what you loved or loathed about this book. Although we cannot reply individually to postal submissions, we always guarantee that your feedback goes straight to the appropriate authors, in time for the next edition. Each person who sends us information is thanked in the next edition – and the most useful submissions are rewarded with a selection of digital PDF chapters.

Visit **lonelyplanet.com/contact** to submit your updates and suggestions or to ask for help. Our award-winning website also features inspirational travel stories, news and discussions.

Note: We may edit, reproduce and incorporate your comments in Lonely Planet products such as guidebooks, websites and digital products, so let us know if you don't want your comments reproduced or your name acknowledged. For a copy of our privacy policy visit lonelyplanet.com/privacy.

OUR READERS

Many thanks to the travellers who used the last edition and wrote to us with helpful hints, useful advice and interesting anecdotes:

Carly Joanne Botterill, Christian Cantos, William Chang, Eric Danziger, Theresa Elward, Vincent Foucher, Tim Grady, Lance Hall, Grace Harris, Daniel Imrecke, Neill Ireland, Miss Lamont, Sofia Lundgren, Hayden Opie, Steve Rogowski, Jairo Romero, Johannes Röwert, Karine Van Malderen, Chet Wah, Wayne Yee

AUTHOR THANKS

Daniel McCrohan

Thank you to my darling wife Taotao and our two incredible children Dudu and Yoyo for making everything worth doing. For ideas and recommendations, huge thanks to Iain Shaw, Gil Miller, David Goodman-Smith, Mao and Sydney, Daryl Snow, Guy Taylor and Keith Bradbury. And thanks to Kevin Li for his advice on hiking the Great Wall. Much appreciation to my co-author David Eimer for all his work, and to Damian Harper for his sterling efforts on previous editions. Thanks too to Emily Wolman for her patience and support.

David Eimer

Thanks to Daniel McCrohan for his input and patience, and also to Damian Harper for his fine work on previous editions. Thanks to Emily Wolman, Barbara Delissen and Mark Griffiths at Lonely Planet for their guidance. Special gratitude goes to Li Xinying for her invaluable assistance.

ACKNOWLEDGMENTS

Illustration pp54-5 by Michael Weldon.
Cover photograph: Buddhist Fragrance Pavilion, Longevity Hill, Summer Palace; Manfred Gottschalk/LPI/Getty Images ©.

THIS BOOK

· ·

This 9th edition of Lonely Planet's *Beijing* was researched and written by Daniel McCrohan and David Eimer. The previous two editions were written by David Eimer and Damian Harper. This guidebook was commissioned in Lonely Planet's Oakland office and produced by the following:

Commissioning Editors Emily K Wolman, Kathleen Munnelly

Coordinating Editors Sam Trafford, Simon Williamson

Coordinating Cartographer Valentina Kremenchutskaya

Coordinating Layout Designer Wendy Wright

Managing Editors Barbara Delissen, Martine Power

Senior Editor Andi Jones

Managing Cartographers Adrian Persoglia, Diana Von Holdt

Managing Layout Designers Jane Hart, Kerrianne Southway

Assisting Editors Alice Barker, Adrienne Costanzo, Andrea Dobbin, Kate Kiely, Anne Mulvaney, Erin Richards

Cover Research Naomi Parker

Internal Image Research Nicholas Colicchia, Kylie McLaughlin

Language Content Branislava Vladisavljevic

Thanks to Sasha Baskett, Lucy Birchley, Janine Eberle, Ryan Evans, Suki Gear, Chris Girdler, Mark Griffiths, Corey Hutchison, Jouve India, Catherine Naghten, Karyn Noble, Darren O'Connell, Trent Paton, Averil Robertson, Laura Stansfeld, Phillip Tang, John Taufa, Gerard Walker, Juan Winata

See also separate subindexes for:

✕ **EATING P273**

🍷 **DRINKING & NIGHTLIFE P274**

☆ **ENTERTAINMENT P275**

🛍 **SHOPPING P275**

🏃 **SPORTS & ACTIVITIES P275**

🛏 **SLEEPING P275**

Index

🍸 DRINKING & NIGHTLIFE

Běijīng Maps

Map Legend

Sights
- Beach
- Buddhist
- Castle
- Christian
- Hindu
- Islamic
- Jewish
- Monument
- Museum/Gallery
- Ruin
- Winery/Vineyard
- Zoo
- Other Sight

Eating
- Eating

Drinking & Nightlife
- Drinking & Nightlife
- Cafe

Entertainment
- Entertainment

Shopping
- Shopping

Sports & Activities
- Diving/Snorkelling
- Canoeing/Kayaking
- Skiing
- Surfing
- Swimming/Pool
- Walking
- Windsurfing
- Other Sports & Activities

Sleeping
- Sleeping
- Camping

Information
- Bank
- Embassy/Consulate
- Hospital/Medical
- Internet
- Police
- Post Office
- Telephone
- Toilet
- Tourist Information
- Other Information

Transport
- Airport
- Border Crossing
- Bus
- Cable Car/Funicular
- Cycling
- Ferry
- Monorail
- Parking
- S-Bahn
- Taxi
- Train/Railway
- Tram
- Tube Station
- U-Bahn
- Underground Train Station
- Other Transport

Routes
- Tollway
- Freeway
- Primary
- Secondary
- Tertiary
- Lane
- Unsealed Road
- Plaza/Mall
- Steps
- Tunnel
- Pedestrian Overpass
- Walking Tour
- Walking Tour Detour
- Path

Boundaries
- International
- State/Province
- Disputed
- Regional/Suburb
- Marine Park
- Cliff
- Wall

Geographic
- Hut/Shelter
- Lighthouse
- Lookout
- Mountain/Volcano
- Oasis
- Park
- Pass
- Picnic Area
- Waterfall

Hydrography
- River/Creek
- Intermittent River
- Swamp/Mangrove
- Reef
- Canal
- Water
- Dry/Salt/Intermittent Lake
- Glacier

Areas
- Beach/Desert
- Cemetery (Christian)
- Cemetery (Other)
- Park/Forest
- Sportsground
- Sight (Building)
- Top Sight (Building)

MAP INDEX

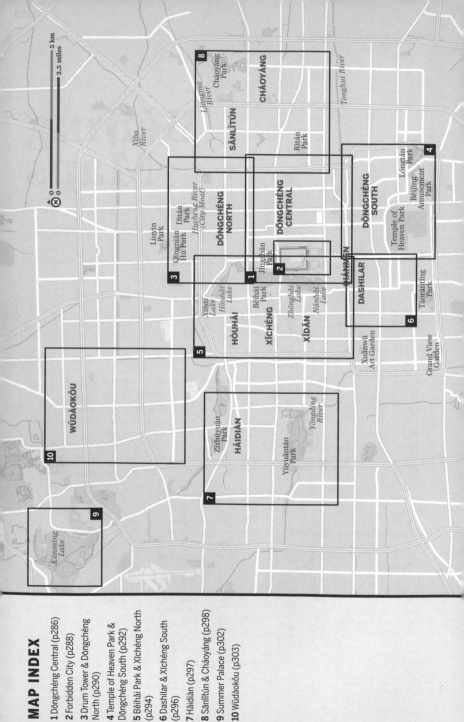

WŬDÀOKǑU

Kūnmíng Lake

9

10

HǍIDIÀN

Zízhúyuàn Park

Yùyuāntán Park

Yǒngdìng River

Xíba River

Liǔyīn Park

3

DŌNGCHÉNG NORTH

Qīngnián Hú Park

Dítán Park

Húchéng River (City Moat)

Liàngmǎ River

SĀNLǏTÚN

Cháoyáng Park

8

CHÁOYÁNG

Rìtán Park

1

Jǐngshān Park

DŌNGCHÉNG CENTRAL

2

5

HòUHǍI

Xīhǎi Lake

Hòuhǎi Lake

Běihǎi Park

XĪCHÉNG

Zhōnghǎi Lake

Nánhǎi Lake

XĪDĀN

QIÁNMÉN

DASHILAR

6

Xuānwǔ Art Garden

Grand View Garden

Táorántíng Park

Temple of Heaven Park

DŌNGCHÉNG SOUTH

Lóngtán Park

Běijīng Amusement Park

4

Tōnghuì River

N

0   5 km
0   2.5 miles

DŌNGCHÉNG CENTRAL

DŌNGCHÉNG CENTRAL

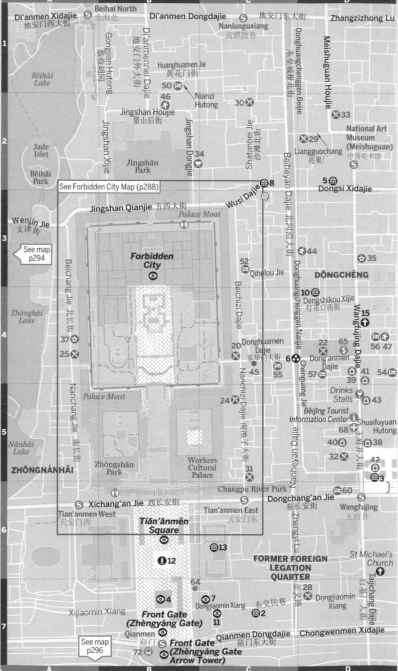

Di'anmen Xidajie 地安门西大街
Beihai North 北海北
Di'anmen Dongdajie 地安门东大街
Zhangzizhong Lu

Nanluoguxiang 南锣鼓巷

Gongjian Hutong 恭俭胡同
Di'anmennei Dajie 地安门内大街

Běihǎi Lake

Huanghuamen Jie 黄花门街
50
46
Nianzi Hutong
30

33

National Art Museum (Meishuguan) 中国美术馆

Jingshan Houjie 景山后街
Jingshan Xijie
Jingshan Dongjie
Jade Islet

Jingshān Park 景山公园
34
Shatanbei Jie 沙滩北街
29
Liangguochang 亮果厂

Běihǎi Park

Meishuguan Houjie

8 @
Dongsi Xidajie 东四西大街

See Forbidden City Map (p288)

Jingshan Qianjie 五四大街
Wusi Dajie
Palace Moat

See map p294

Wenjin Jie 文津街
5
Dongsi Xidajie 东四西大街

44

DŌNGCHÉNG

52
Qihélou Jie
35

Forbidden City

Zhōnghǎi Lake

10
Dengshikou Xijie 灯市口西大街

Beichizi Dajie 北池子大街

37
25

15

Wangfujing Dajie

22 65
56 47

20
Donghuamen Dajie 东华门大街

Chenguang Jie 晨光街

6
Dong'anmen Dajie
57
41 54
39

Nanchang Jie 南长街

45
55

Drinks Stalls
43

Palace Moat

Nanchizi Dajie 南池子大街

24

Běijīng Tourist Information Center
68
Shuaifuyuan Hutong

Zhōngshān Park 中山公园

40
38

Zhōngnánhǎi

Workers Cultural Palace

31

32
42
60
3

Nánhǎi Lake

Chàngpu River Park

ZHŌNGNÁNHǍI

Dongchang'an Jie

Wangfujing 王府井

Xichang'an Jie 西长安街
Tian'anmen West 天安门西

Tian'anmen East 天安门东

Dongchang'an Jie 东长安街
Zhengyi Lu

Tiān'ānmén Square

13

FORMER FOREIGN LEGATION QUARTER

St Michael's Church

12

64
4
7
Dongjiaomin Xiang

2
28
Dongjiaomin Xiang
Tajichang Dajie 台基厂大街

11

Xijiaomin Xiang

Front Gate (Zhèngyáng Gate)

Qianmen 前门

Qianmen Dongdajie 前门东大街
Chongwenmen Xidajie

72
Front Gate (Zhèngyáng Gate Arrow Tower)

See map p296

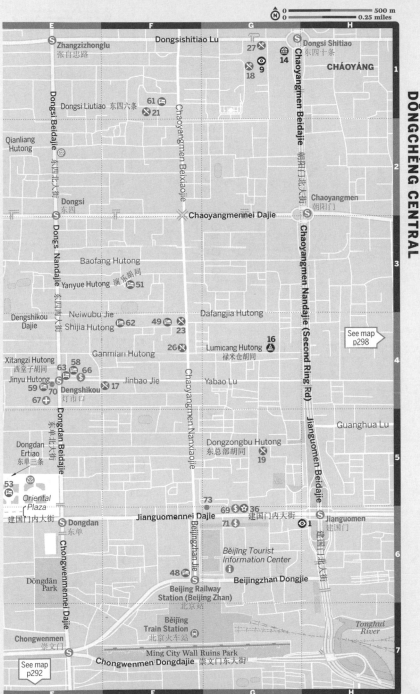

DŌNGCHÉNG CENTRAL

Dongsishitiao Lu

Zhangzizhonglu
张自忠路

Dongsi Shitiao
东四十条

CHÁOYÁNG

Dongsi Beidajie
东四北大街

Dongsi Liutiao 东四六条

Qianliang
Hutong

Chaoyangmen Beixiaojie

Chaoyangmen Beidajie 朝阳门北大街

Chaoyangmen
朝阳门

Dongsi
东四

Chaoyangmennei Dajie

Chaoyangmen Nandajie (Second Ring Rd)

Baofang Hutong

Yanyue Hutong 演乐胡同

Dafangjia Hutong

Dengshikou
Dajie

Neiwubu Jie

Shijia Hutong

Dongs. Nandajie 东四南大街

Ganmian Hutong

Lumicang Hutong
禄米仓胡同

See map
p298

Xitangzi Hutong
西堂子胡同

Jinyu Hutong

Jinbao Jie

Yabao Lu

Dengshikou
灯市口

Dongdan Beidajie 东单北大街

Chaoyangmen Nanxiaojie

Guanghua Lu

Dongdan
Ertiao
东单三条

Dongzongbu Hutong
东总部胡同

Jianguomen Beidajie

Oriental
Plaza
建国门内大街

Beijingzhan Jie

Jianguomennei Dajie

建国门内大街

Jianguomen
建国门

Dongdan
东单

Běijīng Tourist
Information Center

Chongwenmennei Dajie

Dōngdān
Park

Beijingzhan Dongjie

Beijing Railway
Station (Beijing Zhan)
北京站

Běijīng
Train Station
北京火车站

Tonghui
River

Chongwenmen
崇文门

Ming City Wall Ruins Park
Chongwenmen Dongdajie 崇文门东大街

See map
p292

FORBIDDEN CITY

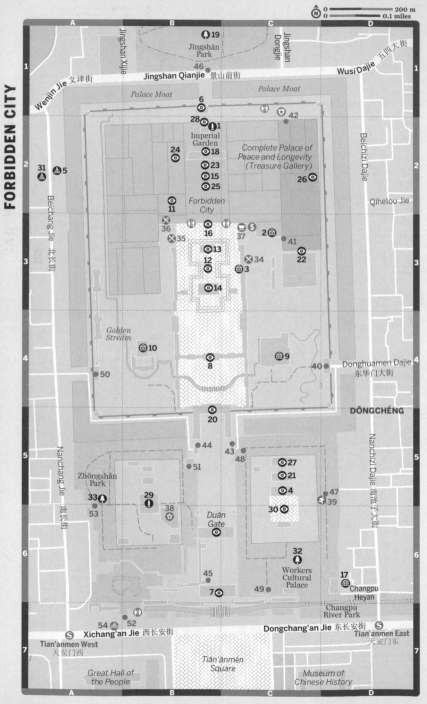

0   200 m
0   0.1 miles

Jingshan Xijie 景山西街

Jingshan Qianjie 景山前街

Wenjin Jie 文津街

Wusi Dajie 五四大街

Beichizi Dajie

Jingshan Dongjie

Jingshan Park

19

46

Palace Moat

Palace Moat

6

28 1

Imperial Garden

18

24

23

15

25

11

Forbidden City

Complete Palace of Peace and Longevity (Treasure Gallery)

26

Qihelou Jie

31 5

Beichang Jie 北长街

36

35

16

37 2

41

13

12

34

3

22

14

Golden Stream

10

9

40

50

8

Donghuamen Dajie 东华门大街

DŌNGCHÉNG

20

Nanchang Jie 南长街

44

43

51

48

Zhōngshān Park

33

53

29

38

Duān Gate

27

21

4

47 39

30

Nanchizi Dajie 南池子大街

32

45

17

Changpu Heyan

7

49

Workers Cultural Palace

Changpu River Park

54 52

Xichang'an Jie 西长安街

Dongchang'an Jie 东长安街

Tian'anmen East 天安门东

Tian'anmen West 天安门西

Tiān'anmén Square

Great Hall of the People

Museum of Chinese History

FORBIDDEN CITY

DŌNGCHÉNG NORTH

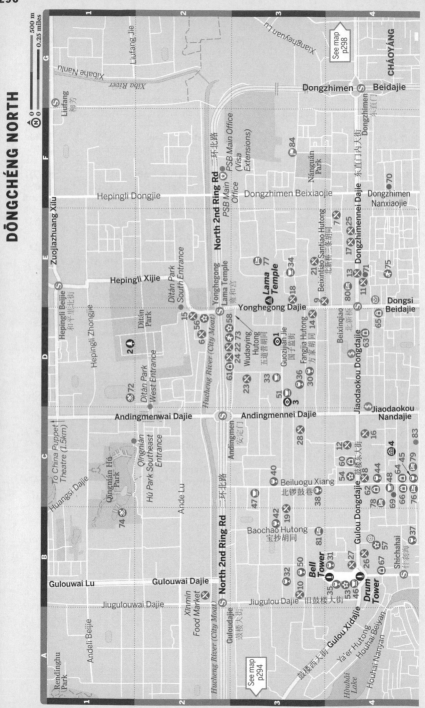

See map p298

See map p294

CHÁOYÁNG

Dongzhimen Beidajie

Dongzhimen Nanxiaojie

Dongzhimen Beixiaojie

Nánguān Park

Liufang Jie

Liufang
柳芳

Xiba River
西坝河

Xibahe Nanlu

Xiangheyuan Lu

North 2nd Ring Rd
环北路

PSB Main Office
(Visa Extensions)

PSB Main Office

Zuojiazhuang Xilu

Hepingli Dongjie

Hepingli Beijie
和平里北街

Hepingli Zhongjie

Hepingli Xijie

Dìtán Park
West Entrance

Dìtán Park
South Entrance

Dìtán Park

Yonghegong
雍和宫

Lama Temple
雍和宫

Lama Temple

Yonghegong Dajie

Dongsi Beidajie

Dongzhimennei Dajie
东直门内大街

Beixintiao Santiao Hutong
北新桥三条胡同

Wudaoying Hutong
五道营胡同

Guozijian Jie
国子监街

Fangjia Hutong
方家胡同

Beixinqiao
北新桥

Beixinqiao

Huangsi Dajie

To China Puppet
Theatre (1.5km)

Qīngnián Hú Park
Southeast Entrance

Qīngnián Hú Park

Ande Lu

Andingmenwai Dajie

Andingmennei Dajie

Andingmen
安定门

Hùchéng River (City Moat)

Jiaodaokou
Nandajie

Jiaodaokou
Dongdajie

Jiaodaokou

Beiluogu Xiang
北锣鼓巷

Baochao Hutong
宝抄胡同

Bell Tower

Gulou Dongdajie

Drum Tower

Gulou Xidajie

Shichahai
什刹海

Houhǎi
Lake

Houhǎi Beiyán

Ya'er Hutong

Houhǎi Nanyán

North 2nd Ring Rd
环北路

Guduodajie
鼓楼东大街

Jiugulou Dajie 旧鼓楼大街

Jiugulou Dajie 旧鼓楼大街

Xinmin
Food Market

Gulouwai Dajie

Gulouwai Lu

Jiuguloawai Dajie

Andeli Beijie

Andeli Dajie

Rendinghu
Park

Rendinghu Park

DŌNGCHÉNG NORTH

DŌNGCHÉNG SOUTH

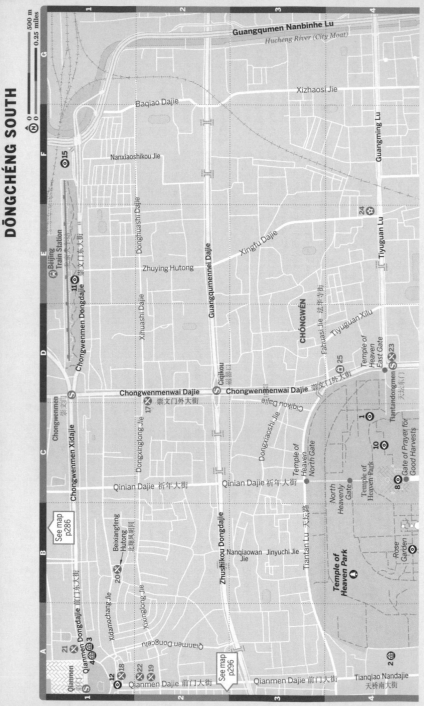

500 m
0.25 miles

Guangqumen Nanbinhe Lu

Hucheng River (City Moat)

Xizhaosi Jie

Baqiao Dajie

Nanxiaoshikou Jie

Guangming Lu

15

Beijing Train Station

Donghuashi Dajie

Xingfu Dajie

Tiyuguan Lu

24

Chongwenmen Dongdajie

Zhuying Hutong

Guangqumennei Dajie

CHÓNGWÉN

Fahuasi Jie

Tiyuguan Xilu

11

Xihuashi Dajie

Temple of Heaven East Gate

23

C'ıqikou

Chongwenmen

Chongwenmenwai Dajie

Chongwenmenwai Dajie

Cíqikou Dajie

25

Tiantandongmen

Chongwenmen Xidajie

17

Dongxinglong Jie

Dongxiaoshi Jie

Temple of Heaven North Gate

1

Gate of Prayer for Good Harvests

Qinian Dajie 祈年大街

Qinian Dajie 祈年大街

10

North Heavenly Gate

8

Temple of Heaven Park

Beixiangfeng Hutong
北香凤胡同

Zhushikou Dongdajie

Tiantan Lu 天坛路

Nanqiaowan Jie

Jinyuchi Jie

Rose Garden

See map p286

20

Xxixinglong Jie

Xidamochang Jie

Temple of Heaven Park

21

Qianmen Dongdajie 前门东大街

3

4

Qianmen Dongcelu

See map p296

2

Qianmen

12

18

22

19

Qianmen Dajie 前门大街

Qianmen Dajie 前门大街

Tianqiao Nandajie 天桥南大街

DŌNGCHÉNG SOUTH

Dongzhong Jie

东直门北大街

Dongsì Shítiáo / 东四一条

交道口南大街

Nanluogu Xiang 南锣鼓巷

Banchang Hutong 板厂胡同

Di'anmen Dongdajie 地安门东大街

Nanluoguxiang 南锣鼓巷

Dongsishitiao Lu

Zhangzizhonglu 张自忠路

Zhangzizhong Lu

See map p286

Qiánhǎi Lake

Qianhai Xiyan

Qianhai Xijie

Beihai North 北海北

Di'anmen Xidajie

Beihai Lake 北海

Mao'er Hutong

XĪCHÉNG NORTH

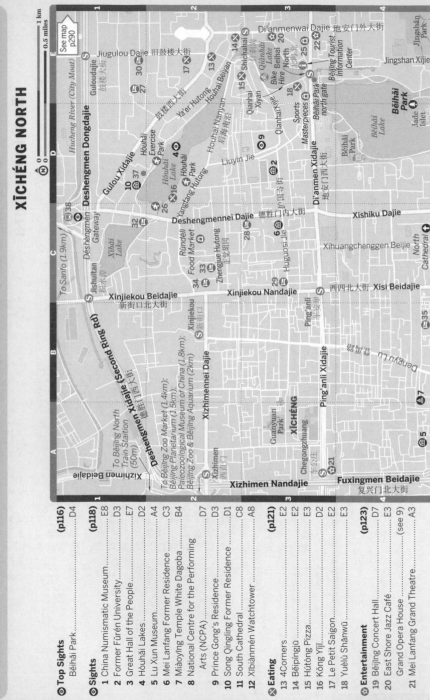

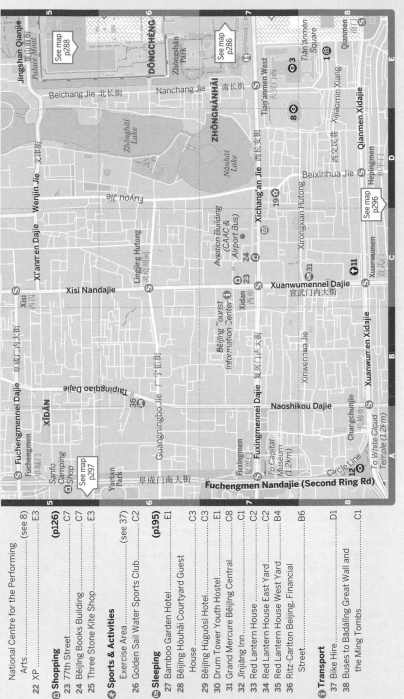

XĪCHÉNG NORTH

HĂIDIĂN

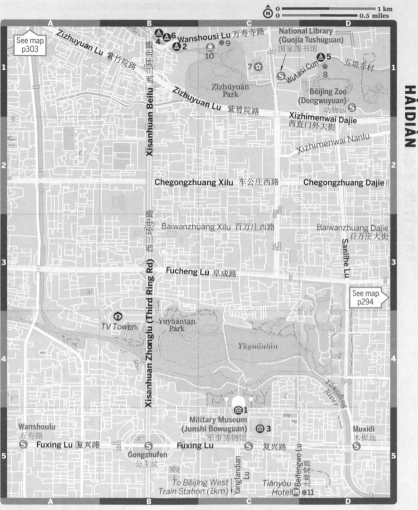

See map p303

See map p294

◎ Sights (p158)

✪ Entertainment (p164)

ℹ Information

ℹ Transport

SĀNLĬTÚN & CHÁOYÁNG

Cháoyáng Park

To French Embassy (200m);
Israeli Embassy (300m);
US Embassy (400m)

To Japanese
Embassy (500m);
Dos Kolegas (2km)

To South Korean
Embassy (400m)

Liangmaqiao Lu

Liangmaqiao
亮马桥

Liangma River
亮马河

Liangmahe Nanlu

SĀNLĬTÚN
EMBASSY
AREA

Sanlitun Dongliujie

Xinyuan Nanlu

Xin Donglu

Agricultural
Exhibition Center
(Nongye Zhanlanguan)
农业展览馆

Agricultural
Exhibition
Center

Dongsanhuan Beilu
(East 3rd Ring Rd North)
东三环北路

Nongzhanguan Nanlu

Tuanjiehu
团结湖

Sanlitun
Xiliujie

Sanlitun
Xiwujie

Sanlitun Beixiaojie

Sanlitun Dongsanjie

Sanlitun Dongsijie
三里屯东四街

Sanlitun Lu
三里屯路

Sanlitun Dongsanjie
三里屯东三街

Sanlitun
Beijie

Sanlitun

Dong'erjie

Nansanlitun Lu

Xindong Lu

Xin Donglu

Dongzhimenwai Dajie
东直门外大街

Dongzhimenwai Xiejie
东直门外斜街

Xiangheyuan Lu

Dongzhimen Beixiaojie
东直门北小街

Chunxiu Lu

Xingfucun Lu

Gongrentiyuchang Beilu

Gongrentiyuchang
Xilu

Workers
Stadium

Workers
Gymnasium

Xinzhong Lu

Xinzhong Jie

Dongzhong Jie

Dongzhong Jie

Dongsishitiao
东四十条

CHÁOYÁNG

Dongzhimen
东直门

See map
p290

Dong'erhuan (East 2nd Ring Rd)
东二环

6

59
81

94

97

77

15

82
93

90

8 19 70

45

50
66

37

30 32

34

51

52

89

23

11

61
9

28

87

78
73

35

5

18

63

16

13

4

68

26

22

21

56
33

24

38

40

44

43

83

104
103

See map p286

Dong'erhuan (East 2nd Ring Rd) 东二环

SUMMER PALACE

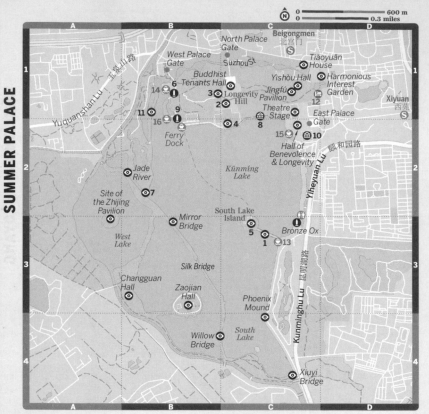

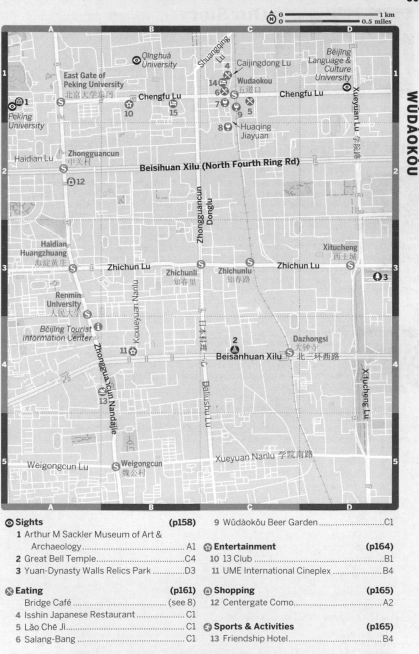

WŬDÀOKŎU

Our Story

A beat-up old car, a few dollars in the pocket and a sense of adventure. In 1972 that's all Tony and Maureen Wheeler needed for the trip of a lifetime – across Europe and Asia overland to Australia. It took several months, and at the end – broke but inspired – they sat at their kitchen table writing and stapling together their first travel guide, *Across Asia on the Cheap*. Within a week they'd sold 1500 copies. Lonely Planet was born.

Today, Lonely Planet has offices in Melbourne, London and Oakland, with more than 600 staff and writers. We share Tony's belief that 'a great guidebook should do three things: inform, educate and amuse'.

Our Writers

Daniel McCrohan

Coordinating Author, Forbidden City & Dōngchéng Central, Drum Tower & Dōngchéng North, Sānlǐtún & Cháoyáng, The Great Wall, Day Trips from Běijīng Daniel moved to Běijīng in 2005 and, more significantly, moved into the *hútòng* in 2007. He has made this fascinating network of ancient alleys his home ever since, and now lives with his wife and two children in a small courtyard tucked away behind the Drum and Bell Towers. He can't imagine ever leaving. Daniel has written more than a dozen Lonely Planet guidebooks. He is also the creator of the smartphone app *Beijing on a Budget*, and the co-host of the television series *Best in China*. Find out more on his website (danielmccrohan.com) or follow him on Twitter (@danielmccrohan). Daniel also wrote the Need to Know, Top Itineraries, With Kids, Like a Local, Běijīng Today, History, Transport and Directory A–Z chapters.

Read more about Daniel at:
lonelyplanet.com/members/danielmccrohan

David Eimer

Temple of Heaven Park & Dōngchéng South, Běihǎi Park & Xīchéng North, Dashilar & Xīchéng South, The Summer Palace & Hǎidiàn David first came to China in 1988, when both Westerners and cars were in short supply. After abandoning the idea of the law as a career, he became a freelance journalist in London and LA, before subsequent return trips to China convinced him to move to Běijīng permanently in early 2005. Now, he contributes to a variety of newspapers and magazines in the UK. David co-wrote the previous two editions of the Běijīng guide, and worked on the last three editions of the China guide. David also wrote the Welcome to Běijīng, What's New, If You Like, Month by Month, For Free, Eating, Drinking & Nightlife, Entertainment, Shopping, Neighbourhoods at a Glance, Historic Hútòng, Arts and Architecture chapters.

Published by Lonely Planet Publications Pty Ltd
ABN 36 005 607 983
9th edition – Apr 2013
ISBN 978 1 74179 846 3
© Lonely Planet 2013   Photographs © as indicated 2013
10 9 8 7 6 5 4 3 2 1
Printed in Singapore